THE

PUBLICATIONS

OF THE

𝕷incoln 𝕽ecord 𝕾ociety

FOUNDED IN THE YEAR

1910

VOLUME 88

ISSN 0267–2634

THE ACTA OF
HUGH OF WELLS

BISHOP OF LINCOLN
1209–1235

EDITED BY

DAVID M. SMITH

The Lincoln Record Society

The Boydell Press

First published 2000

A Lincoln Record Society Publication
published by The Boydell Press
an imprint of Boydell & Brewer Ltd
PO Box 9, Woodbridge, Suffolk IP12 3DF, UK
and of Boydell & Brewer Inc.
PO Box 41026, Rochester, NY 14604–4126, USA
website: http://www.boydell.co.uk

ISBN 0 901503 65 7

A catalogue record for this book is available
from the British Library

Details of other Lincoln Record Society volumes are available
from Boydell & Brewer Ltd

This publication is printed on acid-free paper

Printed in Great Britain by
St Edmundsbury Press Ltd, Bury St Edmunds, Suffolk

CONTENTS

IN MEMORY OF
MY PARENTS

PREFACE

This work has taken a long time to appear in print. It was originally completed as part of my doctoral thesis under the supervision of Professor Kathleen Major in 1970. Shortly afterwards, in 1973 to be precise, the British Academy English Episcopal Acta project was launched and I was very fortunate to be appointed general editor of the series. The immediate consequence was that I devoted my time to editing the earlier post-Conquest *acta* of bishops of Lincoln and Hugh of Wells was put to one side, since his *acta* did not in fact come within the remit of the series.[1] Other research has intervened since then, but a couple of years ago I decided to revisit the Hugh of Wells *acta*, and the result is this present edition.

My greatest debt is to Professor Kathleen Major who first introduced me to the discipline of historical research, and in particular to the rigours of editing medieval records. I shall always be grateful for her supervision of the original thesis and her subsequent help and advice. Mrs Joan Varley, the then County Archivist of Lincolnshire, was also of great assistance when I was undertaking my thesis.

More recently Professor Christopher Brooke and Dr Philippa Hoskin have given up valuable research time of their own to read through the entire edition and I have greatly benefited from their comments. They have saved me from countless errors and effected considerable improvements. I am most grateful to them for their generosity.

I have been greatly helped in my search for episcopal *acta* of Bishop Hugh by the courtesy, helpfulness and advice of custodians of archives in record offices and libraries. I want to record my thanks for their assistance and I also gratefully acknowledge permission granted by them to publish texts in their possession. My thanks must be recorded to the British Library, the Bodleian Library, Oxford, Cambridge University Library, Christ Church, Oxford, the President and Fellows of Magdalen College, Oxford, the Warden and Fellows of New College, Oxford, the Provost and Fellows of the Queen's College, Oxford, Trinity College, Dublin, and the Dean and Chapter of Canterbury, Durham, Exeter, Hereford, Lichfield, Lincoln, Peterborough, Salisbury, Wells, Westminster, and York, the Provost and Chapter of Southwell, Bedfordshire Record Office, Buckinghamshire Record Office, Devon Record Office, Hertfordshire Archives and Local Studies, Lichfield Joint Record Office, Lincolnshire Archives, Northamptonshire Record Office, Oxfordshire Archives, and Wiltshire and Swindon Record Office. Tran-

---

[1] The earlier Lincoln *acta* were published as *English Episcopal Acta I: Lincoln 1067–1185* (Oxford University Press for the British Academy, 1980), and *English Episcopal Acta IV: Lincoln 1186–1206* (Oxford University Press for the British Academy, 1986). The British Academy English Episcopal Acta project encompasses the *acta* of English diocesan bishops from the Norman Conquest to a variable point in the thirteenth century, linked with the introduction of the diocesan registration of acts. In other words the Academy edition will normally stop at the point when the keeping of bishops' registers is introduced in that particular diocese, and the earliest register is still extant.

scripts of Crown copyright records in the Public Record Office appear by permission of the Controller of HM Stationery Office. Private owners have also been very willing to give access to their archives. I particularly wish to thank the Duke of Buccleuch (The Living Landscape Trust), the Marquess of Northampton, Mr Charles Stopford Sackville, and the Spalding Gentlemen's Society.

MANUSCRIPT SOURCES CITED

Original Charters of Hugh of Wells

Boughton House, Northamptonshire
    Buccleuch mun. B.1.470   *360*

Canterbury Cathedral Library and Archives
    Ch. Ant. C115/141   *1*
    Ch. Ant. C115/143   *1*
    Ch. Ant. R40   *8*

Castle Ashby, Northamptonshire
    Compton document 37   *380*
    Compton document 38   *413*

Durham University Library, Archives and Special Collections
    Durham D. & C. 3.4. Ebor. 6   *435*

Hereford Cathedral Library and Archives
    Hereford D. & C. mun. 2040   *257*

Lincoln, Lincolnshire Archives Office
    Lincoln D. & C. archives:
        A/2/18 no. 119   *333*
        Dj/20/1/2   *431*
        Dj/20/1/3   *431*
        Dj/20/1/4   *134*
        Dj/20/1/7   *408*
        Dij/55/3/3   *234*
        Dij/61/4/14   *189*
        Dij/67/1/15   *198*
        Dij/67/2/4   *330*
        Dij/69/1/43   *26*
        Dij/72/2/9   *111*
        Dij/72/2/10   *177*
        Dij/72/3/1   *304*
        Dij/83/2/53   *88*
        Dij/84/2/17   *306*
        Dij/87/3/13   *115*
        Dij/89/1/12   *345A*
        Dij/89/1/24   *371*
        Dij/90/2/27   *136*
    Misc. Dep. 456   *436*

London, British Library
     Add. Ch. 10596   *292*
     Add. Ch. 21999   *280*
     Add. Ch. 47561   *226*
     Add. Ch. 47562   *226*
     Cotton Ch. xi 32   *69*
     Harl. Ch. 43 H 24   *75*

London, Public Record Office
     E210/3084   *305*
     E326/1877   *247*
     E326/3570   *62*
     E326/8781   *154*
     E326/8827   *22*
     SC1/1/54   *109*

Northampton, Northamptonshire Record Office
     SS. 608   *188*
     SS. 2320   *383*

Oxford, Bodleian Library
     DD. Ch. Ch. O.938   *64*

Oxford, Magdalen College
     Aynho Ch. 82   *16*

Oxford, New College
     Newington Longeville deed 101   *303*

Wells Cathedral Library and Archives
     Cathedral charter 22   *8*

Westminster Abbey Library and Muniment Room
     mun. 2578   *63*
     mun. 15683   *3*
     mun. 20622   *345B*

Copies, Transcripts and Mentions of Charters of Hugh of Wells

Bedford, Bedfordshire Record Office
     D.D, GY. 9/2   *39*

Buckingham, Buckinghamshire Record Office
     Boarstall Cartulary   *200*

Cambridge University Library
     Add. ms. 3020   *230, 283*
     Add. ms. 3021   *283*

PRINTED BOOKS AND ARTICLES CITED,
WITH ABBREVIATED REFERENCES

Acta Stephani Langton	K. Major ed., *Acta Stephani Langton, Cantuariensis archiepiscopi A.D. 1207–1228* (Canterbury and York Society 50, 1950).
Ann. mon.	H.R. Luard ed., *Annales monastici*, 5 vols. (Rolls ser. 1864–9).
Barrow, J.	'From the lease to the certificate: the evolution of episcopal acts in England and Wales (*c.* 700 – *c.* 1250)' in J.C. Haidacher and W. Köfler eds., *Die Diplomatik der Bischofsurkunden vor 1250/La Diplomatique épiscopale avant 1250* (Innsbruck 1995), pp. 529–42.
Bedfordshire Feet of Fines	G.H. Fowler ed., *A calendar of the feet of fines for Bedfordshire, preserved in the Public Record Office, of the reigns of Richard I, John and Henry III* (Bedfordshire Historical Record Society 6, 1919).
Blair, J.	*Bampton Deanery* (Bampton Research paper 2, 1988).
Blair, J.	*The Medieval Clergy of Bampton* (Bampton Research Paper 4, 1991).
BM Seals	W. de G. Birch, *Catalogue of Seals in the department of manuscripts in the British Museum*, 6 vols. (London 1887–1900).
Boarstall Cartulary	H.E. Salter ed., *The Boarstall Cartulary* (Oxford Historical Society 88, 1930).
Book of Fees	*The Book of Fees, commonly called Testa de Nevill (1198–1293)*, 2 vols. in 3 (London 1920–31).
Bradenstoke Cartulary	V.C.M. London ed., *The cartulary of Bradenstoke priory* (Wiltshire Record Society 35, 1979).
Bradshaw, H. & Wordsworth, C.	*The statutes of Lincoln cathedral*, 2 vols. in 3 (Cambridge 1892–7).
Brooke, C.N.L.	'English episcopal *acta* of the twelfth and thirteenth centuries' in M.J. Franklin and C. Harper-Bill eds., *Medieval Ecclesiastical Studies in honour of Dorothy Owen* (Woodbridge 1995), pp. 41–56.
Bucks Eyre Roll	J.G. Jenkins ed., *Calendar of the roll of the justices on eyre, 1227* (Buckinghamshire Record Society 6, 1945).
Burger, M.	'*Officiales* and the *familiae* of the bishops of Lincoln, 1258–99', *Journal of Medieval History* 16 (1990), 39–53.
Burger, M.	'Sending, joining, writing, and speaking in the

	diocesan administration of thirteenth-century Lincoln', *Mediaeval Studies* 55 (1993), 151–82.
Burger, M.	'Bishops, archdeacons and communication between centre and locality in the diocese of Lincoln *c.* 1214–99', in P.R. Coss and S.D. Lloyd eds., *Thirteenth Century England V* (Woodbridge 1995), pp. 195–206.
Bushmead Cartulary	G.H. Fowler and J. Godber eds., *The cartulary of Bushmead priory* (Bedfordshire Historical Record Society 22, 1945).
Cal. Ch. R.	*Calendar of Charter Rolls preserved in the Public Record Office*, 6 vols. (London 1903–27).
Canterbury Professions	M. Richter ed. (Canterbury and York Society 67, 1973).
Carpenter, D.A.	*The Minority of Henry III* (London 1990).
Carte Nativorum	C.N.L. Brooke and M.M. Postan eds., *Carte Nativorum: a Peterborough abbey cartulary of the fourteenth century* (Northamptonshire Record Society 20, 1960).
Catto, J.I. ed.	*The History of the University of Oxford, vol. I: The Early Oxford Schools* (Oxford 1984).
CDF	J.H. Round ed., *Calendar of documents preserved in France, illustrative of the history of Great Britain and Ireland, vol. i, A.D. 918–1216* (London 1899).
Cheney, C.R.	'The Church and Magna Carta', *Theology*, lxviii (1965), 266–72.
Cheney, C.R.	*English Bishops' Chanceries 1100–1250* (Manchester 1950).
Cheney, C.R.	*Episcopal Visitation of Monasteries in the thirteenth century* (Manchester 1931).
Cheney, C.R.	*From Becket to Langton: English church government 1170–1213* (Manchester 1956).
Cheney, C.R.	*Hubert Walter* (London 1967).
Cheney, C.R.	*Notaries Public in England in the thirteenth and fourteenth centuries* (Oxford 1972).
Chichester Acta	H. Mayr-Harting ed., *The acta of the bishops of Chichester, 1075–1207* (Canterbury and York Society 56, 1964).
Chichester Cartulary	W.D. Peckham ed., *The chartulary of the high church of Chichester* (Sussex Record Society 46, 1946).
Church, C.M.	'Jocelin, bishop of Bath, 1206–1242', *Archaeologia* 51 (1878), 281–346.
Cirencester Cartulary	C.D. Ross and M. Devine eds., *The cartulary of Cirencester abbey, Gloucestershire*, 3 vols. (Oxford 1964–77).
Clanchy, M.	*From Memory to Written Record: England 1066–1307* (2nd edn, Oxford 1993).
Close Rolls 1227–31	*Close rolls of the reign of Henry III (1227–1272)* 14 vols. (London 1902–38), vol. i.

Colvin, *White Canons*	H.M. Colvin, *The White Canons in England* (Oxford, 1951).
Complete Peerage	G.E. Cokayne and others eds., *The Complete Peerage, or a history of the House of Lords and all its members from the earliest times* 14 vols. in 15 (London 1910–98).
Connor, R.D.	*The Weights and Measures of England* (London, Science Museum, 1987).
Coss, P. R. and Lloyd, S.D. eds.	*Thirteenth Century England V* (Woodbridge, 1995).
Councils and Synods	F.M. Powicke and C.R. Cheney eds., *Councils and synods with other documents relating to the English Church, vol. ii: A.D. 1205–1313*, 2 vols. (Oxford, 1964).
CPL	W.H. Bliss, C. Johnson, J.A. Twemlow, M.J. Haren eds., *Calendar of entries in the papal registers relating to Great Britain and Ireland: papal letters* (1893–in progress).
CPR	*Calendar of Patent Rolls preserved in the Public Record Office* (London 1901–).
CRR	*Curia regis rolls . . . preserved in the Public Record Office* (London 1922–).
Daventry Cartulary	M.J. Franklin ed., *The cartulary of Daventry priory* (Northamptonshire Record Society 35, 1988).
Derbyshire Charters	I.H. Jeayes, *Descriptive catalogue of Derbyshire charters in libraries and muniment-rooms (c. 1129–1550)* (London 1906).
Dunkin, J.	*Oxfordshire: the history and antiquities of the Hundreds of Bullington and Ploughley*, 2 vols. (London, 1823).
Dunstable Cartulary	G.H. Fowler ed., *A digest of the charters preserved in the cartulary of the priory of Dunstable* (Bedfordshire Historical Record Society 10, 1926).
Durham Annals and Documents	F. Barlow ed., *Durham annals and documents of the thirteenth century* (Surtees Society 155, 1945 for 1940).
Edwards, K.	*The English secular cathedrals in the middle ages: a constitutional study with special reference to the fourteenth century* (2nd edn, Manchester 1967).
EEA	*English Episcopal Acta 1: Lincoln 1072–1185*, ed. D.M. Smith (Oxford 1980); *2: Canterbury 1162–1190*, eds. C.R. Cheney and B.E.A. Jones (Oxford 1986); *3: Canterbury 1193–1205,* eds. C.R. Cheney and E. John (Oxford 1986); *4: Lincoln 1186–1206*, ed. D.M. Smith (Oxford 1986); *5: York 1070–1154*, ed. J.E. Burton (Oxford 1988); *6: Norwich 1070–1214*, ed. C. Harper-Bill (Oxford 1990); *7: Hereford 1079–1234*, ed. J. Barrow (Oxford 1992); *8: Winchester 1070–1204*, ed. M.J. Franklin

(Oxford 1993); *9: Winchester 1205–1238*, ed. N. Vincent (Oxford 1994); *10: Bath and Wells 1061–1205*, ed. F.M.R. Ramsey (Oxford 1995); *11: Exeter 1046–1184*, ed. F. Barlow (Oxford 1996); *12: Exeter 1186–1257*, ed. F. Barlow (Oxford 1996); *13: Worcester 1218–1268*, ed. P.M. Hoskin (Oxford 1997); *14: Coventry and Lichfield 1072–1159*, ed. M.J. Franklin (Oxford 1997); *15: London 1076–1187*, ed. F. Neininger (Oxford 1999); *16: Coventry and Lichfield 1160–1182*, ed. M.J. Franklin (Oxford 1998); *17: Coventry and Lichfield 1183–1208*, ed. M.J. Franklin (Oxford 1998); *18: Salisbury 1078–1217*, ed. B.R. Kemp (Oxford 1999).

EHR — *English Historical Review.*

English, B. — *The Lords of Holderness 1086–1260* (Oxford 1979).

EPNS — Publications of the English Place-Name Society.

EYC — *Early Yorkshire Charters* i–iii, ed. W. Farrer (London 1914–16); iv–xii and index to i–iii, ed. C.T. Clay (Yorkshire Archaeological Society record ser., extra ser., 1935–65).

Eynsham Cartulary — H.E. Salter ed., 2 vols. (Oxford Historical Society 49, 51, 1907–8).

Farmer, D.H. — 'The cult and canonization of St Hugh' in H. Mayr-Harting ed., *St Hugh of Lincoln: lectures delivered at Oxford and Lincoln to celebrate the eighth centenary of St Hugh's consecration as bishop of Lincoln* (Oxford 1987), pp. 75–87.

Fasti Lincoln — D.E. Greenway ed., *John Le Neve: Fasti Ecclesiae Anglicanae 1066–1300: iii Lincoln* (London 1977).

Fasti St Paul's London — D.E. Greenway ed., *John Le Neve: Fasti Ecclesiae Anglicanae 1066–1300: i St Paul's, London* (London 1968).

Fasti Salisbury — D.E. Greenway ed., *John Le Neve: Fasti Ecclesiae Anglicanae 1066–1300: iv Salisbury* (London 1991).

Feodarium Prioratus Dunelmensis — W. Greenwell ed., *Feodarium prioratus Dunelmensis: a survey of the estates of the priory and convent of Durham, compiled in the fifteenth century* (Surtees Society 58, 1872).

Foedera — T. Rymer, *Foedera, conventiones, litterae, et cujuscunque generis acta publica inter reges Angliae et alios imperatores, reges, pontifices, principes, vel communitates . . .* 20 vols. (London 1727–35).

Franklin, M.J. and Harper-Bill, C. eds. — *Medieval Ecclesiastical Studies in honour of Dorothy Owen* (Woodbridge 1995)

Galbraith, V.H. — *Studies in the Public Records* (London 1949).

Gilbertine Charters — F.M. Stenton ed., *Transcripts of charters relating to Gilbertine houses of Sixle, Ormsby, Catley, Bullington and Alvingham* (Lincoln Record Society 18, 1922).

Gir. Camb.	J.S. Brewer, J.F. Dimock and G.F. Warner eds., *Giraldi Cambrensis Opera*, 8 vols. (Rolls ser., 1861–91).
Glastonbury Cartulary	A. Watkin ed., *The great chartulary of Glastonbury*, 3 vols. (Somerset Record Society 59, 63–4, 1947–56).
Godstow English Register	A. Clark ed., *The English register of Godstow nunnery near Oxford*, 3 vols. (Early English Text Society, original ser., 129, 130, 142, 1905–11).
Gorham, G.C.	*History and antiquities of Eynesbury and St Neot's*, 2 vols. and supplement (London 1824).
Graham, R.	'An appeal for the church and buildings of Kingsmead Priory *c.* 1218', *Antiquaries Journal* xi (1931), 51–4.
Gransden, A. ed.	*Bury St Edmunds: Medieval Art, Architecture, Archaeology and Economy* (British Archaeological Association conference transactions xx, 1998).
Gray, M.	*The Trinitarian Order in England: excavations at Thelsford priory*, eds. L. Watts and P. Rahtz (BAR British ser. 223, 1993).
Guide to Bishops' Registers	D.M. Smith, *Guide to bishops' registers of England and Wales: a survey from the middle ages to the abolition of episcopacy in 1646* (Royal Historical Society guide and handbook 11, 1981).
Haidacher, J.C. and Köfler, W. eds.	*Die Diplomatik der Bischofsurkunden vor 1250/La Diplomatique épiscopale avant 1250* (Innsbruck 1995).
Hallam, H.E.	'Salt-making in the Lincolnshire Fenland during the middle ages', *LAASRP* new ser. 8 (1960), 85–112.
Harrold Cartulary	G.H. Fowler ed., *Records of Harrold priory* (Bedford shire Historical Record Society 17, 1935).
Harvey, J.	*English Mediaeval Architects* (revised edn, London 1987).
Hastings, A.	*Elias of Dereham, architect of Salisbury Cathedral* (Salisbury 1997).
Heads	D. Knowles, C.N.L. Brooke and V.C.M. London eds., *The heads of religious houses: England and Wales 940–1216* (Cambridge 1972).
Heales, A.	*The records of Merton priory in the county of Surrey* (London 1898).
Hector, L.C. and Hager, M.E. eds.	*Year Books of Richard II: 8–10 Richard II, 1385–1387* (Ames Foundation 1987).
HMC Wells	*Calendar of the manuscripts of the dean and chapter of Wells*, 2 vols. (Royal Commission on Historical Manuscripts 1907–14).
Holt, J., *Magna Carta*	(Cambridge 1965).
Kennett, *Parochial Antiquities*	W. Kennett, *Parochial antiquities attempted in the history of Ambrosden, Burcester, and other adjacent parts in the counties of Oxford and Bucks* (Oxford 1695).

KH	D. Knowles and R.N. Hadcock eds., *Medieval Religious Houses: England and Wales* (2nd edn, London 1971).
LAARSP	*Lincolnshire Architectural and Archaeological Society Reports and Papers.*
Leicester Abbey	A. Hamilton Thompson, *The abbey of St Mary of the Meadows, Leicester* (Leicester 1949).
Letters of Guala	N. Vincent ed., *The letters and charters of Cardinal Guala Bicchieri, papal legate in England 1216–1218* (Canterbury and York Society 83, 1996).
Letters of Innocent III	C.R. Cheney and M.G. Cheney eds., *The letters of Pope Innocent III (1198–1216) concerning England and Wales: a calendar* (Oxford 1967).
Lib. Ant.	A. Gibbons ed., *Liber antiquus de ordinationibus vicariarum tempore Hugonis Wells, Lincolniensis episcopi, 1209–1235* (Lincoln 1888).
Lincoln Final Concords	W.O. Massingberd and W.K. Boyd eds., *Lincolnshire Records: abstracts of final concords, Richard I, John, and Henry III (1193–1244), vol. I* (London 1896).
Lincolnshire Eyre Roll	D.M. Stenton ed., *Rolls of the justices in eyre for Lincolnshire 1218–19 and Worcestershire 1221* (Selden Society 53, 1934).
Lincolnshire Notes and Queries	Anon., 'The will of Hugh of Wells, bishop of Lincoln, A.D. 1212', *Lincolnshire Notes and Queries* ii (1890–1), 172–6.
List of Sheriffs for England and Wales from the earliest times to A.D. 1831	(Public Record Office List and Index ix, 1898).
Logan, F.D.	*Excommunication and the Secular Arm* (Toronto 1968).
Luffield Priory Charters	G.H. Elvey ed., 2 vols. (Northamptonshire Record Society 22, 26, 1968–75).
Magnum Registrum Album	H.E. Savage ed., *The great register of Lichfield cathedral known as the Magnum Registrum Album* (William Salt Archaeological Society, 3rd ser., 1928 for 1926).
Major, K.	'The *familia* of Archbishop Stephen Langton', *EHR* xlviii (1933), 529–553.
Major, K.	*The D'Oyrys of South Lincolnshire, Norfolk and Holderness 1130–1275* (Lincoln 1984).
Maxwell-Lyte, *Great Seal*	H.C. Maxwell-Lyte, *Historical notes on the use of the great seal* (London 1926).
Mayr-Harting, H. ed.	*St Hugh of Lincoln: lectures delivered at Oxford and Lincoln to celebrate the eighth centenary of St Hugh's consecration as bishop of Lincoln* (Oxford 1987).
McKechnie, *Magna Carta*	W.S. McKechnie, *Magna Carta: a commentary on the Great Charter of King John* (2nd edn, Glasgow 1914).
Medieval Deeds of Bath	B.R. Kemp and D.M.M. Shorrocks eds., *Medieval Deeds of Bath and district: I Deeds of St John's*

	hospital, Bath; II Walker-Heneage Deeds (Somerset Record Society 73, 1974).
Mon. Angl.	W. Dugdale, Monasticon Anglicanum, J. Caley, H. Ellis and B. Bandinel eds., 6 vols. in 8 (London 1817–30).
MPCM	H.R. Luard ed., Matthaei Parisiensis, monachi sancti Albani: chronica majora, 7 vols. (Rolls ser. 1872–83).
MPHM	F. Madden ed., Matthaei Parisiensis, monachi sancti Albani, historia Anglorum, sive, ut vulgo dicitur, historia minor, 3 vols. (Rolls ser. 1866–9).
Neilson, N. ed.	A Terrier of Fleet, Lincolnshire (British Academy records of social and economic history 4, 1920).
Newington Longeville Charters	H.E. Salter ed. (Oxfordshire Record Society 3, 1921).
Newnham Cartulary	J. Godber ed., Cartulary of Newnham priory (Bedfordshire Historical Record Society 43, 1963–4).
Offer, C.J.	The Bishop's Register (London 1929).
Oseney cartulary	H.E. Salter ed., Cartulary of Oseney abbey, 6 vols. (Oxford Historical Society 89–91, 97, 98, 101, 1929–36).
Oseney English Register	A. Clark ed., The English register of Oseney abbey, by Oxford, written about 1460, 2 vols. (Early English Text Society, original ser., 133, 144, 1907–13).
Owen, A.	'St Edmund in Lincolnshire: the abbey's lands in Wainfleet and Wrangle' in A. Gransden ed., Bury St Edmunds: Medieval Art, Architecture, Archaeology and Economy (British Archaeological Association conference transactions xx, 1998), pp. 122–7.
Painter, S.	The Reign of King John (Baltimore 1945).
Peck, F.	Academia Tertia Anglicana, or the Antiquarian annals of Stamford (London 1727).
Pipe Roll 7 John	S. Smith ed., The great roll of the pipe for the seventh year of the reign of King John, Michaelmas 1205 (Pipe Roll Society, new ser., 19, 1941).
Pipe Roll 8 John	D.M. Stenton ed., The great roll of the pipe for the eighth year of the reign of King John, Michaelmas 1206 (Pipe Roll Society, new ser., 20, 1942).
Pipe Roll 11 John	D.M. Stenton ed., The great roll of the pipe for the eleventh year of the reign of King John, Michaelmas 1209 (Pipe Roll Society, new ser., 24, 1948).
PL	J.-P. Migne ed., Patrologiae latinae cursus completus (Paris 1844–64).
Pollard, G.	'The legatine award to Oxford in 1214 and Robert Grosteste', Oxoniensia xxxix (1974), 62–72.
PUE	W. Holtzmann ed., Papsturkunden in England, 3 vols. (Abhandlungen der Gesellschaft der Wissenschaften zu Göttingen, phil.-hist. Klasse, neue Folge, 25, 1930–1; 3 Folge, 14–15, 1935–6; 33, 1952).

Ramsey Cartulary	W.H. Hart and P.A. Lyons eds., *Cartularium monasterii de Rameseia*, 3 vols. (Rolls ser., 1884–93).
Reading Cartularies	B.R. Kemp ed., *Reading abbey cartularies* 2 vols. (Camden Society, 4th ser., 31–2, 1986–7).
Reg. Ant.	C.W. Foster and K. Major eds., *The Registrum Antiquissimum of the cathedral church of Lincoln*, 10 vols. and 2 vols. of facsimiles (Lincoln Record Society 27–9, 32, 34, 41, 42, 46, 51, 62, 67, 68, 1931–73).
Reg. Burghersh	N. Bennett ed., *The Registers of Bishop Henry Burghersh 1320–1342, vol. I* (Lincoln Record Society 87, 1999).
Reg. Lacy	G.R. Dunstan ed., *The register of Edmund Lacy, bishop of Exeter, 1420–1455*, 5 vols. (Canterbury and York Society 60–63, 66; also Devon and Cornwall Record Society, new ser., 7, 10, 13, 16, 18, 1963–72).
Reg. Roff.	J. Thorpe ed., *Registrum Roffense* (London 1769).
Reg. Sutton	R.M.T. Hill ed., *The rolls and register of Bishop Oliver Sutton, 1280–1299*, 8 vols. (Lincoln Record Society 39, 43, 48, 52, 60, 64, 69, 76, 1948–86).
RHW	W.P.W. Phillimore and F.N. Davis eds., *Rotuli Hugonis de Welles, episcopi Lincolniensis, AD mccix–mccxxxv*, 3 vols. (Canterbury and York Society 1, 3, 4, 1907–9, and Lincoln Record Society 3, 6, 9, 1912–14).
Rievaulx Cartulary	J.C. Atkinson ed., *Cartularium abbathiae de Rievalle, ordinis Cisterciensis, fundatae anno mcxxxii* (Surtees Society 83, 1889).
Robinson, J.A.	'Jocelin of Wells and members of his family' in his *Somerset Historical Essays* (London 1921), app. D, pp. 156–9.
Robinson, J.A.	*Somerset Historical Essays* (London 1921).
Roger of Wendover	H.E. Hewlett ed., *Chronica Rogeri de Wendover sive Flores Historiarum*, 3 vols. (Rolls ser., 1886–9).
Rot. Chart.	T.D. Hardy ed., *Rotuli chartarum . . . vol. i, pars i, 1199–1216* (Record Commission 1837).
Rot. Grav.	F.N. Davis, C.W. Foster and A. Hamilton Thompson eds., *Rotuli Ricardi Gravesend, episcopi Lincolniensis, AD mcclviii–mcclxxix* (Canterbury and York Society 31 and Lincoln Record Society 20, 1925).
Rot. Litt. Claus.	T.D. Hardy ed., *Rotuli litterarum clausarum in turri Londinensi asservati*, 2 vols. (Record Commission 1833–4).
Rot. Litt. Pat.	T.D. Hardy ed., *Rotuli litterarum patentium in turri Londinensi asservati* (Record Commission 1835).
Rot. Cur. Reg.	F. Palgrave ed., *Rotuli Curiae Regis*, 2 vols. (Record Commission 1835).
RRG	F.N. Davis ed., *Rotuli Roberti Grosseteste, episcopi Lincolniensis, AD mccxxxv–mccliii* (Canterbury and

	York Society 10, 1913, and Lincoln Record Society 11, 1914).
St Frideswide's Cartulary	S.R. Wigram ed., *The cartulary of the monastery of St Frideswide at Oxford*, 2 vols. (Oxford Historical Society 28, 31, 1895–6).
Salisbury Charters	W.D. Macray ed., *Charters and documents illustrating the history of the cathedral, city, and diocese of Salisbury, in the twelfth and thirteenth centuries* (Rolls ser. 1891).
Salter, H.E. ed.	*Mediaeval Archives of the University of Oxford*, 2 vols. (Oxford Historical Society 70, 73, 1917–21).
Sanders	I.J. Sanders, *English Baronies: a study of their origin and descent 1086–1327* (Oxford 1960).
Smith, 'Rolls'	D.M. Smith, 'The rolls of Hugh of Wells, bishop of Lincoln 1209–35', *Bulletin of the Institute of Historical Research* xlv (1972), 155–95.
Smith, D.M.	'The *Officialis* of the bishop in twelfth- and thirteenth-century England: problems of terminology' in M.J. Franklin and C. Harper-Bill eds., *Medieval Ecclesiastical Studies in honour of Dorothy Owen* (Woodbridge 1995), pp. 201–20.
Smith, D.M.	'Hugh's administration of the diocese of Lincoln' in H. Mayr-Harting ed., *St Hugh of Lincoln: lectures delivered at Oxford and Lincoln to celebrate the eighth centenary of St Hugh's consecration as bishop of Lincoln* (Oxford 1987), pp. 19–47.
Thompson, S.	*Women Religious: the founding of English nunneries after the Norman Conquest* (Oxford 1991).
Thurgarton Cartulary	T. Foulds ed., *The Thurgarton Cartulary* (Stamford 1994).
Trotman, F.H.	*The Trotman Family 1086–1963* (priv. pd 1965).
VCH	*Victoria County History.*
Walter of Coventry	W. Stubbs ed., *Memoriale fratris Walteri de Coventria: the historical collections of Walter of Coventry (from Brutus to 1225)*, 2 vols. (Rolls ser. 1872–3).
Wells thesis	D.M. Smith, 'The administration of Hugh of Wells, bishop of Lincoln, 1209–1235' (unpublished Ph.D. thesis, University of Nottingham, 1970).
Werner, J.	'Nachlese aus Zuricher Handschriften – I. Die Teilnehmerliste des Laterankonzils vom Jahre 1215', *Neues Archiv der Gesellschaft für altere deutsche Geschichtskunde* xxxi (1906), 575–93.

OTHER ABBREVIATIONS

Add.	Additional	Lib.	Library
app.	appendix	m.	membrane
archbp(s)	archbishop(s)	misc.	miscellanea, miscellaneous
archdn(s)	archdeacon(s)	ms.	manuscript
BL	British Library, London	Mun.	muniment(s)
Bodl.	Bodleian Library, Oxford	opp.	opposite
bp(s)	bishop(s)	pd	printed
CCC	Corpus Christi College	PRO	Public Record Office,
cat.	catalogue		London
Ch.	Charter	repd	reprinted
Ch. Ant.	Charta Antiqua	RO	Record Office
CUL	Cambridge University	s. - ex.	late-century
	Library	s. - in.	early-century
D. & C.	Dean and Chapter	s. - med.	mid-century
dioc.	diocese	ser.	series
doct	document	Trans.	Transactions
ed.	edited, editor	transl.	in translation, translated
edn	edition		
LAO	Lincolnshire Archives		
	Office		

INTRODUCTION

This collection of some four hundred and fifty episcopal *acta* or mentions of such *acta* brings together the surviving charters issued in the name of Hugh of Wells, bishop of Lincoln 1209–1235. A few charters still survive in original form but for the most part they are to be found as later copies entered into the registers and cartularies of cathedrals and monasteries and other ecclesiastical and governmental bodies with which the bishop had dealings. Taken together with the fourteen surviving enrolments of the bishop (an internal working record of his episcopal clerks comprising in the main brief summaries of transactions rather than transcripts of outgoing charters) and a composite register recording vicarage endowments and appropriations, this represents a formidable archival source for the episcopate of Hugh of Wells, much more documentary evidence than is available for the majority of twelfth- and thirteenth-century English bishops.[1] That being said, it must be emphasised that this collection is a mere fraction of what was issued or enrolled by the episcopal secretariat, and it is fortunate that at least one archdeaconry 'charter roll' has survived to mitigate to some extent the scale of the losses of *acta*. At a conservative estimate it is probable that a minimum of ten further rolls of the bishop's enactments have been lost, maybe many more.[2] When the number of original documents issued during the episcopate is considered then the enormous losses can only be hazarded. For instance, in the series of institution rolls there are summary references to almost 1,200 (written) mandates for induction being despatched to archdeacons and their officials: only one such induction mandate has survived![3] Given that most of the original *acta* or transcribed copies survive among the archives of institutional recipients – monasteries, cathedrals, collegiate churches etc. – then that archival bias in itself can easily distort the extent of our knowledge of diocesan administration and give undue prominence to certain categories of record to the detriment of others. At the same time the supplementing of the enrolments by material not customarily

---

[1] For the bishop's enrolments and the *Liber Antiquus* see *Guide to Bishops' Registers*, pp. 106–7; D.M. Smith, 'The rolls of Hugh of Wells, bishop of Lincoln 1209–35', *Bulletin of the Institute of Historical Research* 45 (1972), 155–95 (hereafter Smith, 'Rolls').

[2] Based on the likely existence of seven further archdeaconry charter rolls from 1219 x 20, and two earlier ones for the whole diocese *c.* 1214 x 1218, 1218 x 19, and at least one (probably more) memoranda roll for the whole diocese, arranged chronologically. References occur to charter rolls from the bishop's sixth pontifical year (1214 x 15) and to the memoranda roll from the bishop's sixteenth year (1224 x 25) but it is probable that they were coeval developments (charter rolls – *RHW* i 199, 232; ii 84, 210, 226; iii 8, 40, 56 (on original roll, omitted by editor), 79, 80, 82, 125; memoranda roll – ibid. iii 137, also ii 34, 87, 159, 244; iii 201).

[3] For induction mandates, both written and verbal, see Wells thesis i 11–12; M. Burger, 'Sending, joining, writing, and speaking in the diocesan administration of thirteenth-century Lincoln', *Mediaeval Studies* 55 (1993), 151–82; and his 'Bishops, archdeacons and communication between centre and locality in the diocese of Lincoln, *c.* 1214–99' in P.R. Coss and S.D. Lloyd eds., *Thirteenth Century England V* (Woodbridge 1995), pp. 195–206.

registered or which might have once been found in the missing rolls provides a welcome additional source and, as I hope to show when discussing the dating of documents, creates a unique opportunity for comparison and analysis.

HUGH OF WELLS, BISHOP OF LINCOLN 1209–1235

The future Bishop Hugh II of Lincoln was the eldest son of Edward of Wells, and was presumably a native of the cathedral city in Somerset from which he took his name.[4] Edward held land of the bishop of Bath in Lancherley, a village close by Wells, and in the 1180s was also granted property in Wells itself.[5] It is not known in which year Hugh was born but it is probable that he was an old man at the time of his death in 1235. As far as can be determined from the extant sources, he never left his episcopal residence of Stow Park near Lincoln after March 1233 and this long period of immobility would seem to suggest incapacity due to old age or physical infirmity. Hugh had at least one brother, Jocelin, who became bishop of Bath in 1206 and remained there until his death in 1242. A niece, Agatha is mentioned (no. 408). Walter of Wells, later canon of Lincoln, and Hugh of Wells, canon of Lincoln and archdeacon of Bath, and the latter's *nepos*, Hugh son of Osbert of Wells, feature prominently during Bishop Hugh's episcopate but it is unclear whether they were relatives.[6] It is hazardous, without any other confirmatory evidence, to place much reliance on similar territorial surnames. The future Bishop Hugh began his ecclesiastical career in the service of Bishop Reginald FitzJocelin of Bath (1174–1191) – his earliest occurrences in a witness list can be dated 1189 x 1191[7] – and after the bishop's death, he is found as a clerk in the household of his successor, Bishop Savaric (1192–1205).[8] He first occurs as a canon of Wells cathedral at the end of the century.[9] Hugh maintained close links with his native diocese throughout his life and drew on many clerks from the region for his own episcopal *familia*.

With the accession of King John in 1199 Hugh entered the royal chancery. It may be conjectured that his entry into the royal administration was connected with Simon of Wells *alias* FitzRobert, archdeacon of Wells, and a close adherent of Hubert Walter, archbishop of Canterbury.[10] When Archbishop Hubert was appointed royal chancellor in May 1199, Archdeacon Simon and Hugh were

---

[4] See *HMC Wells* ii 548, charter no. 9; *EEA* 10 no. 68, dated *c.* 1184 x 1188 with Hugh described as Edward's heir. cf. Cambridge, Trinity College ms. R.5.33, fo. 41r '. . . Iocelino natione Wellen' fratre Hugonis Lincoln' presulis . . .' Tradition has ascribed to Jocelin of Wells the surname of Trotman and Dean Armitage Robinson was led to assume a connexion with the family of Tortesmains who held fees in Pilton and elsewhere (*Ann. mon.* i 28; J.A. Robinson, 'Jocelin of Wells and members of his family' in his *Somerset Historical Essays* (1921), app. D., pp. 156–9; see also F.H. Trotman, *The Trotman Family 1086–1963* (priv. pd 1965). Bishop Hugh mentions a bequest to relatives in Pilton in his 1233 will (no. 408).

[5] *HMC Wells* ii 548, charters nos. 9–10.

[6] See index under their names; *Reg. Ant.* ix nos. 2540–1; *Fasti Lincoln*, 88, 129.

[7] *EEA* 10 nos. 68–9, 145, 157, 159–60, 162–3, 166, 178; also no. 72 (date 1186 x 91) and nos. 114–15 (1189).

[8] Ibid. no. 263.

[9] Ibid. no. 234; cf. *Rot. Cur. Reg.* ii 179.

[10] See C.R. Cheney, *Hubert Walter* (London 1967), pp. 43–4, 85, 160, 171. Hugh is found in Simon's company around this time (*Salisbury Charters* no. lxxiii).

brought into the chancery, the former acting as datary and a deputy of the chancellor, in which capacity Hugh eventually succeeded him, when Simon was elevated to the bishopric of Chichester in 1204. Hugh spent the decade from 1199 in active service to the king, both in England and abroad, and it is probable that he was one of the administrators responsible for the implementation of Archbishop Hubert's chancery innovations, close knowledge of which he brought to his diocese with the introduction of episcopal registration there.[11]

Loyal service to the king produced its expected rewards in ecclesiastical preferment – including a prebend in Lincoln cathedral and the prebend of Ealdstreeet in St Paul's, London, and the archdeaconry of Wells, as well as several parochial benefices;[12] in addition he was granted the Somerset manors of Cheddar and Axbridge and the hundreds of Cheddar and Winterstoke in feefarm.[13] He also acted as a royal custodian of the vacant bishopric of Lincoln between 1200 and 1203 and in a similar capacity in the diocese of Bath and Glastonbury during the 1205–6 vacancy.[14] Early in 1209 Pope Innocent III commanded the cathedral chapter of Lincoln to elect a new bishop in place of William of Blois who had died in 1206 and by 12 April 1209 Hugh is found styled as bishop-elect of Lincoln.[15] The election of a prominent royal official aroused papal suspicions that the king had exerted pressure on the chapter and the pope commissioned the exiled Archbishop Stephen Langton of Canterbury to examine the elect and certain charges made against him.[16] Hugh's breach with the excommunicate King John came later in the year after he, along with other royal officials, had urged the king to come to terms with the pope. King John was excommunicated in November 1209 and many former supporters took themselves abroad. Hugh was among this number and on 20 December at Melun he was consecrated as bishop of Lincoln by Langton.[17] The new bishop remained in exile for three and a half years during the papal interdict on England. Of the intervening period little is known. Apart from his consecration the only other recorded appearance Hugh made during his enforced stay abroad was in November 1212 at St Martin de Garenne near Paris when he drew up his testament (below, no. 2). In early 1213 Hugh (together with fellow-exiles, the archbishop of Canterbury and the bishops of London, Ely, and Hereford) was the recipient of a papal missive ordering the suspension of all those clergy who had failed to observe the excommunication of the king.[18] On 24 May 1213, a few days after King John's submission to the pope, royal letters were directed to Bishop Hugh promising peace and safety and urging him to return to England.[19] The bishop

[11] Hugh's first appearance in the royal records is on 26 August 1199 (*CDF* no. 1103). See *Rot. Chart.*, *Rot. Litt. Pat.* and *Rot. Litt. Claus. passim*. He first occurs as joint-datary with John of Brancaster in 1200 (*Rot. Chart.* 74b). Cf. S. Painter, *The Reign of King John* (Baltimore 1945), pp. 104–5. See also Wells thesis i 182–7.
[12] *Fasti Lincoln* 129; *Fasti St Paul's London* 48; *EEA* 10 p. 219; *Rot. Chart.* 129. For parochial benefices see ibid. 140b; *Rot. Litt. Pat.* 43.
[13] *Rot. Chart.* 129.
[14] Ibid. 99b; *Rot. Litt. Pat.* 57b, 63b; *Rot. Litt. Claus.* i 49, 52, 56, 61, 63b, 66b, 67, 72b; *Pipe Roll 7 John*, pp. 144–5.
[15] *Letters of Innocent III* no. 829; *Rot. Chart.* 185.
[16] *Letters of Innocent III* nos. 851, 853; *CPL* i 34; cf. *MPCM* iii 526.
[17] *MPCM* iii 528; *Gir. Camb.* vii 5.
[18] *Letters of Innocent III* no. 908, cf. no. 905.
[19] *Reg. Ant.* i no. 207.

returned to England in June or July 1213[20] and his active episcopate dates from then. His earliest *actum* after his return dates from October 1213 (no. 3) and later that month he is found dedicating the conventual church of Dunstable.[21] Presumably diocesan duties took up much of his time. The see of Lincoln had in effect been without a pastor for over seven years; during the interdict the temporalities has been entrusted to a royal custodian, Brian de Insula, and mention is made of the bishop's official, master Richard of Berkhamsted, in 1209. Certainly letters of presentation were addressed to 'offic' domini Linc' episcopi' or 'offic' episcopatus Linc' in this period. Perhaps also, as in the case of episcopal vacancies, certain non-sacramental spiritual duties were carried out by the dean of Lincoln cathedral and the eight archdeacons of the diocese (acting as agents of the cathedral chapter).[22] Hugh was present when Magna Carta was issued and he joined his episcopal colleagues in protesting when the barons refused to honour the promise to give surety for the maintenance of the peace (nos. 23–5). In September 1215 the bishop again left England, this time to attend the Fourth Lateran Council, and was abroad for some eighteen months.[23] He is next found in England in early February 1217 when he was the recipient of a royal mandate concerning Newnham priory.[24]

Although he never totally ceased to be active in public affairs, the task of restoring normality to diocesan government and introducing new methods in administrative practice and procedure consumed Hugh's energies for the rest of his episcopate. His tenure of the geographically extensive see was marked by transition and innovation in the sphere of episcopal government.[25] The introduction of episcopal registration at Lincoln has already been mentioned and I have dealt with this subject in more detail elsewhere.[26] References are found to his visitations of monastic houses and despite Matthew Paris's strictures on him as *monachorum gravator indefessus, canonicorum, sanctimonialium et omnium religiosorum malleus*,[27] no evidence survives to indicate a particular antipathy to the monastic orders, over and above an understandable anxiety to maintain the rights of his see. Indeed, the St Albans chronicler's comments probably reflect the particular feelings at that powerful (and canonically exempt) abbey following

---

[20] *Walter of Coventry* ii 213; *Roger of Wendover* ii 81. For King John's restitution to the bishopric of Lincoln see *Reg. Ant.* i nos. 205–6, 211.

[21] *Ann. mon.* iii 42.

[22] For Brian de Insula *CRR* vi 361; vii 197–8; *Reg. Ant.* ii no. 615; for Richard of Berkhamsted *Pipe Roll 11 John* p. 121; and for royal presentations *Rot. Litt. Pat.* 95b, 96b. For vacancy practice see also D.M. Smith, 'The *Officialis* of the bishop in twelfth- and thirteenth-century England: problems of terminology' in M.J. Franklin and C. Harper-Bill eds., *Medieval Ecclesiastical Studies in honour of Dorothy Owen* (Woodbridge 1995), pp. 201–20, especially 208–12.

[23] *Cal. Ch. R.* i 131; Hugh was in Rome in January 1216 (*Acta Stephani Langton* no. 42).

[24] *CPR 1216–25*, p. 29.

[25] The Lincoln diocese was divided into eight archdeaconries: Bedford, Buckingham, Leicester and Oxford which covered their respective civil counties; Huntingdon (Huntingdonshire and the northern part of Hertfordshire), Lincoln (all Lincolnshire except for the portion covered by Stow archdeaconry), Northampton (Northamptonshire and Rutland), and Stow (West Riding of Lindsey). Bishop Hugh had (in addition to the palace at Lincoln) residences at Stow Park, Buckden, Fingest, Kilsby, Dorchester, Cropredy, Spaldwick, Nettleham and Lyddington (all within the diocese), castles at Sleaford, Banbury and Newark on Trent, and a London residence at the Old Temple, Holborn.

[26] Smith, 'Rolls'.

[27] *MPHM* ii 375–6.

the 1219 composition with Bishop Hugh over the ordination of a perpetual vicar-age in Luton church and the appointment of priors in the abbey's dependent cells of Belvoir, Hertford and Beadlow within the Lincoln diocese (appendix, no. 3). A similar clash with the exempt Gilbertine order centred on the appropriation of parish churches belonging to the order.[28] In this regard Hugh was particularly active in appropriations and the proper ordination of vicarages and provision of pastoral care, building upon the foundations of twelfth-century bishops. Those earlier efforts had been acknowledged and confirmed in the enactments of the Fourth Lateran Council of 1215 and in the later provincial Council of Oxford of 1222. These enactments gave conciliar authority to the subsequent actions of the diocesan and thereby accelerated the process of extending the system and, wher-ever possible, of re-ordaining existing vicarages to the required standard, activi-ties well-represented in Hugh's register known as the *Liber Antiquus* and his vicarage rolls.[29] The extant enrolments and this present collection of *acta* together provide evidence of a man with a remarkable talent for administration.

The bishop died at his residence of Stow Park on 7 February 1235 and was buried in the north choir aisle of his cathedral three days later.[30] A plain stone slab still marks his place of burial. His later testament, dated 1 June 1233 (below, no. 408), is a lengthy document, dealing with bequests to family and household clerks, the fabric of Lincoln cathedral, numerous religious houses in the diocese, and the poor. The residue of his estate was to be divided between the poor relig-ious and leper houses of the diocese, the masters and scholars from Oxford, con-verts from Judaism in his diocese, and poor men on the episcopal manors.

THE EPISCOPAL CLERKS AND DATARIES

The fact that the vast bulk of Hugh's *acta* were witnessed and dated is of great help when trying to discover details of the episcopal household staff and secretar-iat. However, previous studies of the Lincoln diocese in the twelfth and early thir-teenth centuries have already emphasised the shortcomings and limitations of witness-lists as a source and it is still important to bear this in mind.[31] It is, for example, very difficult to distinguish, among the many clerks who witness these documents, between those who are attached to the bishop and those who are in the service of other witnesses. The term *clericus domini episcopi* is rarely used and regularity of appearance in these lists must of necessity remain the principal criterion for judging the membership of the *familia*. It need hardly be stressed that this method is by no means foolproof. Walter of Crombe attests episcopal charters in 1226 (nos. 247–8, 251, 253–4, 263) but the fact that he only occurs

---

[28] *Acta Stephani Langton* no. 43.

[29] For appropriations and vicarages in the twelfth century see C.R. Cheney, *From Becket to Langton* (Manchester 1956), pp. 131–2, 182–5; and for the Lincoln diocese in particular *EEA* 1 and 4 *passim*; D.M. Smith, 'Hugh's administration of the diocese of Lincoln' in H. Mayr-Harting ed., *St Hugh of Lincoln: lectures delivered at Oxford and Lincoln to celebrate the eighth centenary of St Hugh's con-secration as bishop of Lincoln* (Oxford 1987), pp. 19–47, especially 35–9.

[30] *MPHM* ii 376.

[31] *EEA* 1 xli–ii; *EEA* 4 xxvi–vii. See also M. Burger, '*Officiales* and the *familiae* of the bishops of Lincoln, 1258–99', *Journal of Medieval History* 16 (1990), 39–53.

when William of Bardney, archdeacon of Wells, is attesting would seem to suggest a link with the Somerset archdeacon rather than with Bishop Hugh. Similarly William of Winchcombe occurs in the vicarage rolls in 1218 described as the clerk of Robert of Hailes, archdeacon of Huntingdon,[32] but he is found attesting Hugh's *acta* regularly without such designation from 1217, the year before he received the foregoing description in the enrolments. Robert of Hailes was an important member of the episcopal *familia*, occasionally acting as datary, and this association between William of Winchcombe and the archdeacon – a natural enough association if credence can be given to the geographical proximity of their territorial surnames – clearly indicates a method of recruitment of household personnel and raises the question of the exact relationship between the bishop and the *clerici* who witnessed his charters and assisted him in diocesan administration. Perhaps a more 'pyramidal' arrangement, with clerks of prominent members of the *familia* being also at the disposal of the bishop, should be considered.

As might be expected, the majority of members of Hugh's clerical staff in the early years of his episcopate had been associated with him at various stages of his career before 1209. Roger de Bohun is found as a contemporary of the future bishop's as a canon of Wells in the time of Bishop Reginald of Bath before 1191.[33] William de Thornaco, Peter of Bath, Nicholas of Evesham, Richard of Cernay, Philip of Langport, John of Taunton, and Walter of Wells all had definite Somerset connections and they may have been known to Hugh when he was in the service of Bishops Reginald and Savaric or later when he was archdeacon of Wells.[34] Another source of recruits was the royal chancery and Hugh's particular connection with Simon FitzRobert, archdeacon of Wells and bishop of Chichester. Peter of Wilton is found in the royal records as Hugh's clerk as early as 1205[35] and Roger of Bristol is known to have been chaplain of Bishop Simon of Chichester.[36] Master Stephen of Chichester may have been connected with Bishop Simon, although it is more likely that he was a connection of Peter of Chichester, a future dean of Wells and erstwhile companion of the two Wells brothers.[37] Six clerks bore territorial surnames indicative of Lincoln diocesan origin – master William of Lincoln, master William of Benniworth, Warin of Kirton, master Robert of Graveley, Richard of Fingest and master Amaury of Buckden, the last two places being the sites of episcopal residences. In addition Thomas of Fiskerton was inherited from Hugh's immediate predecessor, Bishop William of Blois (1203–1206) and remained active in Hugh's service until 1222, while other clerks of St Hugh (1186–1200) and Bishop William seem to have retired to Lincoln as residentiary canons and are occasionally found attesting later *acta* in full chapter of the cathedral. Some like Hugh of St Edward, Adam of

32 *RHW* i 191.
33 J.A. Robinson, *Somerset Historical Essays*, p. 87; *EEA* 10, pp. l, lii; *Fasti Lincoln*, p. 94.
34 For Thornaco see *Lincoln Fasti*, pp. 10 & n. 1 (Thornaco), 133 (Bath), 83 (Evesham), 14, 113 (Taunton); 61 & n. 2 (Wells). For other probable members of the Thornaco family *EEA* 10 xlii–iii, xlv, xlvii–viii, li–ii; for Cernay and Langport see the present index.
35 *Rot. Litt. Claus.* i 46, cf. *CRR* i 436.
36 *Rot. Litt. Claus.* i 398b; *Pipe Roll 8 John*, p. 65; *Chichester Acta* nos. 143, 152–4.
37 *Fasti Lincoln*, p. 145; *HMC Wells* i 432, 480, 491.

St Edmund and William son of Fulk received archdeaconries from Hugh and assisted him in the diocesan administration.[38]

One feature of Bishop Hugh's witness-lists is that they are remarkably full and a close scrutiny of over two hundred and fifty acta in the bishop's active period 1215–1233 found that the numbers of *clerici* who regularly attest – and consequently can be considered possible members of the *familia* – remained fairly constant throughout this period. Twenty-five of the clerks who are assumed to have been members of the bishop's staff were described as *magistri* and twenty-nine were eventually rewarded with canonries in Lincoln cathedral, an understandable action since this was one of the simplest means the diocesan possessed of recompensing clerks for their services. The more prominent members of the group received higher preferment: eight obtained archdeaconries, one became precentor of Lincoln, three succeeded one other as subdean of Lincoln, and William de Thornaco ultimately rose to be dean of the cathedral. Besides making use of his rights of collation to prebends and dignities and parish churches in his own gift, the bishop also took advantage of his diocesan right to collate vacant benefices *per lapsum temporis* to reward his staff. William of Benniworth, Oliver Chesney, Amaury of Buckden, Richard of Kent, Nicholas of Evesham, John of Crakehall and Ralph de Waravill all benefited from this practice. At the same time some clerks were presented by religious houses to rich benefices in their gift – whether owing to episcopal pressure or with a desire to ingratiate can only be conjectured. The duration of service of these household clerks differed considerably. Some like Richard of Oxford and Robert of Graveley remained in the bishop's service for between fifteen and twenty years; others occur only for a year or two. Some may have moved on to other households or returned to parochial benefices: Oliver Chesney attests fifty-nine *acta* of the bishop between 1218 and 1223 and latterly acted as episcopal datary, but then disappears from the Lincoln records until his death as rector of Bottesford is announced in 1260 x 1261.

While there is no trace among Hugh's *acta* of an official called the bishop's chancellor, it is possible that the supervision of the bishop's secretarial staff fell to the datary.[39] These dataries were seemingly no mere clerks of the bishop – two were already archdeacons when they acted in this capacity, and another was subdean of the cathedral; with one solitary exception, all the others were canons of the cathedral church. In the first half of Hugh's episcopate there seems to have been some flexibility in that although there was probably a regular datary (e.g. William de Thornaco) it was not unusual for another to carry out such functions during presumed absences. In the latter half of Hugh's pontificate it seems to have been customary for a datary to hold office for several years without interruption, and 'temporary substitutes' are not found.[40] William de Thornaco continued to act until he was transferred from Stow archdeaconry to the extensive archdeaconry of Lincoln; there is a strong possibility that Thomas of Fiskerton's period of office was terminated by death; his successor, John of Taunton, relin-

---

[38] *Fasti Lincoln*, pp. 46, 36, 46 respectively; see also *EEA* 4 xxvii–viii.

[39] So far the earliest reference to an episcopal chancellor at Lincoln dates from 1260 (PRO, E210/11014), cf. *Rot. Grav.* p. 244 (1269).

[40] It is perhaps significant that, apart from two isolated (and solemnly enacted) examples in 1220, the *datum per manum nostram* clause is found only from 1226 onwards. This supports the idea that one of its uses was during the absence of the regular datary (see below).

quished his duties after two years on his promotion to the precentorship of the cathedral, and Ralph de Waravill was replaced after six years by Warin of Kirton, who remained as datary until the bishop's death. A full list of episcopal dataries is appended:

ROGER [OF BRISTOL], CHAPLAIN
Occurs 5 October 1213 (no. 3).

WILLIAM DE THORNACO, ARCHDEACON OF STOW
Occurs from 27 February 1214 (no. 5) to 1 September 1215 (no. 41), and from 24 August 1217 (no. 62) to 25 May 1219 (no. 112).

MASTER ROBERT OF HAILES, ARCHDEACON OF HUNTINGDON
Occurs from 7 February 1215 (no. 16) to 21 August 1215 (no. 33).

MASTEr REGINALD OF CHESTER, SUBDEAN OF LINCOLN
Occurs on 5–6 August 1215 (nos. 30–1) and then from 10 December 1218 (no. 94) to 13 July 1219 (no. 115).

PETER OF BATH, CANON OF LINCOLN
Occurs 23 September 1217 (no. 63) and then from 23 September 1219 (no. 117) to 12 March 1223 (no. 199).

THOMAS OF FISKERTON, CANON OF LINCOLN
Occurs from 21 July 1219 (no.116) to 15 August 1222 (no. 188).

OLIVER CHESNEY, CLERK
Occurs from 25 November 1222 (no. 189) to 2 September 1223 (no. 204).

JOHN OF TAUNTON, CHAPLAIN, CANON OF LINCOLN
Occurs from 29 September 1223 (no. 206) to 25 August 1225 (no. 232).

RALPH DE WARAVILL, CANON OF LINCOLN
Occurs from 26 September 1225 (no. 233) to 9 September 1232 (no. 383).

WARIN OF KIRTON, CHAPLAIN, CANON OF LINCOLN
Occurs from 7 March 1233 (no. 393) to 25 January 1235 (no. 439).

THE DIPLOMATIC OF THE ACTA

The *acta* of Hugh of Wells fit well into the general development of episcopal diplomatic in the English Church as revealed by previous studies of earlier Lincoln *acta* and in the wider provincial aspect.[41] Indeed, any study of the main features of the documents issued by Hugh's clerical staff would have to give particular emphasis to their (almost monotonous) regularity and uniformity. There are few surprises or puzzles, virtually no evidence (as one might expect to be the case at this date) of compilation by recipients rather than the episcopal clerks, and while

[41] See the sections on diplomatic in the series of *EEA* volumes; C.N.L. Brooke, 'English Episcopal *acta* of the twelfth and thirteenth centuries' in M.J. Franklin and C. Harper-Bill eds., *Medieval Ecclesiastical Studies in honour of Dorothy M. Owen* (Woodbridge 1995), pp. 41–56; J. Barrow, 'From the lease to the certificate: the evolution of episcopal acts in England and Wales (*c.* 700 – *c.* 1250)' in J.C. Haidacher and W. Köfler eds., *Die Diplomatik der Bischofsurkunden vor 1250/La Diplomatique épiscopale avant 1250* (Innsbruck 1995), pp. 529–42.

there are new developments (chief among them being the use of the dating clause
in the *acta* and of course in the wider context diocesan registration) the general
picture is one of almost routine, professional document production. This being
the case I will deal quickly with the pertinent diplomatic features of the *acta* and
concentrate on special problems or questions that deserve a more thorough investigation – in particular, the dating clause and the significance of the date. Hugh's
clerks used *Dei gratia Lincolniensis episcopus* for the episcopal style, a usage
which first occurs at Lincoln under Bishop Alexander (1123–48)[42] and which
was employed by his successors with remarkable consistency until being finally
superseded as the standard diplomatic form at Lincoln by *permissione divina* or
miseratione divina Lincolniensis episcopus from the episcopate of Henry Lexing-
ton (1254–58) onwards. Variations in this episcopal style in Hugh's time are rare
and only occur when the bishop is addressing king or pope.[43] The general address
had come to be used for all manner of 'public' diocesan business, save for mandates and commissions and letters of restricted application which were naturally
directed to specific individuals. A similar monotony of form prevails in the
general address: the brief *Omnibus Cristi fidelibus ad quos presens scriptum pervenerit* being the most frequently used throughout the entire episcopate, *Universis sancte matris ecclesie filiis* only rivalling it as a standard form before 1218,
and very occasional use being found of *carta* in place of *scriptum*, and once
littere presentes. The succinct and formal *salutem in Domino* is the most regular
formula used by the episcopal clerks to the virtual exclusion of all other forms,
with a slight alternative *eternam in Domino salutem* being found on only eleven
occasions. The use of the *arenga* or pious preamble, never an essential part of the
charter, was severely curtailed under Bishop Hugh (generally it appears to have
been falling out of fashion) and only twenty-five *acta* have been found with it, on
the whole indulgences with observations on almsgiving, pious donations and
charitable works. The episcopal secretariat also attained a considerable degree of
uniformity in the notification clause used with a general address. Over three
hundred *acta* in this collection contain the simple clause *Noverit universitas
vestra*. Forms of the verb *scire* are only found in the notification in connection
with a few grants of property and possessions, most of which it must be said concerned the bishop's brother, Jocelin of Wells, bishop of Bath and Glastonbury.
The formula of corroboration announced the form of authenticity of the document, validating the business described in the dispositive clauses, and almost
invariably the episcopal seal is mentioned. The episcopal clerks at Lincoln in
Hugh's time mainly preferred three such corroboration clauses: *Quod ut perpetuam obtineat firmitatem, presenti scripto et sigilli nostri appositione duximus
apponendum*; *In huius rei (robur et) testimonium presenti scripto sigillum
nostrum apposuimus*; and *Et ut hec nostra concessio* (and variants) *perpetue firmitatis robur optineat, eam presenti scripto et sigilli nostri appositione duximus
confirmandum*. Such a clause affords ample opportunity for minor scribal variations, which fortunately do not need rehearsing: indeed, fifty-two different ver-

---

[42] *EEA* 1 liii.
[43] *Devotus suus H. divina miseratione Lincolniensis ecclesie minister humilis* when addressing
Henry III (*RHW* ii 204; no. 210); *Devotissimus sanctitatis sue servus H. miseratione divina Lincolniensis ecclesie minister humilis* when addressing Pope Honorius III (*LAASRP* n.s. 6 (1956), 111; no.
127).

sions of the corroboration clause have been found in Hugh's *acta*, but in the main they vary with the choice of words to describe the document (*scriptum/ carta/ littere/ pagina/ institutio/ concessio/ ordinatio/ confirmatio/ compositio/ donatio*), or the verbs employed (*roborare/ corroborare/ confirmare/ apponere/ munire/ communire*). The bulk of the *acta* have witness-lists, invariably introduced by *Hiis testibus*. Those that evidently did not require attestation fall mainly into the category of routine administrative business, such as mandates for induction, the report of enquiries into the patronage of a church or the matrimonial status of litigants etc., the appointment of sequestrators, a notification of excommunication, and so on. Exceptionally a few letters of institution to benefices did not have witnesses (the vast majority did so). Indulgences also fall into this group and clearly, in Hugh's case, merely required a dating-clause. In general the witnesses follow the corroboration clause and precede the date. On formal occasions the *acta* can have up to thirty witnesses but on average the regular number of witnesses is about ten.

Hugh of Wells, with his experience of royal methods of dating documents (introduced in the chancery under Richard I), was the first bishop of Lincoln to include a dating-clause with any regularity in the bulk of his *acta*. The date of each document is always to be found in the eschatochol – even in the case of awards and judgments where a tendency is found elsewhere to include a date in the introductory clauses – and with one solitary exception it constitutes the last sentence of the charter, being immediately preceded by the names of witnesses. Over three hundred of the *acta* in this collection contain a dating-clause, a further forty show evidence of having once had a date and the rest are in truncated cartulary copies. As a general rule, *datum* introduces the date and *actum* is only found on seven occasions. Bishop Hugh's clerks copied the royal sequence of dating by inserting the datary's name before the place-date. The day and month were expressed according to the Roman method and in this Hugh followed papal rather than royal precedents. The royal practice of using the numbering of days within the month is never employed at Lincoln at this time and the use of ecclesiastical festivals also found little favour. Apart from two documents issued while he was in exile in France during the interdict, only two later *acta* mention an ecclesiastical festival (Easter), issued on the same occasion in 1220 (nos. 134–5). The bishop's pontifical year is also used, rather than the year of the Christian era. The combined evidence of the *acta* and the enrolments confirm that Hugh's pontifical year dated from his consecration on 20 December.

THE EPISCOPAL SEAL

Only fifteen specimens of Bishop Hugh's seal have been found and several are in an advanced state of deterioration (nos. 3, 16, 22, 63, 64, 69, 88, 188, 280, 303, 345B, 380, 413, 435, 436). Nevertheless fine impressions of the seal and counterseal are appended to a confirmation for Osney abbey (no. 64) and the 1229 grant of a pension for Newton Longville priory (no. 303). On the obverse, the bishop stands full-length, vested in alb, chasuble, and mitre, with the right hand raised in blessing and the left hand holding his pastoral staff. On the right hand side of the seal, half way up, is the Roman numeral II, distinguishing Hugh II from his predecessor and namesake, St Hugh of Avalon. The reverse (counterseal) has the

Virgin Mary seated, with the child Jesus, and in the base, under an arch, the bishop half-length in profile to the right, vested, with mitre, holding a scroll.[44] A fairly detailed medieval description of the bishop's seal and counterseal and the legends on each is to be found in the *registrum commune* of Bishop Edmund Lacy of Exeter (1420–55), following the inspeximus of Hugh's charter concerning the dean and chapter of Exeter and the Oxfordshire church of Bampton (no. 151):

> . . . primo videlicet sigillo oblongo predicte (*sic*) sancte memorie domini Hugonis dudum Lincolniensis episcopi in quo parte anteriori magna est insculpta sive impressa ymago cuiusdam pontificis vestibus sacerdotalibus induta, baculum pastoralem in manu sua sinistra tenens ac manu dextra benedicens; in cuius sigilli circumferencia scriptum est HUGO DEI GRACIA LINCOLNIENSIS EPISCOPUS et in dorso eiusdem sigilli est alterum sigillum oblongum impressum in cuius medio ymago Virginis gloriose sedentis et Filium in brachio sinistro tenentis ac ubera manu dextera Filio propinantis; insculpta sub cuius pede similitudo est cuiusdam episcopi mitrati genuflectensis et iunctas manus sursum tenentis, et in ipsius sigilli circumferencia metrice scriptum est: VITA SIT HUGONIS HIIS INFORMATA PATRONIS.[45]

To complete the description of seal, it may be added that examples of the episcopal seal have survived in green, natural, and varnished natural wax. The method of attachment is generally on a parchment tag (method 1) but on occasion strings have been used and there are instances of sealing on a tongue. Two methods of sealing by parchment have been found as described by Professor Cheney.[46] The first (the most popular with Hugh's clerks) involved a single horizontal cut through the two thicknesses of parchment in the fold or turn-up, and then a parchment tag was drawn through the slit to carry the seal; in the second case, two parallel cuts were made in the double thickness of the turn-up and a third being made on the crease itself. The tag was passed through the two thicknesses at the upper slit, its tails turned inwards at the second slit and emerging together at the slit on the crease to carry the seal. These are described as method 1 and method 2 respectively in the descriptions in the text. It is difficult to establish whether there were any strict rules regulating the method of applying the seal to specific categories of *acta* according to their purport, and clearly the number of extant originals is not proportionately large. Certainly based on the surviving examples confirmations and grants of appropriation and pensions appear to have always been sealed on a parchment tag, as were those letters of institution which contained both witnesses and dating clause. Letters of institution which bore a date but were not attested were sealed on a tongue and this method of attachment seems to have applied to routine administrative mandates and, if we can judge from the sole surviving example in original, indulgences. The customs of the royal chancery whereby grants in perpetuity were authenticated by attaching the seal on laces or strings was clearly not followed at Lincoln, for such grants could be sealed indiscriminately by laces or on a parchment tag.[47] The grant to Bishop

---

[44] See also *Reg. Ant.* ii p. 338, with a facsimile of the seal and counterseal as a frontispiece to the volume; *BM Seals*, no. 1712.

[45] *Reg. Lacy* ii 342.

[46] *EEA* 2 xlvii.

[47] Maxwell-Lyte, *Great Seal*, p. 302.

Jocelin of Bath of half a knight's fee in Rowberrow and Draycott (no. 8) had seal strings, whereas in the case of a grant of land to the bishop's butler a parchment tag was used (no. 88).

The specimen of the bishop's seal attached to the charter confirming the grant of the advowson of Water Stratford to Luffield priory (no. 63) has aroused interest, for although resembling exactly the normal seal and counterseal in its device and legend, it is nevertheless of much smaller dimensions. The date of this charter is 23 September 1217 and perhaps the explanation of the different-sized matrix may hinge upon the arrangement made by the bishop while he was abroad at the Lateran Council and elsewhere from September 1215 to early 1217. This solitary example of the smaller seal is found, as it happens, on the first document issued after the bishop's return to his diocese with its seal still intact. Examples of the 'normal-sized' seal are found on documents dated 5 October 1213, 7 February 1215 and 20 April 1215 (nos. 3, 16, 22) and the episcopal clerks had reverted to this larger matrix by 14 October 1217 (no. 64), using it continuously until the end of Hugh's episcopate. There is no information available on the arrangements made for the sealing of documents while Hugh was absent abroad. Certainly the vicegerent, master Reginald of Chester, would appear to have been using his personal seal for administrative business[48] but whether the episcopal seal was left in his custody or whether the bishop took a smaller matrix with him and continued to use it for a few months after his return is impossible to ascertain. There is certainly no mention of a *secretum* or *privatum sigillum*.[49] Interestingly, when Bishop Hubert Walter of Salisbury (1189–93) was absent from England his officials used either his counterseal (which was a mirror image of his seal in design but smaller) or else a replica of it.[50] Perhaps something like this happened while Hugh was at the Lateran Council.

DATUM PER MANUM NOSTRAM

The datary is normally named in most of the dating-clauses, but on thirty-three occasions *datum per manum nostram* is found. This personal authorisation of a document by the bishop has been found from time to time in other early

---

[48] *RHW* I 30–1. Simon Islip, the vicar-general of Bishop Henry Burghersh (1320–40), used the episcopal seal (*Reg. Ant.* iii no. 1084).

[49] In the fourteenth century Bp Hugh's seal was connected with an interesting attempt at forgery. In 1319 Edward II inspected a charter for the Gilbertine priory of St Katharine outside Lincoln, dated at Salisbury in 1210, in which it was stated in the corroboration clause that: 'quia sigillum nostrum pro futuris temporibus pluribus est incognitum sigillum . . . nostri domini Iohannis Dei gratia regis Anglie et sigillum venerabilis patris domini Hugonis permissione divina Lincolniensis episcopi . . . (*and others named*) procuravimus' (*CPR 1317–21*, p. 357). Twenty-nine years after the inspeximus, Edward III caused the document and seals to be examined. It was subsequently found out that: 'sigilla predicta aliunde acquisita in superioribus eorum partibus ingeniose aperta fuerant et inscisis infra ceram alteris partibus fili et pergameni per que dicta sigilla pendebant, dicta filum et pergamenum per medium plicature scripti predicti transmissa in dictis aperturis sigillorum predictorum reposita et in cera ipsorum sigillorum predictorum est aperta cum glutino reconjuncta . . .' (*CPR 1348–50*, p. 131). It may also be added in proof of the forgery that at the time the document was supposedly drawn up, Bp Hugh was in exile in France!

[50] *EEA* 18 cvii and app. ii, no. 1.

thirteenth-century episcopal *acta* but it is still highly exceptional.[51] The common link between the bishops who employed this clause was their previous connexion with the royal chancery, where it has been found in use from 1197 at least. Professor Galbraith attributed its use in the royal chancery specifically to cancellarial vacancies and whenever the particular solemnity of the act or occasion demanded the personal assumption of responsibility for the written record by the king.[52] Professor Cheney, discussing its use in episcopal chanceries, suggested that it merely meant that the usual datary was absent and the bishop authorised the document in his place.[53] In addition to these circumstances can be added (as far as the royal chancery is concerned) those occasions where the regular datary was also the beneficiary of the royal grant (presumably to avoid any semblance of impropriety).[54] The introduction of the term seems initially to have been one of expediency – the formulation of an alternative method of dealing with temporary difficulties or specific situations out of the ordinary.

The *datum per manum nostram* clause is found in thirty-three of Bishop Hugh's *acta* and there is no evidence to show that the formula was used at Lincoln before 1220, when two isolated examples have come to light (nos. 134–5). It is not until the employment of Ralph de Waravill as datary from 1226 to 1232 that *per manum nostram* is found with any frequency. Thirteen letters of institution of this period bear the formula and it is perhaps significant that Ralph de Waravill is missing from the witness-lists of these charters (nos. 251, 275, 276, 288, 289, 310, 318, 329, 331, 334, 335, 340, 367). It is most probable that Ralph's absence was instrumental in the use of the episcopal authorisation in these particular cases.

As mentioned above, it seems to have become the acknowledged practice among clerks in the royal chancery that the personal authorisation of the king would be employed whenever the datary was a party to, or a recipient of, a specific royal grant. This precedent is followed at Lincoln towards the end of the bishop's pontificate. At first other means of overcoming this problem had been attempted. In 1220 Thomas of Fiskerton the datary was instituted to the church of St Peter, Northampton; his letter of institution is merely dated by another episcopal clerk, Peter of Bath (no. 148). By 1233 this had given way to *per manum*

---

[51] For its use by John de Gray, bishop of Norwich (1200–14) see *EEA* 6 lxxiii–iv. The *per manum nostram* formula is also found in the *acta* of Jocelin of Wells, bishop of Bath and Glastonbury (Wells D. & C., Liber Albus II, fos. 10r, 13r, 128v, 192v; Liber Ruber, fos. 14r, 15r, 43v; Hereford D. & C. mun. 2042; PRO E164/20, f. 91r; BL, ms. Harl. 3650, fo. 51v; *Glastonbury Cartulary* i 21); Richard Marsh, bishop of Durham (Durham D. & C. Cartuarium Vetus, f. 148r; *Rievaulx Cartulary*, p. 223; *Feodarium Prioratus Dunelmensis*, pp. lxxxvii–viii); Walter de Gray, archbishop of York (Durham D. & C. Cartuarium Vetus, fo. 157v); Ralph Neville, bishop of Chichester (*Chichester Cartulary* no. 246); Walter Mauclerc, bishop of Carlisle (Hereford D. & C. mun. 2039); Eustace of Fauconberg, bishop of London (ibid., no. 2043); and Thomas de Blundeville, bishop of Norwich (BL, ms. Cotton Faustina A iv, fo. 110r (dat '. . . manu nostra . . .').

[52] V.H. Galbraith, *Studies in the Public Records* (London 1949), pp. 126–9.

[53] C.R. Cheney, *English Bishops' Chanceries*, p. 89.

[54] In 1204 King John conferred upon Hugh of Wells, then royal datary, the church of Edington – the formula *per manum nostram* was used (*Rot. Chart.* p. 140b). At Hugh's wishes, John also conferred the vicarage of Adisham on Jocelin of Wells, his brother. The personal authorisation of the king is used, even though on the same day Hugh of Wells is found acting as the regular datary (ibid. 157). In 1205 when Jocelin of Wells was the regular datary, a royal grant of the church of Meriden merited the *per manum nostram* formula (ibid. 142).

nostram as can be verified by the use of the term in the letter of admission of Warin of Kirton, the then current datary, to the church of Nettleham (no. 398).

Although the episcopal datary's absence or the vacancy of the office would seem to account adequately for a fair number of such *acta* of royal chancery-trained prelates, it is equally certain that in several cases the solemnity of the occasion or the document was alone responsible for the use of the formula. In 1210 Bishop Jocelin of Bath and Glastonbury augmented the endowments of the deanery and subdeanery of Wells; four years later he enacted that the chapter should have the custody and fruits of vacant prebends while the bishop retained similar rights in respect of the dignities of the cathedral.[55] These two charters are of considerable importance for the bishop's relations with the chapter and for the capitular constitution. In accordance with the solemnity of these episcopal ordinances, the relevant parts of the dating clauses read respectively: *dat' per manum nostram et Alexandri decani et capituli Wellensis* and *dat' in capitulo Wellensi per manum nostram et decani et capituli*. There could be no better examples illustrating the use of the personal authorisation to lend added weight and authority to a particular transaction. Subsequent enactments of Bishop Jocelin relating to the vicars choral of Wells and the augmentation of the common fund of the canons are also dated in chapter *per manum nostram*.[56]

The first occurrence of *per manum nostram* in Hugh's acta is in two charters issued in the chapter of Lincoln on Easter Day 1220 (nos. 134–5). Both concern episcopal grants of pensions from churches in the bishop's collation to augment the common fund of the canons of Lincoln. In one version of the second charter, Thomas of Fiskerton, the current episcopal datary, is to be found in the witness list. Twenty-five charters issued *in capitulo Lincolniensi* have survived before this date and a further sixteen from 1220 to 1227, which are authorised by the current datary. The only difference between these two charters and the other forty-one is that the former are the only documents to contain a grant to the chapter, and the use of the episcopal authorisation can thus be attributed either to the solemnity of the enactments and the bishop's desire to symbolically ensure their provisions (as at Wells) or to the fact that Thomas of Fiskerton the datary was also a canon of Lincoln and consequently a member of the body to whom the charters were directed. From 1226 onwards the situation at Lincoln becomes more complex with the apparent extension of the scope of the personal authorisation, the reason for which is still far from clear. Thirteen charters are found which not only contain the *datum per manum nostram* clause but at the same time include the attestation of the regular datary – Ralph de Waravill or Warin of Kirton. These examples obviously do not fit easily into any of the previously-discussed categories. It is just conceivable that a general confirmation of the possessions of the Augustinian priory of Fineshade (no. 247) and the grant to Bishop Jocelin of the custody of the land and heirs of Ralph Cromwell and William de Dive (no. 407) were considered matters of sufficient importance and solemnity to require *per manum nostram*, but against this one must set the fact that in 1221 a grant of wardship was held to be such a sufficiently routine piece of administrative business that it was dated by Thomas of Fiskerton (no. 155). It can be argued

---

55 Wells D. & C., Liber Albus II, fos. 43v, 14r respectively.
56 Ibid., fos. 128v, 14v.

that the administrative changes taking place in the episcopal chancery in the time of Ralph de Waravill and his successor as datary, Warin of Kirton, could have involved a change in attitude towards the significance of specific types of document but this is really venturing too far into the hypothetical and the point should not be laboured. The eleven remaining charters were all issued *in capitulo Lincolniensi*. In 1220 the reason for this usage appeared to be dependent upon the contents of the *acta* and the circumstances of their issue – the solemnity of the grants to the common fund of the canons made in full chapter. In the later period only three of the enactments could have been so described – the ordination of the bishop's anniversary (no. 378), grants of pensions from the churches of Brattleby and Hambleton in augmentation of the common fund (no. 379) and, in addition, a grant of six marks from Kilsby church to provide for the maintenance of two servants to guard the cathedral day and night (no. 381). The remaining documents fall into categories of business which earlier in the pontificate would have been authorised by the regular datary, even when they were issued in the chapter of Lincoln. The following table comparing the dating clauses of similar types of documents issued both in the early years and towards the end of the episcopate will convincingly illustrate my point. It is important to realise that from 1229 onwards, every charter issued in the chapter of Lincoln was dated *per manum nostram* without any apparent regard to its contents:

Acta dated 'in capitulo Lincolniensi'

1. 12 July 1219　Appropriation of Marston St Laurence church to the abbey of St Evroul. Dated 'by the hand of Reginald of Chester'. (no. 113)
     9 Apr. 1230　Appropriation of Rushden church to Lenton priory. Dated *per manum nostram*. Ralph de Waravill, regular datary, a witness. (no. 320)

2. 28 Dec. 1217　Grant of a pension from the church of Beesby to Greenfield priory. Dated 'by the hand of William de Thornaco'. (no. 75)
     2 April 1229　Grant of a pension from Horwood church to Newton Longville priory. Dated *per manum nostram*. Ralph de Waravill, regular datary, a witness. (no. 303)
     8 Sept. 1232　Grant of a pension from Great Paxton church to Holyrood abbey. Dated *per manum nostram*. Ralph de Waravill, regular datary, a witness. (no. 377)
     9 Sept. 1232　Grant of a pension from Moulsoe church to Goring priory. Dated *per manum nostram*. Ralph de Waravill, regular datary, a witness. (no. 380)

3. 16 Dec. 1220　Confirmation of Bampton church to the dean and chapter of Exeter and ordination of a vicarage. Dated 'by the hand of Thomas of Fiskerton'. (no. 151)
     9 Sept. 1231　Confirmation of Haddenham church and its chapels to Rochester cathedral priory and ordination of a vicarage. Dated *per manum nostram*. Ralph de Waravill, regular datary, a witness. (no. 346)

4. The following *acta* are similar in content, though not identical.

     25 Dec. 1221　Permission for a private chapel. Dated 'by the hand of Thomas of Fiskerton'. (no. 177)
     2 Apr. 1229　Permission for Hockliffe hospital to have a chapel and burial rights.

Dated *per manum nostram*. Ralph de Waravill, regular datary, a witness. (no. 304)

? 2 Apr. 1229 Permission for Stonely hospital to have a chapel and burial rights. Dated *per manum nostram*. Ralph de Waravill, regular datary, a witness. (no. 305)

5. 15 Aug. 1222 Grant of tithes of Fleet to Castle Acre priory. Dated 'by the hand of Thomas of Fiskerton'. (no. 187)

9 Sept. 1232 Grant of tithes of Thornton by Horncastle to the dean and chapter of Lichfield. Dated *per manum nostram*. Ralph de Waravill, regular datary, a witness. (no. 382)

How can these apparent illogicalities be explained? Professor Cheney and others have questioned the meaning of witness-lists and have tentatively suggested that the datary might not have been present when the drafting of the act was authorised, even though he attested the document.[57] This may be the case. However, I am more inclined to believe that the reason for the use of the *per manum nostram* formula in these eight instances cited above lies not in their contents, but rather is related to the circumstances surrounding the redaction of these acts and the place of issue – namely *in capitulo Lincolniensi*. Under Ralph de Waravill there seems to have been a deliberate extension of the use of this personal episcopal authorisation as far as charters enacted in the cathedral chapter of Lincoln are concerned. Whereas, initially, the apparent criterion for the use of this dating clause seems to have been the solemnity of the document in itself, this was gradually superseded by the notion that the clause applied to the solemnity of the occasion – the fact that the documents were authorised in full chapter – irrespective of the tenor of the charters that were issued at these times. It may well have been a conscious development, attributable to the datary of the time.

In this preliminary investigation I have attempted to offer a plausible explanation for the introduction and use of *datum per manum nostram*. However, it must be emphasised that my findings are only tentative and their corroboration and disproof will only be possible when much more research has been undertaken into the administration of the other royal chancery-trained prelates who are known to have employed the personal authorisation in their *acta*. The real irony of the situation lies in the fact that *datum per manum nostram* came to be employed far beyond its original scope by the royal chancery clerks in the later years of Henry III and to the exclusion of all other methods of dating, but in the episcopal chanceries the formula rapidly disappeared. At Lincoln the use of the *per manum* formula with the name of a datary has been found only infrequently in documents issued by Hugh's immediate successor, Robert Grosseteste (1235–53),[58] and it very soon gave way to a simpler form of dating with the time and the place-date and the pontifical year only. *Per manum nostram* is not found at Lincoln after Bishop Hugh's death.

---

[57] C.R. Cheney, *English Bishops' Chanceries*, p. 89.
[58] *RRG* 58, 138, 141, 190, 207, 252, 316–17, 343.

WHAT DOES THE DATE ACTUALLY MEAN?

Editors of medieval texts are probably so delighted to be presented with precisely dated documents, particularly after the problems of attempting to date undated material of the twelfth century from often meagre internal evidence, that too little attention has been devoted to what the date of the document actually means in relation to the act the document describes. It may seem bizarre, even perverse, to insert a note of caution here about the significance of such precise dates as those found in the dating-clauses of Bishop Hugh's *acta*, but it has become apparent from these Lincoln records that all is not what it seems.

In his seminal work *From Memory to Written Record*, Dr Michael Clanchy has provided a detailed and cogent analysis of the factors leading to dating English documents in the twelfth and thirteenth centuries.[59] One important reason for dating documents and being precise about the place and time dates was to provide a check in case of future disputes about authenticity. The evidentiary nature of documents, that is, putting into written form details of acts that may have taken place some time before, may be considered one reason why dating was not more widespread, but, as Dr Clanchy points out: 'The difficulty with this explanation is that even when a charter was written after the event, it would still have been prudent, if the draftsman really had that regard for posterity which his preamble claimed, to specify in the text the date of the transaction itself and distinguish that from the date on which the charter was written.'[60] Examples of such care over dating do of course exist in the thirteenth century and beyond. In 1298 Bishop Oliver Sutton of Lincoln issued letters patent certifying the institution of the then rector of Middleton Stoney which had taken place in 1295: it runs thus:

> Universis pateat per presentes quod nos. O. permissione divina Lincoln' episcopus ad presentationem abbatis et conventus de Barlinges Willelmum de Luda subdiaconum ad ecclesiam de Midlington nostre diocesis vacantem per mortem quondam Petri Durandi ultimi rectoris eiusdem admisimus et rectorem sextodecimo kalendas Ianuarii anno domini M. CC. nonagesimo quinto instituimus in eadem, tunc pro certo tenentes presentationem de dicto Willelmo factam fuisse canonicam, eo quod facta prout moris est inquisitio super vacatione dicte ecclesie, iure patronatus dictorum religiosorum et persona presentati ac aliis articulis huiusmodi presentationis negotium contingentibus pro presentatione eadem et presentato plenius faciebat, nullo se tunc eidem presentato nec presentationi de se facte nec etiam patronis presentatibus aliqualiter opponente. In cuius rei testimonium sigillum nostrum presentibus est appensum. Datum apud Bukeden' quarto nonas Septembris anno domini M. CC. nonagesimo octavo.[61]

There is nothing very remarkable about this. It is typical of the form of document called *littera testimonialis* supplying information about a past event or act. The bishop's clerks have checked their records and, whatever the reason for the request for such letters testimonial three years after the actual event, have com-

---

[59] M.T. Clanchy, *From Memory to Written Record: England 1066–1307* (2nd edn, Oxford 1993), pp. 299–304.
[60] Ibid., p. 301.
[61] Lincoln, Ep. Reg. I, fo. 186r, pd in *Reg. Sutton* vi 105–6; the 1295 institution is recorded in the Oxford archdeaconry institution roll (ibid., viii 190).

piled a document recording the full details of the 1295 institution, together with the current date for the compilation of the letters patent testifying to the event. Of course Sutton's staff were able to create such a record in this form because his rolls and register of institutions were the first Lincoln enrolments where each summarised institution record was systematically dated. Before Sutton's time (1280–99) these institution records were only arranged by pontifical year of the bishop and not individually dated. That, in itself, is not an obstacle as later responses to royal writs *certiorari* prove when searches were made of the rolls of thirteenth-century bishops of Lincoln. The royal officials were quite content to have information about earlier institutions (normally requested in assizes of darrein presentment) provided with no closer dating than the episcopal year.[62] Can we project this attitude to records back to the early thirteenth century?

A series of chance survivals have made the present documentary material available for Hugh of Wells unique. Diocesan registration of selective categories of acts is very much a phenomenon of the thirteenth century in England, and Hugh of Wells has the earliest surviving examples of registration from *c.* 1214 x 1217, closely followed by Walter de Gray, archbishop of York, whose enrolments are extant from 1225.[63] Previous collections of *acta* have understandably concentrated on twelfth and thirteenth-century bishops who did not keep registers or whose registers have not chanced to survive. This is the first collection of *acta* of an English bishop who actually did keep a register and the majority of whose enrolments still survive, and it can be seen how much the collection of *acta* supplements the registered entries. So, unlike any other English bishop so far, comparison is possible between the *acta* and the enrolments. The result of such a comparison, in the case of the dating of a great many routine letters of institution to parochial benefices, is disturbing. The pioneering aspect of Hugh's enrolments, as opposed to Walter de Gray's whose clerks followed royal chancery precedents and entered transcripts of the selected outgoing letters, is that the Lincoln clerks devised a precise summary of the act for the series of archdeaconry institution and vicarage rolls, reserving 'royal chancery type' transcripts for the more selective charter rolls, which I have argued elsewhere were to a great extent used as an additional safeguard for the incumbents and patrons of benefices and most probably involved them in a registration fee.[64] The summary of the acts in the institution rolls was the internal 'working record' sufficient for the purposes of the diocesan administrators but there may have been initial doubt about the legal effectiveness of such a précis form which led to the charter roll transcripts of full letters of institution etc. in selected cases. In the earlier article on Hugh's enrolments I drew attention to the discrepancies of dating between the institution roll and charter roll entries[65] and I have been able to add further details both for Hugh and his immediate successor, Robert Grosseteste. The results of this comparison throw serious doubt on what the Lincoln clerks (at least) meant by the dating-clause to the episcopal letters of institution. It is clear from the many examples found that it sometimes bore no relation to the actual date of the

[62] PRO, C269; see *Guide to Bishops' Registers*, p. viii.
[63] See ibid., pp. vii–viii, 105–7, 234.
[64] See Smith, 'Rolls'; *Reg. Burghersh* I, pp. xxv–vi.
[65] Ibid., 189–92. I am grateful to the Institute of Historical Research for permission to incorporate part of the 1972 table in this present introduction.

act of institution recorded in the institution rolls, on occasion by a matter of several years.

Let us actually look at two dated letters of institution entered on Bishop Hugh's Northampton archdeaconry charter roll, one a straightforward institution to a parish church, the other slightly more complicated with detailed provision made for the vicar's portion and the annual pensions he is to pay to the patrons. The general address and episcopal style and the corroboration clause may be truncated since they were obviously considered common form unnecessary to transcribe in full but the important elements of the text are there in each case:

> Omnibus etc. Noverit universitas vestra nos, ad presentationem abbatis et conventus de Seleby, patronorum ecclesie de Stanford', dilectum in Cristo filium magistrum Willelmum de Linc' ad eandem ecclesiam admisisse, ipsumque in ea canonice personam instituisse; salvis in omnibus etc. Quod ut etc. Hiis testibus: magistris Willelmo de Cantuar', Willelmo de Linc', Nicholao de Evesham' et Rogero de Laccock' et Radulfo de Warevill', canonicis Linc', Philippo de Langeport' et Iohanne de Bannebir', clericis. Dat' per manum Oliveri de Chedn' clerici, apud Cildesby iii kalendas Martii pontificatus nostri anno xiiii°. [i.e. 27 February 1223][66]

> Omnibus etc. Noverit universitas vestra nos, ad presentationem dilectorum filiorum abbatis et conventus sancti Iacobi Norhampt', patronorum ecclesie de Duston', dilectum in Cristo filium Warnerium capellanum ad ipsius ecclesie vicariam admisisse, ipsumque in ea canonice vicarium perpetuum instituisse, cum onere ministrandi personaliter in eadem. Habebit autem nomine vicarie sue totum altaragium de Duston' cum manso ecclesie, reddendo inde dictis patronis suis i marcam annuam. Habebit etiam totam capellam beate Margarete cum manso, reddendo ii marcas antedictis patronis annuatim et habebit idoneum capellanum socium in dicta capella continue ministrantem et solvet sinodalia; salvis in omnibus etc. Quod ut perpetuum etc. Hiis testibus: Warino de Kirketon' et Roberto de Bollesour', capellanis, magistris Waltero de Werm' et Ricardo de Wendour', W. de Winchecumb' et R. de Oxon', canonicis Linc', magistris A. de Arundell', Iohanne de Kralcohal' et aliis. Dat' per manum R. de Warr', canonici Linc', apud Lidingt' iiii nonas Iulii pontificatus nostri anno xxiii. [i.e. 4 July 1232][67]

On the face of it there is nothing suspicious about these two dated documents and an editor coming across such transcripts in, say, a monastic cartulary, would be totally justified in ascribing the acts of institution of William of Lincoln to Stanford on Avon and Warner the chaplain to Duston to 27 February 1223 and 4 July 1232 respectively.

Unfortunately, the institution roll evidence creates serious difficulties for this interpretation, for the Stanford on Avon entry is entered in summary form among the Northampton archdeaconry business of the bishop's eleventh pontifical year (which ran from 20 December 1219 to 19 December 1220) and the Duston vicarage entry is entered on the same institution roll under entries for the bishop's eighteenth year (from 20 December 1226 to 19 December 1227):

> STANFORD' Magister Willelmus de Linc', presentatus per abbatem et conventum de Seleby ad ecclesiam de Stanforton', facta prius inquisitione per R. archidiaconum Norh', per quam negotium fuit in expedito, ad eandem est admissus et in ea

---

[66] No. 197 below.
[67] No. 373 below.

canonice persona institutus. Et injunctum est dicto archidiacono tunc presenti quod ipsum W. in corporalem illius ecclesie possessionem inducat.
Annus Undecimus [20 December 1219 x 19 December 1220][68]

DUSTON' VICARIA Warnerius cappellanus, presentatus per dictos abbatem et conventum [sancti Iacobi Norhampt'] ad perpetuam vicariam ecclesie de Duston', vacantem per resingnationem (sic) Willelmi supradicti, ad eandem admissus cum onere et pena vicariorum etc. Fuit autem hec vicaria auctoritate Concilii per dominum episcopum ordinata sic: Vicarius habebit nomine vicarie sue perpetue totum altaragium de Duston' cum manso ecclesie, reddendo inde dictis canonicis i marcam annuam. Habebit etiam totam cappellam beate Margarete cum manso, reddendo inde ii marcas eisdem annuatim; et habebit cappellanum socium in dicta cappella continue ministrantem, et solvet sinodalia. Canonici vero hospitium archidiaconi procurabunt. Et mandatum est archidiacono Norh' ut etc. Memorandum de candela de qua nichil in ordinatione.
Annus XVIII [20 December 1226 x 19 December 1227][69]

The circumstances and the details in these two sets of entries confirm that they relate to the same acts, but the considerable dating discrepancies cannot be easily glossed over. They are also not isolated examples. A comparison of the institution rolls of Bishop Hugh with entries on the charter roll and in other sources found eighty-three examples where the letter of institution was dated years after the institution roll entry. This survey was extended to Hugh's successor at Lincoln, Robert Grosseteste (1235–53), by comparing his institution roll entries with the selective full transcripts of letters of institution endorsed on the *Carte* section of his enrolments. That produced another eighty examples of such irreconcilable dating discrepancies, which are set out below:

Institutions to Benefices and the Dating of Letters of Institution at Lincoln 1217–1235

Benefice	Date of institution roll entry	Date of letter of institution	Reference in RHW, and other sources
1 Kilsby	*c.* Dec. 1217–Dec. 1218	Dec. 1219–Dec. 1220	i. 121; ii. 185
2 Easton Maudit	Dec. 1218–Dec. 1219	17 Jan. 1220	i. 139; ii. 183
3 Everdon	Dec. 1218–Dec. 1219	3 Aug. 1220	i. 171; ii. 185–6
4 Whitfield	Dec. 1218–Dec. 1219	5 Sept. 1220	i. 172; ii. 186
5 St Peter, Northampton	*c.* Dec. 1217–Dec.1218	20 Oct. 1220	i. 122–3; ii. 187–8
6 Thrapston	Dec. 1218–Dec. 1219	26 Dec. 1220	i. 169–70; ii. 190
7 Maxey	*c.* Dec. 1217–Dec. 1218	5 Aug. 1221	i. 90; ii. 192
8 Pickworth	Dec. 1218–Dec. 1219	12 Aug. 1221	i. 167–8; ii. 193
9 Ashley	*c.* Dec. 1217–Dec. 1218	27 Sept. 1221	i. 63; ii. 194
10 St Peter, Northampton	Dec. 1220–Dec. 1221	23 Jan. 1223	ii. 108, 199–200

[68] *RHW* ii 98 (slightly modified after checking with original enrolment).
[69] Ibid. 135 (slightly modified after checking with original enrolment).

11 Stanford	Dec. 1219–Dec. 1220	1 March 1223	ii. 98, 200
12 Checkendon	Dec. 1221–Dec. 1222	12 March 1223	ii. 7–8; *Boarstall Cartulary*, no.6
13 Overstone	Dec. 1221–Dec. 1222	22 May 1223	ii. 107–8, 201
14 Kislingbury	18 Nov. 1223	4 Jan. 1224	ii. 113, 204
15 Litchborough	Dec. 1222–Dec. 1223	1 July 1224	ii. 110–11, 205
16 Hannington	Dec. 1223–Dec. 1224	Dec. 1224–Dec. 1225	ii. 118, 208
17 Harpole	Dec. 1223–Dec. 1224	Dec. 1224–Dec. 1225	ii. 117, 208
18 Edith Weston	Dec. 1223–Dec. 1224	27 March 1225	ii. 119, 209
19 Woodford Halse	Dec. 1223–Dec. 1224	7 June 1226	ii. 119, 214
20 Boddington	Dec. 1224–Dec. 1225	Dec. 1225–Dec. 1226	ii. 125, 211
21 Earls Barton	Dec. 1222–Dec. 1223	22 June 1226	ii. 111, 214
22 Desborough	Dec. 1224–Dec. 1225	23 Feb. 1227	ii. 127, 220–1
23 Stanwick	Dec. 1224–Dec. 1225	2 Apr. 1227	ii. 124, 221
24 Broughton	Dec. 1219–Dec. 1220	12 May 1227	ii. 101, 221
25 Cranford	*c*. Dec. 1217–Dec. 1218	12 May 1227	i. 65; ii. 221–2
26 Holcot	Dec. 1225–Dec. 1226	Dec. 1227–Dec. 1228	ii. 131, 226
27 Hanging Houghton	Dec. 1226–Dec. 1227	4 Jan. 1228	ii. 137, 225–6
28 Woodford	Dec. 1225–Dec. 1226	4 Jan. 1228	ii. 128, 226
29 Harlestone	Dec. 1226–Dec. 1227	Dec. 1227–Dec. 1228	ii. 139, 227
30 Warkton	Dec. 1226–Dec. 1227	Dec. 1227–Dec. 1228	ii. 140, 226–7
31 Little Bowden	14 Sept. 1224	5 Oct. 1228	ii. 118, 227
32 Great Creaton	Dec. 1225–Dec. 1226	Dec. 1227–Dec. 1228	ii. 132, 227
33 St John, Peterborough	Dec. 1224–Dec. 1225	Dec. 1228–Dec. 1229	ii. 126, 230–1
34 Cottesmore	Dec. 1227–Dec. 1228	16 Aug. 1229	ii. 144, 232
35 Stuchbury	Dec. 1227–Dec. 1228	25 Aug. 1229	ii. 142, 231
36 Brackley	Dec. 1227–Dec. 1228	31 Aug. 1229	ii. 141, 232
37 Clipston	Dec. 1228–Dec. 1229	7 June 1230	ii. 150, 237
38 Islip	Dec. 1228–Dec. 1229	5 Sept. 1230	ii. 151, 236
39 Collyweston	Dec. 1228–Dec. 1229	5 Sept. 1230	ii. 150–1, 236
40 St Giles, Northampton	Dec. 1228–Dec. 1229	5 Sept. 1230	ii. 152, 236
41 North Aston	Dec. 1226–Dec. 1227	1 Dec. 1230	ii. 25–6; BL, Stowe 925, f. 29v
42 Winwick	Dec. 1229–Dec. 1230	Dec. 1230–Dec. 1231	ii. 155, 240
43 Clapton	Dec. 1229–Dec. 1230	Dec. 1230–Dec. 1231	ii. 156, 239–40
44 Hargrave	Dec. 1228–Dec. 1229	29 March 1231	ii. 156, 239–40
45 Lyndon	Dec. 1229–Dec. 1230	1 Apr. 1231	ii. 158, 239
46 Church Brampton	Dec. 1229–Dec. 1230	13 Apr. 1231	ii. 154–5, 238–9
47 Wadenhoe	Dec. 1225–Dec. 1226	21 May 1231	ii. 127, 239

48 Bradden	Dec. 1229–Dec. 1230	29 May 1231	ii. 156, 242
49 Whiston	Dec. 1229–Dec. 1230	19 June 1231	ii. 155, 240
50 All Saints, Northampton	Dec. 1228–Dec. 1229	1 Aug. 1231	ii. 148, 241
51 Lilford	Dec. 1228–Dec. 1229	14 Oct. 1231	ii. 150, 242
52 Charwelton	Dec. 1229–Dec. 1230	14 Oct. 1231	ii. 155–6, 242
53 Thornby	Dec. 1227–Dec. 1228	Dec. 1231–Dec. 1232	ii. 142, 253
54 Rushden	Dec. 1229–Dec. 1230	Dec. 1231–Dec. 1232	ii. 152–3, 250–1
55 Great Harrowden	Dec. 1225–Dec. 1226	6 Feb. 1232	ii. 136–7, 246
56 Weekley	Dec. 1227–Dec. 1228	26 Feb. 1232	ii. 144, 247
57 Weedon Lois	Dec. 1229–Dec. 1230	26 Feb. 1232	ii. 153–4, 247
58 Duston	Dec. 1226–Dec. 1227	4 July 1232	ii. 135, 249
59 Quinton	Dec. 1230–Dec. 1231	31 July 1232	ii. 162, 250
60 Roade	Dec. 1231–Dec. 1232	Dec. 1232–Dec. 1233	ii. 167, 265
61 Pattishall	Dec. 1225–Dec. 1226	Dec. 1232–Dec. 1233	ii. 130, 265
62 Wicken	Dec. 1231–Dec. 1232	7 March 1233	ii. 171, 261
63 Braybrooke	Dec. 1231–Dec. 1232	2 Apr. 1233	ii. 170, 262
64 Farthingstone	Dec. 1231–Dec. 1232	7 March 1233	ii. 167–8, 261
65 Nettleham	Dec. 1223–Dec. 1224	Mar./Apr. 1233	i. 221–2; *Reg. Ant.* ii. no. 378
66 Edith Weston	Dec. 1231–Dec. 1232	16 Apr. 1233	ii. 170, 263
67 Ashby Folville	Dec. 1231–Dec. 1232	16 Apr. 1233	ii. 263, 317
68 Helpston	Dec. 1230–Dec. 1231	16 Apr. 1233	ii. 161, 263–4
69 Gumley	Dec. 1228–Dec. 1229	16 Apr. 1233	ii. 264, 308
70 Ashby St Ledgers	Dec. 1226–Dec. 1227	16 Apr. 1233	ii. 136, 262–3
71 Burley	Dec. 1231–Dec. 1232	Dec. 1232–Dec. 1233	ii. 166–7, 265–6
72 Wellingborough	Dec. 1231–Dec. 1232	July/Aug. 1233	ii. 169, 264–5
73 Thistleton	Dec. 1225–Dec. 1226	Dec. 1233–Dec. 1234	ii. 133, 270
74 South Luffenham	Dec. 1232–Dec. 1233	28 Jan. 1234	ii. 175, 267
75 Walgrave	Dec. 1231–Dec. 1232	21 March 1234	ii. 169, 268
76 East Farndon	Dec. 1229–Dec. 1230	21 March 1234	ii. 156–7, 268
77 Hardingstone	Dec. 1232–Dec. 1233	21 March 1234	ii. 174–5, 268
78 Oxendon	Dec. 1230–Dec. 1231	5 June 1234	ii. 159, 269–70
79 Stanwick	Dec. 1232–Dec. 1233	2 Oct. 1234	ii. 174, 270
80 Great Harrowden	Dec. 1233–Dec. 1234	Dec. 1234–Dec. 1235	ii. 181, 271
81 Holy Trinity, Northampton	10 Dec. 1233	25 Jan. 1235	ii. 176, 272
82 Gayton	Dec. 1233–Dec. 1234	25 Jan. 1235	ii. 180–1, 272
83 Paston	Dec. 1233–Dec. 1234	25 Jan. 1235	ii. 179–80, 272

Addendum

The bishop's collation of the church of Claybrooke produced two letters of collation (which still survive in original) – one without witnesses dated 24 Oct. 1224, one with witnesses dated 6 Dec. 1224 (BL, Add. Chts. 47561–2).

Institutions to Benefices and the Dating of Letters of Institution at Lincoln 1235–1253

Benefice	Date of institution roll entry	Date of letter of of institution	RRG reference
1 Horncastle	June 1235–June 1236	5 Feb. 1237	2, 13–14
2 Glentham	June 1235–June 1236	27 Nov. 1236	134, 14, 137–8
3 Sutterton	June 1235–June 1236	17 July 1237	2, 23–4
4 Laughton	June 1235–June 1236	22 March 1239	133, 139
5 Fillingham	June 1235–June 1236	16 Nov. 1240	148–9, 155–6
6 Great Gidding	June 1235–June 1236	16 June 1238	251, 260
7 Roxton	June 1235–June 1236	25 Aug. 1236	301, 306
8 Bedford St Cuthbert	June 1235–June 1236	22 Sept. 1236	302, 306
9 Wilshamstead	June 1235–June 1236	25 Sept. 1236	302, 306–7
10 Elstow	June 1235–June 1236	25 Sept. 1236	302, 307
11 Biddenham	June 1235–June 1236	29 July 1237	304, 310
12 Dunton	June 1235–June 1236	12 June 1238	304, 311
13 Wrestlingworth	June 1235–June 1236	June 1238–June 1239	304, 314
14 Wymington	June 1235–June 1236	16 Sept. 1239	302, 316
15 Studham	June 1235–June 1236	29 Dec. 1244	303, 323–4
16 Denham	June 1235–June 1236	3 Sept. 1236	341, 343
17 Amersham	June 1235–June 1236	29 May 1237	341, 343
18 Bradenham	June 1235–June 1236	13 July 1240	341, 359
19 Waterstock	June 1235–June 1236	4 July 1241	446, 472
20 Toynton All Saints	June 1236–June 1237	26 June 1237	9, 23
21 Frodingham	June 1236–June 1237	5 June 1238	136, 138
22 Marholm	June 1236–June 1237	26 June 1237	164, 172
23 Hamerton	June 1236–June 1237	July 1237	252, 256–7
24 Little Wolston	June 1236–June 1237	19 Aug. 1238	342, 351
25 Galby	June 1236–June 1237	26 June 1237	392–3, 400
26 Scraptoft	June 1236–June 1237	15 Oct. 1237	394, 401
27 Brington	June 1237–June 1238	27 Aug. 1238	169, 184
28 Glaston	June 1237–June 1238	10 Sept. 1238	170, 185
29 North Luffenham	June 1237–June 1238	17 Nov. 1238	170, 185

30 Brampton Ash	June 1237–June 1238	4 Aug. 1238	165, 186
31 Normanton	June 1237–June 1238	4 Feb. 1239 & 8 May 1239	171, 188, 190
32 Steeple Gidding	June 1237–June 1238	12 May 1239	256, 266
33 Wilden	June 1237–June 1238	22 Nov. 1240	308, 317
34 Hatley Cockayne	June 1237–June 1238	29 Aug. 1241	309, 319
35 King's Norton	June 1237–June 1238	24 July 1238	397, 407
36 Buckminster	June 1237–June 1238	2 Dec. 1240	399, 413–14
37 Chesterton	3 Oct. 1237	31 March 1239	255, 267–8
38 Great Ponton	June 1238–June 1239	26 Nov. 1238 & 30 Nov. 1240	30, 56, 185
39 Ingham	June 1238–June 1239	14 Nov. 1240	140, 56
40 Howell	June 1238–June 1239	22 Nov. 1240	36, 58
41 Moulton	June 1238–June 1239	3 Aug. 1240	177, 207
42 Kingscliffe	June 1238–June 1239	13 Aug. 1244	181, 222
43 Woodstone	June 1238–June 1239	28 Sept. 1240	262, 274–5
44 Aspley Guise	June 1238–June 1239	5 Sept. 1239	313, 316
45 Milton Ernest	June 1238–June 1239	17 Apr. 1241	313–14, 317–18
46 Chellington	June 1238–June 1239	22 Sept. 1249	311–12, 336
47 Eton	June 1238–June 1239	13 July 1240	348, 358
48 Ludgershall	June 1238–June 1239	16 Oct. 1241	346, 359
49 Belgrave	June 1238–June 1239	12 Aug. 1239	405–6, 410
50 Britwell Salome	June 1238–June 1239	18 Feb. 1240	457, 467
51 Brant Broughton	June 1239–June 1240	9 Nov. 1240	47, 57
52 Legsby	June 1239–June 1240	28 July 1240	44, 57–8
53 Seaton	June 1239–June 1240	25 Sept. 1240	196, 206
54 Paston	June 1239–June 1240	30 Nov. 1240	195, 206–7
55 Willian	June 1239–June 1240	2 Aug. 1241	268–9, 277
56 Glenfield	June 1239–June 1240	3 Dec. 1240	409, 414
57 Godington	June 1239–June 1240	5 Aug. 1242	464, 479
58 East Haddon	June 1240–June 1241	22 Apr. 1242	205, 209–10
59 Eydon	June 1240–June 1241	26 Feb. 1243	202, 216
60 Brixworth	June 1240–June 1241	June 1244–June 1245	200, 221
61 Newton Longueville	June 1240–June 1241	June 1241–June 1242	357, 359–60
62 Leire	June 1240–June 1241	27 Apr. 1242	412, 418
63 Ewerby	June 1241–June 1242	13 Oct. 1244	65, 78–9
64 Sutton	June 1241–June 1242	24 Feb. 1244	318, 323
65 Radwell	June 1242–June 1243	10 Nov. 1243	283–4, 285–6
66 Ashwell	June 1243–June 1244	9 Nov. 1244	285, 288–9

67 Loughborough	June 1243–June 1244	9 July 1244	422, 425
68 Bicester	June 1243–June 1244	4 Oct. 1244	481, 487
69 Althorpe	June 1244–June 1245	9 Jan. 1250	148–9, 155–6
70 Thurleigh	June 1245–June 1246	21 Apr. 1247	326, 327–8
71 Linslade	June 1245–June 1246	June 1251–June 1252	372, 382–3
72 Saddington	June 1245–June 1246	25 March 1247	426, 428
73 Cottesbrooke	June 1246–June 1247	3 March 1251	228, 247–8
74 Carlby	June 1247–June 1248	25 Apr. 1249	96–7, 110–11
75 Dunsby	June 1247–June 1248	June 1248–June 1249	102, 112–13
76 Isham	June 1247–June 1248	23 Sept. 1250	233, 243
77 Little Bowden	June 1247–June 1248	June 1249–June 1250	231, 143
78 Aldwincle	June 1247–June 1248	27 July 1250	230, 247
79 Peakirk	June 1249–June 1250	June 1250–June 1251	243, 247
80 Saunderton	June 1250–June 1251	Oct. 1251	380, 382

What does this mean? The immediate answer is that the later dated letter of institution (together with the witnesses and place recorded) relates to the date of *issue*
of the evidentiary documentary only and does not relate to the date of the particular *act* of institution. Unfortunately, the clerks of Hugh and Grosseteste,
unlike those of Bishop Sutton in the example cited above, gave no indication in
the actual document that this was the case – a cause of inevitable confusion if
only the letter of institution had chanced to survive without the enrolment evidence.

Two questions arise immediately: why was there such a delay with the issue of
many letters of institution; and secondly, is this dating discrepancy a quirk of the
Lincoln clerks or should we consider the possibility that such practice was widespread in the issuing of documents in the first half of the thirteenth century? I
hazarded a possible answer to the first question in my original article on Hugh's
enrolments, and I have not changed my opinion in the quarter-century since that
article was published. I would conclude that despite the good intentions of conciliar legislation, the issue of letters of institution (in Lincoln diocese at least) in
the thirteenth century was not automatic (nor incidentally any subsequent registration free).[70] Some incumbents (or patrons) may have only later come to see the
need for formal letters of institution to protect their legal position and rights, if
such letters were not automatically issued at the time of the ceremony. If letters
of institution had been automatically issued then you would have expected a later
episcopal *inspeximus* or letters testimonial, if some form of later registration or
inspection was required. Other circumstances such as accidental loss or the need
for duplication (for incumbent or patron) may have also played their part, but
whatever the reasons they do not detract from the alarming fact that these *later*
letters of institution give no indication that they *are* later and historians could
easily confuse the dates of their issue with the date of the actual act of institution.

The last question (as to how widespread this practice was) must of necessity

[70] Smith, 'Rolls', especially pp. 187–92. Even in Bishop Sutton's time (1280–99) there is evidence
that the issue of letters of institution to new incumbents was not automatic (ibid., p. 192).

be left unanswered. We do not have the example elsewhere afforded by Hugh's summarised enrolments to compare with originals and transcripts of *acta*. Even in the case of Walter de Gray, the only other non-Lincoln register surviving from the first half of the thirteenth century, the nature of the York enrolments (copying transcripts of outgoing letters) means that no comparison can be possible. However, from time to time discrepancies in dating do arise which have up till now been ascribed to scribal error or other reasons. A recent example is in Professor Kemp's edition of the Salisbury episcopal *acta* from 1078 to 1217. Two charters relating to the hospital of Pont-Audemer and the perpetual vicarage of Sturminster Marshall seem to contain dating contradictions. In the first, dated 1 September 1204, reference is made to master Thomas of Chobham as having already been admitted as vicar; in the second, dated 15 October 1206, master Thomas of Chobham is admitted to the perpetual vicarage![71] Now it may be, as has been suggested, that the 1206 document represented a redefinition of the vicarage endowment and hence a re-admission of master Thomas; however, in the view of what has gone before it may not be the only explanation.

EDITORIAL METHOD

This volume attempts to follow the British Academy English Episcopal Acta series in the way that it approaches the edition of this collection of Hugh's *acta*, but with one significant change owing to the introduction of a dating-clause. Since most of the *acta* can be dated precisely and there are very few undated ones which cannot be ascribed to a particular pontifical year of the bishop, the arrangement of the material in this edition is chronological, rather than by beneficiary or recipient. The texts of all original *acta* have been given in full; similarly all unpublished copies and transcripts, where no originals survive. Copies which have been printed in easily accessible editions have been calendared, although the witness-lists and dating-clauses have been retained in their original form. Sigla are used to denote the manuscript sources, A being reserved for original charters and B, C, D etc. being used for copies. In the latter case, the first-named manuscript provides the basis for the printed text and is usually the earliest copy to survive. The later copies are arranged in roughly chronological order. With originals, medieval endorsements are given together with medial measurements (in millimetres) and brief notes on the seals and sealing methods. With cartulary and register copies an approximate indication of the date of the manuscript is provided and a note is made to any former foliation or pagination. The English summary caption is followed by the date, when known. After the manuscript sources, reference is made to any previous publication. Textual and historical notes, where appropriate, follow the *actum*. Mentions of lost charters are denoted by an asterisk placed immediately before the series number; forged charters are marked by a cross immediately before the number.

The spelling of originals and copies has been retained, except that 'i' is treated as the equivalent of 'i' and 'j', and 'u' is used as a vowel, 'v' as a consonant. Classical practice is followed in using 't' where 'c' is found in some manuscripts e.g. *confirmatio*. Modern usage has been adopted in respect of capital letters and

[71] *EEA* 18 nos. 222–3.

punctuation. Editorial corrections are inserted in the text with the manuscript reading indicated in the textual notes. Conjectural readings are placed in square brackets and insertions and interlineations are noted in the printed text by the use of the marks < >. Any missing sections are indicated. Manuscripts have been collated but only significant variant readings and necessary editorial corrections are normally recorded, and where the originals survive the variant spellings are only rarely included.

Modern practice, in starting the year on 1 January, has been used throughout. Certain important works of reference and chronology have considerably assisted the editor, notable among them Professor Diana Greenway's edition of *John Le Neve: Fasti Ecclesiae Anglicanae 1066–1300: iii Lincoln* (London 1977), the *Handbook of British Chronology* (3rd edition, eds. E.B. Fryde, D.E. Greenway, S. Porter and I. Roy, Royal Historical Society guide and handbook 2, 1986), and *Heads of Religious Houses: England and Wales 940–1216*, eds. D. Knowles, C.N.L. Brooke and V.C.M. London (Cambridge 1972).

THE ACTA OF HUGH OF WELLS

1. Profession of obedience

Profession of obedience made to Stephen [Langton], archbishop of Canterbury.

[Melun, 20 December 1209]

(I)

A = Canterbury D. & C. Ch. Ant. C115/141 (facsimile, *Canterbury Professions* pl.
II(b)). Endorsed: Stephanus Archiepiscopus (s. xiii); approx. 174 x 59 mm.;
not sealed.
B = Canterbury D. & C. register A (The Prior's register) fo. 224v. s. xiv med.
Pd from A in *Canterbury Professions* no. 147a.

Ego Hugo ecclesie Lincoln' electus episcopus profiteor.
Ego Hugo ecclesie Lincoln' electus profiteor sancte Cantuariensi ecclesie et tibi,
reverende pater Stephane archiepiscope tuisque successoribus canonice substituendis, canonicam obedientiam et subiectionem per omnia me servaturum esse
promitto, et propria manu signo sancte crucis confirmo.

This document is presumably a draft of Hugh's profession.

(II)

A = Canterbury D. & C. Ch. Ant. C115/143 (facsimile, *Canterbury Professions* pl.
II(c)). Endorsed: Professio Lincoln' episcopi (s. xiii); approx. 172 x 17 mm.;
not sealed.
Pd *Canterbury Professions* no. 147b.

+ Ego Hugo ecclesie Linc' electus episcopus profiteor sancte Cantuariensi ecclesie et tibi, reverende pater Stephane archiepiscope tuisque successoribus
canonice substituendis, canonicam per omnia obedientiam me servaturum et
subiectionem, et propria manu signo sancte crucis confirmo . +

The final cross is presumably autograph. For Bp Hugh's consecration at Melun, see
MPCM iii 528, cf. *Gir. Camb.* vii 5.

2. Testament of the bishop

The first testament of the bishop.

St Martin-de-Garenne, 13 *or* 14 November 1212

B = Wells D. & C. Liber Albus II, fos. 248v–249v. s. xvi in.
Pd (calendar) *HMC Wells* i 431–2; (with transl.), *Lincolnshire Notes and Queries*, II
(1890–1), 172–6. There is also a brief abstract in C.M. Church, 'Jocelin,
bishop of Bath, 1206–1242' in *Archaeologia*, 51 (1888), 281–346, at 312–13.

+ In nomine sancte et individue Trinitatis, ego Hugo divina miseratione Lincoln'
episcopus ecclesie qualiscumque minister condidi testamentum meum de bonis
meis que michi restituenda sunt in Anglia in hunc modum. Inprimis volo ut reddantur debita subscripta, scilicet, cclxi marce et dimidia, si non fuerint solute, de
quodam debito quod scit dominus Bath' domino pape[a], quod ei debetur de episcopatu Lincoln' de tempore meo de denariis beati Petri; domino regi Anglie dc
marce et viii marce et viii solidi et unus denarius de diversis particulis quas scit

dominus Bathoniensis, preter ea si qua debentur de Ludingeland'; lego autem pro
anima mea d marcas ad fabricam ecclesie Lincoln' et d marcas ad emendas terras,
redditus et possessiones ad augmentandam communam eiusdem ecclesie; vicariis
Lincoln' ecclesie lx marcas; et ccc marcas ad distribuendum per domos religiosas
episcopatus Lincoln'; et centum marcas ad distribuendum per domos leprosorum
eiusdem episcopatus; et centum marcas per domos hospitales episcopatus
eiusdem; et ccc marcas distribuendas ecclesiis quas habui ad libros et ornamenta
emenda; domui de Stanleg' xxx marcas; domui de Quarrei xx marcas; domui de
Poleston xxx marcas; domui de Fernleg' decem marcas; domui de Plinton'
centum marcas; pro anima relicte Galfridi de Mand' xx marcas; Thome de Mand'
xx marcas; Willelmo de Mand' xl marcas; Ricardo de Argent' iii marcas; cuidam
militi de Notingehamsire, tenenti de archiepiscopatu Ebor', cuius filiam G. Atyes
habere voluit ad opus filii sui xl marcas; Ricardo cuius fuerat Hill' quam Robertus de Mand' habuit xxx marcas; Willelmo capellano de Niweton' quondam
persone de Trent' x marcas; ad hospitale construendum pro anima Iordani de
Turry vel ad alias elemosynas pro anima sua faciendas per executores testamenti
sui et per consilium executorum huius testamenti ccc marcas; relicte Simonis de
Bugeden' xx marcas; Cristine relicte Hugonis fabri et filie sue iii marcas;
Matillde Blunde de Well' iii marcas; Matillde filie Cristine Sudoure iii marcas;
domui leprosorum de Selewud iii marcas; domui monialium de Berwe x marcas;
domui de Berliz iii marcas; ad fabricam ecclesie de Bocland' xx marcas; [fo.
249r] domui de Caninton' v marcas; ad construendum hospitale apud Well' d
marcas; hospitali Bath' vii marcas et dimidiam; domui leprosorum extra Bath' iii
marcas; leprosis extra Ivelcestr' iii marcas; monialibus de Stodleg' in Oxeneford-
sire vii marcas et dimidiam; Matillde de Berewich' que fuit cum G. Wac vii
marcas et dimidiam ad se maritandam; relicte Ricardi Foliot de Stok vii marcas et
dimidiam; pro anima Eve filie Algari de Well' vii marcas et dimidiam; magistro
Iohanni de Ebor', nisi a me beneficiatus fuerit, centum marcas; filiabus Willelmi
de Stratton' ccc marcas ad eas maritandas; puelle de sancto Edwardo centum et l
marcas ad se maritandam; puero de Evercriz xl marcas ad eum exhibendum; pauperibus de consanguinitate mea centum marcas; Iohanni de Mertoc' lx marcas;
Hereberto de camera l marcas; Rogero mariscallo xxx marcas; Ricardo mariscallo xl marcas; Walensi coco xxx marcas; Ricardo de camera x marcas; Matheo
de coquina iii marcas; Galfrido filio Petri vii marcas et dimidiam; et singulis aliis
garcionibus meis mecum euntibus v marcas; Galfrido Ginenier[b] ii marcas; Alano
le Hottere ii marcas; Willelmo homini Rogeri capellani v marcas; Willelmo scrip-
tori meo x marcas. Volo autem quod restituantur hominibus meis tam militibus
quam aliis facta mihi restitutione que me et eos contingit omnia que ab eis capta
sunt iniuste in hoc interdicto. Item lego canonicis de Moreton' xx marcas;
canonicis de sancta Barbara xx marcas; pro anima filii Stephani persone de
Dokemeref' vii marcas et dimidiam. Huius autem testamenti mei executores constituo dominum Bathon' et magistrum Heliam de Derham ad recipiendum omnia
et distribuendum ut predixi, et dominum Cantuar' et confratres et coexules meos
rogo quatinus pro Deo et honore ecclesie Dei et pro salute animarum suarum et
mee, cum requisiti fuerint, consilium et auxilium efficax apponant ut hoc testamentum meum compleatur. Quod autem ultra hec omnia predicta remanserit tam
de his que michi restituenda sunt quam de aliis bonis meis et his que michi
debentur, volo quod per predictos executores mei testamenti distribuatur pro
anima mea tam pauperibus per episcopatum Lincoln' quam alibi, sicut magis vid-

erint expedire. Qui etiam nichilominus de libris, pannis et vestibus meis disponant sicut commodius noverint faciendum. Si vero interim de domino Bathon' humanitus contigerit, quod dominus avertat, volo quod magister Helias et magister Reginaldus de Cestr' omnia exequantur cum consilio domini Cantuar' et domini Elyensis. Et si de magistro Helia ita contingat humanitus, volo quod dominus Bathon' omnium sit executor, habito inde consilio domini Cantuar' cum viderit expedire. Ad hec lego ad fabricam ecclesie Wellen' ccc marchas et ad communam ecclesie ipsius augmentandam tam ad opus vicariorum quam canonicorum ccc marcas, et xl marcas distribuendas vicariis ecclesie memorate. Act' apud [fo. 249v] sanctum Martinum de Garenn' in die sancti Bricii pontificatus mei anno tertio, presentibus domino I. Bathon' episcopo, magistro Helia de Derham, magistro Iohanne de Ebor', magistro Reginaldo de Cestr', magistro Willelmo, Rogero et Helia capellanis, Petro de Cic' et Willelmo de Ham'.

ᵃ *This word is scored through with red ink.* ᵇ *or possibly* Ginemer.

St Brice's day can be celebrated on either 13 or 14 November (Cheney, *Handbook of Dates*, p. 45). Bp Hugh made a second testament in 1233 (no. 408). For master Elias de Dereham, one of the bp's executors, see K. Major in *EHR* xlviii (1933), 542–4; *EEA* 3 p. 307 (where he occurs as executor of Archbp Hubert Walter of Canterbury); J. Harvey, *English Mediaeval Architects* (rev. edn, 1987), pp. 81–2; A. Hastings, *Elias of Dereham, architect of Salisbury Cathedral* (Salisbury, 1997); N. Vincent, 'Master Elias of Dereham (d. 1245): a reassessment' (forthcoming).

3. Westminster abbey

Institution of master Simon of London to the church of Launton on the presentation of the abbot Ralph and the convent of Westminster, saving the perpetual vicarage of Henry de Colewell. Henry holds the church, paying an annual pension of two marks. London, 5 October 1213

A = Westminster Abbey mun. 15683. Endorsed: Carta *(dotted for deletion and* institutio *interlined)* Lincolnien' episcopi super personatu ecclesie de Langetun' (s.xiii); approx. 147 x 96 + 19 mm.; fragment of seal, green wax, good impression of counterseal, on parchment tag, method 1.
B = ibid. Mun. Bk.11 (Westminster Domesday) fo. 275v (296v). s. xiv in.

Omnibus sancte matris ecclesie filiis ad quos presens carta pervenerit, Hugo Dei gratia Lincoln' episcopus salutem in domino. Noveritis nos, ad presentationem Radulfi abbatis et conventus Westmonasterii patronorum ecclesie de Langetun', dilectum in Cristo filium magistrum Symonem de Lond' ad ecclesiam de Langetun' admisisse, et ipsum in eadem personam instituisse, salva Henrico de Colewell' perpetua vicaria quam habet in eadem: qui dictam ecclesiam tenet, reddendo annuatim duas marcas nomine pensionis et salvis in omnibus episcopalibus consuetudinibus et ecclesie Lincolniensis dignitate. Et ut hec nostra institutio perpetuum firmitatis robur optineat, eam presenti carta sigillo nostro signata duximus confirmandam. Hiis testibus: domino I. Bathoniensi episcopo, magistro Iohanne de Eboraco, magistro Reginaldo de Cestre, magistro Willelmo de Tornay, Elya cappellano, Petro de Cicestria, Willelmo de Hammes, Rogero cappellano, Hereberto camerario, Ricardo marescallo, Rogero marescallo, et multis aliis. Dat' per manum Rogeri cappellani nostri apud London' tertio nonas Octobris anno pontificatus nostri quarto.

+4. Ramsey abbey

Provision concerning the cellarership of Ramsey abbey. During the time of the interdict the cellarership had been in the hands of King John; afterwards it was restored to the monks of Ramsey by the bishop.   [?late 1213]

> B = PRO E164/28, fos. 195v–196r. s. xiv.
> Pd *Ramsey Cartulary* ii no. cccxxi.

Universis sancte matris ecclesie filiis presentibus et futuris notum esse volumus quod ego Hugo Dei gratia Linc' episcopus, quondam regis cancellarius, post reversionem domini Stephani archiepiscopi et nostram ab exilio in Angliam confecta prius pacis concordia inter ipsum regem Iohannem et dominum Stephanum Cantuar' archiepiscopum durante adhuc interdicto, habere fecimus dilectis filiis nostris monachis Ram', non sine gravi nostri corporis dispendio, plenam et integram seisinam et dispositionem celerarie sue quam idem rex in manu sua tunc temporis vacante abbathia aliquamdiu tenuerat de qua ipsos monachos causa interdicti disseisaverat. In huius rei testimonium ut nostri semper memoriam habeant iam dicti monachi in orationibus et beneficiis suis hoc scriptum illis sub sigilli nostri attestatione inposterum munimen contulimus. Predicti vero loci abbas que de manibus celerarii monachorum solebat antiquitus de iure percipere, nec per se nec per aliquem suorum sed per manus celerarii sui propter emergentia obsequentium mala recipiet. Inhibemus ergo ex parte Dei et nostra ne celerarium predictorum monachorum attrectari vel de rebus celerarii illis invitis disponere presumat. Quod si quis contra hanc nostram prohibitionem venire attemptaverit maledictionem omnipotentis Dei et nostram se noverit incursurum.

> If genuine, this document must date after Hugh's return to England after the Interdict in July 1213. Ramsey abbey was vacant between 1206 and 1214 (*Heads* i 62–3). Diplomatically, this charter is extremely dubious. a) The charter was inserted in the cartulary, at the foot of two folios ; it is in a late fourteenth century hand. b) Bp Hugh was never chancellor : he acted as vice-chancellor although never being known by that designation. c) The first person singular is used side by side with the first person plural by the scribe of the charter. The discrepancies and the interpolations cast great doubts on the authenticity of this charter. See also later charter regarding the cellarership of Ramsey (no. 182).

5. Lincoln, St Katharine's priory

Confirmation of the composition made between Hugh (I), bishop of Lincoln (1186–1200) and the chapter of Lincoln on the one hand, and R(oger), Master of the order of Sempringham and the canons of St Katharine's outside Lincoln on the other, concerning the churches of Norton [Disney], Marton, and Newton [on Trent] [EEA 4 no. 109]. G(ilbert) the successor of Roger as master of the order of Sempringham, consents to the composition.   Lincoln, 27 February 1214

> B = LAO Add. Reg. 6 (Liber antiquus) fo. 23r. s. xiii in.
> Pd *Lib. Ant.* 72.

Hiis testibus: Rogero decano, Galfrido precentore, Rogero cancellario, Iohanne subdecano, Hugone de sancto Edwardo, Willelmo filio Fulconis, Reginaldo de Cestr', Waltero de Well', canonicis Linc' ecclesie, Roberto capellano, Roberto de Gravel', Petro de Wileton', Petro de Bathon' et Ricardo, clericis, et multis aliis. Dat' apud Lincoln' iii⁰ kalendas Martii per manum W. de Tornach', archidiaconi Stowe, pontificatus nostri anno quinto.

> For Bp Robert Chesney's grant of these churches, probably c. 1148, see *EEA* 1 no. 163. This confirmation of Bp Hugh is mentioned in *RHW* iii 92.

6. Little Wymondley priory

Grant of the church of St Peter, Little Wymondley to the hospital founded there by Richard de Argentein, and confirmation of all the possessions of the hospital (described in detail).   Sleaford, 27 June 1214

> B = BL ms. Add. 43972 (Little Wymondley cartulary) fo. 12r–v (11r–v). s. xiii med.

Universis sancte matris ecclesie filiis ad quos presens scriptum pervenerit, H. Dei gratia Lincolniensis episcopus salutem in auctore salutis. Noverit universitas vestra quod nos, divine pietatis intuitu zeloque religionis, de consensu Rogeri decani et capituli Lincoln', locum in Parva Wilemundel' in qua fundata est domus hospitalis capelle, que ex dono Ricardi de Argent' est de nostra et successorum nostrorum ac predictorum decani et capituli Lincoln' advocatione, in usum religiose professionis convertimus et locum ipsum sub Dei et beate Marie et nostra protectione ac defensione suscipientes, prefato hospitali capelle et fratribus ibidem deo servientibus ecclesiam beati Petri de eadem villa cum omnibus pertinentiis suis in proprios usus convertendam et habendam inperpetuum; salvo iure et possessione Hugonis Leidet persone et magistri Willelmi de Argent' et Thome capellani vicariorum quoad vixerint in eadem, et salva indempnitate et immunitate vicinarum omnium ecclesiarum; salvis etiam episcopalibus consuetudinibus et ecclesie Lincolniensis dignitate concedimus et concessa nobis a domino auctoritate episcopali confirmamus. Eidem etiam loco et fratribus predictis liberam annuimus habere sepulturam sibi et familie sue ceterisque qui se deliberaverint ibidem sepeliri, salvo iure parochialis ecclesie et aliarum ecclesiarum a quibus corpora mortuorum assumuntur. Omnes etiam possessiones et quecumque bona in presenciarum iuste et canonice possident, vel in futuro largitione fidelium iustis modis poterunt adipisci, firma eis et illibata permaneant; in quibus hec propriis duximus exprimenda vocabulis: triginta quinque acras de bosco de Tipmere in parte, scilicet, orientali et totum servitium Iohannis de Bosco, scilicet, sex solidos per annum, et septem et decem acras terre ad mesuagium faciendum, scilicet, inter Murtelake et Brechineresfurlong' versus austrum a via [fo. 12v] que tendit inter duas Wilemundel'; et triginta et septem acras terre et tres rodas in Chalvecrofte, scilicet, in parte aquilonari illius campi simul in eadem cultura iacentes, ita quod pars eiusdem campi que domino Ricardo de Argent' remanet iacet versus austrum illius campi; et quadraginta et septem acras terre in Brechineresfurlong' et in Chaldewellefurlong', scilicet, versus austrum a via que ducit de Gravele apud Magna Wilemundel'; et triginta acras que iacent inter Mannemede et croftam Iohannis Britonis versus occidentem a via que ducit inter duas Wilemundel'; et totam terram que fuit Godefridi de

Heia, excepto mesuagio suo et crofta; et totam pasturam que est in via de Murtelake usque ad croftam Iohannis Britonis; et duas acras que se abutant super viam
de Gravele ex una parte, et super culturam que vocatur Thritiacre ex alia parte
versus occidentem; et duas acras et dimidiam que se extendunt ad viam que
tendit de Gravele apud Wilie versus orientem; et tres rodas terre in eadem cultura
que iacent iuxta terram Hugonis de Argent' versus austrum; et duas acras terre et
dimidiam de Wudemere versus austrum; et totam terram quam Meinardus de
Holeton' tenuit de domino Ricardo de Argent' in Haleswurth' et in Holeton',
scilicet, decem rodas de marisco inter domum prefati Meinardi et Ricardi Withfot
que se extendunt super ripam de Melnes; et unam acram terre in campis de Holeton'; et totum redditum de molendino de Hicchford' quod vocatur molendinum
de Hida cum omnibus pertinentiis suis, scilicet, mesuagium et unum cotlandum
terre et pratum versus austrum iuxta stagnum et Turefholm versus aquilonem
inter stagnum et Hicchford' et pitellum cum prato quod rusellum transit et
Turefput versus orientem iuxta foveam; et communionem cum hominibus
Ricardi de Argent' super totam terram suam in viis, in semitis, in pascuis, et in
omnibus locis eidem hospitali et fratribus eiusdem domus congruis et utilibus
cum omnibus libertatibus que prefato loco a predicto Ricardo de Argent' vel aliis
quibuscumque rationabiliter collate sunt vel inposterum conferende. Siquis
autem predicto loco et fratribus aliquid boni caritative contulerit, orationum et
beneficiorum suorum omnium particeps efficiatur. Conservantibus autem pacem
et tranquillitatem eorum, gratia dei, pax et nostra benedictio multiplicetur. Si
vero aliquis eorum pacem perturbando vel iniuriam inferendo molestus eis
extiterit, Dei et gloriose virginis indignationem se noverit incursurum. Et ut hec
nostra concessio et confirmatio rata inposterum perseveret, eam tam presenti
scripto quam sigilli nostri et sigilli capituli Lincolniensis appositione duximus
roborandam. Hiis testibus etc. Dat' apud Lafford' v^{to} kalendas Iulii pontificatus
nostri anno quinto.

For charters of Richard de Argentein relating to the hospital see *Reg. Ant.* iii nos.
792–5.

7. Eynsham abbey

*Notification to the mayor and commune of Oxford that the abbot and convent of
Eynsham have taken upon themselves the charge of paying each year in perpetuity the five marks and two shillings which N(icholas), cardinal bishop of Tuscu-
lum and papal legate, had laid upon the town as a penalty for the hanging of
certain clerks. The burgesses are therefore quit of this burden for ever.*

[?c. July 1214]

B = LAO Add. Reg. 6 (Liber antiquus) fo. 23r s. xiii in.
Pd *Lib. Ant.* 73.

The *suspendium clericorum* took place in 1209 and resulted in a general migration
of masters and scholars from Oxford. The legatine ordinance of 20 June 1214
settled the quarrel and, among other provisions, imposed the above fine upon the
citizens. The charter of Adam, abbot of Eynsham about this payment is thought to
have been issued in July 1214 and the episcopal notification may have been issued
shortly afterwards (*Reg. Ant.* ii no. 366; *Eynsham Cartulary* i xx; *Mediaeval
Archives of the University of Oxford*, ed. H.E.Salter, i (Oxford Historical Society
lxx, 1917) nos. 2–5; G. Pollard, 'The legatine award to Oxford in 1214 and Robert

Grosteste', *Oxoniensia* xxxix (1974) 62–72; *VCH Oxfordshire* iii 2); cf. also J.I. Catto ed., *The History of the University of Oxford, vol. I. The Early Oxford Schools* (Oxford, 1984), pp. 26–33.

8. Bishop Jocelin of Bath and Glastonbury

Grant to Jocelin, bishop of Bath and Glastonbury, and his successors, of half a knight's fee in Rowberrow and Draycott (Somerset).   Stow, 11 July 1214

A1 = Canterbury, Christ Church muniments, Chartae Antiquae R. 40. Endorsed: Domini H. Linc' Episcopi super feodo dimidii militis in Roheberg' et Draicot' s. xiii in.; 143/145 mm. x 143/145 mm.; seal missing, two holes for seal strings.

A2 = Wells D. & C. charter 22. Endorsed: Domini H. Linc' Episcopi de feodo dimidii militis in Draicot' et Ruheburg' s. xiii in.; 158 x 102 + 16 mm., seal missing, two holes for seal strings.

B = Wells D. & C. Liber Albus II, fo. 339v. s. xvi in. C = Wells D. & C. Liber Albus II, fo. 349r.

Pd (calendar) from B & C in *HMC Wells*, i 470–1.

Omnibus Cristi fidelibus ad quos presens carta pervenerit, Hugo Dei gratia Linc' episcopus, salutem in domino. Sciatis nos[a] concessisse et dedisse venerabili fratri nostro domino Ioscelino Bathon' et Glaston' episcopo et successoribus suis inperpetuum, in puram et perpetuam elemosinam, feodum dimidii militis in Rugeberg' et Draycot', cum pertinentiis suis quod Mauritius de Benington'[b] et Galfridus Maureward' de nobis tenuerunt et nos de domino rege, cum homagiis et servitiis ipsorum Mauritii et Galfridi et heredum suorum inperpetuum; volentes et concedentes quod predicti Mauritius et Galfridus et heredes sui inperpetuum faciant homagia et servitia sua de predicto feodo ipsi episcopo et successoribus suis. Nos quidem homagia et fidelitates, que nobis fecerunt predicti Mauritius et Galfridus, eis remisimus et ipsos inde quietos clamavimus inperpetuum. Ut autem hec nostra concessio et donatio perpetua firmitate roboretur, eam presenti carta et sigilli nostri appositione confirmavimus. Hiis testibus: Galfrido filio Baldewini senescallo nostro, magistro Hugone de Wilton', magistro Willelmo de Keynesham, Petro de Wilton', Petro de Bathon', Stephano de Baddebir', et multis aliis. Dat' apud Stowam per manum magistri Willelmi de Thornaco, archidiaconi de Stowa, quinto idus Iulii pontificatus nostri anno quinto.

[a] intuitu Dei et pro salute anime nostre *is inserted* B.   [b] Beningtun' A2.

This and the next three charters were inspected and confirmed (but not recited) by King Henry III on 12 Feb. 1227 (*Cal.Ch. R.* i 4–5).

9. Bishop Jocelin of Bath and Glastonbury

Grant to Jocelin, bishop of Bath and Glastonbury, and his successors, of the advowson of the church of Axbridge.   Stow, 12 July 1214

B = Wells D. & C. Liber Albus II, fo. 343r. s. xvi in. C = ibid. fo. 349v.
Pd (calendar) *HMC Wells* i 472.

Omnibus Cristi fidelibus ad quos presens carta pervenerit, Hugo Dei gratia Lincoln' episcopus salutem in domino. Sciatis nos, intuitu dei et pro salute anime nostre, concessisse et dedisse venerabili fratri nostro domino Ioscelino Bathon' et

Glaston' episcopo et successoribus suis imperpetuum[a] advocationem ecclesie de Axebrig'[b] cum pertinentiis, volentes et concedentes quod ipsi de predicta ecclesia ordinent et disponant imperpetuum[a] pro voluntate sua sicut de aliis ecclesiis que de[c] sua advocatione sunt. Ut autem hec nostra concessio et donatio perpetua firmitate roboretur, eam presenti carta et sigilli nostri appositione confirmavimus. His[d] testibus: Galfrido filio Baldewini, senescallo nostro, magistro Hugone de Wilton', magistro Willelmo de Keynesham,[e] Petro de Wilton',[f] Petro de Bathon', Stephano de Baddebir',[g] et multis aliis. Dat' apud Stowam[h] per manum magistri Willelmi de Tornaco [i] archidiaconi de Stowa quarto idus Iulii pontificatus nostri anno quinto.

[a] inperpetuum C.   [b] Axbrig' C.   [c] *omitted* C.   [d] Hiis C.   [e] Kaynesham C.   [f] Wylton' C.   [g] Badbir' C.   [h] Stow' C.   [i] Thornaco C.

10. Bishop Jocelin of Bath and Glastonbury

Grant to Jocelin bishop of Bath and Glastonbury, and his successors, of half a knight's fee in Norton [Hawkfield], lately held of Bishop Hugh by Stephen de Altavilla and after him by Reginald his son, and by Hugh of the king with quitclaim of the homage and service of Reginald. The bishop also grants that this half fee and all other fees, lands and tenements held by Bishop Jocelin in the hundreds of Cheddar and Winterstoke and all the men thereof shall be for ever quit of suits of the aforementioned hundreds and enjoy all such liberties and free customs as his other manors have.   Stow, 12 July 1214

B = Wells D. & C. Liber Albus II fo. 350r. s. xvi in.
Pd (calendar) *HMC Wells* i 475.

Omnibus Cristi fidelibus ad quos presens carta pervenerit, Hugo Dei gratia Lincoln' episcopus salutem in domino. Sciatis nos, intuitu dei et pro salute anime nostre, concessisse et dedisse venerabili fratri nostro domino Ioscelino Bathon' et Glast' episcopo et successoribus suis inperpetuum in puram et perpetuam elemosinam feudum dimidii militis in Nortun' cum pertinentiis suis quod Stephanus de Altavill' de nobis tenuit et post illum Reginaldus filius eius et nos de domino rege, cum homagio et servitio ipsius Reginaldi et heredum suorum inperpetuum, volentes et concedentes quod idem Reginaldus et heredes sui inperpetuum faciant homagia et servitia sua de predicto feudo ipsi episcopo et successoribus suis. Nos quidem homagium et fidelitatem que nobis fecit predictus Reginaldus ei remisimus et ipsum inde quietum clamavimus inperpetuum. Volumus etiam et concedimus quod tam predictum feudum dimidii militis quam omnia alia feuda, terre et tenementa que idem episcopus habet in hundredis de Ceddr' et Wyntescomb' et omnes homines de predictis terris, feudis et tenementis quieti sint inperpetuum de sectis hundredorum predictorum et omnibus gaudeant libertatibus et liberis consuetudinibus quas alia maneria sua habere noscuntur. Ut autem hec nostra concessio et donatio perpetua firmitate roboretur, eam presenti carta et sigilli nostri appositione confirmavimus. Hiis testibus: Galfrido filio Baldewini senescallo nostro, magistro Hugone de Wylton', magistro Willelmo de Keynesham, Petro de Wilton', Petro de Bathon', Stephano de Baddebir' et multis aliis. Dat' apud Stowam per manum magistri Willelmi de Thornaco, archidiaconi de Stowa, quarto idus Iulii pontificatus nostri anno quinto.

11. Bishop Jocelin of Bath and Glastonbury

Grant that all the fees lands and tenements held by Jocelin, bishop of Bath and Glastonbury, in the hundreds of Cheddar and Winterstoke and all the men thereof shall be for ever quit of suits of the aforenamed hundreds and enjoy all such liberties and free customs as his other men and lands have. Stow, 12 July 1214

B = Wells D. & C. Liber Albus II fo. 347v. s. xvi in.
Pd (calendar) *HMC Wells* i 474.

Omnibus Cristi fidelibus ad quos presens carta pervenerit, Hugo Dei gratia Lincoln' episcopus salutem in domino. Volumus et concedimus quod omnia feoda, terre et tenementa que venerabilis frater noster dominus Ioscelinus Bathon' et Glaston' episcopus habet in hundredis de Ceddr' et Wintestok' et omnes homines de predictis feodis, terris et tenementis quieti sint in perpetuum, tam tempore suo quam successorum suorum, de sectis hundredorum predictorum et omnibus gaudeant libertatibus et liberis consuetudinibus quas alia feoda, terre et tenementa sua et alii homines sui habere noscuntur. Ut autem hec nostra concessio perpetua firmitate roboretur, eam presenti carta et sigilli nostri appositione confirmavimus. Hiis testibus: Galfrido filio Baldwini senescallo nostro, magistro Hugone de Wilton', magistro Willelmo de Keynesham, Petro de Wilton', Petro de Bathon', Stephano de Baddebir' et multis aliis. Dat' apud Stowam per manum magistri Willelmi de Thornaco, archidiaconi de Stowa, quarto idus Iulii pontificatus nostri anno quinto.

12. Huntingdon, priory of St Mary

Grant to the prior and canons of St Mary, Huntingdon, of an annual pension of fifty shillings from the church of Offord [Darcy], in the name of a perpetual benefice, saving to William Dacus, the patron, and his heirs, their right of patronage.
Buckden, 5 November 1214

B = LAO Add. Reg. 6 (Liber antiquus) fo. 23r. s. xiii in.
Pd *Lib. Ant.* 72–5.

Hiis testibus: R. archidiacono Hunted', magistro R. de Cestr', magistro W. de Well', R. capellano, canonicis Lincoln', Petro de Wileton', magistro R. de Tingehurst', R. de Bohum', Petro de Bathon', Stephano de Cicestr' et aliis. Dat' per manum W. archidiaconi de Stowa apud Buggeden' nonis Novembris pontificatus nostri anno quinto.

This grant of Bp Hugh is mentioned in *RHW* iii 93.

13. Thrapston Bridge

Indulgence (number of days not specified) for all those who shall contribute towards the construction and repair of Thrapston bridge.
[20 December 1213 x 19 December 1214]

Mention of lost charter issued during the bp's fifth pontifical year in no. 259.
Pd *RHW* ii 220.

For other indulgences for Thrapston bridge, see nos. 220, 256. This reference is possibly an error for the indulgence of the fifteenth pontifical year, not the fifth.

14.   Torre abbey

Confirmation of the grant made by Hugh (I), bishop of Lincoln (1186–1200), of the church of Skidbrook to the canons of Torre [EEA 4 no. 202].
Lincoln, 27 December 1214

> B = LAO Add. Reg. 6 (Liber antiquus) fo. 23r. s. xiii in. C = Dublin, Trinity College Lib., ms. E. 5. 15 (Torre cartulary) fo. 107v, no. cxl. (witnesses omitted). s. xiii med. D = PRO E164/19 (Torre cartulary) fo. 50r (witnesses omitted). s. xv.
> Pd from B in *Lib. Ant.* 73.

Hiis testibus: Roberto archidiacono Hunted', magistro Reginaldo de Cestr', magistro W. de Well', Rogero capellano, canonicis Linc', Martino de Pateshull', magistro R. de Gravel', magistro R. de Thingehurst', <R. de Bohum>, Petro de Wileton', <W. de Henton'>, Petro de Bathon', Stephano de Cicest' et aliis. Dat' per manum W. de Thornac', archidiaconi de Stowa, apud Linc' sexto kalendas Ianuarii pontificatus nostri anno sexto.

> This charter was confirmed by Roger, the dean, and the chapter of Lincoln (fos. 107v–108r, no. cxli of C). This confirmation of Bp Hugh is mentioned in *RHW* iii 93.

15.   Spalding Priory

Institution of Ralph of Westminster, clerk, to the church of Surfleet, on the presentation of the prior and convent of Spalding, saving to the priory its customary pension.
Old Temple, London, 8 January 1215

> B = LAO Ep. Reg. II (institution register of Bp Dalderby, 1300–20) fos. 27v–28r (in an inspeximus of Bp Dalderby, 27 April 1309).

Omnibus Cristi fidelibus ad quos presens scriptum pervenerit Hugo Dei gratia Linc' episcopus salutem in domino. Noverit universitas vestra nos, ad presentationem prioris et conventus de Spalding patronorum ecclesie de Surflet', dilectum in Cristo filium Radulfo de Westm' clericum ad eandem ecclesiam admisisse et ipsum in eadem canonice personam instituisse, salva dictis priori et conventui debita et antiqua pensione de eadem ecclesia; salvis etiam in omnibus episcopalibus consuetudinibus et Lincolniensis ecclesie dignitate.[a] Et ut hec nostra institutio perpetue firmitatis robur optineat, eam presenti scripto sigilli nostri impressione roborato duximus confirmandum. Hiis testibus: Roberto archidiacono Huntedon', magistro Reginaldo de Cestr', magistro Waltero de Welles, Rogero capellano, canonicis Linc', magistro Roberto Gravel, Ricardo de Tinchehirst', Rogero de Boun', Petro de Wylton', Petro de Bath', [fo. 28r] Stephano de Cicestr' et aliis. Dat' per manum Willelmi de Thornac', archidiaconi Stowe, apud Vetus Templum London' vi idus Ianuarii pontificatus nostri anno sexto.

[a] dignita B.

16. Aynho hospital

Grant in proprios usus, made with the consent of Guy de la Haye, the patron, to the hospital of Aynho of the chapel of Croughton.   Banbury, 7 February 1215

> A = Oxford, Magdalen College, Aynho Ch. 82. Endorsed: Confirmacio capelle de Crolton' (s. xv); I. de Clipston' (ss. xiv–xv); pressmarks; approx. 164 x 69 + 12 mm.; fragment of seal on parchment tag (method 1), brownish wax, counterseal.
> B = LAO Add. Reg. 6 (Liber antiquus) fo. 23r. s. xiii in. C = Oxford, Magdalen College, estate records 137/1 (charter roll of Aynho hospital) m. 7 (witnesses omitted). s. xiii.
> Pd from B in *Lib. Ant.* 73–4.

Omnibus Cristi fidelibus ad quos presens scriptum pervenerit, Hug(o) Dei gratia Linc' episcopus eternam in domino salutem . Cum ea que locis religiosis rationabiliter collata sunt pium sit perpetuo roborare, nos intuitu Dei capellam de Croultun', de consensu Guidonis de la Haye patroni eiusdem cappelle, hospitali de Einho in usus proprios habendam concedimus et episcopali auctoritate confirmamus, salvis in omnibus episcopalibus consuetudinibus et Linc' ecclesie dignitate. Quod ut perpetuam optineat firmitatem, presenti scripto sigillum nostrum apposuimus. Hiis testibus: Willelmo de Tornac' archidiacono de Stowa, magistro Reginaldo de Cestr', Rogero cappellano, Petro de Bathon', canonicis Linc', magistro Roberto de Gravel', magistro Ricardo de Tinghurst', Rogero de Bohun, Stephano de Cicestr'et aliis. Dat' per manum Roberti, archidiaconi Huntend', apud Bannebyr' septimo idus Februarii pontificatus nostri anno sexto.

> This charter was confirmed by Roger the dean and the chapter of Lincoln (Oxford, Magdalen College, Aynho Ch. 81; estate records 137/1, m. 7). The charters of Walter the chamberlain and Baldwin de Bulvinia relating to the grant of Croughton chapel are ibid. Aynho Chs. 30, 85. This grant of Bp Hugh is mentioned in *RHW* III 93.

17. Northampton, abbey of St James

Grant in proprios usus, made with the consent of the chapter of Lincoln, to the abbot and convent of St James, Northampton, of the church of Horton.
Lincoln, 21 March /20 April 1215

> B = LAO Add. Reg. 6 (Liber antiquus) fo. 23r–v. s. xiii in.
> Pd *Lib. Ant.* 74.

Hiis testibus: R. decano, G. precentore, Rogero cancellario, Gilberto thesaurario, Reimundo Leic', Roberto Norhampton', Alexandro Bedeford', Iohanne Oxon', Willelmo Stowe, Roberto Huntedon' archidiaconis, magistro Reginaldo de Cestr', magistro Waltero de Well', Rogero capellano, Petro de Bathon', canonicis Lincoln', [fo. 23v] magistro R. de Gravel', magistro R. de Tingehurst, R. de Bohun, Petro de Wylton', P. de Cheuermont, Stephano de Cicestr' et aliis. Dat' apud Linc' duodecimo kalendas Aprilis pontificatus nostri anno vi.

> The transcripts of the following six acta in the *Liber Antiquus* are all dated the 12th calends of April (21 March). However, the survival of an original charter (no. 22) dated the 12th calends of May (20 April) would seem to indicate that the scribe of the *Liber Antiquus* has miscopied the month in the dating clause. This grant of Bp Hugh is mentioned in *RHW* iii 93.

18.   Bourne abbey

Grant in proprios usus, *made with the consent of the cathedral chapter, to the abbot and convent of Bourne of the church of Bitchfield.*

Lincoln, 21 March/20 April 1215

> B = LAO Add. Reg. 6 (Liber antiquus) fo. 23v. s. xiii in.
> Pd *Lib. Ant.* 74.

Hiis testibus: Rogero decano, Galfrido precentore, Rogero cancellario, Gileberto thesaurario, Reimundo Leicestr', Roberto Norhampt', Alexandro Bedeford', Iohanne Oxon', Willelmo Stouwe, Roberto Huntingd' archidiaconis, magistro Reginaldo de Cestr', magistro Waltero de Well', Rogero capellano, Petro de Bathon', canonicis Lincoln', magistro Roberto de Gravel', magistro Ricardo de Tingehurst, Rogero de Bohun, Petro de Wylton', P. de Cheuermont', Stephano de Cicestr' et aliis. Dat' apud Linc' xii° kalendas Aprilis pontificatus nostri anno vi°.

> This grant of Bp Hugh is mentioned in *RHW* iii 93.

19.   Caldwell priory

Grant, with the assent of the chapter of Lincoln, to the prior and convent of Caldwell of an annual pension of three marks from the church of Marsworth, in the name of a perpetual benefice.

Lincoln, 21 March/20 April 1215

> B = LAO Add. Reg. 6 (Liber antiquus) fo. 23v. s. xiii in.
> Pd *Lib. Ant.* 75.

Testibus ut supra in proxima, excepto magistro Ricardo de Tingehurst. Dat' apud Lincoln' xii° kalendas Aprilis pontificatus nostri anno vi^{to}.

> For the date, see no. 17. This grant of Bp Hugh is mentioned in *RHW* iii 93.

20.   Bicester priory

Grant, with the assent of the chapter of Lincoln, to the prior and convent of Bicester of an annual pension of five marks from the church of Little Missenden, in the name of a perpetual benefice.

Lincoln, 21 March/20 April 1215

> B = LAO Add. Reg. 6 (Liber antiquus) fo. 23v. s. xiii in.
> Pd *Lib. Ant.* 75.

Testibus et dat' ut supra in carta canonicorum de Brunn' de ecclesia de Billesfeld' [no. 17].

> For the date, see no. 17. This grant of Bp Hugh is mentioned in *RHW* iii 93.

21.   Norton priory

Grant, with the assent of the chapter of Lincoln, to the prior and convent of Norton of an annual pension of four marks from the church of Castle Donington, in the name of a perpetual benefice.

Lincoln, 21 March/20 April 1215

> B = LAO Add. Reg. 6 (Liber antiquus) fo. 23v. s. xiii in.
> Pd *Lib. Ant.* 75.

Testibus et dat' <addito> per manum W. de Tornac' archidiaconi Stouwe ut <supra> in proxima.

For the date, see no. 17. This grant of Bp Hugh is mentioned in *RHW* iii 93.

22. Canons Ashby priory

Grant, with the assent of the chapter of Lincoln, to the prior and canons of [Canons] Ashby of a pension of three marks a year, in the name of a perpetual benefice, from the church of Moreton [Pinkney].   Lincoln, 20 April 1215

> A = PRO E326/8827. Endorsed: Littera domini Hugonis episcopi Linc' et capituli de pensione ecclesie de Morton' (s. xv); approx. 182 x 103 + 15 mm.; seal brownish-white wax, on parchment tag (method 1), counterseal; slit for another seal tag on the right-hand side of the fold.
> B = LAO Add. Reg. 6 (Liber antiquus) fo. 23v. s. xiii in. C = BL ms. Egerton 3033 (Canons Ashby cartulary) fo. 17r–v. s. xiii ex.
> Pd from B in *Lib. Ant.* 75.

Universis sancte matris ecclesie filiis ad quos presens scriptum pervenerit[a], Hugo Dei gratia Lincoln' episcopus eternam in domino salutem. Noverit universitas vestra nos, de assensu capituli nostri Linc', divine pietatis intuitu concessisse et dedisse dilectis in Cristo filiis . . priori et canonicis de Esseby tres marcas annuas in ecclesia de Morton' nomine perpetui beneficii percipiendas, salvis in omnibus episcopalibus consuetudinibus et Lincoln' ecclesie dignitate. In huius igitur rei robur et testimonium, sigillum nostrum et sigillum capituli nostri Lincoln' huic scripto sunt apposita. Hiis testibus:[b] Rogero decano, Galfrido precentore, Rogero cancellario, Gileberto thesaurario, Reimundo Leicestr', Roberto Norhamton', Alexandro Bedeford', Iohanne Oxon', Willelmo Stowe, Roberto Huntindon' archidiaconis, magistro Reginaldo de Cestr', magistro Waltero de Well', Rogero cappellano, Petro de Bathon', canonicis Lincoln', magistro Roberto de Gravel', magistro Ricardo de Tinchurst', Rogero de Bohum', Petro de Wylton', Petro de Chieuremont' et aliis. Dat' apud Lincoln' duodecimo kalendas Maii pontificatus nostri anno sexto.

> [a] B *has* Universis Christi fideiibus etc.   [b] Testibus et dat' ut supra in carta canonicorum de Brunna de ecclesia de Billesfeld' excepto Stephano de Cicestr' B.

This grant of Bp Hugh is mentioned in *RHW* iii 93.

23. John, king of England

Inspeximus by Stephen archbishop of Canterbury, Henry archbishop of Dublin, William bishop of London, Peter bishop of Winchester, Jocelin bishop of Bath and Glastonbury, Hugh bishop of Lincoln, Walter bishop of Worcester, William bishop of Coventry, Benedict bishop of Rochester and master Pandulph, papal subdeacon, of Magna Carta.   [June 1215]

> B = PRO E164/2 (Red Book of the Exchequer) fos. 234r–236r. s. xiii med.
> Pd *Acta Stephani Langton* no. 16 (and see note on the probable original charter); *EEA* 9 no. 97.

For the background see C.R. Cheney, 'The Church and Magna Carta', *Theology*, lxviii (1965), 266–72.

24. John, king of England

Testimony of Stephen archbishop of Canterbury, Henry archbishop of Dublin, William bishop of London, Peter bishop of Winchester, Jocelin bishop of Bath and Glastonbury, Hugh bishop of Lincoln, Walter bishop of Worcester, William bishop of Coventry, Richard bishop of Chichester and Pandulph, papal subdeacon, to the unwillingness of the barons to give King John a charter declaring their obligations of fealty.   [15 June 1215 x September 1215, ? July 1215]

> B = PRO C66/14 (patent roll, 17 John) m. 21d.
> Pd from B in *Rot. Litt. Pat.* i 181; *Acta Stephani Langton* no. 17; *Foedera* 134; McKechnie, *Magna Carta* 497 no. 7; Holt, *Magna Carta*, 498 no. 13 (cf. ibid. 486–7); *EEA* 9 no. 99.

25. John, king of England

Testimony by S(tephen) archbishop of Canterbury, H(enry) archbishop of Dublin, W(illiam) bishop of London, P(eter) bishop of Winchester, J(ocelin) bishop of Bath and Glastonbury, H(ugh) bishop of Lincoln, W(alter) bishop of Worcester and W(illiam) bishop of Coventry acknowledging the king's intention to reform the laws of the forest.   [15 June 1215 x September 1215, ? July 1215]

> B = PRO C54/12 (close roll, 17 John) m. 27d. C = PRO C54/13 (ibid.) m. 21d.
> Pd from B in *Rot. Litt. Claus.* i 269; *Foedera* 134; McKechnie, *Magna Carta* 496 no. 6; Holt, *Magna Carta* 498–9 no. 14; *EEA* 9 no. 98.

For the background see Holt, *Magna Carta* 352, 486–7.

26. Lincoln cathedral: prebend of Clifton

Acknowledgement that the bishop is bound to pay two marks a year to Marchisius d'Aubigny, canon of Lincoln and prebendary of Clifton, in exchange for the mill of Haleclive in [North] Clifton and a fishery which Marchisius and his predecessors held.   Newark, 8 July 1215

> A = LAO Lincoln D. & C. Dij/69/1/43. Endorsed: De piscaria de Clifton' (s. xiii); De piscaria in Trenta pro qua solebant episcopi Linc' solvere .ii. marcas (s. xiv); approx. 178 x 85 + 18 mm.; seal missing, parchment tag.
> Pd *Reg. Ant.* iii no. 912.

Omnibus Cristi fidelibus ad quos presens scriptum pervenerit, Hug(o) Dei gratia Lincoln' episcopus eternam in domino salutem. Noverit universitas vestra nos teneri dilecto filio nostro Marchisio de Albinico canonico Linc' et successoribus suis [ca]nonicis prebende de Clifton' ad solvendas annuas duas marcas argenti inperpetuum per manus ballivi nostri de Stowa ad terminum sancti Michaelis in nundinis de Stowa, in excambium molendini de Haleclive et piscarie cum pertinenciis suis: que ipse Marchisius et predecessores sui tenuerant, reddendo nobis et predecessoribus nostris episcopis Linc' tres marcas argenti, que idem Marchisius nobis quieta clamavit. Et hec acta sunt de consensu Rogeri decani et capituli Linc'. In huius igitur rei robur et testimonium presenti scripto sigillum nostrum apposuimus. Dat' per manum Roberti, archidiaconi Huntendon', apud Newer' viii⁰ idus Iulii pontificatus nostri anno sexto. Hiis testibus: Rogero decano, G. precentore, I. subdecano, magistro W. filio Fulconis, Thoma de Fiskerton', Rogero cappellano, Gileberto de Scartheb', magistro Waltero de Well', Petro Bathon', canonicis Linc', Petro de Wylton', magistro Ricardo de Tinge-hurst, clericis, et multis aliis.

> This charter was inspected by Roger, dean and chapter of Lincoln (ibid. no. 913). The square brackets indicate a small hole in the document. For Marchisius see *Fasti Lincoln* 61.

27. Castle Acre priory

Institution of master Hugh de Bereford to the perpetual vicarage of [Long] Sutton, on the presentation of the prior and convent of Castle Acre, saving to the priory an annual pension if it is ancient and due.   Boddington, 12 July 1215

> B = BL ms. Harl. 2110 (Castle Acre cartulary) fos. 122v–123r (116v–117r). s. xiii med.

Universis sancte matris ecclesie filiis ad quos presens scriptum pervenerit, Hugo Dei gratia Linc' episcopus salutem in domino. Noverit universitas vestra nos, ad presentationem prioris et conventus de Acra patronorum ecclesie de Sutton', dilectum filium in Cristo magistrum Hugonem de Bereford' ad perpetuam eiusdem ecclesie vicariam vacantem admisisse et ipsum [fo. 123r] in eadem canonice instituisse vicarium, salva dictis priori et conventui de eadem ecclesia annua pensione si qua debita sit et antiqua, salvis etiam in omnibus episcopalibus consuetudinibus et Lincolniensis ecclesie dignitate. Et ut nostra institutio perpe-tuum firmitatis robur optineat, eam presenti scripto et sigilli nostri munimine roboravimus. Hiis testibus: magistro Reginaldo de Cestr', magistro Waltero de Well', Rogero capellano, Petro de Bathon', canonicis Linc', magistro Roberto de Gravel', magistro Ricardo de Tinghurst', Petro de Wilt', Rogero de Bohun', Stephano de Cicestr' et aliis. Dat' per manum Roberti de Heiles, archidiaconi de Huntedon', apud Badinton' iiii idus Iulii pontificatus nostri anno sexto.

28. Stainfield priory

Confirmation, with the assent of the chapter of Lincoln, for the prioress and convent of Stainfield of an annual pension of twenty shillings from the church of Kirmond [le Mire], in the name of a perpetual benefice.   Banbury, 26 July 1215

> B = LAO Add. Reg. 6 (Liber antiquus) fo. 23v. s. xiii in.
> Pd *Lib. Ant.* 75.

Testibus: magistro R. de Cestr', Rogero capellano, Petro de Bathon', canonicis Lincoln', magistro Roberto de Gravel', magistro Ricardo de Tingehurst, magistro Willelmo de Staveneby, Rogero de Bohun, Stephano de Cicestr' et aliis. Dat' per manum Willelmi de Thornac', archidiaconi Stouwe, apud Bannebir' vii kalendas Augusti pontificatus nostri anno vi^to.

> This grant of Bp Hugh is mentioned in *RHW* iii 93.

29. Stamford, priory of St Michael

Appropriation, made with the assent of the chapter of Lincoln, to the prioress and nuns of St Michael, Stamford, of the church of All Saints in the market-place of Stamford, saving the vicarage which the bishop has ordained. The vicarage con-

sists of all the income of the altarage. The vicar shall pay to the nuns a pension of two marks a year at Rogationtide and shall bear all episcopal burdens. The prioress and nuns shall have all the land of the church and all garb tithes for their own use.   Banbury, 29 July 1215

> B = LAO Add. Reg. 6 (Liber antiquus) fos. 23v–24r. s. xiii in.
> Pd *Lib. Ant.* 76.

Testibus: Rogero decano, R. Norhampton', R. de Hailes, Huntingdon' archidiaconis, Hugone de sancto Edwardo, magistro Reginaldo de Cestr', Thoma de Fiskarton' et Rogero de Bristoll' capellanis, [fo. 24r] Petro de Bathon', canonicis Lincoln', magistro Willelmo de Brancewell', magistro Roberto de Gravel', magistro Ricardo de Tingehurst', Stephano de Cicestr' et aliis. Dat' per manum W. de Tornac', archidiaconi Stouwe, apud Bannebir' iiii^{to} kalendas Augusti pontificatus nostri anno vi^{to}.

> This grant of Bp Hugh is mentioned in *RHW* iii 93.

30. Thelsford, hospital of St John and St Radegund

Confirmation of the grant made by Philip of Kineton to the hospital of St John and St Radegund, Thelsford, of the advowson of the church of Kirkby [Mallory].
                                                        Kilsby, 5 August 1215

> B = LAO Add. Reg. 6 (Liber antiquus) fo. 24r. s. xiii in.
> Pd *Lib. Ant.* 76.

Hiis testibus: R. de Bristoll' capellano, P. de Bathon', canonicis Linc', magistro Roberto de Gravel', magistro R. de Tingehurst', R. de Bohun, Stephano de Cicestr' et aliis. Dat' per manum magistri Reginaldi de Cestr' apud Kyldeby nonis Augusti pontificatus nostri anno vi^{to}

> This grant does not appear to have taken effect. The house of St John and St Radegund appears to have been of the short-lived order of canons of the Holy Sepulchre. Some time after 1224 it passed to the Trinitarian order (*KH* 175; M. Gray, *The Trinitarian Order in England: excavations at Thelsford priory*, eds. L. Watts and P. Rahtz (BAR British series 226, 1993)). In the *matricula* of the Leicester archdeaconry, Philip of Kineton is still described as the patron of the church (*RHW* i 246) and in 1225 the patronage was in the possession of Thomas Mallory (ibid. ii 298). This grant of Bp Hugh is mentioned in *RHW* iii 93.

31. Lavendon abbey

Grant in proprios usus, *made with the assent of the chapter of Lincoln, to the abbot and convent of Lavendon of the chapel of Tattenhoe.*
                                                        Kilsby, 6 August 1215

> B = LAO Add. Reg. 6 (Liber antiquus) fo. 24r. s. xiii in.
> Pd *Lib. Ant.* 76–7.

Hiis testibus: Rogero de Bristoll' capellano etc. ut supra in carta proxima [no. 30]. Dat' per manum magistri Reginaldi de Cestr' apud Kyldeby octavo idus Augusti pontificatus nostri anno sexto.

> This grant of Bp Hugh is mentioned in *RHW* iii 94.

32. Oxford, priory of St Frideswide

Grant, with the assent of the chapter of Lincoln, to the prior and convent of St. Frideswide, Oxford, of a pension of three marks a year from the church of All Saints, Oxford, in the name of a perpetual benefice.   Oxford, 18 August 1215

> B = LAO Add. Reg. 6 (Liber antiquus) fo. 24r. s. xiii in. C = Oxford, Bodl. C.C.C. ms. 160 (St Frideswide's cartulary) p. 298, no. 453. s. xiii ex.
> Pd from B in *Lib. Ant.* 77; from C in *St Frideswide's Cartulary* i no. 371.

Testibus:[a] Roberto de Heiles archidiacono [b] Huntindon'[b], magistro Reginaldo de Cestr'[c] etc. ut supra in carta proxima [no. 31][d]. Dat'[e] per manum Willelmi de Tornac'[f] archidiaconi[g] Stow'[h] apud Oxon' quintodecimo[i] kalendas Septembris pontificatus nostri anno vi°.[j]

> [a] Hiis testibus C.   [b] de Huntindone C.   [c] Cest' C.   [d] Rogero de Bristolle capellano, Petro de Baton', canonicis Linc', magistro Roberto de Gravel', magistro Ricardo de Tinghurst, Rogero de Bohum, Stephano de Cicestre et aliis C.   [e] datum C.   [f] Tornaco C.   [g] archidiaco (*sic*) C.   [h] Stowe C.   [i] xv C.   [j] sexto C.

This grant of Bp Hugh is mentioned in *RHW* iii 94.

33. Tupholme abbey

Confirmation of the grant made by Geoffrey de Nevill to the abbey of Tupholme of the advowson of the church of [Great] Sturton.   Oxford, 21 August 1215

> B = LAO Add. Reg. 6 (Liber antiquus) fo. 24r. s. xiii in.
> Pd *Lib. Ant.* 77.

Hiis testibus: Willelmo de Tornaco archidiacono Stow', magistro R. de Cestr', R. de Bristoll' capellano, magistro Waltero de Well', P. de Bath', canonicis Linc', magistris R. de Gravel' et W. de Staveneby, Petro de Wilton', R. de Bohun, Stephano de Cic' et aliis. Dat' per manum Roberti de Heill', archidiaconi Huntind', apud Oxon' duodecimo kalendas Septembris pontificatus nostri anno vi°.

This grant of Bp Hugh is mentioned in *RHW* iii 93.

34. Worksop priory

Grant, with the assent of the chapter of Lincoln, to the prior and convent of Worksop of an annual pension of three marks from the church of Rushton, in the name of a perpetual benefice. Previously they had only enjoyed a pension of one mark a year.   Old Temple, London, 28 August 1215

> B = LAO Add. Reg. 6 (Liber antiquus) fo. 24r–v. s. xiii in.
> Pd *Lib. Ant.* 77.

Hiis testibus: Rogero decano Linc', Reimundo Leirc', Roberto Norh't, Alexandro Bedef', Iohanne Oxon', Roberto Hunt' archidiaconis, magistris R. de Cestr' et W. de Well', Rogero de Bristoll' et Thoma de Fiskert' capellanis, Petro de Bath',canonicis Linc', magistris R. de Gravel', W. de Staveneby, R. de Tingherst et Stephano de Cic' et aliis. Dat' per manum W. de Tornac', [fo.24v] archidiaconi

Stow', apud Vetus Templum Lond' quinto kalendas Septembris pontificatus nostri anno vi°.

This grant of Bp Hugh is mentioned in *RHW* i 26, and ibid., iii 94.

35. Northampton, priory of St Andrew

Grant in proprios usus, made with the assent of the chapter of Lincoln, of the church of Preston [Deanery] to the prior and convent of St Andrew, Northampton, saving the vicarage which the bishop has ordained. This vicarage consists of the altarage, a manse and all other land pertaining to the church. The prior and convent shall have a barn in which to store their corn each year.

Old Temple, London, 28 August 1215

> B = LAO Add. Reg. 6 (Liber antiquus) fo. 24v. s. xiii in. C = BL ms. Royal 11 B ix (cartulary of St Andrew, Northampton) fo. 28r. s. xiii ex. D = BL ms. Cotton Vespasian E xvii (cartulary of St Andrew, Northampton) fo. 70v (67v). s. xv med. E = ibid. fo. 292r (275r).
> Pd from B in *Lib. Ant.* 78.

Hiis testibus:[a] Rogero decano Linc', Reimundo Leicestr',[b] Roberto Norh't,[c] Alexandro Bedeford',[d] Iohanne Oxon',[e] Roberto Huntend'[f] archidiaconis, magistro Reginaldo de Cestr', Rogero de Bristoll'[g] capellano,Thoma de Fiskerton'[h], Petro de Bathonia, canonicis Linc', magistro Roberto de Gravel', magistro Ricardo de Tinghurstr'[i], Stephano de Cicestr' et aliis. Dat' per manum Willelmi de Tornaco, archidiaconi Stow'[j], apud Vetus Templum Lond'[k] v° kalendas Septembris pontificatus nostri anno vi° .[m]

> [a] Testibus etc. ut supra in carta proxima, exceptis magistris W. de Welles et W. de Staveneby. Dat' ut in carta proxima precedenti [no. 33] B. Witness list and date from C.   [b] Leyrcestr' D; Leycestr' E.   [c] North' D; Northampton' E.   [d] Bedeford D; Bedford E.   [e] Oxen' E.   [f] Huntyndon' D; Huntyngd' E.   [g] Brystoll' D; Brystell' E.   [h] Fylkerton' DE.   [i] Tinghurst' D; Tynghurston' E.   [j] Stowe E.   [k] London' DE.   [l] quinto DE.   [m] sexto DE.

This grant of Bp Hugh is mentioned in *RHW* iii 94.

36. Caldwell priory

Grant, made with the assent of the chapter of Lincoln, to the prior and canons of Caldwell, patrons of the church of Marsworth, of all the tithes of corn belonging to the same church. This grant is to take effect on the death or cession of master Richard of Fingest, saving to the vicar who shall be instituted to the church the third part of the garb tithes of the demesne of Thurstan Basset, the entire altarage and all the land that belongs to the church except for four acres assigned to the prior and convent for building purposes. The vicar shall minister in the priestly office and shall bear all episcopal burdens.

Old Temple, London, 28 August 1215

> B = LAO Add. Reg. 6 (Liber antiquus) fo. 24v. s. xiii in.
> Pd *Lib. Ant.* 78.

Testibus et dat' etc. ut supra in carta prioris et conventus de Wirksop' super ecclesia de Riston' [no. 34].

Richard of Fingest was a member of Bp Hugh's *familia*. No record survives of his institution to Marsworth; since he is also found attesting *acta* of St Hugh in the late 1190s and of William of Blois, bp of Lincoln 1203–1206 (*EEA* 4 nos. 3, 73, 251), it is conceivable that he received this parish church long before Hugh II's election. This grant of Bp Hugh is mentioned in *RHW* iii 93.

37. Freiston priory

Confirmation, with the assent of the chapter of Lincoln, for the prior and convent of Freiston of an annual pension of twelve marks from the church of Toft, in the name of a perpetual benefice. This pension shall be paid by Peter of Bath, parson of the church, and his successors and replaces the pension of six marks which the monks used to receive.   Old Temple, London, 28 August 1215

B = LAO Add. Reg. 6 (Liber antiquus) fo. 24v. s. xiii in.
Pd *Lib. Ant.* 78.

Testibus ut supra in carta proxima excepto Petro de Bathon'. Dat' ut supra in carta proxima [no. 36].

Peter of Bath was an episcopal clerk and canon of Lincoln cathedral (*Fasti Lincoln,* p. 133). This grant of Bp Hugh is mentioned in *RHW* iii 94.

38. Newnham priory

Confirmation, with the assent of the chapter of Lincoln, for the prior and convent of Newnham of an annual pension of twelve shillings from the church of All Saints, Bedford, in the name of a perpetual benefice.
                                         Old Temple, London, 29 August 1215

B = LAO Add. Reg. 6 (Liber antiquus) fo. 24v. s. xiii in. C = BL ms. Harl. 3656
(Newnham cartulary) fo. 57r–v. s. xv in.
Pd from B in *Lib. Ant.* 79; from C in *Newnham Cartulary* i no. 93.

Hiis testibus: Rogero decano Linc', Roberto Norh't[a], [b-]Reimundo Leirc'[-b], Alexandro Bedef' et Roberto Hunt' archidiaconis, magistris R. de Cestr' et W. de Well', Thoma de Fiskerton' et P. de Bath', canonicis Linc', magistris R.de Gravel', Th. officiale Norh't, Willelmo de Brancewell', Simone de Elnestow' et aliis. Dat' per manum magistri Willelmi[d] de Tornac', archidiaconie[e] Stow'[f], apud Vetus Templum Lond' quarto[g] kalendas Septembris pontificatus nostri anno vi[to].

[a] de Norhampt' C. [b-b] *omitted* C. [c] Bed' C *and witness list ends here with* et aliis. [d] W. C. [e] C-*adds* de. [f] Stowa C. [g] iiii[to] C.

This grant of Bp Hugh is mentioned in *RHW* iii 94.

39. Bushmead priory

Inspeximus of the confirmation of his predecessor, Bishop Hugh (I) [EEA 4 no. 29] for Bushmead priory and confirmation to prior Joseph and the canons of all their present possessions and any which they may acquire in future.
                                              Maidstone, 30 August 1215

B = LAO Add. Reg. 6 (Liber antiquus) fos. 24v–25r. s. xiii in. C = Bedfordshire
Record Office, D.D.GY.9/2 (Bushmead cartulary) fo. 4r–v. s. xiv med.

Pd from B in *Lib. Ant.* 79–80; from C in *Bushmead Cartulary* no. 13.

Hiis testibus: Roberto archidiacono Hunt',[a] magistro Reginaldo de Cestr', Rogero capellano, Petro de Bath'[b], canonicis Linc', magistro Ricardo de Tingherst,[c] Petro de Wilton', Rogero de Bohun,[d] Stephano de Cicestr' et aliis. Dat' per manum Willelmi de Tornac'[e], archidiaconi Stow'[f], apud Meidestan' tertio[g] kalendas Septembris pontificatus nostri anno vi[o] [h]

[a] C *reads* Rogero decano Lincolniensi, Roberto de Heyles, archidiacono de Huntend'.   [b] Bathon' C.   [c] Tinghurst C.   [d] Bohum' C.   [e] Tourac' C.   [f] Stowe C.   [g] iii C.   [h] sexto C.

Bp Hugh I's charter is dated 1197 x 1198. It was inspected by Hubert Walter, archbp of Canterbury (*EEA* 3 no. 363) and by Bp William of Lincoln (*EEA* 4 no. 228) before Hugh II's inspection.

40.   Keynsham abbey

Grant, with the assent of Roger the dean and the chapter of Lincoln, to the abbot and convent of Keynsham of all the garb tithes of the church of Burford and of the chapel of Fulbrook, together with a messuage of the mother church which belongs to the parson. All the land of the church and chapel, a messuage, and all other appurtenances (except for the aforementioned garb tithes and messuage) are assigned for the provision of a perpetual vicar, who shall be presented by the abbot and convent to the bishop for institution.   Maidstone, 31 August 1215

B = LAO Add. Reg. 6 (Liber antiquus) fo. 25r. s. xiii in.
Pd *Lib. Ant.* 80.

Hiis testibus: Ioscelino Bath' et Glaston' episcopo, Rogero decano Linc', <Iohanne Oxon'>, Roberto Huntind' archidiaconis et testibus aliis supra in carta proxima prenotatis [no. 41]. Dat' per manum W. de Tornac', archidiaconi Stow', apud Meidestan' pridie kalendas Septembris pontificatus nostri anno sexto.

This grant of Bp Hugh is mentioned in *RHW* iii 94.

41.   Goring priory

Grant in proprios usus, made with the assent of the chapter of Lincoln, of the church of Nuffield to the prioress and convent of Goring, the patrons, in order to provide for their clothing. A perpetual vicarage of five marks is reserved and the vicar shall serve personally.   Canterbury, 1 September 1215

B = LAO Add. Reg. 6 (Liber antiquus) fo. 25r. s. xiii in.
Pd *Lib. Ant.* 80.

Testibus ut supra in carta proxima [no. 39], adiecto hic magistro R. de Gravel'. Dat' per manum Willelmi de Tornac', archidiaconi Stow', apud Cant' kalendis Septembris pontificatus nostri anno vi[o].

This grant of Bp Hugh is mentioned in *RHW* iii 94.

42. Wells hospital

Grant, with the assent of Jocelin, bishop of Bath and Glastonbury, of all his lands and rents in the manor of Wells, within and outside the borough, to establish a hospital at Wells, saving to the bishop of Bath and Glastonbury and his successors and other lords all rents and services due to them.

Troyes (?), 29 September 1215

B = PRO C53/25 (charter roll 15 Henry iii), m. 9 (in an inspeximus dated at Westminster, 17 April 1231).
Pd (calendar), *Cal.Ch.R.* i 131.

Omnibus Cristi fidelibus ad quos presens scriptum pervenerit, H. Dei gratia Linc' episcopus salutem eternam in domino. Sciatis nos pro salute[a] anime nostre et antecessorum et heredum nostrorum, de assensu et voluntate venerabilis fratris nostri domini I. Bath' et Glaston' episcopi et ecclesiarum suarum, concessisse et presenti carta nostra confirmasse in puram et perpetuam elemosinam omnes terras et redditus quos habemus in manerio de Welles, sive in burgo sive extra burgum, ad faciendum unum hospitale apud Welles, salvis inde dicto episcopo et successoribus suis et aliis eiusdem hereditatis dominis redditibus et servitiis debitis. Testibus: domino Willelmo Lond' episcopo, Roberto Elyens[i] electo, Willelmo archidiacono de Stowe, Rogero Wellensi, Thoma de Fiskerton', Petro de Bath', Linc' canonicis, magistris Nicholao de Evesham, Iohanne de Houton' et multis aliis. Dat' Tretis in festo sancti Michaelis pontificatus nostri anno vi, per manum dicti W. archidiaconi Stowe.

[a] nostra *is written here and is dotted for deletion.*

'Tretis' is possibly an English scribe's version of Troyes (*civitas Trecensis*), a city which lay on the Simplon route to Rome (via Paris – Troyes – Dijon – Simplon – Milan – Pavia – Piacenza – Bologna), cf. *PUE* ii p. 152, no. 13. This charter would seem to indicate that William de Ste Mere Eglise, bp of London (1199–1221), can be enumerated among those English prelates who attended the Fourth Lateran Council. Previous episcopal attendance lists for the Council have not included his name and of course there is no proof that he actually arrived in Rome. In English records the last mention of him that I have found occurs on 2 September 1215 (*Rot. Litt. Claus.* i 227b). There is silence as to his whereabouts until 10 October 1216 (*Rot. Litt. Pat.* i 199). A mandate of Pope Innocent III to be dated to the period December 1215 x January 1216 and addressed to the bps of Chichester and London could well have been issued personally to them at Rome (C.R. and M.G. Cheney, *The Letters of Pope Innocent III concerning England and Wales* (Oxford 1967), no.1051). Richard Poore of Chichester certainly attended the Council and was definitely still in Rome in January 1216 (*Acta Stephani Langton* no. 42). For the episcopal attendance lists see J. Werner, 'Nachlese aus Züricher Handschriften – I. Die Teilnehmerliste des Laterankonzils vom Jahre 1215' in *Neues Archiv der Gesellschaft für altere deutsche Geschichtskunde* xxxi (1906) 575–93.

43. Bardney abbey

Collation, by authority of the Lateran Council, of a mediety of the church of Cranwell to master Robert of Graveley, saving in future the right of the patron and saving also a pension of sixteen shillings to the abbot and convent of Bardney, if it is customary. [*c.* 1214 x 1215]

B = BL ms. Cotton Vespasian E xx (Bardney cartulary) fo. 231v (226v). s. xiii ex.

Universis sancte matris ecclesie filiis ad quos presens scriptum pervenerit, Hugo
Dei gratia Linc' episcopus eternam in domino salutem. Noverit universitas vestra
nos, auctoritate concilii Lateran', dilectum in Cristo filium magistrum Robertum
de Gravel' in medietate ecclesie de Cranewell' canonice personam instituisse,
salvo iure cuiuslibet qui ius patronatus sibi vendicat in eadem, et salva pensione
sexdecim solidorum abbati et conventui de Bard' si debita fuerit et antiqua; salvis
in omnibus episcopalibus consuetudinibus et Linc' ecclesie dignitate. Et ut hec
institutio nostra perpetuam optineat firmitatem, eam presenti scripto et sigilli
nostri duximus appositione confirmandam. Hiis t(estibus): Roberto de Heil',
archidiacono Huntendon' etc.

> The record of the collation is entered on the first membrane of Wells roll x, com-
> mencing c. 1214 x 1215 (*RHW* i 2, cf. Smith, 'Rolls'). Robert of Hailes first occurs
> as archdeacon of Huntingdon on 5 November 1214. Robert of Graveley was a
> member of Bp Hugh's *familia*. The Council referred to was the the Third Lateran of
> 1179, c. 17.

*44.   Harrold priory

*Appropriation, made with the consent of the dean and chapter of Lincoln, to the
nuns of Harrold of the church of Stevington, and endowment of a vicarage.*
                              [20 December 1214 x 19 December 1215]

> B = BL ms. Lansdowne 391 (Harrold cartulary) fo. 12r (abstract of charter). s. xv
>   in.
> Pd (calendar) *Harrold Cartulary* no. 36.

Appropriatio Hugonis dei gratia Lincoln' episcopi cum consensu decani et capituli super ecclesia de Steventon' facta monialibus huius loci ad uberiorem earum
sustentationem et in ista litera continetur. Dotatio vicarie etc.

> This is most probably to be identified with the Harrold charter of the bp's sixth
> pontifical year [20 December 1214 x 19 December 1215] noted on the vicarages
> roll: 'Monialibus de Harewode: sedecim marcas annuas in ecclesia de Stiventon',
> anno vi⁰' (*RHW* iii 93).

*45.   Templars

Grant to the Templars of three marks a year from the church of North Carlton.
                              [20 December 1214 x 19 December 1215]

> Mentioned in the list of churches, pensions and grants made by Bp Hugh to the
> religious in LAO Wells roll xi, pd *RHW* iii 93, dated to the bp's sixth pontifical
> year.

*46.   Mavis Enderby church

*Mandate to R. of Cawkwell, [rural] dean of Louthesk, and A., [rural] dean of
Bolingbroke, to enquire if William Malebise, patron of the church of [Mavis]
Enderby, was with the barons against the king, and to certify their findings to the
bishop.*   [c. 1217]

Mention of letter being sent in LAO, Wells roll x, m. 4d, pd. *RHW* i 20, cf. Smith, 'Rolls' for probable date.

*47. Mavis Enderby church

Mandate to the [rural] dean of Bolingbroke to induct Robert Malebise to the church of [Mavis] Enderby, on the presentation of William de Malebise, his father.   [*c.* 1217]

> Mention of written mandate in LAO Wells roll x, m. 4d, pd *RHW* i 20, cf. Smith, 'Rolls' for probable date.

*48. Sudborough church

Grant of a pension of one aureus *to master Nicholas son of Simon, parson of the church of Sudborough, in the name of his parsonage.*   [*c.* 1217]

> Mention of charter in LAO Wells roll x, m. 4, pd *RHW* i 21, cf. Smith, 'Rolls' for probable date.

*49. Walgrave church

Letter to master Th., official of the archdeacon of Northampton, to certify whether G. de Malesoures consented to the presentation of master Geoffrey of Dodford to the church of Walgrave by the prior and convent of Daventry, while he was not excommunicated.   [*c.* 1217]

> Mention of charter in LAO Wells roll x, m. 4d, pd *RHW* i 25, cf. Smith, 'Rolls' for probable date. See also no. 77 for the letter of institution dated 26 October 1218 (see introduction for the dating problems surrounding letters of institution).

50. St Neots priory

Record of the institution of master William of Wakerley to the church of Wing, on the presentation of the prior and convent of St Neots, saving the perpetual vicarage of master Reginald of Weston. Master William having then died, William of Bath, clerk, was admitted to the church on the same presentation, saving the perpetual vicarage of master Reginald. The vicar shall pay an annual pension of four marks to the parson and shall bear all charges.   [*c.* 1217]

> B = BL ms. Cotton Faustina A iv (St Neots cartulary) fos. 40v–41r (39v–40r), no. xxvi. s. xiii med.

Omnibus Cristi fidelibus ad quos littere presentes pervenerint, Hugo Dei gratia Lincol' episcopus salutem eternam in domino. Noverit universitas vestra nos, ad presentationem dilectorum filiorum Rogeri prioris et conventus sancti Neoti, admisisse dilectum in Cristo filium magistrum Willelmum de Wakerl' ad ecclesiam de Weng', ipsumque in ea personam instituisse, salva perpetua vicaria magistri Reginaldi de Westun' in eadem quoad vixerit. Defuncto quoque dicto magistro Willelmo, ad eorundem presentationem, admisimus Willelmum de Bathon' clericum ad eandem ecclesiam et in ea personam instituimus, salva similiter perpetua vicaria dicti magistri Reginaldi quoad vixerit, qui quidem dictam ecclesiam cum pertinentiis possidebit, reddendo [fo. 41r] eidem Willelmo quatuor marcas nomine pensionis annuatim et omnia honera eiusdem ecclesie sustinebit; salvis etiam in omnibus episcopalibus consuetudinibus et Lincol' ecclesie dignitate. In huius autem rei testimonium, presentes litteras nostras patentes fecimus. Valete.

The institution of William of Bath is recorded in the first institution roll *c.* 1217 (*RHW* i 42, cf. Smith, 'Rolls').

51. Crowland abbey

Institution of Roger of Wellingborough, chaplain, to the perpetual vicarage of Sutterton, on the presentation of H(enry), abbot, and the convent of Crowland, saving to the abbey all the garb tithes of the church and the customary pension of two marks. [*c.* 1217]

B = Spalding Gentlemen's Society, Crowland cartulary fo. 123v. s. xiv med.

Omnibus Cristi fidelibus ad quos presens scriptum pervenerit, Hugo Dei gratia Lincoln' episcopus salutem in domino. Noverit universitas vestra nos, ad presentationem H. abbatis et conventus Croiland' patronorum ecclesie de Suterton' in Hoyland, dilectum in Cristo filium Rogerum de Wendlingburgh' capellanum ad perpetuam eiusdem[a] ecclesie vicariam admisisse et ipsum in eadem canonice vicarium instituisse perpetuum, salvis dicto abbati et conventui decimis omnibus garbarum illius ecclesie et debita et antiqua duarum marcarum pensione; salvis etiam episcopalibus consuetudinibus et Lincoln' ecclesie dignitate. Et ut hec institutio nostra perpetue firmitatis robur optineat, eam presenti scripto et sigilli nostri appositione duximus confirmandam. Hiis testibus etc.

[a] eius B.

Roger of Wellingborough was given custody of the benefice by the Official of the bp during the latter's absence abroad (September 1215–1217) and was instituted by the bp on his return (*RHW* i 85).

52. Reading abbey

Institution of Thomas de Camel, clerk, to the church of Stanton Harcourt, on the presentation of the abbot and convent of Reading, saving to the abbey an annual pension of twenty marks to be paid by Thomas and his successors as parsons. The parson shall bear all due and customary charges of the church. [*c.* 1217]

B = BL ms. Harl. 1708 (Reading cartulary) fo. 202r. s. xiii med. C = BL ms. Cotton Vespasian E xxv (Reading cartulary) fo. 123r. s. xiv in.
Pd Kennett, *Parochial Antiquities* i 194; (calendar) from BC in *Reading Cartularies* i no. 543.

Omnibus Cristi fidelibus ad quos presens scriptum pervenerit, Hugo Dei gratia Linc'[a] episcopus salutem[b]. Noverit universitas vestra nos, ad presentationem dilectorum in Cristo abbatis et conventus Rading'[c] patronorum ecclesie de Stanton'[d], dilectum in Cristo filium Thomam de Camel clericum ad eandem ecclesiam admisisse, ipsumque in ea canonice personam instituisse, salvis xx marcis annuis dictis abbati et conventui per manum ipsius Thome et successorum suorum de eadem ecclesia nomine perpetui beneficii percipiendis. Idem vero Thomas et successores sui omnia onera ipsius ecclesie debita et consueta sustinebunt, salvis etiam in omnibus consuetudinibus episcopalibus et Linc' ecclesie dignitate. Quod ut ratum sit et firmum, presenti scripto sigillum nostrum duximus apponendum. Testibus[e]

[a] Lyncoln' C. [b] C *adds* in domino. [c] Radyng' C. [d] Staunton' C. [e] *omitted* C.

The institution is recorded on the fifth membrane of the first institution roll *c.*1217 (*RHW* i 31, cf. Smith, 'Rolls'). For Thomas de Camel's promise and obligation to pay the above annual pension see *Reading Cartularies* i no. 544.

*53. Horton church

Mandate to the archdeacon of Buckingham to induct H. of Windsor, clerk, to the church of Horton. [*c.* 1217]

Mention of written mandate in LAO Wells roll x, m. 6, pd *RHW* i 34, cf. Smith, 'Rolls' for probable date.

*54. Beeby church

Mandate to the [rural] dean of Rearsby to induct master Henry of Stanford to the church of Beeby. [*c.* 1217]

Mention of written mandate in LAO Wells roll x, m. 6, pd *RHW* i 34, cf. Smith, 'Rolls' for probable date.

*55. Weston on the Green church

Mandate to the archdeacon of Oxford to induct Gilbert son of Robert, clerk, to the church of Weston [on the Green]. [*c.* 1217]

Mention of written mandate in LAO Wells roll x, m. 6, pd *RHW* i 32, cf. Smith, 'Rolls' for probable date.

*56. Fulbeck church

Mandate to G., [rural] dean of Stubton to induct David the clerk to the church of Fulbeck. [*c.* 1217]

Mention of written mandate in LAO Wells roll x, m. 6, pd *RHW* i 34, cf. Smith, 'Rolls' for probable date.

*57. Bishop of Coventry

Letter to the bishop of Coventry to see what is to be done about John of Birmingham's benefice of Birmingham, following his institution to the church of Iffley. [*c.* 1217]

Mention of letter in LAO Wells roll x, m. 6, pd *RHW* i 38, cf. Smith, 'Rolls' for probable date.

*58. Sheepy church

Mandate to master R. of Blois, official of the archdeacon of Leicester, to induct William Burdet to a mediety of the church of Sheepy. [*c.* 1217]

Mention of written mandate in LAO Wells roll x, m. 6, pd *RHW* i 40, cf. Smith, 'Rolls' for probable date.

59. Newnham priory

Institution of Elias of Evesham, chaplain, to the church of Gravenhurst, on the presentation of the prior and convent of Newnham, saving to the priory an annual pension if it shall be proved to be customary.   [*c.* 1217 x 1218]

> B = BL ms. Harl. 3656 (Newnham cartulary) fo. 58v. s. xv in.
> Pd *Newnham Cartulary* i no. 99.

Hiis testibus: Humfrido de Bassyngburne archidiacono Sarr' et magistro Waltero de Wellys, canonicis Lincolniensibus et aliis multis.

> The institution is recorded on the tenth membrane of Wells roll x, *c.* 1217 x 1218 (*RHW* i 73, cf. Smith, 'Rolls'). Elias later made an arrangement with Newnham to pay an annual pension of fourteen shillings (*Newnham Cartulary* ii no. 943). He was apparently a clerk of the archdn of Salisbury (ibid.).

60. Bury St Edmunds abbey

Settlement of a dispute between abbot H(ugh) and the convent of St Edmunds and master R[obert] of Graveley, rector of the church of Wainfleet, over the chapel on the land of the monks within the said parish and over forty sesters of salt which the monks claim should be paid to them by the church. This case had been delegated by pope Honorius to the abbot of [West] Dereham and his fellow judges. With the assent of Roger the dean and the chapter of Lincoln, the bishop ordains that the monks of St Edmunds shall receive the forty sesters of salt each year from the rector of the church of Wainfleet. However, during the time that master Robert of Graveley is rector, he shall pay twenty shillings a year to the abbey in place of the salt. Free access to the chapel is to be allowed to the monks, where they can celebrate divine service, without prejudice to the mother church, which shall possess all the obventions of the chapel. When divine service is over each day, the keys of the chapel are to be restored to the chaplain of the church or his servant.
[*c.* 1217 x 1218, prob. *c.* 20 June 1218]

> B = PRO DL42/5 (Bury cellarer's cartulary) fo. 75r–v (fo. 52r–v). s. xiii ex. C = CUL ms. Add. 4220 (Bury register) fo. 521v. s. xv.

Omnibus etc. H. Dei gratia Lincoln' episcopus salutem. Cum inter viros venerabiles H. abbatem sancti Aedmundi[a] et eiusdem loci conventum, ex una parte, et magistrum R. de Gravell' rectorem ecclesie de Wayneflet,[b] ex altera, super capella in fundo prefatorum monachorum intra predicte ecclesie parochiam constituta et super quadraginta[c] sextaria salis ab eadem ecclesia sibi annuatim ut dicebant prestandis, coram abbate de Derham et coniudicibus suis a domino papa Honorio delegatis questio verteretur, tandem lis inter eos in hunc modum conquievit.[d] Supradicte videlicet partes in ordinationem quam, de consensu Rogeri decani et capituli nostri, faceremus pure et liberaliter[e] consenserunt. Nos igitur super hoc habita deliberatione de assensu R.[f] decani et capituli nostri super premissis taliter duximus ordinandum, scilicet, quod monasterium beati Aedmundi[a] de ecclesia de Wayneflet[g] quadraginta[c] sextaria salis imperpetuum singulis annis percipiet, per manum ipsius qui eiusdem ecclesie pro tempore rector extiterit. Ita tamen quod predictus R. de Gravell' pro tempore regiminis sui in ecclesia illa xx[ti] solidos annuos pro supradicto sale prestabit, decem solidos ad festum sancti Petri ad Vincula et x.[h] solidos ad festum Purificationis beate Virginis. De capella autem sic ordinavimus:[i] quotiens monachum aliquem vel monachos aliquos de monasterio supradicto ob domus sue necessitates illuc venire contigerit, per capellanum matricis ecclesie in capellam liber et absque difficultate eis pateat ingressus ut ibi possint celebrare divina sine preiudicio tamen matricis ecclesie, ad quam omnes obventiones quas illuc deferri contigerit cum omni integritate volumus pertinere. Expletis divinis claves[j] capelle sub eadem facilitate capellano ecclesie vel eius ministro singulis diebus restituendi etc.

> [a] Edmundi C.   [b] Waynflete C.   [c] xl. C.   [d] quievit C.   [e] conce *written after this word and then crossed out* C.   [f] Rogeri C.   [g] Waynflet C.   [h] decem C.   [i] ordinamus C.   [j] clave B.

> The church of Wainfleet was collated to master Robert of Graveley, an episcopal clerk, by authority of the Lateran council (*RHW* i 2). It is recorded (ibid. 114–15) that on the 'Wednesday before the Nativity of St John the Baptist' the abbot of Bury St Edmunds came to the bishop at Stanground with letters of the legate Guala concerning the chapel of St Edmund, Wainfleet and the forty sesters of salt. It is impossible to determine with complete certainty whether the year in question is 1217 (21 June) or 1218 (20 June), although the latter is perhaps more likely if it is accepted that the membranes of roll X are in roughly chronological order. This preceding information is entered on membrane 12 towards the end of the roll. The latter date is confirmed in *Letters of Guala* no. 122. Hugh son of Pinzun, steward of Bp Hugh du Puiset of Durham, gave the abbey of Bury certain property in Wainfleet so that the monks might build a chapel there in honour of St Edmund (CUL ms. Add. 4220, fo. 520r–v). For further details see H. E. Hallam. 'Salt-making in the Lincolnshire Fenland during the middle ages', *LAASRP* new ser. 8 (1960) 85–112, at 107–8; and A. Owen, 'St Edmund in Lincolnshire: the abbey's lands in Wainfleet and Wrangle' in A. Gransden ed., *Bury St Edmunds: Medieval Art, Architecture, Archaeology and Economy* (British Archaeological Association conference transactions xx, 1998), pp. 122–7.

*61.   Thornton church

Mandate to the archdeacon of Buckingham to induct Henry of Lewknor to the church of Thornton.   [*c.* June 1217]

> Mention of written mandate in LAO Wells roll x, m. 6, pd *RHW* i 37, cf. Smith, 'Rolls' for probable year, and the entry for two June dates.

62.   Chacombe priory

Confirmation of the grant made by Robert of Boddington, knight, to the prior and canons of Chacombe of the advowson of a mediety of the church of Boddington.

Banbury, 24 August 1217

> A = PRO E326/3570 (damaged. Words in square brackets supplied from B). Endorsed: Botyngdon' (s. xv); approx. 142 x 93 +15mm.; seal missing, slit for seal tag.
> B = LAO Add. Reg. 6 (Liber antiquus) fo. 25r–v. s .xiii in.
> Pd from B in *Lib. Ant.* 81.

Omnibus Cristi fidelibus has litteras visuris et audituris, Hug(o) Dei gratia Linc' episcopus salutem in domino.[a] Noverit universitas vestra quod Robertus de Bottendon'[b] miles, in nostra presentia constitutus, confessus est se dedisse pro salute anime sue et suorum et carta sua confirmasse priori et canonicis de Chaucumb' ius advocacionis in medietate ecclesie de Bottendon'[b] et eidem priori cartam super hoc [confecta]m in presentia nostra sponte liberavit. Nos igitur predictam advocacionem coram nobis eis collatam et co[nces]sam, au[c]toritate episcopali con[fir]mamus.[c] Quod ut ratum et stabile perseveret, presens scriptu[m sigilli nostri muni]mine roboravimus. Hiis testibus: magistro Reginaldo de Cestr' sub-decano Linc', [d] [Thoma de F]iskerton' cappellano, magistro R[oberto] de Gravel', [e] canonicis Linc', magistro Nicholao de Evesh[am et magist]ro Ricardo de Tinghurst', Radulfo de Chendeduit, [f] Willelmo de Ferendun', [g] Symone de Cropper', [Rogero] de Leonibus, Ricardo de Cliftun',[h] Radulfo de Chaucumb', clerico, Stephano de Cicestr' et aliis. Dat' per manum Willelmi de Thornaco,[i] archidiaconi de[j] Stowa,[k] apud Bannebyr'[l] nono[m] kalendas Septembris pontifica-tus nostri anno octavo.

[a] B *has* Omnibus Christi fidelibus etc.   [b] Botend' B.   [c] confirmavimus B.
[d] Subdecano Lincolniensi *omitted* B.   [e] *Thomas of Fiskerton and Robert of Grave-ley are in reverse order in* B.   [f] Chenduit B.   [g] Ferendon' B.   [h] Clifton' B.
[i] Torn' B.   [j] *omitted* B.   [k] Stow B.   [l] Bannebir' B.   [m] ix B.
The document has suffered from some damage by rodents. Conjectural reconstruc-tions are placed in square brackets.

This grant of Bp Hugh is mentioned in *RHW* iii 94.

63. Luffield priory

Confirmation of the grant made by William of Stratford to the priory of Luffield of the advowson of the church of [Water] Stratford.   Kilsby, 23 September 1217

> A= Westminster Abbey mun. 2578. Endorsed: Confirmacio . ecclesie de Strafford (s. xiii); Confirmacio H. Lincoln' episcopi (s.xiii); approx. 140 x 78 + 14mm.; 'smaller' seal on parchment tag, method 1, brownish-white wax, in seal-bag.
> B = LAO Add. Reg. 6 (Liber antiquus) fo. 25v. s. xiii in. C = Westminster Abbey mun. bk. 10 (Luffield cartulary) fo. 26v. s. xv ex.
> Pd from A in *Luffield Priory Charters* i no. 41; from B in *Lib. Ant.* 81.

Universis sancte matris ecclesie filiis ad quos presens scriptum pervenerit, H. Dei gratia Linc' episcopus salutem in domino. Quoniam pia facta fidelium digno sunt prosequenda favore, noveritis quod nos collationem dilecti filii Willelmi de Strafford' quam super advocatione ecclesie de Strafford' domui religiose de Luf-feld' fecit et monachis ibidem deo servientibus et in perpetuum regulariter ser-vituris, ratam et gratam habemus et eam sicut rationabiliter facta est eis auctoritate episcopali confirmamus: salvis in omnibus episcopalibus consuetu-dinibus et Linc' ecclesie dignitate. Quod ut perpetuam obtineat firmitatem, presens scriptum sigilli nostri duximus appositione roborandum. Hiis testibus: Thoma de Fiskerton' cappellano, magistro Roberto de Gravel', canonicis Linc', Radulfo de Warevill', Willelmo de Kainesham', canonico Wellens[i], Stephano de Cicestr' et aliis. Dat' per manum Petri de Bathon', canonici Linc', apud Kildeby nono kalendas Octobris pontificatus nostri anno octavo.

> The grant of the advowson to the priory by William II of Stratford is in *Luffield Priory Charters* i no. 66. Since his charter was read aloud in the chapter of Archdn Stephen of Buckingham, no doubt about the time the grant was made, William's charter must date from *c.* 1194 to *c.* 1202 (Archdn Stephen's tenure of office) (ibid.

no. 43). With the position of witnesses in the episcopal confirmation it would be expected that Ralph of Waravill should be described as a canon of Wells, as well as William of Keynsham, but 'canonico' is definitely written. Ralph was certainly a canon of Wells by 3 November 1218 (see below, no. 93). See also no. 449 below. This grant of Bp Hugh is mentioned in *RHW* iii 94.

64. Osney abbey

Confirmation, made with the assent of the dean and chapter of Lincoln, for the abbot and canons of Osney of the church of [Steeple] Barton and the chapel of Sandford in proprios usus *for the provision of hospitality for poor people and travellers: saving the life interest of William of St John, the present rector. After William's death, the abbey shall present suitable clergy to the perpetual vicarages of [Steeple] Barton and Sandford. The vicar of Steeple Barton shall have the altarage, half a hide of land, and the house which Thomas* senex *holds. The vicar of Sandford shall have the altarage, small tithes, and four and a half acres of land. The vicar serving the chapel of Ledwell shall take one third of the tithes of Grove. The vicars are to bear all ecclesiastical charges, except hospitality for the bishop and the archdeacon.*   Osney abbey, 14 October 1217

> A = Oxford, Bodl. DD. Ch.Ch. O. 938. Endorsed: Confirmacio <sancti> H. Lin-coln' . episcopi <et capituli> quondam archidiaconi. Well' . super ecclesia de Berton' in proprios usus possidenda . (s. xiii) et de Sandford' . et Ledwelle (*added later*); k (s. xiii); 9; approx. 177 x 174 + 21 mm.; two seals on parch-ment tags, method 1, excellent specimen of episcopal seal, green wax, coun-terseal; capitular seal (chipped at edges), green wax, counterseal.
> B = LAO Add. Reg. 6 (Liber antiquus) fo. 25v (abbreviated witness list). s. xiii in.
> C = BL ms. Cotton Vitellius E xv (Osney cartulary) fo. 48r. s. xiii in. D = Oxford, Ch. Ch. Lib., Osney cartulary, fo. 52r–v (witnesses omitted). s. xiii ex. E = PRO E164/26 (Osney cartulary, English version) fo. 30r. s. xv med.
> Pd from B in *Lib. Ant.* 81–2; from CD in *Oseney Cartulary* iv no. 123; from E in *Oseney English Register* i no. 134; cf. *RHW* i 65.

Omnibus Cristi fidelibus ad quos presens carta pervenerit, Hug(o) Dei gratia Lin-colniens' episcopus salutem in domino. Attendentes religionem et honestam con-versationem dilectorum filiorum abbatis et canonicorum de Osen', divine pietatis intuitu decrevimus eis de consensu decani et capituli Linc' ecclesiam de Berton' cum pertinentiis suis, cuius advocationem habent ex dono Rogeri de sancto Iohanne eiusdem ecclesie patroni, in usus proprios ad sustentationem pauperum et peregrinorum concedere et episcopali autoritate confirmare. Verum quia quidam dicebant ecclesiam de Sanford' matricem esse ecclesiam, alii vero asserebant eam esse capellam ad ecclesiam de Berton' pertinentem, volentes super hiis plenius certificari, inquisitionem exinde fieri fecimus diligentem per archidiaconum loci et per viros fide dignos in capitulo. Qui omnes iurati sub debito iuramenti sui asseruerunt ipsam esse pertinentem tanquam capellam ad ecclesiam de Berton' sed tamen tanquam matricem ecclesiam invenimus eam de omnibus oneribus et consuetudinibus episcopalibus et archidiaconalibus respon-dentem. Unde habito consensu decani et capituli nostri de consilio virorum pru-dentum predictam ecclesiam de Berton' cum capella de Sanford et aliis pertinenciis predicto abbati et conventui in perpetuum concessimus in proprios usus ad sustentationem hospitalitatis memorate convertendam: salvis episcopali-bus et archidiaconalibus consuetudinibus de predicta capella de Sanford tanquam de ecclesia matrice ut prediximus; salva etiam Willelmo de sancto Iohanne persone ecclesie de Berton' et de Sanford pacifica possessione sua quoad vixerit. Statuimus autem quod post decessum predicte persone capellanus idoneus nobis et successoribus nostris ad perpetuam vicariam ecclesie de Barton' ab abbate et conventu presentetur, qui percipiet nomine perpetue vicarie totum altalagium eiusdem ecclesie cum dimidia hida terre ad eandem ecclesiam pertinente et cum domo quam Thomas senex tenet. Ad perpetuam vero vicariam capelle de Sanford' similiter presentetur nobis et successoribus nostris idoneus capellanus ab eisdem, qui percipiet omnes obventiones altaris eiusdem capelle cum minutis decimis et cum quatuor acris et dimidia ad eandem capellam pertinentibus. Vicarius autem ad quem pertinet offitiare capellam de Ledwell' ei faciet prout debet deserviri et percipiet terciam partem omnium decimarum de Grava pro necessaria sustentatione capellani. Sustinebunt autem predicti vicarii omnia onera predictarum ecclesie et capelle de Sanford episcopalia et archidiaconalia consueta, preter hospitium episcopi et archidiaconi. Ut igitur omnia premissa rata et inconcussa permaneant, ea presenti scripto et sigillo nostro duximus confirmanda; salvis in omnibus episcopalibus consuetudinibus et Lincolnien' ecclesie dignitate. Hiis testibus: Reginaldo subdecano Linc' ecclesie, Roberto archidiacono Huntingdon', Thoma de Fiskerton' capellano et Petro de Bathon', canonicis Lincolnien' ecclesie, magistro Ricardo de Tinghurst', Willelmo de Wynchelcumb' et Stephano de Cicestr', clericis, et aliis. Dat' per manum Willelmi de Thornaco, archidiaconi de Stowa, apud domum de Oseneya Oxon' ii idus Octobris pontificatus nostri anno octavo.

For the confirmation of this document by the legate Guala on 19 January 1218 see *Letters of Guala* no. 75. This grant of Bp Hugh is mentioned in *RHW* iii 94.

65. Osney abbey

Grant, with the consent of Roger the dean and the chapter of Lincoln, to the abbot and convent of Osney of an annual pension of two shillings from the church of [Black] Bourton, which is of their patronage, in the name of a perpetual benefice. Lincoln, in chapter, 28 December 1217

B = LAO Add. Reg. 6 (Liber antiquus) fos. 25v–26r. s. xiii in.
Pd. *Lib. Ant.* 82–3.

Hiis testibus: Roberto archidiacono Hunt', Hugone de sancto Edwardo, magistro Willelmo filio Fulconis, magistro Ada de sancto Edmundo, Thoma de Fiskert' et Rogero de Brist', capellanis, magistro Waltero de Well', canonicis Linc', magistro Theobaldo et aliis. Dat' per manum W. de Tornac', archidiaconi Stowe, in capitulo Linc'[fo. 26r] apud Linc' v^{to} kalendas Ianuarii pontificatus nostri anno nono.

This grant of Bp Hugh is mentioned in *RHW* iii 94.

66. Godstow abbey

Grant, with the consent of Roger the dean and the chapter of Lincoln, to the abbess and convent of Godstow of an annual pension of two marks from the church of Easington, which is of their patronage, in the name of a perpetual bene-

fice. The pension is to be paid by William of Chinnor the parson and his succes-
sors.   Lincoln, in chapter, 28 December 1217

> B = LAO Add. Reg. 6 (Liber antiquus) fo. 26r. s. xiii in.
> Pd *Lib. Ant.* 83.

Hiis testibus: Rogero decano et aliis ut supra carta proxima [no. 65]. Dat' per manum eiusdem eadem die et loco pontificatus nostri anno ix⁰.

67.   Chacombe priory

Grant, with the consent of Roger the dean and the chapter of Lincoln, to the prior and convent of Chacombe of an annual pension of one mark from a mediety of the church of Boddington, which is of their patronage, in the name of a perpetual benefice. The pension is to be paid by Roger the chaplain, parson of the mediety, and his successors.   Lincoln, in chapter, 28 December 1217

> B = LAO Add. Reg. 6 (Liber antiquus) fo. 26r. s. xiii in.
> Pd *Lib. Ant.* 83.

Testibus ut supra carta proxima [no. 66]. Dat' per manum eiusdem eadem die et loco pontificatus nostri anno ix⁰.

This grant of Bp Hugh is mentioned in *RHW* iii 94.

68.   Northampton, abbey of St Mary

Grant, with the consent of Roger the dean and the chapter of Lincoln, to the abbess and convent of St Mary de Prato, Northampton, of a pension of two marks in the name of a perpetual benefice from the church of [Earl's] Barton, which is of their patronage. This pension is to be paid each year by Peter, the parson of the church and his successors.   Lincoln, in chapter, 28 December 1217

> B = LAO Add. Reg. 6 (Liber antiquus) fo. 26r. s. xiii in.
> Pd *Lib. Ant.* 83.

Testibus, dat' etc. ut supra carta tertia [no. 66].

This grant of Bp Hugh is mentioned in *RHW* iii 94.

69.   Godstow abbey

Grant in proprios usus, *made with the consent of Roger the dean and the chapter of Lincoln, to the abbess and convent of Godstow of a mediety of the church of Pattishall, saving a vicarage assigned by the bishop. The vicarage consists of the land, meadow, messuage and altarage of the mediety. John of Milcombe, chaplain, is admitted perpetual vicar, on the presentation of the nuns.*
Lincoln, in chapter, 28 December 1217

> A = BL Cotton Ch. xi 32. Endorsed: Exhibeantur ista 'domino' pro medietate eccle-
> sie de Patushull (ss. xiv–xv); Confirmacio ecclesie de Pateshull' (s. xv);
> Pateshelle (ss. xiv–xv); approx. 185 x 127 + 15mm.; episcopal seal missing,
> fragment of capitular seal survives, reddish-brown wax, parchment tags,
> method 1.

B = LAO Add. Reg. 6 (Liber antiquus) fo. 26r (with truncated witness list and
dating clause (testibus. Dat' etc. ut supra carta quarta [no. 66]). s. xiii in.
Pd from A in *Mon. Angl.* iv 365, no.xii; from B in *Lib. Ant.* 83–4.

Universis sancte matris ecclesie filiis ad quos presens scriptum pervenerit, Hugo
Dei gratia Lincolniensis episcopus eternam in domino salutem. Noverit universitas vestra nos, de consensu Rogeri decani et capituli nostri Linc', divine pietatis
intuitu concessisse et presenti carta confirmasse dilectis in Cristo filiabus abbatisse et conventui de Godestow' medietatem ecciesie de Pateshull' quam prius
habuerunt in proprios usus habendam et in perpetuum possidendam: salva vicaria
in eadem medietate per nos assignata. Que consistit cum in terra tum in prato,
tum in mesuagio et altalagio eiusdem medietatis ad quam ad presentationem
earum Iohannem de Mildecumb' capellanum perpetuum vicarium admisimus.
Debebunt autem predicta abbatissa et conventus nobis et successoribus nostris ad
eandem vicariam semper cum vacaverit capellanum idoneum presentare: salvis
etiam in omnibus episcopalibus consuetudinibus et Linc' ecclesie dignitate. Et ut
hec nostra confirmatio perpetuam obtineat firmitatem, presenti scripto sigillum
nostrum una cum sigillo predicti capituli nostri Linc' duximus apponendum. Hiis
testibus: Rogero decano, Galfrido precentore, Rogero cancellario, Reginaldo subdecano, Roberto Norhamton', Reimundo Leircestr', Alexandro Bedeford',
Iohanne Oxon', Willelmo Bukingh', Roberto Huntingd' archidiaconis, Hugone
de sancto Edwardo, magistro Willelmo filio Fulconis, magistro Ada de sancto
Edmundo, Thoma de Fiskerton' et Rogero de Bristoll', capellanis, magistro
Waltero de Wellis, canonicis Linc', magistro Theobaldo et aliis. Dat' per manum
Willelmi de Thornac', archidiaconi Stow', in capitulo Linc' apud Linc' quinto
kalendas Ianuarii pontificatus nostri anno nono.

This grant of Bp Hugh is mentioned in *RHW* iii 94.

70. Leicester abbey

*Grant, with the assent of Roger the dean and the chapter of Lincoln, to the abbot
and convent of St Mary de Prato, Leicester, of an annual pension of twenty shillings from the church of Narborough, in the name of a perpetual benefice. This
pension, which is to be paid by the parson, is to take effect after the death of John,
the present parson of the church. While John is alive, the monks shall receive
twelve pence a year. A further annual pension of twenty shillings is also granted
to the same abbey, in the name of a perpetual benefice, from the church of [Clay]
Coton to take effect after the death of the present parson, master Stephen de
Manecestre. Until then, the abbey shall receive half a mark each year from
master Stephen.* Lincoln, in chapter, 28 December 1217

B = LAO Add. Reg. 6 (Liber antiquus) fo. 26r. s. xiii in.
Pd *Lib. Ant.* 84.

Testibus et dat' ut in carta quinta precedenti [no. 66].

This charter is to be identified with the *Concessio Hugonis episcopi Lincolniensis
et capituli super annua pensione xx solidorum de ecclesiis de Norbor' et de Cotys*
noted in the Leicester abbey rental (Oxford, Bodl. ms. Laud misc. 625, fo. 182v).
This grant of Bp Hugh is mentioned in *RHW* iii 94.

71. Little Marlow priory

Confirmation, with the consent of Roger the dean and the chapter of Lincoln, for the prioress and convent of Little Marlow of the gift made to them by the lords of Sudbiry of the demesne tithes of Sudbiry. An enquiry held in the local chapter had found that the lords were accustomed to give these tithes to whomsoever they wished without prejudice to any church.   Lincoln, in chapter, 28 December 1217

> B = LAO Add. Reg. 6 (Liber antiquus) fo. 26r–v. s. xiii in.
> Pd *Lib. Ant.* 84.

Testibus et dat' ut supra in carta septima [no. 66].

> The place-name is spelled 'Yuebir' or 'Ynebir' in B, but it is possibly a scribal error for 'Suebir', the form found in the reference to this charter, *RHW* iii 94, cf. *Rot. Grav.* 177, Sudbiry hermitage, Beds., cf. *EPNS Beds & Hunts*, p. 59.

72. St Neots priory

Grant in proprios usus, made with the assent of Roger the dean and the chapter of Lincoln, to the prior and convent of St Neots of a mediety of the church of Turvey, which is of their patronage, in the name of a perpetual benefice. The priory shall have for their own use all the garb tithes of the demesnes of Hugh de Alneto and William le Mansel, all the small tithes of the curia *of the prior in the same village, and half the garb tithes of the rest of the parish, together with the tenements of William de Alno, Richard Bigebon, Hervey and Sailde, with their services. The remaining mediety shall be possessed by Richard of Wigston, clerk, whom the bishop has instituted as parson of the mediety, on the presentation of the priory. His successors as parsons shall be presented by the prior and convent of St Neots to the bishop and his successors for institution. The parson's mediety consists of the remaining half of the garb tithes of the parish, the entire altarage, and the tenements of William the monk, Turbnus, and Hugh the shoemaker, with their services. The priory have granted the messuage and garden lately held by master Warin of the demesne of St Neots to the parson and his successors. The tithe of mills and anything else that may be acquired later shall be equally divided between the priory and the parson. Likewise, the priory and the parson shall bear equally all episcopal and archidiaconal charges.*

Lincoln, in chapter, 28 December 1217

> B = LAO Add. Reg. 6 (Liber antiquus) fo. 26v. s. xiii in. C = BL ms. Cotton Faustina A iv (St Neot's cartulary) fo. 40r (39r), no. xxi. s. xiii med.
> Pd from B in *Lib. Ant.* 84–5, from C (abridged) in G.C. Gorham, *History and antiquities of Eynesbury and St Neot's* 308.

Testibus et dat' ut supra in carta viii[a] [no. 66] pontificatus nostri anno nono[a].

> [a] Hiis testibus C.

> This grant of Bp Hugh is mentioned in *RHW* iii 94.

73. Trentham priory

*Grant, with the assent of Roger the dean and the chapter of Lincoln, to the prior
and convent of Trentham of an annual pension of one hundred shillings from the
church of Donington [-on-Bain], which is of their patronage, in the name of a
perpetual benefice. This pension is to be paid by Solomon the chaplain, whom the
bishop has instituted to the church on the priory's presentation, and his successors as parson. The parson and his successors are also to bear all the episcopal
and archidiaconal burdens of the church.*

Lincoln, in chapter, 28 December 1217

B = LAO Add. Reg. 6 (Liber antiquus) fo. 26v. s. xiii in.
Pd *Lib. Ant.* 85.

Testibus et dat' ut supra in carta nona anno nono [no. 66].

At one point the incumbent is named as Solomon (Salom'), at another as Sampson.
This grant of Bp Hugh is mentioned in *RHW* iii 94.

74. Markby priory

*Grant, with the consent of Roger the dean and the chapter of Lincoln, to the prior
and convent of Markby of a pension of one* aureus *from a mediety of the church of
Beesby[-in-the-Marsh], which is of their patronage, in the name of a perpetual
benefice. The pension is to be paid each year at Michaelmas by Thomas of
Norton, the parson of the church, and his successors, who shall be instituted on
the common presentation of the aforesaid prior and convent and the prioress and
convent of Greenfield.*   Lincoln, in chapter, 28 December 1217

B = LAO Add. Reg. 6 (Liber antiquus) fo. 26v. s. xiii in.
Pd *Lib. Ant.* 85–6.

Testibus et dat' ut supra in carta decima anno ix° [no. 66].

This grant of Bp Hugh is mentioned in *RHW* iii 95.

75. Greenfield priory

*Grant, with the consent of Roger the dean and the chapter of Lincoln, to the pri-
oress and convent of Greenfield of a pension of one* aureus *from the other mediety
of the church of Beesby [-in-the-Marsh], which is of their patronage, in the name
of a perpetual benefice. The pension is to be paid each year at Michaelmas by
Thomas of Norton, the parson of the church, and his successors, who shall be
instituted on the common presentation of the aforesaid prioress and convent and
the prior and convent of Markby.*   Lincoln, in chapter, 28 December 1217

A = BL Harl. Ch. 43 H 24. Endorsed: Concessio unius aurei in medietate ecclesie
   de Beseby (s.xvi); approx. 153 x 95 +20 mm.; episcopal seal missing, fragment of capitular seal survives, green wax, parchment tags.
B = LAO Add. Reg. 6 (Liber antiquus) fo. 26v (witnesses omitted). s. xiii in.
Pd from B in *Lib. Ant.* 86.

Universis sancte matris ecclesie filiis ad quos presens scriptum pervenerit,
Hug(o) Dei gratia Lincolniensis episcopus salutem in domino. Noverit universitas vestra nos, de consensu Rogeri decani et capituli nostri Linc', divine pietatis

intuitu dedisse et concessisse dilectis in Cristo filiabus priorisse et conventui monialium de Grenefeld' unum aureum in medietate ecclesie de Beseby, que medietas de earum est advocatione, nomine perpetui beneficii, singulis annis in festo sancti Michaelis percipiendum per manum Thome de Norton' capellani, persone illius ecclesie et successorum suorum, qui ad communem presentacionem dictarum priorisse et monialium et dilectorum in Cristo filiorum prioris et conventus de Markeby in tota ecclesia pro tempore fuerint instituti: salvis in omnibus episcopalibus consuetudinibus et Linc'ecclesie dignitate. Et ut hec nostra concessio perpetuam obtineat firmitatem, presenti scripto sigillum nostrum una cum sigillo capituli nostri Linc' duximus apponendum. Hiis testibus:[a] Rogero decano, Galfrido precentore, Rogero cancellario, Reginaldo subdecano, Roberto Norhamton', Reimundo Leircestr', Alexandro Bedeford', Iohanne Oxon', Willelmo Bukingeham', Roberto Huntingd', archidiaconis, Hugone de sancto Edwardo, magistro Willelmo filio Fulconis, magistro Ada de sancto Edmundo, Thoma de Fiskerton' et Rogero de Bristoll', capellanis, magistro Waltero de Well', canonicis Linc', magistro Theobaldo et aliis. Dat' per manum Willelmi de Thornac', archidiaconi Stow', in capitulo Linc' apud Linc' quinto kalendas Ianuarii pontificatus nostri anno nono.

[a] Testibus et dat' ut supra in carta decima [no. 66] B.

76.   York, hospital of St Peter [and St Leonard]

Grant,with the assent of the dean and chapter of Lincoln, to the hospital of St Peter [and St Leonard], York, of a pension of two shillings in the name of a perpetual benefice, from a mediety of the church of Althorpe which is of their patronage. The pension is to be paid each year by Adam, the parson of the mediety and his successors.   Lincoln, in chapter, 28 December 1217

B = LAO Add. Reg. 6, fo. 27v. s. xiii in. C = BL ms. Cotton Nero D iii (cartulary of
St Leonard, York) fo. 16r. ss. xiv–xv.
Pd from B in *Lib. Ant.* 88.

Hiis testibus: R. decano, Galfrido precentore, Rogero cancellario, Reginaldo subdecano, Roberto de Norh't, Reimundo Leirc', Alexandro Bedeford', Iohanne Oxon', Willemo Buck' [archidiaconis] et aliis ut supra in carta xiiii[a] [no. 65]. Dat' per manum Willelmi, archidiaconi Stow', in capitulo Linc' apud Linc' v kalendas Ianuarii pontificatus nostri anno ix°.

This grant of Bp Hugh is mentioned in *RHW* iii 95.

77.   Huntingdon priory

Grant in proprios usus, made with the assent of Roger the dean and the chapter of Lincoln, to the prior and convent of Huntingdon of a mediety of the church of Stoke [Goldington], which is of their patronage, in the name of a perpetual benefice. Richard the chaplain, who has been instituted parson on the priory's presentation, and his successors, shall possess the other mediety. The parson and his successors, who shall serve personally, shall receive the entire altarage with the small tithes and the curia *and a virgate and a half of land belonging to the church, together with the land that Richard Maufras held of W. the late parson. The canons of Huntingdon shall have the other* curia *of the church with a*

*messuage of one rood of land that Hugh de Crawl' held, and in recompense for
the altarage, small tithes, land and* curia *belonging to the parsons, they shall
have the garb tithes of the whole fee of Robert de Saucey in Eakley. All the other
garb tithes shall be equally divided between the priory and the parson, as shall
any other possessions that the church may acquire. The parson and his successors shall pay three shillings a year for synodals: the canons and the parson shall
share equally the archidiaconal and other burdens of the church.*

Lincoln, in chapter, 28 December 1217

B = LAO Add. Reg. 6, fo. 27v. s. xiii in.
Pd *Lib. Ant.* 88–9.

Testibus et dat' ut supra carta proxima [no. 76].

This grant of Bp Hugh is mentioned in *RHW* iii 93. Peter of Goldington recovered
the advowson of Stoke Goldington from the prior of Huntingdon before the itinerant justices at Wycombe 20 December 1232 x 19 December 1233 (ibid., ii 89).

78. Northampton, abbey of St James

*Grant, in the name of a perpetual benefice, made with the assent of Roger the
dean and the chapter of Lincoln, to the abbot and convent of St James, Northampton, patrons of the church of Rothersthorpe (from which previously they had
received only six marks) of all the garb tithes of thirty virgates of land of the
demesne of Walter of Pattishall in the village, half of the arable land with appurtenances, and all the orchard on the west part of the* curia *of the church in which
to construct buildings. The remainder shall be in the possession of Roger the
chaplain, whom the bishop has instituted to the church on the presentation of the
abbey, and his successors, who shall minister in the church in person. Roger and
his successors shall pay to the abbot and convent of St James five shillings a year,
which is owed by the abbey to the prior and convent of St Andrew, [Northampton]
for two garbs of tithes of four virgates of land in the village which are of the
demesne of the hospital of St John, Northampton. Roger and his successors shall
pay synodal dues but the abbey shall find hospitality for the archdeacon.*

Lincoln, in chapter, 28 December 1217

B= LAO Add. Reg. 6 (Liber antiquus) fo. 28r. s. xiii in. C = BL ms. Cotton Tiberius
E v (cartulary of St James, Northampton, badly damaged by fire), fos.
128v–129r. s. xiv in. D = Oxford, Bodl. ms. Top. Northants. c 5 (extracts
from the cartulary) p. 406 (much abridged). s. xviii in. The witnesses agree
with C, except that Gilbert the treasurer is omitted and replaced by Roger the
chancellor.
Pd from B in *Lib. Ant.* 90.

(B version)
Testibus et dat' ut supra in carta domus hospitalis sancti Petri de Ebor' super
duobus solidis in medietate ecclesie de Alethorp' [no. 76].

(C version)
Hiis testibus: Rogero decano, Galfrido precentore, [Gilberto] thesaurario,
Reginaldo subdecano, Roberto Norh', Reimundo Leicestr', Alexandro [Bede-
ford'], Iohanne Oxon', Roberto Huntingdon', archidiaconis, Hugone de sancto
Ed[wardo], magistro Ada de sancto Edmundo, magistro Waltero de Well',

canonicis Linc'. [Dat' per] manum Willelmi Thornac', archidiaconi Stow', in capitulo Linc' apud [Linc] quinto kalendas Ianuarii pontificatus nostri anno nono.

This grant of Bp Hugh is mentioned in *RHW* iii 93.

79. Alvingham priory

Institution of Ralph de Waravill, clerk, to the church of Grainthorpe, on the presentation of the prioress and convent of Alvingham. Ralph has obtained a dispensation from the legate Guala, enabling him to hold an additional benefice with cure of souls. [*c.* 1217 x 1218]

B = Oxford, Bodl. ms. Laud misc. 642 (Alvingham cartulary) fo. 98v. s. xiii ex.

Omnibus Cristi fidelibus ad quos presens scriptum pervenerit, Hugo Dei gratia Linc' episcopus salutem in domino. Noverit universitas vestra nos, ad presentationem dilectarum in Cristo filiarum priorisse et monialium de Al. patronarum[a] ecclesie de Germethorp', dilectum in Cristo filium Radulfum de Warravill' clericum, dispensante cum eo venerabili patre domino Guala tunc legato, ut illud beneficium simul cum aliis curam animarum annexam habentibus que prius habuit possit obtinere, ad eandem ecclesiam admisisse et ipsum in ea canonice personam instituisse: salvis in omnibus episcopalibus consuetudinibus et Linc' ecclesie dignitate. Quod ut perpetuam obtineat firmitatem, presenti scripto sigillum nostrum duximus apponendum. Hiis testibus.

[a] personarum B.

The church of Grainthorpe was initially collated to Ralph de Waravill by the bp, saving the right of the nuns of Alvingham (*RHW* i 127–8). As the entry is at the end of roll x, the date must be *c.* 1217 x 1218, after the bp's return from abroad (see Smith, 'Rolls'). Ralph de Waravill was a member of the episcopal *familia*, acted as datary from 1226 to 1232 and was a canon both of Lincoln and Wells (see *Fasti Lincoln* p. 102). For the legate's dispensation see *Letters of Guala* no. 93.

*80. Derby, Kingsmead priory

Indulgence of fifteen days for the priory of St Mary, Kingsmead, outside Derby. [20 December 1209 x 18 March 1227, ? *c.* 1218]

Mention of indulgence in a letter of R., prior of King's Mead, *temp.* Pope Honorius III (1216–27), BL Woolley Ch. xi 25, pd by R. Graham, 'An appeal for the church and buildings of Kingsmead Priory *c.* 1218', *Antiquaries Journal*, xi (1931) 51–4; calendared in *Derbyshire Charters*, pp. 119–20, no. 969. S. Thompson, *Women Religious*, p. 238, likewise suggests the date of this document is *c.* 1218.

81. Newark castle

Agreement made between the bishop and Henry de Nevill that, whereas the bishop claimed against Henry the guard of five knights at his castle of Newark [-on-Trent] in respect of the fee of five knights which Henry holds of him, the bishop agrees that Henry during his lifetime shall henceforth perform the guard of three knights at the episcopal castle of Sleaford in war or when the peace of the

*realm is disturbed, for forty days a year; and the bishop remits to Henry for his
lifetime the guard of two of the five knights, saving the bishop's right to the guard
of the two knights after Henry's death.*   [*c.* 1218]

> B = LAO Lincoln D. & C. A/1/5 (Registrum Antiquissimum) no. 237. s. xiii in.
> Pd *Reg. Ant.* ii no. 379.

Hiis testibus: Galfrido de Salicosa Mara, Iohanne Bonet tunc vicecomite,
Jodlano de Nevil', Alano de Multon', Iohanne de Nevill' filio Galfridi de Nevill',
Symone de Chancy, Willelmo de Bilingh', Iocelino de Chanci, Gilberto de
Riggeb', Osberto Arsic, Iordano de Brakeb', Iohanne de Hamb', Iollano de
Heilling', Willelmo filio Roberti, Hereveo Darci, Rogero de Torpel, Haraldo filio
Umfridi, Lamberto de Buss', Radulfo de Crombwell', Nigello de Lisur', Wil-
lelmo de Charnel', Radulfo Selveyin, Girardo de Howell', Henrico de Colevil',
Ricardo Selveyn, Hugone de Ringesdon', Roberto camerario, Galfrido de
Campan, Ada de Merlo, Radulfo de Hoyland, Gilberto Cusyn, Alexandro de
Laford', Waltero Malerb', Iordano de Luda.

> Most of the witnesses are episcopal knights. John Bonet occurs as (under-)sheriff of
> Lincolnshire in Michaelmas 1218 *(List of Sheriffs for England and Wales from the
> earliest times to A.D. 1831* (Public Record Office List and Index ix, 1898) 78).

82.   Wroxton priory

Confirmation to the canons at Wroxton of the site (the place called locus sancte
Marie*) with the chapel of St Mary and the houses and the whole* curia *with yardlands* (virgulte) *and fishponds* (vivaria) *and the area contained with the the the cir-
cumference of the wall which is around the vineyard* (vinea) *and the* curia, *and all
that is contained within the* curia, *together with the advowson of the parish
church of Wroxton, all of which has been granted to them in pure and perpetual
alms by master Michael Belet son of Michael Belet.*   Kilsby, 9 January 1218

> B = LAO Add. Reg. 6, fo. 28r. s. xiii in.
> Pd *Lib. Ant.* 90.

Hiis testibus: Thoma de Fiskerton', P. de Bath', magistro W. de Well', R. de
Bohun, Stephano de Cic', canonicis Linc', magistro Ricardo de Tinghurst' et
Olivero de Chednet' et aliis. Dat' per manum W. de Torn', archidiaconi Stow',
apud Kildeby v idus Ianuarii pontificatus nostri anno ix°.

> For the foundation of Wroxton priory see *Reg. Ant.* iii no. 955; *VCH Oxfordshire* ii
> 101. This *actum* of Bp Hugh is mentioned in *RHW* iii 95.

83.   Fosse priory

*Confirmation of the grant made by John de Fontineto to the nuns of Fosse outside
Torksey of the advowson of the church of [Cherry] Willingham. John's grant has
previously been confirmed to the nuns by Robert Marin the elder and afterwards
by his son Robert, chief lords of the fee.*   Sleaford, 9 February 1218

> B = LAO Add. Reg. 6 (Liber antiquus) fos. 26v–27r. s. xiii in.
> Pd *Lib. Ant.* 86.

Hiis testibus: Rogero decano, Rogero cancellario Linc', Thoma de Fiskerton' et

Rogero de Brist' capellanis, canonicis Linc', magistris W. de Linc', Petro de Bath', Ricardo de Oxon', Stephano de Cicestr' et Olivero de Chesney, clericis, et aliis. Dat' per manum Willelmi de Thorn', archidiaconi Stowe, apud Lafford' v idus Februarii pontificatus nostri anno ixº.

This confirmation of Bp Hugh is mentioned in *RHW* iii 95.

84. Sempringham priory

Notification that master Reginald of Chester, the bishop's Official when he was abroad, had ordained a vicarage in the church of Billingborough on the bishop's authority. The vicar was to serve the cure in person. The vicarage consisted of the entire altarage and all the land of the church with houses and other appurtenances and liberties in meadows, pastures and turbaries. The nuns of the house of Sempringham were to receive all the garb tithes of the parish and to pay synodal dues, provide hospitality for the archdeacon and bear all other charges of the church. The Official had then admitted and instituted Robert of Owmby, chaplain, as perpetual vicar on the presentation of prior G(ilbert) and the convent of Sempringham (made by Nicholas the canon, their proctor). The bishop now confirms his Official's ordination. Sleaford, 15 February 1218

> B = LAO Add. Reg. 6 (Liber antiquus) fo. 27r. s. xiii in.
> Pd from B in *Lib. Ant.* 86–7.

Hiis testibus: Thoma de Fiskerton' capellano, P. de Bathon', canonicis Linc', magistris W. de Linc', T. de Cantia et Ricardo de Tingh', Olivero de Chedn' et Stephano de Cic'. Dat' per manum W. de Tornac', archidiaconi Stow', apud Lafford' xv kalendas Martii pontificatus nostri anno ixº.

This confirmation is mentioned in *RHW* iii 93.

85. Bardney abbey

Institution of Henry de Coleville, clerk, to the church of Heckington on the presentation of Matthew, the abbot and the convent of Bardney; saving a customary pension to the abbey and the perpetual vicarage of Simon the chaplain. There follows a description of the vicarage, ordained by the bishop. Sleaford, 4 March 1218

> B = BL ms. Cotton Vespasian E xx (Bardney cartulary), fos. 33v–34r (29v–30r). s. xiii ex.

Universis sancte matris ecclesie filiis ad quos presens scriptum pervenerit, Hugo Dei gratia Linc' episcopus salutem in domino. Noverit universitas vestra nos, ad presentationem dilectorum in Cristo filiorum Mathei abbatis et conventus de Bard' patronorum ecclesie de Hekington', dilectum in Cristo filium Henricum de Collevill' clericum ad eandem ecclesiam de Hekingt' admisse et ipsum in ea personam instituisse; salva dictis abbati et conventui de Bard' debita antiqua pensione annuatim ab eodem solvenda, et salva perpetua vicaria eiusdem ecclesie Symoni capellano, quam de consensu predictorum abbatis et conventus et ipsius H. persone ordinavimus in eadem ecclesia. Consistit autem dicta vicaria in toto altalagio, scilicet, in oblationibus omnibus et obventionibus eiusdem altaris cum omnibus minutis decimis et in tota terra eiusdem ecclesie, remanentibus integre predicto H. persone et successoribus suis omnibus decimis garbarum ad eandem ecclesiam pertinentibus. Habebit etiam idem vicarius quoad vixerit domum quam propriis sumptibus construxit ibidem in fundo ecclesie; salvo tamen in ea hospitio persone tanquam domino suo, cum ipsum illuc venire contigerit, et salvis eidem persone horreis suis; que quidem domus post decessum ipsius vicarii, debet in usus cedere persone. Predictus igitur vicarius debet hospitium archidiacono facere, et alia omnia onera illius ecclesie tam episcopalia quam archidiaconalia consueta et debita sustinere, et preterea eidem persone et successoribus suis de eadem vicaria quadraginta solidos annuatim reddere, videlicet, ad Pascha xx.solidos et ad festum sancti Michaelis xx solidos: salvis etiam in omnibus episcopalibus consuetudinibus et Linc' ecclesie dignitate. Et ut hec nostra institutio perpetuam obtineat firmitatem, eam presenti scripto sigilli nostri munimine roborato confirmavimus. Hiis testibus: Thoma de Fiskerton' canonico Lincoln', Rogero de Castro Lafford', Henrico decano de Aswrdesburn' capellanis, magistro Willelmo de Linc', Ricardo de Oxon', Olivero de Chedn' et Stephano de Cicecestr',[a] clericis. Dat' per manum Willelmi de Thornac', archidiaconi Stou, apud Lafford' quarto nonas Martii pontificatus nostri anno nono.

[a] Cicecestr' *with the first 'ce' dotted for deletion* B.

The record of the institution is to be found in *RHW* i 89. The 'due and ancient' pension mentioned in this document is presumably the pension of five marks which features in Bp Hugh I's confirmation of 1194 x 1195 (*EEA* 4 nos. 14–15).

86. Haverholme priory

Notification that master Reginald of Chester, the bishop's Official when he was abroad, had made an ordination respecting five parts of the church of Anwick on the bishop's authority. saving to Robert le Simple, clerk, the sixth part of the church. The perpetual vicar ministering in the church was to have all the altarage of the five parts, all offerings and obventions, the garb tithes of all the demesne of the village, the tithes of one bovate of land which Fulk held, and all the land belonging to the five parts of the church with meadows, pastures, turbaries, and all other appurtenances and liberties. The prior and canons and nuns of Haverholme were to receive the rest of garb tithes to use to provide drink for themselves. The priory were to provide the church with books and ornaments when necessary, to maintain the chancel, to provide hospitality for the archdeacon and to bear all other charges except synodal dues, which the vicar should pay. The Official had then instituted Gerard the chaplain to the perpetual vicarage of the five parts on the presentation of the priory, and had admitted the prior and convent to their portion. The bishop now confirms his Official's ordination.

Sleaford, 4 March 1218

B = LAO Add. Reg. 6 (Liber antiquus) fo. 27r–v. s. xiii in.
Pd from B in *Lib. Ant.* 87–8.

Hiis testibus: Thoma de Fiskerton' capellano, canonico Linc', magistro Willelmo de Linc', Stephano de Cic', Ricardo de Oxon' et Olivero de Chesney, clericis, et aliis. Dat' per manum W. archidiaconi Stow' apud Lafford' iiii[to] nonas Martii pontificatus nostri anno nono.

This grant of Bp Hugh is mentioned in *RHW* iii 93.

87. Haverholme priory

A similar confirmation of the Official's ordination of five parts of the church of Anwick, except that the assent of Roger the dean and the chapter of Lincoln was recorded, and the document was sealed with the capitular seal as well as Bishop Hugh's. Sleaford, 4 March 1218

> B = LAO Add. Reg. 6 (Liber antiquus) fo. 28r. s. xiii in.
> Pd *Lib. Ant.* 89.

Testibus: Rogero decano, G. precentore, Rogero cancellario, H. de sancto Edwardo, magistris W. filio Fulconis et A. de sancto Edmundo, R. de Bristoll' et aliis ut in predicta carta vicarii predicti et dat' eadem [no. 86].

88. Richard the butler

Grant, made with the assent of Roger the dean and the chapter of Lincoln, to Richard, the bishop's butler, of five roods of land in Marton, being the bishop's escheat, which Hacon father of John Toht held, together with the manses belonging thereto. Richard is to pay the bishop and his successors ten shillings a year for all service. Lincoln, 12 June 1218

> A = LAO Lincoln D. & C. Dij/83/2/53 (damaged by rodents). No ancient endorsement; approx. 202 x 129 + 22 mm.; bp's seal and counterseal (green wax, chipped, lower half missing) and capitular seal (green wax, chipped) on parchment tags (method 1).
> B = Lincoln D. & C. A/1/6 (Registrum) no. 178. s. xiv med. (words in square brackets have been supplied from B).
> Pd from A in *Reg. Ant.* ii no. 586.

Omnibus Cristi fidelibus ad quos presens carta pervenerit, Hugo Dei gratia Lincol[n' episcopus salutem in domi]no. Noverit universitas vestra nos, de assensu Rogeri decani et capituli nostri Linc', concessisse et dedisse et presenti carta confirmasse d[ilecto et] fideli Ricardo pincerne nostro pro homagio et servitio suo quinque rodas terre in villa de Martun' tanquam exscaetam nostram, quas Haconus pater Iohannis Toht tenuit in eadem villa; simul cum mansis ad eandem terram pertinentibus, uno scilicet manso versus partem australem et occidentalem eiusdem ville a manso qui fuit Willelmi clerici cum curtillis [et cro]ftis ad mansum illum pertinentibus, sicut villa se extendit et ex transverso quantum extenditur crofta eiusdem mansi et alio manso ex par[te bori]ali cum saliceto et mora extendentibus se quantum se extendit ipse mansus, cum pratis etiam pascuis et pasturis et omnibus aliis a[isia]mentis ad terram illam tam infra villam quam extra pertinentibus: habendas et tenendas ei et heredibus suis de nobis et successoribus nostris in per[petuum] iure hereditario, bene et in pace, libere et quiete cum omnibus libertatibus et liberis consuetudinibus suis: reddendo inde nobis et successoribus nostris pro omni servitio ad nos pertinente decem solidos annuatim ad quatuor anni terminos, videlicet ad festum sancti Michaelis duos solidos et sex denarios; ad Natale Domini duos solidos et sex denarios; ad Pascha duos solidos et sex denarios; ad festum sancti Iohannis Baptiste duos solidos et sex denarios. Quod ut ratum sit et stabile, sigillum nostrum una cum sigillo predicti capituli nostri Linc' presenti carte duximus apponendum. Hiis testibus: Rogero decano, Galfrido precentore, Rogero cancellario, Reginaldo subdecano, Reimundo Leircestr', Roberto Norhamt', Alexandro Bedeford', Willelmo Bukingeh' archidiaconis, Hugone de sancto Edwardo, magistris Willelmo filio Fulconis et Adam de sancto Edmundo, Thoma de Fiskerton' et Rogero de Bristoll', cappellanis, Petro de Bathon', canonicis Linc', Galfrido filio Baldwini, Willelmo Walen', Willelmo de Burton', servientibus, et aliis. Dat' per manum Willelmi de Thornac', archidiaconi Stow', apud Linc' ii idus Iunii pontificatus nostri anno nono.

> This land no doubt formed part of the property Richard the butler's daughter, Alice of Marton, granted to Bp Oliver Sutton of Lincoln (1280–99) ('omnes terras et tenementa que habui iure hereditario in villa et in territorio de Marton', together with lands in Ormsby and Utterby, *Reg. Ant.* ii no. 599, cf. no. 594 and ibid. iv no. 1243). Bp Oliver regranted them to the dean and chapter of Lincoln for the maintenance of a chaplain for his own chantry (ibid. ii no. 604).

89.   Alvingham priory

Grant, made with the assent of Roger the dean and the chapter of Lincoln, to the prioress and convent of Alvingham of a pension of three marks a year, payable at Michaelmas, in the name of a perpetual benefice, from the church of Grainthorpe, which is of their patronage. This arrangement is to take effect after the death of Ralph de Waravill, the present parson of the church.

Lincoln, in chapter, 14 June 1218

> B = LAO Add. Reg. 6 (Liber antiquus) fo. 27v. s. xiii in. C = Oxford, Bodl. ms. Laud misc. 642 (Alvingham cartulary) fo. 98v. s. xiii ex.
> Pd from B in *Lib. Ant.* 89.

Testibus:[a] Rogero decano et aliis ut supra in carta canonicorum de Huntind' super medietate ecclesie de Stok' [no. 77] exceptis hic R. Norh't et I. Oxon', W. Buck' et R. Huntind' archidiaconis et adiectis I. de Ebor', P. de Bath' et magistro W. de Linc'. Dat' per manum W. de Torn', archidiaconi Stow', apud Linc' in capitulo Linc' xviii° kalendas Iulii pontificatus nostri anno ix°.

> [a] Hiis testibus C.

> For Ralph de Waravill's institution to Grainthorpe, see no. 79 above. This grant of Bp Hugh is mentioned in *RHW* iii 93.

90.   Bardney abbey

Institution of master William of Benniworth to the church of Howell and of Richard of Oxford, clerk, to a mediety of the church of Claypole, both on the presentation of Gerard of Howell, the patron; saving to the abbot and convent of Bardney their right in the aforesaid churches.   [*c.* late 1217 x 1218]

> B = BL ms. Cotton Vespasian E xx (Bardney cartulary) fos. 35v–36r (31v–32r). s. xiii ex. C = ibid., fos. 224v–225r (219v–220r).

Omnibus Cristi fidelibus ad quos presens scriptum pervenerit[a], Hugo Dei gratia Linc' episcopus salutem in domino. Noverit universitas vestra nos, presente dilecto in Cristo filio Matheo abbate de Bard', ad presentationem Gerardi patroni ecclesie de Huwell' et medietatis ecclesie de Claipol, [fo. 36r] admisisse dilectum nobis magistrum Willelmum de Beningwrd' ad eandem ecclesiam de Huwel'[b] et

Ricardum de Oxon' clericum ad dictam medietatem ecciesie de Claipol vacantes; salvo dicto abbati et conventui de Bard' iure suo quod eis rationabiliter competit in ecclesiis memoratis. In huius igitur rei testimonium, presenti scripto sigillum nostrum apponi fecimus. Valete.

ᵃ Omnibus Cristi fidelibus etc. C.   ᵇ Huwell' C.

This document was evidently issued after the admission of the two incumbents, since the collations of both livings by the bp are recorded on roll x (*RHW* i 69–70). Gerard of Howell the patron was excommunicate at the time of the collations but was later absolved at Sleaford. Both William and Richard were members of Hugh II's *familia*, the former eventually becoming subdean of Lincoln. I have argued elsewhere that the date of roll x is *c.* 1214 x 1218 (Smith, 'Rolls' 157–70). Matthew first occurs as abbot on 4 March 1218 (above, no. 71); his predecessor, Peter of Lenton, was still in office *c.* late April 1217 (*Heads*). The document certainly dates from before 20 December 1218, when the first dated institution roll of the bp survives. For the settlement of a dispute between Bardney abbey and Gerard of Howell over these two benefices *c.* 1195 x 1197 see *EEA* 4 no. 17.

91. Rochester cathedral priory

Institution of Ralph the chaplain to the perpetual vicarage of Haddenham with the chapel of Cuddington, on the presentation of the prior and convent of Rochester, and ordination of the vicarage. The vicarage consists of the whole altarage of the church of Haddenham and the chapel of Cuddington (except the small tithes of the demesne of the monks of Rochester), a virgate of land and the manse belonging to it in Cuddington, the garb tithes of three hides of land of the fee of Richard the younger in the village of Haddenham, and the manse of William, sometime chaplain of the village, with all the curia *belonging to the manse. The bishop, however, has retained for the use of the monks the third garb of the tithes of Cuddington which was formerly allotted to the vicar. The vicar is bound to minister personally in the church of Haddenham and to find a suitable chaplain to serve the chapel of Cuddington, and to bear all other charges of the church, both episcopal and archidiaconal, except the bishop's aid if it shall fall, for which he shall answer according to his proportion, and except the reparation of the choir for which the sacrist of Rochester shall be liable.*

Eynsham, 18 August 1218

B = Lincoln D. & C. Dij/73/1/31 (transcript of 2 charters, much damaged). s. xiii in.
C = BL ms. Cotton Domitian A x (Rochester cartulary) fo. 202r. s. xiii in.
Pd from B in *Reg. Ant.* iii no. 659(i); from C in *Reg. Roff.* 385–6.

Hiis testibus:ᵃ Thoma de Fiskerton' et Rogero de Bristoll' capellanis, magistro Waltero de Welles et Stephano de Cicestr', canonicis Lincoln', et multis aliisᵇ. Datum per manum Willelmi de Thornaco, archidiaconi Stowe, apud Egnesham quinto decimo kalendas Septembris pontificatus nostri anno nono.

ᵃ *Witness list taken from* C, B *has* et cetera.   ᵇ multi alii C.

This is the charter mentioned *RHW* iii 95.

92. Daventry priory

Institution of master Geoffrey of Dodford, clerk, to the church of Walgrave, on the presentation of the prior and convent of Daventry.   Uxbridge, 26 October 1218

> B = BL ms. Cotton Claudius D xii (Daventry cartulary) fo. 144v (cxlv). s. xiv ex.
> Pd *Daventry Cartulary* no. 880.

Hiis testibus: Thoma de Fiscerton', magistro Waltero de Well', Rogero de Bohum' et aliis. Dat' per manum Willelmi de Thornac', archidiaconi Stow', apud Uxebrigg' septimo kalendas Novembris et pontificatus nostri anno nono.

> The record of Geoffrey's institution is pd *RHW* i 25 (cf. Smith, 'Rolls'). Geoffrey is perhaps to be identified with Geoffrey Dodford, clerk of the archdn of Northampton, who witnesses 1215 x 1217 (*Daventry Cartulary* no. 652).

93. Gosberton church

Collation of the church of Gosberton, in the bishop's gift, to Richard de Atteberg, clerk, saving the vicarage of Hugh of Burgundy. Hugh shall hold the church for as long as he lives, paying to Richard as parson an annual pension of thirteen marks. A croft is assigned to Richard for a parsonage.
Dorchester, 3 November 1218

> B = Wells D.& C. Liber albus II, fo. 189r. s. xvi in.
> Pd (calendar), *HMC Wells* i 401.

Universis sancte matris ecclesie filiis ad quos presens scriptum pervenerit, Hugo Dei gratia Linc' episcopus salutem in domino. Noverit universitas vestra nos ecclesiam de Gosebertkirk', que de nostra est advocatione, cum omnibus pertinentiis, libertatibus et liberis consuetudinibus dilecto nobis Ricardo de Atteberg' clerico contulisse et ipsum in eadem canonice personam instituisse, salva Hugoni Burgun' vicaria sua quam habet in eadem: qui dictam ecclesiam tenebit quoadvixerit, reddendo eidem Ricardo tanquam persone tredecim marcas annuatim de eadem ecclesia nomine pensionis. Remanebit etiam nichilominus eidem Ricardo crofta ad edificium persone assignata; salvis etiam in omnibus episcopalibus consuetudinibus et Linc' ecclesie dignitate. Et ut hec institutio nostra perpetue firmitatis robur obtineat, eam presenti scripto et sigilli nostri munimine duximus confirmandam. Hiis testibus: domino Ioscelino Bathon' et Glaston' episcopo, Willelmo de Hammes precentore Wellensi, Thoma de Fiskerton' capellano, magistro Waltero de Well', Rogero de Bohum' et Stephano de Cicestr', canonicis Linc', magistro Adam de Clanefeld' et Radulfo de Warevill', canonicis Wellen', magistro Willelmo de Linc' et Ricardo de Tinghurst', Olivero de Chedneto et aliis. Dat' per manum Willelmi de Thornaco, archidiaconi Stowe, apud Dorkecestr' tertio nonas Novembris pontificatus nostri anno nono.

> The collation is recorded in the bp's institution roll (*RHW* i 123).

94. Crowland abbey

Confirmation, with the assent of Roger the dean and the chapter of Lincoln, to the abbot and convent of Crowland of the annual pensions of four shillings from the church of Sutton and four shillings from the church of West Keal, which they were previously accustomed to receive.   Lincoln, 2 December 1218

B = LAO Add. Reg. 6 (Liber antiquus) fo. 28r. s. xiii in.
Pd *Lib. Ant.* 91.

Hiis testibus: Rogero decano, G. precentore, Rogero cancellario, I. archidiacono Bedef', H. de sancto Edwardo, Gilberto de Scaldeburg, Thoma de Fiskert', R. de Brist', magistro R. de Gravel', Waltero Blundo, Stephano de Cic', R. de Waravill', can(onico) Well', Olivero de Chednet' et aliis. Dat' per manum Reginaldi subdecani apud Linc' quarto nonas Decembris pontificatus nostri anno ix°.

This confirmation of Bp Hugh is mentioned in *RHW* iii 95.

95. Chacombe priory

Grant, with the assent of Roger the dean and the chapter of Lincoln, to the prior and convent of Chacombe of a pension of three marks, in the name of a perpetual benefice, from the church of St Leonard, Aston[-le-Walls], which is of their patronage. This pension is to be paid each year by master Adam of St Bridget, the parson of the church, and his successors.   Lincoln, 15 December 1218

B = LAO Add. Reg. 6 (Liber antiquus) fo. 28r–v. s. xiii in.
Pd *Lib. Ant.* 91.

Testibus ut supra in carta proxima [no. 94], apposito hic magistro Reginaldo subdecano. Dat' per manum W. de Torn', archidiaconi Stow', apud Linc' idibus Decembris pontificatus nostri anno nono.

This grant of Bp Hugh is mentioned in *RHW* iii 94.

*96. Rockingham bridge

Indulgence (number of days not specified) for all those who contribute alms towards the construction and repair of Rockingham bridge.
[20 December 1217 x 19 December 1218]

Mention of lost charter issued in the bp's ninth pontifical year in similar indulgence granted in 1226, no. 242. The charter roll for the ninth pontifical year, upon which this indulgence was recorded, has not survived, pd *RHW* ii 218.

*97. Bishop of Coutances

Letter to the bishop of Coutances about the institution of Stephen, archdeacon of Coutances, to the church of Stenigot, subject to the provisions of the [Lateran] Council (sub pena Concilii).   [20 December 1217 x 19 December 1218]

Mention of written mandate in LAO Wells roll x, m. 10d, pd *RHW* i 86, cf. Smith, 'Rolls' for probable year. See also C.R. Cheney, *From Becket to Langton*, p. 132 et seq. for the Fourth Lateran Council and parochial benefices.

*98. Launde priory

Institution of Alan Costein, clerk, to the church of Ab Kettleby, on the presentation of the prior and convent of Launde.
[20 December 1217 x 19 December 1218]

Mention of letter of institution in LAO Wells roll x, m. 11, pd *RHW* i 90, cf. Smith, 'Rolls' for probable date.

*99.   Thornholm priory

Charter to the priory of Thornholm about the third part of the garb tithes of Cadney.   [20 December 1217 x 19 December 1218]

> Mentioned in the list of churches, pensions and rents granted by Bp Hugh to the religious in LAO Wells roll xi, pd *RHW* iii 94, dated to the bp's ninth pontifical year.

*100.   Newnham priory

Charter to the priory of Newnham about the church of Ravensden.
          [20 December 1217 x 19 December 1218]

> Mentioned in the list of churches, pensions and rents granted by Bp Hugh to the religious in LAO Wells roll xi, pd *RHW* iii 94, dated to the bp's ninth pontifical year.

101.   Laurence of S. Nicolo

Letter of the bishop and his brother, Jocelin bishop of Bath and Glastonbury, acknowledging that they have borrowed from master Laurence of S. Nicolo, clerk of the cardinal legate Guala, for the use of their churches, the sum of seven hundred marks sterling from the money of the cardinal and that they are bound to repay the same sum to the use of the aforenamed cardinal at St Germain-des-Prés, Paris, at the nativity of the Virgin next ensuing (8 September 1219). Should the money not be repaid at that time, the legate may claim damages and expenses.
          London, 15 January 1219

> B = LAO Wells roll xii, m. 1d.
> Pd *RHW i* 140–1; (calendar) *Letters of Guala* no. 145. No witnesses or datary.

Act' London' octavodecimo kalendas Februarii pontificatus domini Honorii pape tertii anno tertio.

> For the Italian master Laurence de S. Nicolo see *Letters of Guala* lxvi–vii, lxxiv, lxxxvi–vii and nos. 16, 23, 48, 149, 153–7.

102.   Abbey of St Evroul

Confirmation, with the assent of Roger the dean and the chapter of Lincoln, for the abbot and convent of Saint-Evroul of the customary pension of three marks from the church of Nettleham, to be paid by the parson each year at the feast of St John the Baptist; saving in perpetuity to the bishop of Lincoln and his successors the advowson of the church.   Lincoln, in chapter, 30 January 1219

> B = LAO Add. Reg. 6 (Liber antiquus) fo. 28v. s. xiii in.
> Pd *Lib. Ant.* 91–2.

Hiis testibus: Rogero decano, G. precentore, Rogero cancellario, Reginaldo subdecano, Willelmo filio Fulconis, Hugone de sancto Edwardo, G. de Scardeb', Iohanne de Ebor', Ada de sancto Edmundo, magistris Thoma de Fiskerton', R. de Bristoll', Theobaldo de Bosell', W. de Avalon', P. de Bath', R. de Bohun, canonicis Linc', magistris R. de Tinghurst et O. de Cheinduit, clerico, et aliis. Dat' per manum W. de Tornac', archidiaconi Stowe, in capitulo Linc' apud Linc' tertio kalendas Februarii pontificatus nostri anno decimo.

This confirmation of Bp Hugh is mentioned in *RHW* iii 95.

103. Knights Hospitallers

Confirmation, with the assent of Roger the dean and the chapter of Lincoln, for the prior and brethren of the Hospitallers in England of all the garb tithes belonging to the fourth part of the church of Kirton, which they had previously from Robert de Hardres, at that time Official of the archdeaconry of Lincoln, for the use of the prior and brethren of the hospital outside Boston. Furthermore they shall receive, in the name of a perpetual benefice, from the parson of the church two marks a year from the small tithes and obventions of the altarage of that fourth part. Previously they had been accustomed to receive four marks.

Lincoln, 7 February 1219

B = LAO Add. Reg. 6 (Liber antiquus) fo. 28v. s. xiii in.
Pd *Lib. Ant.* 92.

Testibus ut supra carta proxima [no. 102] appositis hic Ricardo de Lindwud' et Roberto de Holm' et Stephano de Cic'. Dat' per manum W. de Tornac', archidiaconi Stow', apud Linc' septimo idus Februarii pontificatus nostri anno x°.

For Robert de Hardres, vice-archdn of Lincoln and later archdn of Huntingdon see *Reg. Ant.* vii app. i, 206; *Fasti Lincoln* pp. 27, 81. This confirmation of Bp Hugh is mentioned in *RHW* iii 95.

104. Blanchelande abbey

Grant in proprios usus, made with the assent of Roger the dean and the chapter of Lincoln, to the abbot and convent of Blanchelande of the church of Cammeringham, which is of their patronage, saving the perpetual vicarage assigned by the bishop to Gilbert the chaplain who was instituted on their presentation. The vicar and his successors shall serve personally. The vicarage consists of the entire altarage of the church, a toft, three bovates of the demesne land of the church which Robert Tumin held, and the tithe of eight bovates of land in the village (namely the land of Richard son of Hervey, Robert Beaufiz, Richard Bachel and Richard the tanner, each of whom holds two bovates). The vicar and his successors shall pay no tithes from the demesne of the church belonging to them. He shall be responsible for the payment of synodal dues each year but the abbot and convent shall bear all other charges both episcopal and archidiaconal.

Lincoln, 9 February 1219

B = LAO Add. Reg. 6 (Liber antiquus) fo. 28v. s. xiii in.
Pd *Lib. Ant.* 92–3.

Testibus etc. ut supra carta proxima [no. 103]. Dat' per manum W. de Thornac', archidiaconi Stowe, apud Linc' v^to idus Februarii pontificatus nostri anno x°.

The institution of Gilbert of Willingham as vicar is recorded in the institution roll for the bp's tenth pontifical year, beginning 20 December 1218 (*RHW* i 133). This grant of Bp Hugh is mentioned in *RHW* iii 95.

105.   Lincoln, priory of St Katharine

Notification that master Reginald of Chester, the bishop's Official when he was abroad, had made an ordination respecting the church of Alford and the chapel of Rigsby on the bishop's authority. The perpetual vicar was to have all the land of the church and chapel with meadows, pastures and turbaries and all other appurtenances and liberties, except half a manse at Alford which the canons of the hospital outside Lincoln have for making a barn to store the garb tithes of the church and chapel which they were granted in proprios usus. *The vicar was to have the altarage of the church and chapel, except the aforesaid garb tithes. He was to minister in the church of Alford personally and should find a suitable chaplain to serve the chapel of Rigsby. The vicar was to bear all customary and ordinary charges, on account of which he was to receive ten shillings each year from the canons, five shillings at Easter and five at Michaelmas. The Official had then instituted master John son of Gurred, clerk, to the perpetual vicarage on the presentation of the prior and canons, and had admitted the canons to their portion. The bishop now confirms his Official's ordination.*

Lincoln, in chapter, 17 February 1219

B = LAO Add. Reg. 6 (Liber antiquus) fo. 29r. s. xiii in.
Pd *Lib. Ant.* 93.

Testibus ut supra in prima carta anni decimi [no. 102] appositis hic Reimundo archidiacono Leirc', R. de Hulm', R. de Lindwud', W. Blundo, et magistro W. de Linc'. Dat' per manum W. de Torn', archidiaconi Stowe, in capitulo Linc' apud Linc' xiii° kalendas Martii pontificatus nostri anno x°.

This grant of Bp Hugh is mentioned in *RHW* iii 92.

106.   Adam the lorimer

Grant to Adam the lorimer of half a toft belonging to the bishop's mill upon the Cherwell at Banbury, namely that half to the west near the town ditch, and the small toft to the north of it. He shall pay to the bishop and his successors three shillings a year for all service, namely ninepence at Michaelmas, ninepence at Christmas, ninepence at Easter, and ninepence at the Nativity of St John the Baptist. Thame abbey, 27 February 1219

B = LAO Lincoln D. & C. Dij/66/3/6 (in an inspeximus of Roger the dean and the chapter of Lincoln, 1219 x 1223).
Pd *Reg. Ant.* iii no. 925.

Hiis testibus: Roberto archidiacono Huntendon', Thoma de Fiskerton' capellano et Petro de Bathon', canonicis Linc', Radulfo de Warvill', canonico Wellen', magistro Willelmo de Linc' et Olivero de Chedneto, clericis, Galfrido filio Baldewini senescallo nostro, Willelmo de Burton', Willelmo Walensi, Iohanne de Cestria, Rogero Marescallo, servientibus, et aliis. Dat' per manum Willelmi de Thornac', archidiaconi Stow', apud abbatiam de Tham' tertio kalendas Martii pontificatus nostri anno decimo.

107. Caldwell priory

Confirmation of the grant made by Thurstan Basset, knight, to the prior of Cald-
well of the advowson of the church of Marsworth.   Buckden, 11 April 1219

B = LAO Add. Reg. 6 (Liber antiquus) fo. 29r. s. xiii in.
Pd *Lib. Ant.* 93–4.

Hiis testibus: Roberto Huntind' et Willelmo Buk' archidiaconis, Thoma de Fiskert' capellano, magistris R. de Gravel' et Theobaldo de Cant', P. de Bath', canonicis Linc', magistris W. de Linc' et Ricardo de Tinghurst, Olivero de Chedn',
clericis, et aliis. Dat' per manum W. de Thorn', archidiaconi Stowe, apud Bugged'
iii⁰ idus Aprilis pontificatus nostri anno x⁰.

108. Hockliffe, hospital of St John

Confirmation of the grant made by John Malherbe, knight, to the hospital of St
John the Baptist at Hockliffe of the advowson of the church of St Nicholas, Hock-
liffe.   Buckden, 12 April 1219

B = LAO Add. Reg. 6 (Liber antiquus) fo. 29r. s. xiii in.
Pd *Lib. Ant.* 94.

Testibus: Reginaldo subdecano et aliis ut supra in carta proxima [no. 107]. Dat'
per manum W. de Thorn', archidiaconi Stowe, apud Buged' ii idus Aprilis anno
x⁰.

John Malherbe held land in Hockliffe of the honour of Bedford (*Book of Fees* ii
887). The foundation date of the hospital at Hockliffe, –1277 (*KH* 323), is clearly in
need of revision. This confirmation of Bp Hugh is mentioned in *RHW* iii 95.

109. William de Fortibus, Count of Aumale, and Gilbert de Gant

Letter of Bishop Hugh, John Marshal, Walter Mauclerc, and William de Cressy,
justices itinerant in Lincolnshire, addressed to P(eter des Roches), bishop of Win-
chester, William Marshal, earl of Pembroke, the regent (rector domini regis et
regni), *and H(ubert) de Burgh, the justiciar of England, complaining against the*
royal letters which they have received from them, which suggest that in the matter
of the assize of novel disseisin brought by Gilbert de Gant against William de
Fortibus, count of Aumale, the itinerant justices acted contrary to the law. They
strongly protest that the bishop of Winchester, the regent and the justiciar should
not so readily believe evil of the justices made at the suggestion of Fulk D'Oyry
or another. The itinerant justices are sending their clerk, G. Cusin, to lay the
matter before Bishop Peter, the regent and the justiciar.
[December 1218 x 14 May 1219]

A = PRO, SC1/1/54.
Pd, *Royal Letters* i no. xvi.

This letter of protest is discussed in detail in *Lincolnshire Eyre Roll*, pp. li–lvi. The
political background to this case is provided in D.A. Carpenter, *The Minority of*
Henry III (1990), pp. 99, 102–3; B. English, *The Lords of Holderness 1086–1260*
(Oxford, 1979), p. 42. Gilbert de Gant, a member of the baronial party, had recently
been a prisoner of the count of Aumale. The case of novel disseisin was over
Edenham church. Neither the count nor his steward put in an appearance and the

case was adjudged by default to Gilbert. Fulk D'Oyry was the steward of the count of Aumale (see K. Major, *The D'Oyrys of South Lincolnshire, Norfolk and Holderness 1130–1275* (Lincoln, 1984), esp. pp. 16–24). The eyre began in December 1218 and William Marshal, the regent, died on 14 May 1219.

110.   Chester, priory of St Mary

Confirmation of the grant made by Matilda de Mouhaut to the prioress and nuns of [St Mary's,] Chester, of the advowson of the church of Sutterby.

Newhouse, 22 May 1219

> B = LAO Add. Reg. 6 (Liber antiquus) fo. 29r. s. xiii in.
> Pd *Lib. Ant.* 94.

Testibus: Iohanne de Eboraco archidiacono Stowe, Thoma de Fiskerton' capellano, magistro R. de Gravel' et P. de Bathon', canonicis Linc', W. de Keynesham et Radulfo de Warravill', canonicis Well', magistro Gilberto de Stowa et Olivero de Chedn', clericis, et aliis. Dat' per manum W. de Thorn', archidiaconi Lincoln', apud Neuhus xi° kalendas Iunii pontificatus nostri anno x°.

> This confirmation of Bp Hugh is mentioned in *RHW* iii 95.

111.   Harthey wood

Grant, with the assent of Roger the dean and the chapter of Lincoln, to Walter son of Robert and his heirs of all the assart made or to be made in the bishop's wood of Harthey, for an annual payment of ten pounds at the terms in which the render of the manor of Buckden is accustomed to be made. The assart shall be a possession of this manor.

Lincoln, in chapter, 25 May 1219

> A = LAO Lincoln D. & C. Dij/72/2/9. Endorsed: Carta episcopi et capituli Linc'
>   facta Waltero filio Roberti super assarto faciendo in bosco de Hertheye (s.
>   xiii); Boggeden' (s. xiii); .ij. ; approx. 214 x 100 + 25mm.; seal missing, three
>   slits for seal-tags.
> B = LAO Lincoln D. & C. A/1/5 (Registrum Antiquissimum) no. 233. s. xiii in.
> Pd from A in *Reg. Ant.* ii no. 375.

Omnibus Cristi fidelibus ad quos presens carta pervenerit, Hugo Dei gratia Linc' episcopus salutem in domino. Noverit universitas vestra nos, de assensu Rogeri decani et capituli nostri Linc', concessisse et dedisse Waltero filio Roberti totum assartum factum et faciendum de bosco nostro de Herteya: habendum et tenendum sibi et heredibus suis de nobis et successoribus nostris iure hereditario inperpetuum bene et in pace, libere, integre, et honorifice cum omnibus pertinentiis, libertatibus, et liberis consuetudinibus suis; reddendo inde nobis et successoribus nostris inperpetuum decem libras esterlingorum singulis annis in quatuor anni terminis, in quibus redditus manerii nostri de Buggeden' reddi consuevit. Cuius manerii pertinenciam totum predictum assartum cum hominibus in eo mansuris et omnibus pertinenciis suis esse volumus et perpetuo attornamus ad faciendum ibidem sectas et consuetudines que alia huiusmodi libera tenementa facere debent. Quod ut ratum sit et firmum, presenti carta nostra et sigillo nostro et capituli nostri Linc' duximus confirmandum. Hiis testibus: Rogero decano Linc', Willelmo archidiacono Linc', Rogero cancellario, Reginaldo subdecano,

Reimundo archidiacono Leicestr', magistro Iohanne archidiacono Stowe, magistro Willelmo filio Fulconis, magistro Gilberto de Scardeburg', Hugone de sancto Edwardo, magistro Roberto de Holm, magistro Roberto de Gravel', Petro de Hungar', Petro de Bath', Petro de Keuermunt, canonicis Linc', et multis aliis. Dat' per manum Willelmi de Thorn', archidiaconi Linc', apud Linc' in capitulo octavo kalendas Iunii pontificatus nostri anno decimo.

112.   Fosse priory

Grant in proprios usus, with the assent of Roger the dean and the chapter of Lincoln, of the church of [Cherry] Willingham to the religious house and nuns of Fosse by Torksey, the patrons of the church, saving the possession of Stephen of Hungate, clerk. A pension of two marks a year is to be paid to the nuns after Stephen's death, namely, one half for the provision of clothing and the other half for the kitchen. The perpetual vicarage, which the bishop ordains, shall consist of the entire altarage of the church, two bovates of land and all the meadow belonging to the church, and the tithes of all the land called Holm'. Upon each vacancy of the church the nuns shall present a suitable chaplain to the bishop for institution. The vicar shall serve personally and shall bear all ordinary and customary burdens.   Lincoln, 25 May 1219

> B = LAO Add. Reg. 6 (Liber antiquus) fo. 29v. s. xiii in.
> Pd *Lib. Ant.* 94–5.

Hiis testibus: R. decano Linc', R. cancellario, R. subdecano, R. Leirc' et I. Stowe archidiaconis, G. de Scardeburg', H. de sancto Edwardo, R. de Holmo, R. de Gravel', P. de Hungar', P. de Bath', P. de Kevermunt, canonicis Linc', et multis aliis. Dat' per manum W. de Thorn', archidiaconi Linc', apud Linc' viii⁰ kalendas Iunii pontificatus nostri anno decimo.

113.   Wellow abbey

Confirmation of the grant made by Gilbert de Turribus to the abbot and convent of Grimsby [Wellow] of the advowson of the church of Cabourne.
                                                 Lincoln, 5 July 1219

> B = LAO Add. Reg. 6 (Liber antiquus) fo. 29v. s. xiii in.
> Pd *Lib. Ant.* 96.

Testibus: I. archidiacono Bedef', Thoma de Fiskerton', magistris R. de Gravel' et W. de Well', canonicis Linc', Wiilelmo de Keynesham et Radulfo de Warravill', canonicis Wellen', et Olivero de Chedn', clerico, et aliis. Dat' per manum R. de Cestr', subdecani Linc', apud Linc' iii nonas Iulii pontificatus nostri anno x⁰.

This confirmation of Bp Hugh is mentioned in *RHW* iii 95.

114.   Abbey of St Evroul

Graant in proprios usus, made with the consent of Roger the dean and the chapter of Lincoln, of the church of Marston [St Lawrence] to the abbot and convent of St Evroul, saving the vicarage assigned by the bishop. The vicarage consists of the altarage of the church and of the chapels pertaining to it and of the small tithes of the whole parish, the whole garb tithe of Warkworth, one virgate of land with a

manse which Robert of Alkerton held, and the garb tithes of Middleton [Cheney].
The vicar shall pay twenty shillings to the monks of St Evroul each year and shall
answer for episcopal customs. If the monks happen to have stock at Marston for
their own use, they shall be exempt from the payment of tithes for that stock.
Upon each vacancy of the vicarage, the abbot and convent shall present a suit-
able chaplain to the bishop for institution.   Lincoln, in chapter, 12 July 1219

> B = LAO Add. Reg. 6 (Liber antiquus) fo. 29v. s. xiii in.
> Pd *Lib. Ant.* 95.

Hiis testibus: Rogero decano, G. precentore, Rogero cancellario, R. subdecano, I.
archidiacono Bedef', magistro W. filio Fulconis et aliis ut in carta proxima
precedenti [no. 112] exceptis R. Leirc' et I. Stowe archidiaconis. Dat' per manum
Reginaldi, subdecani Linc', in capitulo Linc' apud Linc' quarto idus Iulii pontificatus nostri anno decimo.

> This must be the document referred to in the inventory of muniments of Sheen (BL
> ms. Cotton Otho B xiv fo. 113v (111v, cix v) – 'Item appropriatio ecclesie de Mer-
> ston' sancti Laurentii et dotatio vicarie facta per episcopum Lincolniensem et capi-
> tulum eiusdem.'). It is also mentioned in *RHW* iii 95.

115.   Gilbert of Sutton

Grant that Gilbert of Sutton, clerk, and his heirs shall hold a messuage and sev-
enteen acres of land and meadow in Sutton[-le-Marsh] of the church of Sutton
and master William of Lincoln, the parson, and his successors for free service of
eight shillings and six pence a year. Six acres of meadow called Suxedeiles *shall*
remain to the church and parson as free, pure and perpetual alms (as is contained
in the chirograph made between William and Gilbert in the king's court).
Lincoln, 13 July 1219

> A = LAO Lincoln D. & C. Dij/87/3/13 (faded in parts, slightly damp stained and a
> few rodent holes). Endorsed: debita rectori de Sutton viii s. vi d. (? s. xv);
> Sutton (s. xvi); approx. 195 x 79 + 14 mm.; seal missing, slit for seal tag
> (method 1).

Omnibus Cristi fidelibus ad quos presens carta pervenerit, Hugo Dei gratia Linc'
episcopus salutem in domino. Noverit universitas vestra nos pro bono pacis concessisse quod Gilebertus de Sutton' clericus et heredes sui habeant et teneant
imperpetuum de ecclesia de Sutton' et de magistro Willelmo de Linc' persona
eiusdem ecclesie et successoribus suis unum mesagium cum decem et septem
acris tam de terra quam de prato in Sutton', per liberum servitium octo solidorum
et sex denariorum per annum pro omni servicio; ita quod sex acre prati que
vocantur Suxedeiles cum pertinentiis remaneant imperpetuum predictis ecclesie
de Sutton' et Willelmo ipsius ecclesie persone et successoribus suis tanquam
libera pura et perpetua elemosina prefate ecclesie, sicut in cyrographo inter
eosdem Willelmum et Gilebertum in curia domini regis confecto plenius continetur: salvo iure si quod predicta ecclesia de Sutton' et magister Willelmus vel successores sui habent vel habituri sunt in aliis terris et tenementis que idem
Gilebertus tenet. Quod ut perpetuam optineat firmitatem, presenti carte sigillum
nostrum apposuimus. Hiis testibus: Iohanne archidiacono Bedeford', Thoma de
Fiskerton' capellano, magistris Roberto de Gravel' et Waltero de Well', Petro de

Bathon', canonicis Linc', Petro de Wilton' capellano, Iohanne de Renham' clerico, Olivero de Chenedt' [sic] et Martino de Eston', clericis, et aliis. Dat' per manum Reginaldi de Cestr', subdecani Linc', apud Linc' tertio idus Iulii pontificatus nostri anno decimo.

> Master William of Lincoln, a future archdn of Leicester, was instituted to Sutton-le-Marsh c.1218 (*RHW* i 117). For the suit against Gilbert of Sutton see *Lincoln-shire Eyre Rolls*, pp. 200, 213–14, 390, 492; for the chirograph between master William and Gilbert see *Lincoln Final Concords*, i 139–40 no. 84. It is dated 25 June 1219 and notes that Bp Hugh was present and granted the agreement.

116. Ramsey abbey

Confirmation, with the assent of Roger the dean and the chapter of Lincoln, for the abbot and convent of Ramsey, for the use of the almonry, of a pension of three marks from the church of Warboys, in the name of a perpetual benefice. This pension, which the monks have been accustomed to receive for a long time past, is to be paid to them in perpetuity by the parson of the church.

Lincoln, 21 July 1219

> B = LAO Add. Reg. 6 (Liber antiquus) fos. 29v–30r. s. xiii in. C = BL ms. Cotton Vespasian E ii (Ramsey cartulary) fo. 41v (39v, xxxvi). s. xiii med.
> Pd from B in *Lib. Ant.* 96.

T(estibus):[a] Rogero decano, G.[b] precentore, R.[c] cancellario,[d] I. archidiacono Stow', Hugone de sancto Edwardo, magistris W. filio Fulconis, R. de Holm', R. de Ludwud'[e] et A. de sancto Edmundo, Waltero Blundo et R. de Bristoll', capellanis, P. de Hung', W. de Avalun, R. de Boh' et P. de Cheuemunt, canonicis Linc', et O. de Chedn', clerico. Dat' per manum Thome de Fiskerton', capellani, canonici Linc', apud Linc' xii kalendas Augusti pontificatus nostri anno x°.

> [a] Hiis testibus C. [b] Gaifrido C. [c] Rogero C. [d] C *ends here with* etc. [e] *sic, recte* Lindwud' B.

> For confirmations of Bp Robert Chesney (1148–1166) concerning this church see *EEA* 1 nos. 226–7. This confirmation of Bp Hugh is mentioned in *RHW* iii 95.

117. Newstead on Ancholme priory

Grant, made with the assent of Roger the dean and the chapter of Lincoln, to the prior and convent of Newstead [on Ancholme] of four marks a year, in the name of a perpetual benefice, from the church of Barnetby [-le-Wold], to be paid by master Hugh of Duffield, the parson, during his lifetime, and of half the garb tithes of thirteen bovates of land in Barnetby to be in their possession during master Hugh's lifetime. After the latter's death, the priory shall have one mediety of the church in proprios usus, on condition thereafter that the aforesaid pension of four marks shall cease and the entire altarage shall remain to the parsons of the church. The value of half of the altarage shall be recompensed to the priory by all the garb tithes of the thirteen bovates of land which the canons hold and the garb tithes of eight bovates of land which Adam de Thorn holds and the garb tithes of thirteen bovates of land which Henry son of Walter holds, except the one bovate held of Henry by William son of Wulstan. Moreover, all other garb tithes, lands and tofts belonging to the church, except the chief manse of the parson, shall be equally divided between the priory and the parson. The latter will be instituted to the other mediety of the church on the presentation of the aforesaid prior and convent. He shall bear all ordinary charges of the church; the canons shall answer proportionally for extraordinary charges.

Lincoln, in chapter, 23 September 1219

> B = LAO Add. Reg. 6 (Liber antiquus) fo. 30r. s. xiii in.
> Pd *Lib. Ant.* 96–7.

T(estibus): Rogero decano, Willelmo archidiacono Linc', G. precentore, Rogero cancellario, G. thesaurario, Iohanne subdecano, Reimundo Leirc', Roberto Hunt', Hugone Stow' archidiaconis, magistris Willelmo de Barden', Roberto de Gravel', W. de Linc' et Waltero de Well' et aliis ut supra carta proxima [no. 116]. Dat' per manum Petri de Bath', canonici Linc', in capitulo Linc' apud Linc' nono kalendas Octobris pontificatus nostri anno decimo.

> This grant of Bp Hugh is mentioned in *RHW* iii 93.

## 118.	Dunstable priory

Grant, made with the assent of Roger the dean and the chapter of Lincoln, to the prior and convent of Dunstable of an annual rent of one hundred shillings in that mediety of the church of Pattishall which Roger of Lutterworth held, in the name of a perpetual benefice. It consists of the tithes of corn and a rent of seven shillings from the cottars holding of the church: saving to Nigel his vicarage and an annual pension of one mark which Nigel used to pay to Roger. During Nigel's lifetime this pension shall go to supplement the needs of the church; after his death it shall go to augment the vicarage. The canons shall provide hospitality for the archdeacon.					Lincoln, in chapter, 23 September 1219

> B = LAO Add. Reg. 6 (Liber antiquus) fo. 30r. s. xiii in. C = BL ms. Harl. 1885
> 	(Dunstable cartulary) fo. 67v (66v, p.146) (witnesses omitted). s. xiii in.
> Pd from B in *Lib. Ant.* 97–8; (calendar) from C in *Dunstable Cartulary* no. 768.

Testibus et dat' ut supra carta proxima [no. 117].

> This grant of Bp Hugh is mentioned in *RHW* iii 95.

## 119.	Chicksands priory

Grant, made with the assent of Roger the dean and the chapter of Lincoln, to the prior and nuns of Chicksands of an annual pension of one silver mark, in the name of a perpetual benefice, from the church of Astwick, to come into effect after the death of Robert of Durham, clerk, to whom the bishop has collated the church by authority of the Lateran council. The pension is to be paid in two instalments, half a mark at Michaelmas and half at Easter.

Lincoln, in chapter, 23 September 1219

> B = LAO Add. Reg. 6 (Liber antiquus) fo. 30r–v. s. xiii in.
> Pd *Lib. Ant.* 98.

Testibus et dat' ut supra carta proxima [no. 118].

Astwick was originally a chapel of Stotfold (see *EEA* 4 no. 41; *VCH Beds.*, i 318, ii 206) and indeed is still described as one in 1250 x 1251 (*RRG* p. 337) and 1266 (*Rot. Grav.* p. 193). It had been given to Chicksands by Simon Beauchamp, son of the founder of the priory. The collation of the church to Robert of Durham is in *RHW* i 126 (wrongly identified as Eastwick, Herts.). This grant of Bp Hugh is mentioned in *RHW* iii 93.

120. Wroxton priory

Confirmation, with the assent of the dean and chapter of Lincoln, of all the grants and gifts of Michael Belet to the priory of St Mary, Wroxton, which he had founded, and also of all lands, rents and tenements given by other benefactors to the priory.   Lincoln, in chapter, 23 September 1219

> B = LAO Add. Reg. 6 (Liber antiquus) fo. 30v. s. xiii in.
> Pd *Lib. Ant.* 98.

Testibus et dat' ut supra carta quarta ab ista [no. 117].

121. Kingsthorpe, hospital of Holy Trinity outside Northampton

Grant, with the assent of Roger the dean and the chapter of Lincoln, and the consent of Robert and Katherine Baret, the patrons, and Walter de Cantilupe, the parson of the church of Barby, to the brethren of the hospital of Holy Trinity outside Northampton (Kingsthorpe) of a pension of half a silver mark from the aforesaid church, in the name of a perpetual benefice. This pension is to be paid each year at Easter by the parson and his successors.   Lincoln, in chapter, 23 September 1219

> B = LAO Add. Reg. 6 (Liber antiquus) fo. 30v. s. xiii in.
> Pd *Lib. Ant.* 98–9.

Testibus et dat' ut supra carta quinta ab ista [no. 117].

> This grant of Bp Hugh is mentioned in *RHW* iii 95. See also PRO, C146/11014.

122. Wroxton priory

Grant in proprios usus, *made with the assent of Roger the dean and the chapter of Lincoln, to the prior and convent of St Mary, Wroxton, of the church of Wroxton, which is of their patronage, saving a suitable vicarage which the bishop shall ordain, and saving to Michael Belet, the parson, the possession of the church for his lifetime.*   Lincoln, in chapter, 23 September 1219

> B = LAO Add. Reg. 6 (Liber antiquus) fo. 30v. s. xiii in.
> Pd *Lib. Ant.* 99.

Testibus: Rogero decano, Galfrido precentore etc. ut supra in carta sexta ab ista anno decimo [no. 117].

*123. Beatrice de Munfichet

Notification to the royal justices that Beatrice de Munfichet and her accomplices are excommunicate.   [Michaelmas term 1219]

Mention of letters patent in *CRR* viii 66, in a case between Beatrice and master Robert (of Hailes), archdn of Huntingdon in a plea of prohibition, Michaelmas term 1219: 'eo quod dominus Lincolniensis mandavit per literas suas patentes quod ipsa et fautores sui sunt excommunicati pro sacrilegio et non pro laico feodo'.

*124. Bullington priory

Charter to the nuns of Bullington about the church of Spridlington.
[20 December 1218 x 19 December 1219]

Mentioned in the list of churches, pensions and rents granted by Bp Hugh to the religious in LAO Wells roll xi, pd *RHW* iii 93, dated to the bp's tenth pontifical year.

125. Brampton bridge

Indulgence of seven days to all travellers who give alms towards the construction and repair of Brampton bridge. The indulgence is to last for one year.
Buckden, 27 December 1219

B = LAO Wells roll ix, m. ld (no witnesses).
Pd *RHW* ii 188.

Dat' per manum Thome de Fiskerton' cappellani, canonici Linc', apud Bugg' sexto kalendas Ianuarii pontificatus nostri anno xi°.

126. Hugh of Avalon, Bishop of Lincoln

Letter from the bishop and the chapter of Lincoln to the Roman cardinals thanking them for the benefits already granted and recommending to their attention the matter of Bishop Hugh (I) of Lincoln.   [27 April 1219 x 17 February 1220]

B = BL Cotton roll xiii 27, no. 3. s. xiii in.
Pd *LAASR* 6 (1956), 113–14.

The dates are those of Pope Honorius III's original commission to enquire into the life and miracles of Bp Hugh I and the papal bull of canonization. See also D.H. Farmer, 'The cult and canonization of St Hugh' in H. Mayr-Harting ed., *St Hugh of Lincoln: lectures delivered at Oxford and Lincoln to celebrate the eighth centenary of St Hugh's consecration as bishop of Lincoln* (Oxford 1987), 75–87.

127. Hugh of Avalon, Bishop of Lincoln

Letter from the bishop and chapter of Lincoln to Pope Honorius III on the matter of the proposed canonization of Bishop Hugh (I). The enquiry into his life and miracles has been diligently carried out by the archbishop of Canterbury and the abbot of Fountains. Raymond, archdeacon of Leicester, Hugh the chaplain, and Theobald, canons of Lincoln, are being sent to the pope with this letter in connection with the business.   [27 April 1219 x 17 February 1220]

B = BL Cotton roll xiii 27, no. 1. s. xiii in.
Pd *LAASRP* 6 (1956) 111–12.

For the date see above.

128. Kilsby church

Collation of the church of Kilsby, in the bishop's gift, to Hugh de Cambio, clerk.
[20 December 1219 x 19 December 1220]

B = LAO, Wells roll ix, m. 1.
Pd *RHW* ii 185.

Hiis testibus ut in carta Willelmi de Eboraco super ecclesia de Ripton' in archidiaconatu Huntigdon' et eadem data.

This entry comes under the bp's eleventh pontifical year; the collation is noted earlier in the institution rolls *c.* 1218 (*RHW* i 121). The Huntingdon archdeaconry charter roll no longer exists, but the record of William of York's collation to Ripton in the institution roll for this pontifical year is ibid. iii 33.

129. St Neots priory

Notification that a dispute in the king's court between the prior of St Neots and the abbot of Peterborough over the right of patronage of the church of Clapton has been settled. The patronage shall remain to the abbot of Peterborough, saving to the prior and monks of St Neots their due and ancient pension. Rannulf of Clapton and William Dacus, who had also claimed the patronage, renounced their appeals. An inquisition held by the archdeacon [of Northampton] found that the monks of St Neots had received twenty-five shillings and eightpence each year from the church for the past forty or so years. Buckden, 14 January 1220

B = LAO, Add. Reg. 6 (Liber antiquus) fo. 31r (slightly abridged). s. xiii in. C = LAO, Wells roll ix, m. 1d. D = BL Cotton ms. Faustina A iv (St Neots cartulary) fo. 41r (40r), no. xxviii. s. xiii med.
Pd from B in *Lib. Ant.* 101; from C in *RHW* ii 190.

Dat' per manum Thome de Fisk'ᵃ capellani, canonici Linc',ᵇ apud Bugged'ᶜ xixᵒ ᵈ kalendas Februarii pontificatus nostri anno xiᵒ.ᵉ

ᵃ Fiskerton' C; Fiskenton' D. ᵇ Lincolnienc' D. ᶜ Bugg' C; Buggeden' D.
ᵈ decimo nono D. ᵉ undecimo D.

130. Easton Maudit church

Institution of Peter the chaplain to the church of Easton [Maudit], on the presentation of Robert Morin, Robert de Legh and Thomas Salvagius (le Sauvage), each being patron of a third part of the church. Spaldwick, 17 January 1220

B = LAO, Wells roll ix, m. 1.
Pd *RHW* ii 183.

Hiis testibus: magistro Stephano de Cicestr' capellano, magistro Willelmo de Linc' et Petro de Bath', canonicis Linc', magistris Willelmo de Cant' et Amaurico de Bugd', Olivero de Chedn' et Willelmo de Winchelcumb, clericis. Dat' per manum Thome de Fiskerton', canonici Linc', apud Spaldewich' sextodecimo kalendas Februarii pontificatus nostri anno undecimo.

The institution is noted in the institution rolls among entries for the bp's tenth pontifical year, 20 December 1218 x 19 December 1219 (ibid. i 139).

131. Northampton, hospital of St Leonard

Indulgence of seven days to all travellers who contribute alms to the leper hospital of St Leonard outside Northampton. The indulgence is to last for two years.
Wellingborough, 21 January 1220

    B = LAO, Wells roll ix, m. 1d (no witnesses).
    Pd *RHW* ii 189.

Dat' per manum Petri de Bath', canonici Linc', apud Wenlingburg' duodecimo kalendas Februarii pontificatus nostri anno xi^mo.

> St Leonard's hospital, Northampton is said to have been founded in the 11th century (*KH*, 380).

132. Haselbech church

Institution of William of Dudley, clerk, to the church of Haselbech, on the presentation of William Burdet.   Banbury, 22 February 1220

    B = LAO, Wells roll ix, m. 1.
    Pd *RHW* ii 183–4.

Hiis testibus: magistris Stephano de Cicestr', Theobaldo de Cantia et Willelmo de Linc', Petro de Bathon', canonicis Linc', Radulfo de Warevill', canonico Wellen', magistro Willelmo de Cant', Willelmo de Winchelcumb, Ricardo de Oxon' et Olivero de Chedn', clericis. Dat' per manum Thome de Fiskerton' capellani, canonici Linc', apud Banneb' viii^vo kalendas Martii pontificatus nostri anno xi^mo.

> The institution is recorded ibid. 98.

133. Bugbrooke church

Collation, by authority of the Council, of the church of Bugbrooke to master Amaury of Buckden, clerk, saving in future the right of the patron.
Biggleswade, 11 March 1220

    B = LAO, Wells roll ix, m. 1.
    Pd *RHW* ii 185.

Hiis testibus: domino Ioscelino Bath' episcopo, Willelmo precentore Wellen', magistris Stephano de Cicestr' et Willelmo de Linc', canonicis Linc', Rogero cappellano, magistro Ada de Clenefeld' et Gilberto de Dulting', canonicis Wellen', magistro Willelmo de Cant', Willelmo de Winchecumba et Olivero de Chedn', clericis. Dat' per manum Thome de Fiskerton' cappellani, canonici Linc', apud Bicleswaud' quinto idus Martii pontificatus nostri anno xi°.

> The collation is recorded in the institution rolls ibid. 99. Amaury of Buckden was an episcopal clerk and witnesses some sixty *acta*. He became archdn of Bedford in 1231 until his death 1245 x 1246. He resigned Bugbrooke church June 1239 x June 1240 (*Fasti Lincoln*, pp. 42, 93; *RRG*, p. 196).

134. Lincoln cathedral

Grant, made with the assent of Roger the dean and the chapter of Lincoln, to the [cathedral] church of Lincoln of a perpetual render of one hundred shillings from the church of Kilsby, five marks from the church of Fingest, and ten marks from the church of Asfordby, in augmentation of the maintenance of the clerks of the choir by whom the office of the Virgin Mary is celebrated in the church of Lincoln. This arrangement is to take effect at the next vacancies of these churches.   Lincoln, in chapter, Easter Day [29 March] 1220

> A = LAO Lincoln D. & C. Dj/20/1/4. Endorsed: De pensione ministrorum misse beate Marie. Salue (s. xiv); approx. 216 x 190 mm. (badly damaged at the base of the document); no sign of sealing visible, seal missing.
> Pd *Reg. Ant.* ii no. 362.

Omnibus Cristi fidelibus ad quos presens scriptum pervenerit, Hugo Dei gratia Linc' episcopus salutem in domino. Noverit universitas vestra nos, ad honorem Dei et gloriose virginis matris sue cuius inutiles servi sumus, de assensu Rogero decani et capituli nostri Linc', concessisse et dedisse ecclesie Linc' redditum subscriptum in liberam, puram et perpetuam elemosinam pro salute anime nostre et omnium antecessorum et successorum nostrorum, in augmentum perpetue sustentationis clericorum de choro Linc' per quos celebretur officium de ipsa Virgine gloriosa in ecclesia Linc' in loco certo ad hoc deputato: videlicet, missa sollempnis singulis diebus mane et alia officia de eadem secundum horas similiter constituta: de ecclesia de Kildesby centum solidos; de ecclesia de Tinghurst' quinque marcas; de ecclesia de Esfordeby decem marcas: reddendas annuatim de ipsis ecclesiis cum proximo vacaverint in quatuor anni terminis preposito officii illius per manus illorum qui pro tempore ipsas ecclesias tenuerint per nos vel successores nostros qui de ipsis ecclesiis et omnibus pertinentiis earum disponemus et ordinabimus pro voluntate nostra inperpetuum libere et quiete et absque omni contradictione, salvo predictis clericis predicto redditu annuatim de eisdem. Constituimus autem, de assensu ipsius decani et capituli nostri, ut cappellanus de choro vir s*[small damaged section]* vite laudabilis et opinionis probate prepositus huius officii a decano et capitulo constitutus integre tam redditum prenominatum quam omnem alium redditum ad hec officia exequenda iam assignatum et inposterum assignandum pia largitione fidelium terminis statutis recipiat et fideliter et bona fide distribuat singulis septimanas predictis clericis de choro executoribus officii memorati secundum ordinationem nostram et predicti capituli nostri salubri volente Domino factam provisione. Statuimus etiam quod unusquisque eorum qui quamcunque predictarum ecclesiarum tenuerit ut dictum est sacramentum faciat fidelitatis decano et capitulo Linc' de predicto redditu integre et sine diminutione aliqua predicto preposito suis terminis persolvendo; decernentes insuper quod si aliquis eorum maliciose contra hoc unquam venire presumpserit et legittime commonitus id emendare negglexerit, ipsum tam diu ab officio et beneficio fore suspensum, donec super hiis satisfecerit competenter maiori etiam pena feriendum iuxta arbitrium nostrum et successorum nostrorum si nec sic errorem suum duxerit corrigendum. Nos vero ad eliminandam prorsus omnem maliciam et ad perpetuam huius concessionis et constitutionis nostre firmitatem, una cum omnibus sacerdotibus ecclesie Linc' sollempniter excommunicavimus omnes illos qui fraudulenter et maliciose hanc elemosinam nostram vel aliorum huic officio ut diximus assignatam vel assignandam subtraxerint, diminuerint vel ad alios usus minus licite converterint contra nostram et capituli nostri ordinationem. Ut igitur hec omnia perpetua gaudeant stabilitate, presenti scripto sigillum nostrum una cum sigillo predicti capituli nostri Linc' duximus apponendum. Hiis testibus: domino Ioscelino episcopo Bathon', Willelmo precentore Wellensi, magistris Iohanne de Hoyland', Willelmo de Cant', Amaurico de Buggeden', Lamberto de Beverlaco et Hugone de Mareseia, Huberto Hesey, Roberto de Caumvill' et Gilberto fratre eius, Laurentio de Wilton', Willelmo de Winchecumb', et Olivero de Ch[edne]to, clericis. Dat' per manum nostram [in] capitulo Linc' die Pasche [pontificatus nostri] anno undecimo.

135. Lincoln cathedral

Grant, made with the assent of Roger the dean and the chapter of Lincoln, to the canons of Lincoln, in augmentation of their common, of an annual render of thirty marks from the church of Nettleham, forty marks from the church of Gosberton, one hundred shillings from the church of Grayingham, one hundred shillings from the church of Stilton, and fifteen marks from the church of Woburn. This arrangement is to take effect at the next vacancies of the churches and the pensions are to be paid each year in four instalments by their respective parsons, who shall each swear to the dean and chapter that they will pay the abovementioned sums.   Lincoln, in full chapter, Easter day [29 March] 1220

> B = LAO, Add. Reg. 6 (Liber antiquus) fo. 31r. s. xiii in. C = LAO Lincoln D. & C. A/1/5 (Registrum Antiquissimum) no. 222. s. xiii in. D = ibid. no. 995. E = ibid. no. 1094. F = LAO Lincoln D. & C. Dj/20/1/1 (in an inspeximus of Archbp Walter de Gray of York, 12 November 1251).
> Pd from B in *Lib. Ant.* 99–100; from C in *Reg. Ant.* ii no. 358.

(B version)
Hiis testibus: Rogero decano, W. archidiacono Linc', G. precentore, Rogero cancellario, I. subdecano, R. Norh't, R. Hunt', I. Bedeford' et Hugone Stow' archidiaconis, magistris W. filio Fulconis, Ricardo de Lindwud', W. Blundo, H. Burgund', R. de Bristoll', Thoma de Fisk' et S. de Cicestr', capellanis, W. de Aval', P. de Hung', magistris R. de Gravel' et W. de Linc', P. de Bath' et P. de Cheuremunt, canonicis Linc', R. de Warr', canonico Well', magistris W. de Cant' et A. de Buged', W. de Winch', R. de Ox' et Olivero de Chedn', clericis. Dat' per manum nostram in pleno capitulo Linc' die Pasche pontificatus nostri anno undecimo.

(C–F versions)
Hiis testibus: domino Iocelino[a] Bathon' episcopo, Willelmo precentore Wellen', magistris Iohanne de Hoyland', Willelmo de Cant', Amarico[b] de Buggeden'[c], Lamberto de Beverlac' et Hugone de Mareseya, Huberto Husey[d], Roberto de Campvill'[e] et Gilberto fratre eius, Laurentio de Wilton'[f], Willelmo de Winchecumbe et Olivero de Chedneto, clericis. Datum per manum nostram in pleno capitulo Linc' die Pasche pontificatus nostri anno undecimo.

> [a] Iocellino DF; Ioscellino E.   [b] Amaurico E.   [c] Bugden' E.   [d] Hesey E.   [e] Camvill' E.   [f] Willeton' E.

The very marked divergence in the lists of witnesses in versions B and C–F is curious. Being dated in full chapter on Easter Day the B version would seem to be the more probable; yet, while versions C–F are not attested by a single canon of Lincoln, the survival of an original actum [no. 134] of the same date with the same witnesses does not allow us to dismiss these versions as the result of scribal errors.

136. Nicholas son of Roger

Grant, made with the assent of Roger the dean and the chapter of Lincoln, to Nicholas son of Roger of two bovates of land and a toft in Newark [on Trent], which Eustace son of Wynald held of the bishop and lost through felony. He shall pay to the bishop and his successors five shillings a year for all service.

Lincoln, in chapter, 31 March 1220

A = LAO Lincoln D. & C. Dij/90/2/27. No ancient endorsement; approx. 143 x 115 + 20 mm.; seals missing, two parchment tags for episcopal and capitular seals (method 1).
Pd from A in *Reg. Ant.* iii no. 919.

Omnibus Cristi fidelibus ad quos presens scriptum pervenerit, Hugo Dei gratia Linc' episcopus salutem in domino. Noverit universitas vestra nos, de assensu Rogeri decani et capituli nostri Linc', concessisse, dedisse et presenti carta confirmasse Nicholao filio Rogeri duas bovatas terre et unum toftum cum omnibus pertinentiis in Newerk', que Eustachius filius Wynaldi de nobis tenuit et amisit per feloniam: habenda et tenenda eidem Nicholao et heredibus suis iure hereditario inperpetuum, libere et quiete, bene et in pace, integre et honorifice in omnibus locis et rebus ad terram illam pertinentibus: reddendo inde nobis et successoribus nostris annuatim quinque solidos argenti pro omni servicio ad nos pertinente, videlicet ad festum sancti Andree apostoli quindecim denarios; ad Pascha Floridum quindecim denarios; ad nativitatem sancti Iohannis Baptiste quindecim denarios; et ad festum sancti Michaelis quindecim denarios. Quod ut ratum sit et firmum, presenti carte sigillum nostrum una cum sigillo predicti capituli nostri Linc' duximus apponendum. Hiis testibus: Rogero decano, Galfrido precentore, Gilberto tesaurario, Roberto Norh', Iohanne Bedeford', Willelmo Bukyng' et Roberto Huntingdon' archidiaconis, Iohanne subdecano, Hugone archidiacono Stowe, magistris Willelmo filio Fulconis et Ada de Sancto Edmundo, Rogero de Bristoll', Roberto de Wassingburne, Waltero Blundo, Petro de Hungar', Petro de Bathon' et Petro de Cheuremunt, canonicis Linc', Olivero de Chedneto, clerico. Dat' per manum Thome de Fiskerton' cappellani, canonici Linc', in capitulo Linc' apud Linc' pridie kalendas Aprilis pontificatus nostri anno undecimo.

137. Reading abbey

Grant, made with the assent of Roger the dean and the chapter of Lincoln, to the abbot and convent of Reading of a pension of twenty marks a year, in the name of a perpetual benefice, from the church of Stanton [Harcourt], namely the pension of ten marks granted to them recently by the bishop, plus the pension of ten marks which they have previously received from the church. This pension is to be paid by Thomas de Kamel, the parson of the church, and his successors.The parson is also to bear all ordinary and customary burdens of the church.

Lincoln, in chapter, 31 March 1220

B = LAO Add. Reg. 6 (Liber antiquus) fo. 31r–v. s. xiii in. C = BL ms. Egerton

3031 (Reading cartulary) fo. 107v (lxxxxiiii v). s. xiii in. D = BL ms. Harl. 1708 (Reading cartulary) fo. 201v (200v) (witnesses omitted). s. xiii med. E = BL ms. Cotton Vespasian E xxv (Reading cartulary) fos. 122v–123r (66v–67r) (witnesses omitted). s. xiv in.

Pd from B in *Lib. Ant.* 101; from C–E in *Reading Cartularies* i no. 542; Kennett, *Parochial Antiquities* i 194.

T(estibus):[a] Rogero decano, Galfrido precentore, Gilberto thesaurario, Roberto Norh', I. Bedef'[b], Willelmo Buck'[c], et R. Hunt'[d] archidiaconis, I.[e] subdecano, H.[f] archidiacono Stowe, magistris W.[g] filio Fulconis et A.[h] de sancto Edmundo, W.[i] Blundo, R. de Brist'[j], Roberto de Wassingb'[k], P. de Hung'[l], P. de Bath'[m] et P. de Cheuemunt[n], canonicis Linc', et Olivero de Chedn'[o], clerico. Dat' per manum Thome de Fisk'[p] capellani, canonici Linc', in capitulo Linc' apud Linc' ii[q] kalendas Aprilis pontificatus nostri anno undecimo.

[a] Hiis testibus C.   [b] Iohanne Bedeford' C.   [c] Buking'C.   [d] Roberto Huntigd'C.   [e] Iohanne C.   [f] Hugone C.   [g] Willelmo C.   [h] Ada C.   [i] Waltero C.   [j] Rogero de Bristoll''et C.   [k] Wassingburne C.   [l] Petro de Hungar' C.   [m] Petro de Bathon' C.   [n] Petro de Cheuremunt C.   [o] Chedneto C.   [p] Fiskertone C.   [q] pridie C.

Allusion is made to this grant in *RHW* iii 96. Thomas was instituted to the church *c.* 1217–18 (ibid. i 31), at which time he was inhibited by Bp Hugh from paying the pension until it was established that it was 'due and ancient'.

138.   Mont-Sainte-Cathérine abbey

Notification that a dispute has been heard before the bishop between Robert of Preston, rector of the church of Tingewick, and the abbot and convent of Mont-Sainte-Cathérine, Rouen, concerning a manse and two virgates of land which Robert said belonged to his church of old, the tithes of the ancient demesne of the abbot and monks, and a pension of three marks imposed, according to Robert, contrary to the statutes of the Lateran Council. However, the dispute has been amicably settled. The abbey are to retain in perpetuity the tithes of the ancient demesne as before and are to receive from the church of Tingewick, in the name of a perpetual benefice, five shillings a year each Whitsun from Robert and his successors. Robert and his successors shall possess as the endowments of the church the said manse and the two virgates of land. The bishop confirms this composition.   Thame, 30 April 1220

B = LAO Add. Reg. 6 (Liber antiquus), fo. 32r. s. xiii in.
Pd *Lib. Ant.* 104.

Hiis testibus: magistro W. de Linc' et P. de Bath', canonicis Linc', R. de Warr', canonico Well', magistris W. de Cant' et A. de Buged' et R. de Tingherst, W. de Winch', R. de Ox' et O. de Chedn', clericis. Dat' per manum Thome de Fisk', capellani, canonici Linc', apud Tham' ii kalendas Maii pontificatus nostri anno xi[mo].

Robert's assertion regarding the pension refers to canon 32 of the Fourth Lateran Council of 1215 which laid down that a sufficient portion of the profits of the church should be assigned to the priest ministering in the church.

139. Lindores abbey

Institution of master William of Kent, clerk, to the perpetual vicarage of Whissendine, on the presentation of the abbot and convent of Lindores. William shall hold the church for life, paying to the abbot and convent as parsons an annual pension of ten marks, payable in two instalments, namely five marks at Easter and five at the feast of St Peter ad Vincula. Northampton, 24 May 1220

B = LAO, Wells roll ix, m. 1.
Pd *RHW* ii 184–5.

Hiis testibus: .. abbate sancti Iacobi extra Norh' et Radulfo priore sancti Andree de Norh', Roberto Norh' et Roberto Huntingdon' archidiaconis, Martino de Patt'hull', magistro Stephano de Cicestr', canonicis Linc', magistris Amaurico et Ricardo de Tinghurst', Willelmo de Raelegh', Willelmo de Winchecumba et Olivero de Chedneto, clericis. Dat' per manum Thome de Fiskerton' cappellani, canonici Linc', apud Norh' ix kalendas Iunii pontificatus nostri anno xi°.

The institution is recorded ibid. 99–100.

140. Brampton Ash church

Confirmation of the grant of a quarter of an acre of land in 'Nether Brampton', which is of the fee of the church of Brampton Ash, made by Martin of Pattishall, rector of the church, to Vincent the carpenter. Kilsby, 25 May 1220

B = LAO, Wells roll ix, m. 1d.
Pd *RHW* ii 189.

Hiis testibus: Roberto archidiacono Huntingd', magistro Stephano de Cicestr' et Petro de Bath', canonicis Linc', Radulfo de Warevill', canonico Wellen', magistro Willelmo de Cant', Willelmo de Winchelcumb, Ricardo de Oxon' et Olivero de Chednet', clericis. Dat' per manum Thome de Fiskerton', capellani, canonici Linc', apud Kildeby viii^to kalendas Iunii pontificatus nostri anno xi^mo.

141. Stamford, St Michael's priory

Institution of Agnes of Boothby, elected as prioress of St Michael's outside Stamford, with the consent of the abbot and convent of Peterborough, the patrons.
[Lincoln, house of the archdeacon of Lincoln, 5 June 1220]

B = CUL Peterborough D. & C. ms. 1 (Swaffham's register) fo. 116v (civ). s.xiii med.

H. Dei gratia Lincolniensis episcopus dilectis in Cristo filiabus konventui sancti Michaelis extra Stanford' salutem, gratiam et benedictionem. Sciatis nos ad canonicam electionem vestram, de consensu dilectorum in Cristo abbatis et conventus de Burgo monasterii vestri patronorum, dilectam in Cristo filiam Agnetem de Boby sanctimonialem vestram ad prioratum admisisse et ipsam in dicto monasterio vestro priorissam canonice instituisse, curam interiorum et exteriorum eidem committentes, salvo dictis^a abbati et conventui iure quod habent in patronatu et in custodia monasterii vestri memorati. Vobis igitur mandamus quatinus memorate A. tamquam priorisse vestre obedientes de cetero et ut decet sitis intendentes. Valete.

^a dicti B.

The record of this institution is to be found in the Lincoln archdeaconry institution roll, where the date is given: 'die veneris ante festum sancti Barnabe in domo archidiaconi Lincoln' apud Lincoln' . . .' (*RHW* iii 107).

142. Beauport abbey

Grant in proprios usus, made with the assent of Roger the dean and the chapter of Lincoln, to the abbot and convent of Beauport of the church of West Ravendale, saving a perpetual vicarage which the bishop has ordained. The vicar shall receive the yearly food allowance of one canon from the aforesaid abbey and one mark a year for clothing. The canons shall bear all ordinary charges of the church.   Lincoln, in chapter, 6 June 1220

> B = LAO Add. Reg. 6 (Liber antiquus) fo. 51r. s. xiii in.
> Pd *Lib. Ant.* 100–1.

Hiis testibus: Rogero decano, Galfrido precentore, R. Huntind', I. Bed' et H. Stowe archidiaconis, Iohanne subdecano, magistris A. de sancto Edmundo, Ricardo de Lindwud', W. Blundo, R. de Gravel', H. Burg', R. de Bristoll', W. de Avalun, P. de Hung' et Petro de Cheuremunt, canonicis Linc', et Olivero de Chedn', clerico. Dat' per manum Thome de Fisk', capellani, in capitulo Linc' apud Linc' viii° idus Iunii pontificatus nostri anno xi°.

143. Eydon church

Collation, by authority of the Council, of the portion of the church of Eydon which was Philip's to Robert de Hamelden, clerk, saving in future the right of the patron.   Fingest, 19 July 1220

> B = LAO Wells roll ix, m. 1.
> Pd *RHW* ii 184.

Hiis testibus: magistro Willelmo de Linc', canonico Linc', Radulfo de Waravill', canonico Wellen', magistris Willelmo de Cant' et Amaurico de Bugeden', Ricardo de Oxon', Olivero de Chednet' et Willelmo de Winchelcumb, clericis. Dat' per manum Thome de Fiskerton' capellani, canonici Linc', apud Tinghirst' xiiii kalendas Augusti pontificatus nostri anno xi^{mo}.

> The collation is recorded in the institution rolls ibid. 98. There was a dispute over the advowson between the abbot of Leicester and Richard son of Walo of Eydon (*CRR* viii 117–18, 264).

144. Everdon church

Institution of master Reginald of Oundle, clerk, to the church of Everdon, on the presentation of master Rannulph, the patron, saving to Silvester the clerk his perpetual vicarage. Silvester shall hold the church in the name of his vicarage, paying to master Reginald and his successors as parsons an annual pension of five marks, and to the monks of Bernay their customary pension, if there is one. The vicar shall bear all ordinary and customary burdens of the church.
                                                  ? Middleton, 3 August 1220

B = LAO Wells roll ix, m. 1.
Pd *RHW* ii 185–6.

Hiis testibus: magistro Willelmo de Linc', canonico Linc', Radulfo de Warravill', canonico Wellen', magistris Willelmo de Cant' et Amaurico de Bugg', Willelmo de Winchecumba, Ricardo de Oxon' et Olivero de Chedneto, clericis. Dat' per manum Thome de Fiskerton' cappellani, canonici Linc', apud Middelton' iii nonas Augusti pontificatus nostri anno xi⁰.

> The institution is recorded in the institution roll for the bp's tenth pontifical year, 20 December 1218 x 19 December 1219 (ibid. i 171).

145.   Eynsham abbey

Institution of Guy son of Ralph, clerk, to the church of Whitfield, on the presentation of the abbot and convent of Eynsham, saving the monks' right to their pension, if it is proved that such a pension belongs to them; if not, then the bishop shall make an ordination respecting the pension.   Cropredy, 5 September 1220

B = LAO Wells roll ix, m. 1.
Pd *RHW* ii 186.

Hiis testibus: Radulfo de Warravill', canonico Wellen', magistro Willelmo de Cant', Willelmo de Winchecumba, Ricardo de Cernay et Olivero de Chedn', clericis. Dat' per manum Thome de Fiskerton' cappellani, canonici Linc', apud Cropperie nonis Septembris pontificatus nostri anno xi⁰.

> The institution is recorded in the institution roll for the bp's tenth pontifical year, 20 December 1218 x 19 December 1219 (ibid. i 172).

146.   Abbey of St Evroul

Institution of William de Hembir', chaplain, to the perpetual vicarage of Marston [St Lawrence] ordained by the bishop, on the presentation of the abbot and convent of St Evroul. The vicarage consists of the altarage of the church and of the chapels belonging to it, the small tithes of the whole parish, all the garb tithes of Warkworth belonging to Marston church, a virgate of land with the manse which Robert of Alkerton held and the garb tithes of Middleton [Cheney], likewise belonging to Marston church. William and his successors as vicar shall pay to the abbey an annual pension of twenty shillings. If the aforesaid monks shall have stock at Marston for their own use, they shall be exempt from the payment of tithes on that stock.   Cropredy, 7 September 1220

B = LAO Wells roll ix, m. 1.
Pd *RHW* ii 186–7.

Hiis testibus: magistro Willelmo de Linc' et Petro de Bath', canonicis Linc', Radulfo de Warravill', canonico Wellen', magistro Willelmo de Cant', Willelmo de Winchecumba et Olivero de Chedn', clericis. Dat' per manum Thome de Fiskerton', cappellani, canonici Linc', apud Cropperie vii idus Septembris pontificatus nostri anno xi⁰.

147. Dunstable priory

Ordination, by authority of the Council, of perpetual vicarages in the churches of Stodham, Totternhoe, Chalgrave, Husborne Crawley and Segenho and institution of perpetual vicars in them on the presentation of the prior and convent of Dunstable. [October 1220]

B = BL ms. Harl. 1885 (Dunstable cartulary) fo. 14r (13r, p. 37). s. xiii in.
Pd (calendar), *Dunstable Cartulary* no. 15.

Omnibus Cristi fidelibus etc. Hugo Dei gratia etc. salutem in domino. Ad universitatis vestre notitiam volumus pervenire nos vicarias perpetuas in ecclesiis de Stodham', de Toternho, de Chaugrava, de Hesseburn' et de Segenho auctoritate Concilii ordinasse et ad presentationem dilectorum[a] in Cristo filiorum prioris et conventus de Dunstapl' ad ipsas vicarias sic ordinatas vicarios perpetuos admisisse et in eisdem instituisse, ita tamen quod nichil iuris predictis priori et canonicis acrescet[b] in ipsis ecclesiis per hanc nostram ordinationem et institutionem sive per eorum presentationem. Sunt autem predicte vicarie ordinate in hunc modum: scilicet, quod vicarius perpetuus ecclesie de Stodham' habebit nomine vicarie sue totum alteragium eiusdem ecclesie cum manso competente et continente circiter septem acras, salvis priori et canonicis de Dunstapl' de prefato alteragio una marca[c] annua et agnis. Vicarius vero perpetuus de Toternho habebit nomine vicarie sue totum alteragium illius ecclesie et redditum decem denariorum de terra Ricardi Cadwer et medietatem decime feni de tota parochia. Vicarius similiter perpetuus de Chaugrava habebit nomine vicarie sue totuit alteragium illius ecclesie et duas croftas et gardinum que sunt iuxta ecclesiam, quarum maior crofta que est ex parte occidentali continet in se quatuor acras et minor crofta cum gardino que est ex parte australi assignabitur ei pro manso. Vicarius etiam perpetuus de Hesseburn' habebit nomine vicarie sue totum alteragium ipsius ecclesie cum crofta et prato ex parte australi. Vicarius insuper perpetuus de Segenho habebit nomine vicarie sue totum alteragium eiusdem ecclesie, exceptis agnis qui dictis priori et canonicis remanebunt. In hiis autem omnibus quinque vicariis sic ordinatis predicti prior et canonici omnia onera ordinaria dictarum ecclesiarum debita et consueta sustinebunt, preter sinodalia que vicarii persolvent; salvis in omnibus super prefatis quinque vicariis et ecclesiis premissis episcopalibus consuetudinibus et Linc' ecclesie dignitate. Et in huius rei t(estimonium) etc. Hiis testibus.

[a] dilectionis B. [b] acrescat *originally written, with the last 'a' dotted for deletion and 'e' interlined.* [c] an *written at the end of the line, before* annua.

The annals of Dunstable date the ordination of these vicarages to October 1220 (*Ann. mon.* iii 59).

148. Northampton, priory of St Andrew

Institution of Thomas of Fiskerton, chaplain, to the church of St Peter, Northampton, on the presentation of the prior and convent of St Andrew, Northampton, saving to the priory their customary pension of six marks.

Banbury, 20 October 1220

B = LAO Wells roll ix, m. 1.
Pd *RHW* ii 187–8.

Hiis testibus: magistris Stephano de Cycestr' et Willelmo de Linc', canonicis Linc', magistro Nicholao de Evesham' et R. de Warevill', canonicis Wellens', magistris W. de Cant' et A. de Buged' et Rogero de Well', Willelmo de Winch' et Olivero de Chedn', clericis. Dat' per manum Petri de Bath', canonici Linc', apud Banneb' xiii kalendas Novembris pontificatus nostri anno xi^{mo}.

> Thomas' institution is noted in the first institution roll *c.* 1218 (ibid. i 122–3, cf. Smith, 'Rolls'). See also no. 193 below.

149. Braybrooke tithes

Collation, by authority of the Council, of the demesne tithes of John de Monte Acuto in Braybrooke to Richard de Cernay, clerk, saving in future the right of the patron.   Louth, 2 December 1220

> B = LAO Wells roll ix, m. 1.
> Pd *RHW* ii 188.

Hiis testibus: domino Ioscelino Bath' episcopo, magistris Stephano de Cicestr' et Willelmo de Linc', canonicis Linc', Rogero capellano, magistro A. de Clenefeld', Radulfo de Warevill' et Gileberto de Tanton', canonicis Wellen', magistro W. de Cant', Willelmo de Winch' et Olivero de Chedn', clericis. Dat' per manum Thome de Fiskerton' capellani, canonici Linc', apud Ludam iiii^{to} nonas Decembris pontificatus nostri anno xi^{mo}.

> The printed edition gives '. . . de dominico Iohanne de Monte Acuto' but the original roll states 'Iohannis'.

150. Goring priory

Grant in proprios usus, made with the assent of Roger the dean and the chapter of Lincoln to the prioress and nuns of Goring of the church of Stanton [Barry], saving the perpetual vicarage which the bishop has ordained by authority of the Council. This vicarage consists of the entire altarage of the church with a suitable manse, two virgates of land belonging to the church, the tithes of two virgates of land which Gerard held and of another two which Samson and Richer held. The vicar shall pay synodal dues and the nuns shall bear all ordinary burdens of the church.   Lincoln, 16 December 1220

> B = LAO Add. Reg. 6 (Liber antiquus) fo. 32r. s. xiii in.
> Pd *Lib. Ant.* 103–4.

Hiis testibus: Rogero decano, W. archidiacono Linc', G. precentore, Ricardo cancellario, R. Hunt' et H. Stow' archidiaconis, magistris W. filio Fulconis et G. de Scardeburg', Ricardo de Lindwud', W. Blundo, Rogero de Bristoll', magistro R. de Gravel', R. de Wassingeb' capellano, P. de Hung', R. de Boh' et P. de Cheuremunt, canonicis Linc', et Olivero de Chedn', clerico. Dat' per manum Thome de Fisk' capellani^{a}, canonici Linc', apud Linc' xvii kalendas Ianuarii pontificatus nostri anno xi^{mo}.

> ^{a} capellano B.

> This grant of Bp Hugh is mentioned in *RHW* iii 94.

151. Exeter cathedral

Confirmation, with the assent of the dean and chapter of Lincoln, to the dean and chapter of Exeter of their ancient portion in the church of Bampton in proprios usus, *in the name of a perpetual benefice, and provision for the remaining two portions, namely, the one held by Robert de Lucy and the other portion which John son of John the former archdeacon of Totnes holds. The vicar of the portion formerly held by Robert is to hold it for life paying to the chapter one hundred shillings a year, in the name of a benefice; John is likewise to hold his portion for life paying to the chapter his present payment of three marks a year. If the two portions chance to fall vacant simultaneously their endowments are to be constituted into three equal portions, each of which is to be a perpetual vicarage and all in the patronage of the dean and chapter of Exeter. Each vicar shall pay to the dean and chapter of Exeter an annual pension of five marks from his portion, in the name of a perpetual benefice. Continual residence is laid down for the vicars and they shall be responsible each in turn for hospitality and other charges of the bishop of Lincoln and the archdeacon of Oxford. If one portion becomes vacant before the other, the chapter of Exeter is to present a perpetual vicar to two-thirds of it. The vicar shall pay five marks a year to the chapter and shall hold the remaining third until the other portion becomes vacant, paying two and a half marks a year. When the remaining portion falls vacant, two further perpetual vicarages shall be formed, one out of two-thirds of that portion, the other out of the union of the remaining thirds of the two portions. The patronage and the annual payments are to be the same as in the simultaneous endowment arrangement described above.* Lincoln, in chapter, 16 December 1220

> B = LAO Add. Reg. 6, fo. 3lv and fos. 1v–2r (slightly abbreviated). s. xiii in. C = Exeter, Devon Record Office, Diocesan records, Chanter catalogue 1002 (copy, s. xiii ex., omits witnesses and date). D = Exeter, Devon Record Office, Episcopal Register of Bishop Lacy, *Registrum Commune*, fos. 266v–267r. s. xv med. E = Exeter D. & C. doct. 651, original inspeximus of Bp Lacy dated 4 October 1445. F = Exeter D. & C. ms. 3672 (chapter cartulary), pp. 3–5. s. xv. G = Exeter D. & C. ms. 3672, pp. 5–7 (omits witnesses and date).
>
> Pd from B in *Lib. Ant.*, 102–3 and 4–5; from D in *Reg. Lacy* ii 339–41; J. Blair, *The Medieval Clergy of Bampton* (Bampton research paper 4, 1991), app. B, pp. 37–40.

T(estibus)[a]: Rogero decano, G.[b] precentore, G.[c] thesaurario, Ricardo cancellario, Roberto Norh',[d] R.[e] Leirc',[f] R.[g] Hunt',[h] I.[i] Oxon', I.[i] Bedef'[j] et H.[k] Stowe archidiaconis, I.[i] subdecano, H.[l] de Bassingeburn[m] archidiacono Sar'[n] et H.[k] de Well'[o] archidiacono Bath',[p] magistris W.[q] filio Fulconis et G.[c] de Scardeburg[r], R.[s] de Lindwud'[t], W.[u] Blundo, R.[v] de Brist',[w] magistris R.[g] de Gravel' et S.[x] de Cic',[y] R.[g] de Wassingeburn'[z] capellanis[aa], magistro A.[bb] de sancto Edmundo, P.[cc] de Hung',[dd] magistro W.[q] de Linc', W.[q] de Aval',[ee] magistro W.[u] de Well'[o], R.[v] de Bohun et P.[cc] de Cheuemunt,[ff] canonicis Linc', et Olivero de Chedn',[gg] clerico. Dat' per manum Thome de Fisk'[hh] capellani[ii], canonici Linc', in capitulo Linc' apud Linc' xvii°[jj] kalendas Ianuarii pontificatus nostri anno xi°.[kk]

> [a] Hiis testibus DEF. [b] Galfrido DEF. [c] Gilberto DEF. [d] Northampton' DF; Norhampton' E. [e] Reymundo DEF. [f] Linc' D; Lenc' EF. [g] Roberto DEF.
> [h] Huntyngdon' DE; Huntingdon' F. [i] Iohanne DEF. [j] Bedford D; Bedeford' EF.

^k Hugone DEF. ^l Humfredo DEF. ^m Bassyngburn D; Bassingburne E; Bassinge-
burne F. ⁿ Sarr' EF. ^o Wellis E. ^p Bathon' DEF. ^q Willelmo DEF. ^r Scardeburgh' F. ^s Ricardo DEF. ^t Lindwod' E; Lindwode F. ^u Waltero DEF.
^v Rogero DEF. ^w Bristoll' DEF. ^x Stephano DEF. ^y Cicestria D; Cicestr' EF.
^z Wassingburg' DE; Wassingburgh' F. ^{aa} cappellanis E. ^{bb} Ada DEF. ^{cc} Petro
DEF. ^{dd} Hungaria D; Hungar' EF. ^{ee} Avalon DE; Avelon' F. ^{ff} Cherenint D;
Cheuremunt EF. ^{gg} Chedneto DEF. ^{hh} Fiskerton DE; Fisketon' F. ⁱⁱ cappellani
E. ^{jj} decimo septimo DEF. ^{kk} undecimo DEF.

Cf. *RHW* i 129, the report of an inquisition held by John of Tynemouth, archdn of
Oxford, concerning the portion of the church of Bampton which belongs to the
dean and chapter of Exeter. This confirmation is mentioned in *RRG*, p. 450 and *Rot.
Grav.*, p. 214. For Bampton church see J. Blair, *Bampton Deanery* (Bampton
Research Paper 2, 1988) and for the vicarage endowment and history J. Blair, *The
Medieval Clergy of Bampton*, pp. 16–19.

152. Bourne abbey

*Institution of Walter de Dunigton, clerk, to the church of Thrapston, on the presentation of the abbot and convent of Bourne, saving to the abbey its customary
pension of four shillings a year.* Buckden, 26 December 1220

B = LAO Wells roll ix, m. 1.
Pd *RHW* ii 190.

Hiis testibus: Willelmo archidiacono Buking', magistris Willelmo de Linc' et
Theobaldo de Cant', Petro de Bath', canonicis Linc', magistris Willelmo de Cant'
et Amaurico de Buggeden', Willelmo de Winchecumba et Olivero de Chedneto,
clericis. Dat' per manum Thome de Fiskerton' cappellani, canonici Linc', apud
Buggeden' septimo kalendas Ianuarii pontificatus nostri anno xii°.

The institution is noted in the institution rolls among entries for the bp's tenth pontifical year, 20 December 1218 x 19 December 1219 (Ibid. I 169–70).

153. Peterborough abbey

Institution of master Roger de Well, clerk, to the church of Tinwell, on the presentation of the abbot and convent of Peterborough, saving to the monks their customary pension. Lincoln, 24 February 1221

B = LAO Wells roll ix, m. 1.
Pd *RHW* ii 191.

Hiis testibus: W. archidiacono Linc' et Petro de Bath', canonicis Linc', magistris
Nicholao de Evesham' et Amaurico de Buggeden', Willelmo de Winchecumba,
Ricardo de Oxon' et Olivero de Chedn', clericis. Dat' per manum Thome de Fiskerton' cappellani, canonici Linc', apud Linc' sexto kalendas Martii pontificatus
nostri anno xii°.

The institution is recorded ibid. 102–3, among entries for the bp's eleventh pontifical year, 20 December 1219 x 19 December 1220.

154. St Fromond priory

Ordination after the prior of St Fromond had claimed that the churches of Bonby and Saxby had been appropriated to his monastery. The church of Bonby shall be appropriated to the prior and convent, saving a perpetual vicarage in the same church. The prior shall present a parson to the church of Saxby and the latter shall pay to the monastery an annual pension of one mark, in the name of a perpetual benefice, payable in two equal instalments.   Bicester, 3 March 1221

> A = PRO, E326/8781. Endt: Pro ecclesiis de Bondeby et de Saxeby. (s. xiii). decretum sancti Hugonis super ecclesiis de Bonby et Saxby. et ordinacio vicarie de B. (s. xv). No surviving seal: parchment seal-tag remains. Size: 177/180 mm. x 134/136 mm.
>
> B = PRO E326/463 (s. xvi copy on paper). C = Queen's College, Oxford deed 283, in an inspeximus of master Robert of Saint Agatha, Official of the bishop of Lincoln dated at Lincoln 23 September 1255. D = BL Add. Ch. 66079 (roll of charters of St Fromond), m. 1. s. xv.

Omnibus Cristi fidelibus ad quos presens scriptum peruenerit, Hugo Dei gratia Linc' episcopus salutem in domino. Noverit universitas vestra quod cum prior de sancto Fromundo post mortem magistri Iohannis de Bondeby, qui ecclesias de Bondeby et Saxeby possedit, dictas ecclesias vendicaret tanquam domui sue in proprios usus canonice concessas et a multis retro temporibus sic possessas, dicens dictum magistrum Iohannem tantum firmarium earundem ecclesiarum fuisse, et super hoc testes produceret et quedam instrumenta exhiberet, tandem publicatis attestationibus dictus prior pro se et conventu suo de sancto Fromundo super utraque predictarum ecclesiarum se sponte simpliciter et pure nostre subiecit ordinacioni. Nos igitur negotii circumstantiis et domus paupertate pensatis super ipsis ecclesiis ita duximus ordinandum: videlicet, quod dicti prior et conventus de sancto Fromundo ecclesiam de Bondeby cum suis pertinentiis inperpetuum in propriis usibus habeant et possideant; salva perpetua vicaria in eadem ecclesia per nos ordinata. Que consistit in toto alteragio ipsius ecclesie et medietate tofti pertinentis ad ecclesiam et in omnibus decimis toftorum et croftorum eiusdem ville. Ad quam vicariam quociens vacaverit, ipse prior et successores sui clericum idoneum nobis et successoribus nostris presentabunt, a nobis et successoribus nostris in ea canonice vicarium perpetuum instituendum. Vicarius autem solvet sinodalia et monachi omnia alia onera illius ecclesie debita et consueta sustinebunt. Ad ecclesiam vero de Saxeby prefatus prior de sancto Fromundo et successores sui inposterum quotiens vacaverit clericum idoneum nobis et successoribus nostris presentabunt, a nobis et successoribus nostris in eadem canonice personam instituendum. Qui ipsam ecclesiam cum omnibus pertinentiis suis tanquam persona possidebit et de omnibus oneribus ordinariis eiusdem ecclesie respondebit: reddendo inde dictis monachis, nomine perpetui beneficii, unam marcam annuatim ad duos terminos, scilicet, ad festum sancti Michaelis dimidiam marcam, et ad Ascensionem Domini dimidiam marcam; salvis in omnibus tam super utraque dictarum ecclesiarum quam super memorata vicaria episcopalibus consuetudinibus et Linc' ecclesie dignitate. Quod ut perpetuam obtineat firmitatem, presenti scripto sigillum nostrum duximus apponendum. Hiis testibus: Petro de Bath', canonico Linc', Radulfo de Warravill', canonico Wellen', Willelmo de Winchecumba, magistro Iohanne de Winton', Ricardo de Oxon', et Oliuero de Chedneto, clericis. Dat' per manum Thome de Fiskerton' cappellani, canonici Linc', apud Berencestr' quinto nonas Martii pontificatus nostri anno duodecimo.

This is presumably the confirmation of Bp Hugh referred to in *RHW* iii 178, although the participation of the cathedral chapter is not noted in this *actum*; this confirmation is also mentioned ibid. 95.

155. Holyoak (parish of Lyddington)

Grant to Robert Abbe of Drayton of the wardship of William, son and heir of John of Holyoak, and of all the land which he held of the bishop in Holyoak [in Lyddington parish], save for the dowry of John's wife, while she lives, and the bishop's service. He is also granted the maritagium *of the said William, without disparagement.* Lyddington, 31 March 1221

    B = LAO Wells roll ix, m. ld.
    Pd *RHW* ii 195.

Hiis testibus: Petro de Bath', Willelmo capellano de Lidinton', Roberto de Brinchirst', Willelmo filio eius, Hugone de Haliach, Roberto filio Willelmi de Meldeburn', Willelmo fratre eius, Willelmo filio Roberti, Roberto le Sauser, Ricardo filio Willelmi, Laurentio clerico et aliis. Dat' per manum Thome de Fiskerton' capellani, canonici Linc', apud Lidint' ii kalendas Aprilis pontificatus nostri anno xii°.

156. Flamstead priory

Grant, with the assent of Roger the dean and the chapter of Lincoln, to the prioress and nuns of Woodchurch [alias Flamstead] of a pension of three marks a year, in the name of a perpetual benefice, from the parson of the church of Dallington, which is of their patronage, together with the annual pension of two marks which they are already accustomed to receive from the church. Lincoln, in chapter, 12 April 1221

    B = LAO Wells roll ix, m. 1. C = Hertfordshire Archives and Local Studies,
        ms.17465 (Flamstead cartulary), fo. [14v]. s. xiii med.
    Pd from B in *RHW* ii 191.

Hiis testibus: Rogero decano, Galfrido precentore, Ricardo cancellario, Roberto Norh', Roberto Huntingdon'[a], Reimundo[b] Leirc', Willelmo Buking', et Hugone Stowe archidiaconis, Iohanne subdecano, Galfrido de Bocland'[c] Martino de Patt'hull'[d], magistris Willelmo filio Fulconis, Gilberto de Scardeburg' et Ricardo de Lindwod'[e], Rogero de Bristoll', cappellanis[f], magistro Ada de sancto Edmundo, Petro de Hungar', Willelmo de Avalon'[g], magistro Waltero de Well'[h], Petro de Bath'[i], Rogero de Bohun' et Petro de Cheuremunt', canonicis Linc', et Olivero de Chedn'[j], clerico. Dat' per manum Thome de Fiskerton' capellani[k], canonici Linc', in capitulo Linc' apud[l] Linc' pridie idus Aprilis pontificatus nostri anno xii°.[m]

    [a] Huntingd'ne C.   [b] Reymundo C.   [c] Boclande C.   [d] Patteshull' C.   [e] Lindwode
    C.   [f] capellanis C.   [g] Avalan' C.   [h] Wellis C.   [i] Bathon' C.   [j] Chedneto C.
    [k] cappellani C.   [l] aput C.   [m] duodecimo C.

This grant of Bp Hugh is mentioned in *RHW* iii 95.

157. Flamstead priory

Institution of Martin nepos of Martin of Pattishall, clerk, to the church of Dallington, on the presentation of the prioress and nuns of Woodchurch [alias Flamstead], saving to the priory an annual pension of three marks together with the two marks a year which was previously paid by the parson of the church, in the name of a perpetual benefice.   Nettleham, 19 April 1221

> B = LAO Wells roll ix, m. 1.

Omnibus etc. Noverit universitas vestra nos, ad presentationem dilectarum in Cristo filiarum priorisse et monialium de Wudecherch' patronarum ecclesie de Daylinton', dilectum in Cristo filium Martinum nepotem domini Martini de Patteshull', clericum, ad eandem ecclesiam admisisse et ipsum in eadem canonice personam instituisse, salvis dicte priorisse et monialibus tribus marcis annuis de eadem ecclesia, una cum duabus marcis quas annuatim de ea prius percipere consueverunt per manum persone ipsius ecclesie nomine perpetui beneficii percipiendis, salvis etiam in omnibus episcopalibus consuetudinibus etc. Quod ut perpetuam obtineat firmitatem, presenti scripto sigillum nostrum duximus apponendum. Hiis testibus: magistro Stephano de Cicestr', domino Martino de Patteshull', Petro de Bath', canonicis Linc', magistro Nicholao de Evesham', canonico Wellen', magistris Willelmo de Cant' et Amaurico de Buggeden', Olivero de Chedneto, Ricardo de Oxon' et Willelmo de Winchecumba, clericis. Dat' per manum Thome de Fiskerton' cappellani, canonici Linc', apud Nettelham xiii kalendas Maii pontificatus nostri anno xii.

> This entry was omitted in the printed edition of the rolls: it should immediately precede the Rothwell entry (*RHW* ii 192). The institution is recorded in the institution roll (ibid. 102), from which it appears that the advowson had been in dispute. See no. 156 for the grant of an additional pension.

158. Charwelton church

Recital of a mandate of the legate, Pandulph, dated at Reading on 3 June, informing the bishop that he has conferred the church of Charwelton, formerly held by Ulian, steward of the abbot of Westminster, on his own clerk, master Bernard, and requesting the latter's induction, saving the right of the true patron of the church. By virtue of this mandate the bishop has caused master Bernard to be inducted by the archdeacon.   Northampton, 7 June 1221

> B = LAO Wells roll ix, m. 2 (no witnesses).
> Pd *RHW* ii 195.

Dat' per manum Thome de Fiskerton', capellani, canonici Linc', apud Norh' vii idus Iunii pontificatus nostri anno xii°.

159. Wansford bridge

Indulgence of ten days to all those who contribute to the repair of Wansford bridge. This indulgence is to last for two years and is not valid outside Wansford.   Lyddington, 30 July 1221

> B = LAO Wells roll ix, m. 2d (no witnesses).
> Pd *RHW* ii 195–6.

Dat' per manum Thome de Fiskerton' capellani, canonici Linc', apud Lidinton' iii⁰ kalendas Augusti pontificatus nostri anno xii⁰.

160. Cirencester abbey

Institution of William of Rothwell, chaplain, to the perpetual vicarage of Roth-well, on the presentation of the abbot and convent of Cirencester. The vicarage consists of the whole altarage of the church and two chapels of St Mary, Rothwell, and Orton, except the entire tithing of wool and half the tithing of lambs, when the lambs are in such numbers that the tenth lamb could be brought. If on account of the paucity of lambs the tenth has to be bought with silver then that silver shall be given for the use of the vicar. The vicar shall have the manse beside the church, which belonged to Roger Marchand, and he shall provide hospitality for the archdeacon and bear all ordinary charges of the church and chapels.

Lyddington, 2 August 1221

> B = LAO Wells roll ix, m. 1. C = Oxford, Bodl. ms. dep. C393 (Cirencester cartu-lary) fo. 205r in a confirmation by Bp Richard Gravesend, 14 February 1278). s. xiv ex.
> Pd from B in *RHW* ii 192; from C in *Cirencester Cartulary* iii no. 861.

Hiis testibus: Roberto archidiacono Huntingd'ᵃ et Matheo archidiacono Oxon', magistro Waltero de Well' et Petro de Bathon', canonicis Linc', magistro Wil-lelmo de Cant', Willelmo de Cava et Olivero de Chedn', clericis.ᵇ Dat' per manum Thome de Fiskerton' capellani, canonici Linc', apud Lidint'ᶜ iiiiᵗᵒ nonas Augusti pontificatus nostri anno xii⁰.

> ᵃ Huntingdon' C.   ᵇ *omitted* C.   ᶜ Lydint' C.

161. Peterborough abbey

Institution of Adam of Pilsgate, clerk, to the perpetual vicarage of Maxey, on the presentation of the abbot and convent of Peterborough. The vicarage consists of the altar offerings and small tithes, the manse and the garb tithes of la Haum. The vicar shall bear all ordinary and customary burdens of the church.

Lyddington, 5 August 1221

> B = LAO Wells roll ix, m. 1.
> Pd *RHW* ii 192.

Hiis testibus: Matheo archidiacono Oxon', magistro Waltero de Well', canonico Linc', Radulfo de Warravill', canonico Wellen', Willelmo de Winchecumb', Wil-lelmo de Tintehell' et Olivero de Chedn', clericis. Dat' per manum Thome de Fiskerton' cappellani, canonici Linc', apud Liddinton' nonis Augusti pontificatus nostri anno xii⁰.

> The institution is recorded on the eleventh membrane of Wells roll x, *c.* 1217 x 1218 (ibid. i 90, cf. Smith, 'Rolls'). The vicarage was ordained by St Hugh (*EEA* 4 nos. 152–3).

162.   Sibbertoft church

Collation, by authority of the Council, of the church of Sibbertoft to master William Blund of Lincoln, saving in future the right of the patron.

Lyddington, 8 August 1221

B = LAO Wells roll ix, m. 1.
Pd *RHW* ii 193.

Hiis testibus: Matheo archidiacono Oxon', magistro Willelmo de Cant', magistro Waltero de Well' et Petro de Bath', canonicis Linc', Radulfo de Warravill', canonico Wellen', Willelmo de Winchecumba, Willelmo de Tintehell', Ricardo de Oxon' et Olivero de Chedn', clericis. Dat' per manum Thome de Fiskerton' capellani, canonici Linc', apud Lidinton' sexto idus Augusti pontificatus nostri anno xii°.

> The collation is recorded in the institution rolls ibid. 104. There it is recorded that the abbot and convent of Sulby claimed the patronage in the king's court and that subsequently master William was instituted on their presentation.

163.   Pickworth church

Institution of Nicholas de Hegham, clerk, to the church of Pickworth, on the presentation of William de Gigneto, knight.

House of the Templars, Witham, 12 August 1221

B = LAO Wells roll ix, m. 1.
Pd *RHW* ii 193.

Hiis testibus[a]: Matheo archidiacono Oxon', magistro Waltero de Well' et Petro de Bath', canonicis Linc', Radulfo de Warravill', canonico Wellen', magistro Willelmo de Cant', Ricardo de Oxon', Willelmo de Tintehell' et Olivero de Chedn', clericis. Dat' per manum Thome de Fiskerton' cappellani, canonici Linc', apud domum fratrum Militie Templi iuxta Widm' pridie idus Augusti pontificatus nostri anno xii°.

> [a] *word omitted* B.

> The institution is recorded in the institution rolls among entries for the bp's tenth pontifical year, 20 December 1218 x 19 December 1219 (ibid. i 167–8).

164.   Pipewell abbey

Institution of master Laurence of Stanwick, clerk, to the church of Ashley, on the presentation of the abbot and convent of Pipewell.

Kilsby, 27 September [1221]

B = LAO Wells roll ix, m. 1.
Pd *RHW* ii 194.

Hiis testibus: Matheo archidiacono Oxon', magistro Stephano de Cicestr', canonico Linc', magistro Nicholao de Evesh', canonico Wellen', Willelmo de[a] Winchelcumb', Willelmo de[a] Tinthill', Ricardo de Oxon' et Olivero de Chedn', clericis. Dat' per manum Thome de Fiskert' capellani, canonici Linc', apud Kildeb' v kalendas Octobris.

ª *word omitted* B.

This institution is placed among entries for the bp's twelfth pontifical year in the charter roll but in the institution roll is recorded on the ninth membrane of Wells roll x, *c.*1217 x 1218 (ibid. i 63; cf. Smith, 'Rolls').

*165.　Geoffrey de Lucy

Letters of the bishop (and the bishops of Salisbury and Worcester) issued in connection with the protection granted to Geoffrey de Lucy by Pope Honorius III.
[17 June 1221 x Michaelmas term 1221]

Mention of letters in *CRR* x 240, in a case between Geoffrey and William de Brigwar' about one carucate of land in Newington near Sittingbourne, Michaelmas term 1221: 'Profert etiam quasdam litteras episcoporum Sarresbiriensis, Wigorniensis et Lincolniensis, in quibus continentur hec verba: Honorius episcopus etc. venerabilibus fratribus in Cristo Sarresbiriensi, Wigorniensi, Lincolniensi episcopis salutem etc. Quia, licet dilectus filius nobilis vir Galfridus de Luci redierit de partibus transmarinis, congruit tamen illi quia dimisit ibidem interim bellatores, nos, volentes ob reverentiam crucis ipsum prosequi gratia speciali, personam suam cum omnibus bonis suis que in presentiarum rationabiliter duximus sub beati Petri et nostra protectione duximus admittendam, statuentes ut ea omnia usque ad annum et dimidium integra maneant et quieta consistant, ac si personaliter existeret in servitio Ihesu Cristi etc.' In the entry the date of the papal protection is given as 21 June 1221.

166.　Rockingham church

Institution of Peter of Wakering, clerk, to the church of Rockingham, on the presentation of King Henry III.　　　Dorchester, 22 November 1221

B = LAO Wells roll ix, m. 2.
Pd *RHW* ii 194.

Hiis testibus: domino Ioscelino Bathon' episcopo, magistro Willelmo de Linc', canonico Linc', Rogero capellano, Radulfo de Warevill' et Gileberto de Dulting', canonicis Wellens', Willelmo de Winchelcumb', Ricardo de Oxon' et Olivero de Chedn', clericis. Dat' per manum Thome de Fiskerton capellani, canonici Linc', apud Dorkecestr' decimo kalendas Decembris pontificatus nostri anno duodecimo.

The institution is recorded in the institution rolls (ibid. 105).

167.　Godstow abbey

Ordination, by authority of the [Lateran] Council, of perpetual vicarages in the churches of [High] Wycombe, Bloxham and St Giles, Oxford, and institution of perpetual vicars in them, on the presentation of the abbess and convent of Godstow.　　　Cropredy, 12 December 1221

B = PRO E164/20 (Godstow cartulary) fos. 17v–18r (5v–6r). s. xv in. C = Oxford, Bodl. ms. Rawlinson B 408 (Godstow cartulary, English version) fo. 16v. s. xv ex.
Pd from C in *Godstow English Register* ii no. 871.

Omnibus Cristi fidelibus ad quos presens scriptum pervenerit, Hugo Dei gratia Linc' episcopus salutem in domino. Ad universitatis vestre notitiam volumus pervenire nos vicarias perpetuas in ecclesiis de Wycumba, de Bloxham et de sancto Egidio Oxon', auctoritate concilii, ordinasse et ad presentationem dilectarum in Cristo filiarum abbatisse et monialium de Godestowa ad ipsas vicarias sic ordinatas perpetuos vicarios admisisse et in eisdem instituisse. Sunt autem predicte vicarie ordinate in hunc modum: scilicet, quod vicarius perpetuus ecclesie de Wycumb' habebit nomine vicarie sue mansum ei assignatum ab occidente domus abbatisse in Wycumb' et medietatem omnium oblationum et obventionum altaris cum tota decima casei et omnibus ovis in vigilia Pasche ad ipsam ecclesiam provenientibus et omnibus decimis aucarum et omnibus decimis gardinorum et ortorum infra burgum, exceptis oblationibus et obventionibus quatuor dierum per annum, scilicet, diei Purificationis, diei Parasceves, diei Pasche et diei Exaltationis Sancte Crucis, et exceptis omnibus decimis lane, lini, agnorum, purcellorum et vitulorum, cum vitulus integer obvenerit, et exceptis omnibus decimis fructuum, gardinorum et hortorum extra burgum et tota decima cardorum qui ad officium fullonum pertinent, tam infra burgum quam extra, exceptis etiam omnibus ovis extra vigiliam Pasche ad ipsam ecclesiam provenientibus et omni oblatione candele per totum annum, preter candelam que provenit die dominica ad altare cum pane benedicto: que omnia superius excepta ad abbatissam et moniales de Godestowa integre pertinebunt. Vicarius vero perpetuus ecclesie de Blokesham habebit nomine vicarie sue totum alteragium illius ecclesie et capelle de Middelcumba, exceptis decimis lane et agnorum matricis ecclesie de Blokesham. Habebit etiam bladum quod solet dari trituratum dictis ecclesie de Blokesham et capelle de Middilcumba quod vocatur Cherecheset. Et habebit mansum quod situm est inter mansum quod fuit Pagani de Bereford' et mansum quod fuit Willelmi Coleman. [fo.18r] Vicarius autem perpetuus ecclesie sancti Egidii in Oxon' habebit nomine vicarie sue medietatem totius alteragii illius ecclesie cum tota decima hortorum, exceptis lana et lino et agnis et excepta candela die Purificationis beate Virginis, que dicte moniales in solidum percipient. Habebit insuper mansum ubi capellanus ecclesie solebat habitare pro quo vicarius solvet ipsi ecclesie sex denarios annuatim. In hiis autem tribus vicariis sic ordinatis prefate moniales omnia onera ordinaria dictarum trium ecclesiarum de vita et consueta sustinebunt, preter sinodalia que vicarii persolvent. Omnes vero vicarii quotiens ad vicarias predictas fuerint admissi memoratis monialibus iuramentum prestabunt fidelitatis. Capellani etiam si quos predicti vicarii in adiutorium suum receperint ad ministrandum secum in dictis ecclesiis similiter iurabunt coram vicariis et procuratore monialium quem ad hoc illuc transmiserint, quod fideles eis erunt quamdiu ibi fuerint, in hiis que ipsas in ecclesiis illis contingunt: salvis in omnibus episcopalibus consuetudinibus et Lincolniensis ecclesie dignitate. Et in huius rei testimonium, presenti scripto sigillum nostrum duximus apponendum. Hiis testibus: Roberto archidiacono Huntingdon', magistro Willelmo de Linc', can(onico), magistris Willelmo de Cant', Hugone de Greneford' et Nicholao de Evesham, Willelmo de Winchecumba et Olivero de Chedneto, clericis. Dat' per manum Thome de Fiskerton' capellani, canonici Linc', apud Cropperiam pridie idus Decembris pontificatus nostri anno duodecimo.

168. Hugh of Boulogne

Notification that all the property of Hugh of Boulogne, knight, a crusader, has been taken into the bishop's protection in accordance with the privilege of crusaders.   [20 December 1220 x 19 December 1221]

> B = LAO Wells roll ix, m. 2d (no witnesses or date), among entries of the twelfth pontifical year.
> Pd *RHW* ii 196.

*169. Elstow abbey

Charter to the nuns of Elstow about the church of Westoning.
                    [20 December 1220 x 19 December 1221]

> Mentioned in the list of churches, pensions and rents granted by Bp Hugh to the religious in LAO Wells roll xi, pd *RHW* iii 96, dated to the bp's twelfth pontifical year. The list also mentions ten shillings from the mill of 'Buggeden' (unidentified, ? Buckden, Bowden). It is not clear whether this pension was the subject of a separate charter or formed part of this present document.

*170. Hospitallers

Charter for the Hospitallers of the advowson of the church of Eaton [Socon].
                    [20 December 1220 x 19 December 1221]

> Mentioned in the list of churches, pensions and rents granted by Bp Hugh to the religious in LAO Wells roll xi, pd *RHW* iii 95, dated to the bp's twelfth pontifical year.

*171. Westminster abbey

Charter to the abbot and convent of Westminster about a mediety of the church of Wheathampstead.   [20 December 1220 x 19 December 1221]

> Mentioned in the list of churches, pensions and rents granted by Bp Hugh to the religious in LAO Wells roll xi, pd *RHW* iii 96, dated to the bp's twelfth pontifical year.

*172. Sixhills priory

Charter to the nuns of Sixhills about the church of Cadeby.
                    [20 December 1220 x 19 December 1221]

> Mentioned in the list of churches, pensions and rents granted by Bp Hugh to the religious in LAO Wells roll xi, pd *RHW* iii 92, dated to the bp's twelfth pontifical year. The ordination of Cadeby vicarage was carried out by master Reginald of Chester, the bp's Official, during the bp's ninth pontifical year, 20 December 1217 x 19 December 1218 (*Lib. Ant.* 57, 66).

80 THE ACTA OF HUGH OF WELLS

*173. Beauport abbey

Charter to the abbot and convent of Beauport, granting twenty shillings from the church of Waltham, one mark from the church of Beelsby, half a mark from the church of Brigsley, half a mark from the church of Hatcliffe, two shillings from the church of Beesby; and the church of West Ravendale.

[20 December 1220 x 19 December 1221]

Mentioned in the list of churches, pensions and rents granted by Bp Hugh to the religious in LAO Wells roll xi, pd *RHW* iii 95, dated to the bp's twelfth pontifical year.

174. Kingsthorpe, Holy Trinity hospital outside Northampton

Confirmation, with the assent of Robert de Bray and Walter of Pattishall, patrons of the church of Bletsoe, and of Martin of Pattishall, the parson, of the confirmation of Bishop W(illiam) of Blois [EEA 4 no. 270] to the master and brethren of the hospital of the Holy Trinity, Northampton, of an annual pension of four silver marks from the church of Bletsoe, in the name of a perpetual benefice. This pension is to be paid by Martin and his successors as parsons in two equal instalments at Easter and Michaelmas; also confirmation of two acres of wood in the wood of Overheya, namely, those which are near the curia of Robert Page, hermit, the whole hermitage which Robert the hermit held, with all that plot of land (placea) in front of Robert's gate where the barn (grangia) of Henry son of Peter was situated, and all the other land which the above hospital has in alms from the free men of Bletsoe (namely,two acres of the gift of Hugh Pipard, five acres of the gift of Stephen son of Robert, eight acres of the gift of William Sly, one acre of the gift of Gervase of Bletsoe, three acres of the gift of William Pepin, thirteen acres and one rood of the gift of Hugh Trunket, and one acre of the gift of Robert son of Hugh). [20 December 1220 x 19 December 1221]

B = LAO Add. Reg. 6 (Liber antiquus), fo. 32r. s. xiii in.
Pd *Lib. Ant.* 104–5.

Hiis testibus: W. archidiacono Linc', R. archidiacono Hunt'. magistris Stephano de Cic', W. de Linc' et W. de Well', canonicis Linc'.

The date of this document is confirmed by the list of churches, pensions and grants made by Bp Hugh to the religious in LAO Wells roll xi, pd *RHW* iii 95, in which the confirmation is dated to the bp's twelfth pontifical year. Kingsthorpe hospital was founded in 1200 and the confirmation of Bp William of Blois mentioned above has not survived (cf. *EEA* 4 no. 270). A final concord of 13 Oct. 1219 survives between Robert de Broy and Walter of Pattishall against John the master of the hospital over the advowson of Bletsoe church. The master recognised it to be the right of Robert and Walter and also quitclaimed to them his right in lands and woods (39 acres of arable land in the field called Bolnohcroft and 9 acres of wood in Overehey wood). With consent of Bp Hugh, Robert and Walter granted the wood to the master, and four silver marks a year in the name of a perpetual benefice, to be received yearly from the parson. Also two acres of wood in Overehey wood, namely those standing next to the court of Robert Perage *sic*, the hermit, the hermitage etc. just as above. When this agreement was made the bp of Lincoln was present and consenting *(Bedfordshire Feet of Fines* pp. 55–6, no. 234).

*175.   Templars

Charter to the Templars granting ten marks a year from the church of Caythorpe.
[?20 December 1220 x 19 December 1221]

Mentioned in the list of churches, pensions and rents granted by Bp Hugh to the religious in LAO Wells roll xi, pd *RHW* iii 93, but without reference to the bp's pontifical year. However, the twelfth year seems most probable since the 1220 x 1221 institution of master Benedict to Caythorpe (ibid. 110) ends with the sentence: 'Dominus episcopus et capitulum Linc' confirmaverunt ipsis Templariis de ecclesia de Cattorp' quinque marcas annuas, quas prius habuerunt, et alias quinque marcas eis de novo concessas'.

176.   Dunstable priory

Grant, made with the assent of Roger the dean and the chapter of Lincoln, to the prior and convent of Dunstable of twenty shillings a year, in the name of a perpetual benefice, from the church of St Mary, Bedford. This pension is to be paid by master Alan, the parson of the church, and his successors.
[20 December 1220 x 19 December 1221]

B = BL ms. Harl. 1885 (Dunstable cartulary) fo. 72v. s. xiii in.
Pd (calendar), *Dunstable Cartulary* no. 875.

Omnibus Hugo episcopus Lincol' salutem. Noverit universitas vestra nos, de assensu dilectorum filiorum Rogeri decani et capituli nostri Linc', divine pietatis intuitu dedisse et concessisse dilectis in Cristo filiis priori et conventui de Dunstapl' xx solidos annuos de ecclesia sancte Marie de Bedeford'[a], nomine perpetui[b] beneficii, per manum magistri Alani persone eiusdem ecclesie et successorum suorum percipiendos in duobus terminis anni, scilicet, in sinodo Pasche x solidos et in sinodo sancti Michaelis x solidos; salvis in omnibus episcopalibus consuetudinibus etc.

[a] Dunstapl' *crossed out.*   [b] perpetue B

The annals of Dunstable (admittedly not always very reliable in matters of chronology) date the appropriation of this church and the institution of master Alan to the year 1217 (*Ann. mon.* iii 52), but the list in *RHW* iii 95 gives the date of issue of this grant as being the twelfth pontifical year of Bp Hugh, 20 December 1220 x 19 December 1221.

177.   Harthey

Ordination, with the assent of Roger the dean and chapter of Lincoln, in settlement of a dispute between Robert archdeacon of Huntingdon, canon of the prebend of Brampton, and Walter son of Robert, knight, whereby the bishop grants his licence to Walter to build a chapel for himself at the place called Harthey and to have a chantry there for himself and his heirs.
Lincoln, 25 December 1221

A = LAO Lincoln D & C doct. Dij/72/2/10. Endt: Herteie in prebenda de Bramton' (s. xiii) The charter is indented and C Y R O G R A P H V M is written through the indentations. No surviving seal. Two parchment seal-tags and a slit for a third seal-tag. size: 238 mm x 197 mm.

B = LAO Lincoln D & C A/1/5 (Registrum Antiquissimum), no. 234, fos. 43v–44r. s. xiii in.
Pd from A in *Reg. Ant.* ii no. 376.

Omnibus Cristi fidelibus ad quos presens scriptum pervenerit, Hugo Dei gratia Linc' episcopus salutem in domino. Noverit universitas vestra quod cum inter dilectum filium Robertum archidiaconum Huntingdon', canonicum prebende de Bramton', ex una parte et Walterum filium Roberti militem ex altera, super quadam capella quam idem miles sibi voluit construere in loco qui dicitur Herthey, quem quidem locum idem archidiaconus ad suam prebendam de Bramton' iure parochiali asseruit pertinere questio verteretur. Tandem utraque pars inde mera et spontanea voluntate appellatione et contradictione cessantibus, se nostre submiserit ordinationi. Nos autem super premissis, de assensu et voluntate Rogeri decani et capituli nostri Linc', ordinavimus in hunc modum: videlicet quod liceat prefato militi libere suis sumptibus sibi capellam construere in predicto loco qui dicitur Herthey matrici ecclesie de Bramton' cum omnibus ad predictum locum de Herthey pertinentibus pleno iure parochiali subiectam; et quod idem W. et heredes sui habeant inperpetuum cantariam suam in eadem per capellanum ibidem residentem quamdiu voluerint et ministrantem. Licebit autem eidem militi et heredibus suis ad hoc sibi eligere capellanum idoneum successive quem voluerint. Quo electo et dicto archidiacono vel successoribus suis qui pro tempore fuerint canonici apud Bramton' per eundem militem vel heredes suos presentato, idem archidiaconus et successores sui ipsum sine contradictione et difficultate admittent ad divinum officium in sepedicta capella ut dictum est exequendum. Concessit autem idem archidiaconus ad onera eiusdem militis et heredum suorum quoad exhibitionem capellani in dicta capella ministrantis ab eis faciendam levius sustentanda, omnes minutas decimas et oblationes provenientes tam de domo dicti militis quam de tenentibus ipsius si processu temporis aliqui fuerint apud Herthey: salvis omnibus decimis garbarum integre et sine diminutione matrici ecclesie de Bramton' de predicto loco de Herthey provenientibus; salvo etiam dicte ecclesie primo et principali legato cum honore sepulture. Sustinebunt etiam dictus W. et heredes sui omnia alia onera eiusdem capelle tam in libris, vestimentis quam in omnibus aliis generaliter ad divinum officium in sepedicta capella exequendum pertinentibus, et quoad ipsam capellam sustentandam et reficiendam. Dicti vero tenentes matricem ecclesiam de Bramton' bis in anno visitabunt, scilicet, die Pasche et die beate Marie Magdalene et omnia ecclesiastica sacramenta percipient de eadem. Similiter et dictus miles et maiores de familia sua eandem ecclesiam bis in anno visitabunt, scilicet, die Pentec' et die beate Marie Magdalene. Iurabunt etiam idem W. et heredes sui qui pro tempore fuerint quod memoratam matricem ecclesiam de Bramton' secundum formam premissam quoad predictam capellam conservabunt indempnem et quod in eadem capella nullum parochianum eiusdem ecclesie aliter quam ut predictum est vel etiam alterius procurabunt vel quantum in ipsis erit scienter sustinebunt in preiudicium matricis ecclesie de Bramt' vel vicinarum ecclesiarum admitti, et hoc idem iurabit presbiter qui pro tempore celebrabit ibidem; salvis in omnibus episcopalibus consuetudinibus et Linc' ecclesie dignitate. Ut autem hec nostra ordinatio perpetuam optineat firmitatem, presenti scripto sigillum nostrum una cum sigillo predicti capituli nostri Linc' simul cum sigillis partium duximus apponendum. Hiis testibus: Rogero decano, Galfrido precentore, Ricardo cancellario, Reimundo Leirc', Matheo Bukingham' et Hugone Stowe archidiaconis,

Iohanne subdecano, magistris Willelmo filio Fulconis, Gilberto de Scardeburg', Ricardo de Lindwud', Roberto de Gravel', Waltero Blundo, Rogero de Bristoll' et Roberto de Wassingburn' et magistro Stephano de Cicestr', Petro de Hungar', et magistro Willelmo de Linc', Willelmo de Avalon', Petro de Bathon' et Petro de Cheueremunt, canonicis Linc'. Datum [per] manum Thome de Fiskerton' capellani, canonici Linc', in capitulo Linc' apud Linc' octavo kalendas Ianuarii pontificatus nostri anno tertio decimo.

The word in square brackets is supplied from the Antiquissimum version.

178. Westminster abbey

Institution of William of Ashwell, clerk, to the church of Sudborough, on the presentation of the abbot and convent of Westminster, saving to Samson of Ashwell, clerk, his vicarage. Samson shall possess the whole church as long as he lives, paying to William the parson an annual pension of two shillings.

Old Temple, London, 24 January 1222

B = LAO Wells roll ix, m. 2.
Pd *RHW* ii 196–7.

Hiis testibus: Roberto Huntingd', I. Bedef' et Hugone Stowe archidiaconis, magistris Ada de sancto Edmundo et Willelmo de Linc', canonicis Linc', magistris Willelmo de Cant', Nicholao de Evesh' et Amaurico de Buged', Willelmo de Winchelcumb' et Olivero de Chedn', clericis. Dat' per manum Thome de Fiskerton', capellani, canonici Linc', apud Vetus Templum Lond' ix^{no} kalendas Februarii pontificatus nostri anno xiii^{mo}.

The institution is recorded in the institution roll among entries for the bp's twelfth pontifical year, 20 December 1220 x 19 December 1221 (ibid. 105).

179. St Fromond priory

Institution of Roger Andeur', clerk, to the church of Saxby, on the presentation of the prior and convent of St Fromond, saving to the monks an annual pension of one mark, in the name of a perpetual benefice, to be paid by Roger.

Thame, 3 February 1222

B = BL Add. Ch. 66079 (roll of charters of St Fromond priory) m. 1. s. xv.

Omnibus Cristi fidelibus ad quos presens scriptum pervenerit, Hugo Dei gratia Lincoln' episcopus salutem in domino. Noverit universitas vestra nos, ad presentationem prioris et conventus de sancto Fromundo patronorum ecclesie de Saxeby, dilectum in Cristo filium Rogerum Andeur' clericum ad eandem ecclesiam admisisse, ipsumque in ea canonice personam instituisse; salva dictis monachis una marca annua per manum eiusdem Rogeri nomine perpetui beneficii persolvenda de ecclesia memorata, scilicet, in festo sancti Michaelis dimidia marca et in festo Ascensionis dimidia marca; salvis etiam in omnibus episcopalibus consuetudinibus et Lincoln' ecclesie dignitate. Quod ut perpetuam optineat firmitatem, presenti scripto sigillum nostrum duximus apponendum. Hiis testibus: Roberto archidiacono Norhampton', magistris Willelmo de Linc', Willelmo Cant' et Amaurico de Buggeden', Radulfo de Warravill', canonico Wellen', Ricardo de Oxon', Willelmo de Winchecomb', et Olivero de Chedneto, cleric(is).

Dat' per manum Thome de Fiskerton'[a], capellani, apud Tham' tertio nonas Februarii pontificatus nostri anno tertiodecimo.

[a] Filkerton' *originally written* B, *then altered to Fiskerton'*.

The institution of Roger de Andevre to Saxby is recorded in *RHW* iii 113.

180. Woburn manor

Inspeximus of the final concord made on 20 January 1222 between the bishop and Oliver de Aencurt concerning the manor of Woburn. Oliver has acknowledged the manor to be the right of the bishop, and moreover has quitclaimed to him ten pounds' worth of land there, namely the third part of his own demesne in the village; and the homage of Robert son of Simon in respect of two and a half virgates, namely, six shillings a year and foreign service and certain villeins and their services. For this the bishop has granted the rest of the manor to Oliver, to hold by the service of two knights, in which shall be reckoned the foreign service which belongs to the land of Robert son of Simon. Oliver has released to the bishop his right in the advowson of the church of the manor, and in the manors of Lyddington, Holme [Spinney} and Corby, in the land of Hungate [in Lincoln], and in three bovates in Cotham, and the lands lying in the fields of Cotham which belong to Balderton. Oliver's wife, Nicholaa, was present in court and has released her right of dower in the property.

Lincoln, in chapter, 13 March 1222

B = LAO, Ep. Reg. XX (register of Bp John Chedworth of Lincoln, 1452–71), fo. 88r–v. The original final concord of 20 January 1222 is LAO, Lincoln D. & C. Dj/20/1/8, pd *Reg. Ant.* iii no. 670; with the foot of fine in PRO, Bucks Fines, CP25/1/14/13, no. 10.

Omnibus Cristi fidelibus ad quos presens carta pervenerit, Hugo Dei gratia Lincoln' episcopus salutem in domino. Noverit universitas vestra quod cum placitum esset in curia domini regis inter nos et Oliverum de Dencourt de toto manerio de Woubourn cum pertinentiis excepta advocatione eiusdem ecclesie eiusdem ville quam antea et tunc habuimus finalis concordia facta est in curia memorata inter nos in forma subscripta: Hec est finalis concordia facta in curia domini regis apud Westm' in octabis sancti Hillarii anno regni regis Henrici filii regis Iohannis sexto, coram Hugone[a] de Burgo tunc iusticiario Anglie, Iohanne de Munem', Martino de Patershull', Radulpho Harang, Stephano de Segrava, Thoma de Heyden, Roberto de Lauxton', iusticiariis et aliis fidelibus domini regis tunc ibidem presentibus, inter Lincoln' episcopum Hugonem secundum petentem et Oliverum de Dencourt tenentem de toto manerio de Woubourn cum pertinentiis excepta advocatione ecclesie eiusdem ville de quo manerio cum pertinentiis recognitio magne assise summonita fuit inter eos in prefata curia: scilicet quod predictus Oliverus recognovit totum predictum manerium cum omnibus pertinentiis suis esse ius ipsius episcopi et ecclesie sue Lincoln'. Et preterea concessit, reddidit et quietas clamavit ipsi episcopo et successoribus suis et ecclesie Lincoln' decem libratas terre cum pertinentiis in predicto manerio, scilicet tertiam partem dominici sui in eadem villa sicud dominicum ubique iacet in campis, videlicet in cultura iuxta portam persone, tertiam partem sicut iacet ubique in eadem cultura versus umbram, et in cultura de Welfeweia tertiam partem sicut iacet ubique in eadem cultura versus umbram, et in cultura que vocatur Southfeld iuxta terram

Walteri clerici, tertiam partem sicut iacet ubique in eadem cultura versus solem,
et in cultura iuxta curiam eiusdem Oliveri, tertiam partem sicut iacet ubique in
eadem cultura versus solem, et in cultura que vocatur Toddeshuth tertiam partem
sicut iacet ubique in eadem cultura versus umbram, et in cultura que vocatur
Blakerichecroft tertiam partem sicut iacet ubique in eadem cultura versus
umbram, et in cultura que vocatur Sepecot' tertiam partem sicut iacet ubique in
eadem cultura versus umbram, et in cultura que vocatur Eldesfeld' tertiam
partem sicut [fo. 88v] iacet ubique in eadem cultura versus solem, et tertiam
partem totius prati quod idem Oliverus habuit in eodem manerio, sicut tertia pars
iacet ubique in pratis versus solem, et tertiam partem totius pasture sue ad boves
scilicet versus umbram et preterea decem acras terre de eodem dominico, videlicet illas que iacent in cultura de Eldesfeld' propinquiores terre eiusdem episcopi
quam habet in eadem cultura; et homagium Roberti filii Simonis[b] et heredum
suorum et totum servitium eorundem de duabus virgatis terre et dimidia quas
idem Robertus tenuit de eodem Olivero, scilicet sex solidos per annum et forinsecum servitium, et Osegodum Anastaus cum dimidia virgata terre quam tenet et
cum tota sequela sua; et Willelmum Anastaus cum dimidia virgata terre et uno
crofto que tenet et cum tota sequela sua; et Gaufridum le Paumer et Godfridum le
Paumer cum dimidia virgata terre quam ipsi tenent et cum tota sequela sua; et
Gaufridum de Widemere cum quarta parte unius virgate terre quam tenet et cum
tota sequela sua; et Iordanum le Paumer cum quarta parte unius virgate terre
quam tenet et cum tota sequela sua; et Radulphum berkarium cum quarta parte
unius virgate terre quam tenet et cum tota sequela sua; et Willelmum Strangbog'
et Walterum King cum una virgata terre quam tenent[c] et cum tota sequela sua; et
Willelmum West cum dimidia virgata terre quam tenet et cum tota sequela sua; et
Alexandrum de la Bournhend' et Iohannem fratrem suum cum dimidia virgata
terre et uno molendino cum pertinentiis que ipsi tenent et cum tota sequela
eorum; et Elizabeth[d] filiam Marie cum dimidia acra terre et uno mesuagio cum
pertinentiis que tenet et cum tota sequela sua; et Haghenildam[e] viduam cum
dimidia acra terre et uno mesuagio cum pertinentiis que tenet et cum tota sequela
sua; et Haghenildam[f] viduam cum uno tofto et uno mesuagio cum pertinentiis
que tenet et cum tota sequela sua: habenda et tenenda ipsi episcopo et successoribus suis et ecclesie Lincoln' tanquam liberam, puram et perpetuam elemosinam
suam. Et sciendum quod omnes sequele villanorum predictorum que fuerunt residentes in terra ipsius Oliveri et de eo terram tenentes die quo concordia ista facta
fuit, remanent ipsi Olivero et heredibus suis quiete de ipso episcopo et successoribus suis. Et pro hac recognitione, concessione, redditione et quieta clamatione,
fine et concordia idem episcopus concessit ipsi Olivero totum residuum predicti
manerii de Woubourn cum pertinentiis unde placitum fuit inter eos: habendum et
tenendum ipsi Olivero et heredibus suis de predicto episcopo et successoribus
suis et ecclesia Lincoln' imperpetuum, faciendo inde plenarium servitium
duorum militum pro omni servitio. Sciendum tamen quod idem episcopus et successores sui et homines sui de eo tenentes in eodem manerio habebunt communam pasture sue in communi pastura eiusdem manerii quantum pertinet ad
tenementa que ipsi tenent in eodem manerio quiete absque disturbio ipsius
Oliveri vel heredum suorum. Et sciendum quod forinsecum servitium quantum
pertinet ad duas predictas virgatas terre et dimidiam quas Robertus filius
Simonis[g] tenet quod servitium idem episcopus sibi retinuit, computabitur et
allocabitur ipsi Olivero et heredibus suis infra predictum servitium duorum

militum. Et pro hac concessione idem Oliverus remisit et quietum clamavit de se et heredibus suis ipsi episcopo et successoribus suis et ecclesie Lincoln' totum ius et clameum quod habuit vel habere potuit in advocatione ecclesie predicti manerii et totum ius et clameum quod habuit vel habere potuit in maneriis de Lidington' et de Hulmo cum pertinentiis et in manerio de Corby cum pertinentiis, et in terra de Hundecate cum omnibus pertinentiis suis et in tribus bovatis terre cum pertinentiis in Cotes, et in illis terris que iacent in campis eiusdem ville de Cotes que pertinent ad villam de Baldretona, quam ipse episcopus tenet. Et sciendum quod predictus Robertus filius Simonis[g] presens fuit in eadem curia et cognovit se debere predictum servitium et predicti Osegod Anastaus, Willelmus Anastaus, Gaufridus le Paumer, Godfridus le Paumer, et Gaufridus de Widemere, Iordanus le Paumer, Radulphus berkarius, Willelmus Strangbog', Walterus King, Willelmus West, Alexander de la Bournhend', Iohannes frater eius, Isabella filia Marie, Hawenilda vidua, Raghenilda vidua presentes fuerunt et cognoverunt se esse villanos. Preterea sciendum quod Nicholaa uxor predicti Oliveri presens fuit in eadem curia et hanc concessit et remisit et quietum clamavit ipsi episcopo et successoribus suis et ecclesie Lincoln' totum ius et clameum quod habuit vel habere poterit versus eundem episcopum vel successores suos nomine dotis in predictis terris, tenementis et serviciis que ipsi episcopo remanent[h] per finem istam, si in processu temporis contigerit quod ipsa supervixerit ipsi Olivero. Et sciendum quod idem episcopus remisit[i] et quietum clamavit ipsum Oliverum de arreragiis servitiorum que idem Oliverus cognovit se debere de predicto manerio de Woubourn et similiter de relevio suo. Nos igitur predictam concordiam ratam et gratam habentes, eam de consensu Rogeri decani et capituli nostri Lincoln' episcopali auctoritate confirmavimus et ipsam similiter tam sigillo nostro quam sigillo predicti capituli nostri Lincoln' communivimus. Hiis testibus: Rogero decano, Galfrido precentore, Ricardo cancellario, Roberto Huntingdon, Remundo Linc'[j], et Hugone Stowie archidiaconis, Iohanne subdecano, magistris Willelmo filio Fulconis, Ricardo de Lindewode, Gilberto de Scardeburgo et Roberto de Gravell', Waltero Blundo, Rogero de Bristoll' et Roberto de Wassingburgh', Petro de Hungar', Willelmo de Avelon', magistris Willelmo de Lincoln' et Waltero de Well', Rogero de Bohun et Petro de Cheurmunt', canonicis Lincoln'. Dat' per manum Thoma de Fyskerton' capellani, canonici Lincoln', in capitulo Lincoln' apud Lincoln' tertio idus Martii pontificatus nostri anno xiii[mo].

[a] *recte* Huberto.　　[b] sui B, Simonis *provided from original final concord.*　　[c] tenet B.　　[d] Isabellam *in original final concord.*　　[e] Hawenildam *in original final concord.*　　[f] Ragenildam *in original final concord.*　　[g] suus B, Simonis *provided from original final concord.*　　[h] remanet B.　　[i] requisivit B.　　[j] *sic. Raymond was archdeacon of Leicester.*

181.　Peterborough abbey

Institution of master W(illiam) de Scotere, clerk, to the church of Tinwell, on the presentation of the abbot and convent of Peterborough, saving to the abbey their customary pension.　　　　　　　　　　　　　　Peterborough, 27 March 1222

B = LAO Wells roll ix, m. 2.
Pd *RHW* ii 197.

Hiis testibus: R. archidiacono Huntingdon', magistro W. de Linc' et R. de Waravill', canonicis Linc', magistris Willelmo de Cant', Rogero de Lacok' et Amaurico de Bugenden', Willelmo de Winchecumb', Olivero de Chednet' et Ricardo de Oxon', clericis. Dat' per manum Thome de Fiskerton' capellani, canonici Linc', apud Burg' vi kalendas Aprilis pontificatus nostri anno xiii.

> The institution is recorded ibid. 106, among entries for the bp's twelfth pontifical year, 20 December 1220 x 19 December 1221.

182. Ramsey abbey

Confirmation of the cellarership of Ramsey abbey. Buckden, 5 April 1222

> B = BL ms. Cotton Vespasian E ii (Ramsey cartulary), fo. 39v (34v, 38v). s. xiii med. C = PRO E164/28 (Ramsey cartulary), fos. 195v–196r. s. xiv.
> Pd *Ramsey Cartulary* ii, p. 195, no. cccxx.

Omnibus Cristi fidelibus ad quos presens scriptum pervenerit[a], Hugo Dei gratia Linc' episcopus salutem in domino[b]. Noverit universitas vestra quod cum vacante abbathia Rames'[c] et in manu I.[d] quondam illustris regis Anglie existente tempore quo fuimus electi in episcopum, monachi eiusdem domus celeraria sua per custodes ibi ab eodem domino rege deputatos fuissent destituti. Nos tandem penes eundem dominum regem tempore vacationis optinentes exigente iustitia procurantes quod eadem ipsis monachis fuerat restituta tanquam obedientia ad ipsos pertinens specialiter. Volentes igitur eorundem monachorum indempnitati quantum in nobis est super hiis in posterum provideri, ad instantiam eorum ut assensu et voluntate dilecti in Cristo filii[e] Hugonis eiusdem loci abbatis, [f-]celerariam predictam sicut eam habuerunt ab antiquo et ut eis sicut predictum est[-f] fuerat restituta, episcopali auctoritate eisdem confirmamus, statuentes ne quis ipsis molestiam inferat aut gravamen: salva in omnibus Linc' ecclesie dignitate. Et in huius rei testimonium, presenti scripto sigillum nostrum una cum sigillis tam predicti abbatis quam conventus memorati duximus apponendum. Dat' per manum Thome de Fisketon' capellani, canonici Linc', apud Buggeden' nonas Aprilis pontificatus nostri anno tertiodecimo.

> [a] Omnibus etc. C. [b] salutem C. [c] Ram' C. [d] Iohannis C. [e] B *repeats* in Cristo. [f-f] *in margin* B. [g] Fiskiton' C. [h] Buked' C. [j] xiii C.

> See also no. 4 above.

183. Elstow abbey

Institution of Elias the chaplain to the perpetual vicarage of Harringworth, on the presentation of the abbess and nuns of Elstow. The vicarage consists of the whole altarage, the garb tithes of two virgates of land belonging to the church and the manse to the north of the church which Robert the clerk held at the end of his life. The vicar shall pay synodal dues and the nuns shall provide hospitality for the archdeacon. Lyddington, 9 June 1222

> B = LAO Wells roll ix, m. 2.
> Pd *RHW* ii 197–8.

Hiis testibus: magistris Willelmo de Linc', Nicholao de Evesh' et Radulfo de Waravill', canonicis Linc', magistro Amaurico de Bugeden', Willelmo de Winchecumb' et Olivero de Chedneto, clericis. Dat' per manum Thome de Fiskerton', capellani, canonici Linc', apud Lidinton' v idus Iunii pontificatus nostri anno xiii°.

184.   Stoke Bruerne church

Institution of Adam of Ilchester, clerk, to the church of Stoke [Bruerne], on the presentation of William Brewer.   Old Temple, London, 11 June 1222

> B = LAO Wells roll ix, m. 2.
> Pd *RHW* ii 197.

Hiis testibus: Roberto de Huntingdon', Ada de Oxon' et Iohanne de Bedeford' archidiaconis, magistro Willelmo de Linc', Petro de Bath' et Radulfo de Waravill', canonicis Linc', magistris Willelmo de Cantuar' et Rogero de Lacok', Olivero de Chedn', clerico. Dat' per manum Thome de Fiskerton' capellani, canonici Linc', apud Vetus Templum, London', iii idus Iunii pontificatus nostri anno xiii.

> The institution is recorded ibid. 106, among entries for the bp's twelfth pontifical year, 20 December 1220 x 19 December 1221.

*185.   Chacombe priory

Confirmation to the priory of Chacombe of the gift made by Thomas de Bosevill of the church of Aston [le Walls].   [20 December 1209 x Trinity term 1222]

> Mention of confirmation in *CRR* x 316, in a case between John Joscelin (nephew of Thomas de Bosevill) and the prior of Chacombe over the church, Trinity term 1222: 'Profert etiam confirmationem Hugonis episcopi Lincolniensis, que donum illud confirmat sicut rationabiliter eis facta fuit'.

186.   Salisbury cathedral: Grantham prebend

Grant, made with the assent of Roger the dean and the chapter of Lincoln, to master William of Ingoldsby, canon of the prebend of Grantham [in Salisbury cathedral] and his successors, of the chapel of Towthorpe with its appurtenances: saving the portion of Adam son of Reginald Ailsi, clerk, who shall hold the chapel during his lifetime, paying to William and his successors as prebendaries an annual pension of four shillings.   Lincoln, in chapter, 15 August 1222

> B = Salisbury D. & C. Liber Evidentiarum C fo. lviir, no. 183. s.xiii ex. C = Trowbridge, Salisbury dioc. records, Liber Evidentiarum B fo. 1r, no. 146. ss. xiv–xv. D = ibid. Liber Ruber fo. 42r, no. 146. ss. xiv–xv.
> Pd from B in *Salisbury Charters* no. cxxxvii.

Hiis testibus: Rogero decano, Galfrido precentore, Ricardo cancellario, Iohanne subdecano, Reymundo Leyrc', Ada Oxon', Hugone Stowe[a] archidiaconis, Willelmo Wellar', Hugone Bath' archidiaconis, magistris Willelmo[b] filio Fulconis, Roberto de Gravel'[c] et Giliberto[d] de Scardebrig'[e], Waltero Blundo, Rogero de Bristoll', Stephano de Cycestr', Petro de Hungar', magistris Willelmo de Linc'[f], Roger de Lacoc,[g] Nicholao de Evesham, Waltero de Well', Rogero de Bohun, Petro de Cheuremon[h], Radulfo de Warivill'[i], canonicis Linc'.[j] Dat'[k] per manum Thome de Fiskaton'[l] capellani, canonici Linc'[m], in capitulo Linc'[j] apud Lincol' xviii kalendas Septembris pontificatus nostri anno tertiodecimo[n].

a Nowe B.   b *word omitted* D.   c Gravell' D.   d Gilberto CD. e Scardeburg' CD.
f Lync' C.   g Lacok' D.   h Cheremon CD.   i Warevill' CD.   j Lync' CD.
k Datum C.   l Fiskton' CD.   m Lync' canonici CD.   n xiii D.

Grantham was divided into two cathedral prebends, and William of Ingoldsby held
the prebend of Grantham Borealis (cf. *RHW* iii 125, 190; *Fasti Salisbury,* pp. 71–2).

187. Castle Acre priory

*Grant, with the assent of Roger the dean and the chapter of Lincoln, to the prior
and monks of Castle Acre, in the name of a perpetual benefice, of all tithes of
sheaves, of corn and of vegetables of the whole parish of Fleet, with certain
exceptions, together with ten measures of salt to be paid by the parson. The
remainder shall be possessed by the parson who will be instituted on the presentation of the priory.*   Lincoln, in chapter, 15 August 1222

B = BL Harley ms. 2110 (Castle Acre cartulary), fo. 122v. s. xiii med.

Omnibus Cristi fidelibus[a] ad quos presens scriptum pervenerit, Hugo Dei gratia
Linc' episcopus salutem in domino. Noverit universitas vestra nos, de assensu
Rogeri decani et capituli nostri Linc', dedisse et concessisse priori et monachis
de Castellacra omnes decimas garbarum bladi et leguminum totius parrochie de
Flet', exceptis decimis garbarum de dominico ecclesie et exceptis decimis garbarum tam bladi quam leguminum de ortis totius parrochie de Flet' predicte integre
et sine diminutione, et propterea decem middos salis quos antiquitus percipere
consueverunt per manum eius qui pro tempore fuerit persona ecclesie de Flet'
percipiendos, cum manso ex occidentali parte ecclesie constituto, nomine perpetui beneficii habenda in proprios usus in perpetuum possidenda. Totum autem
residuum scilicet, tam alteragium quam tota terra pertinens ad ecclesiam cum
decimis eiusdem terre, redditus, decima feni et salis et generaliter omnes alii
proventus eiusdem ecclesie cum manso competente, cedent in usus illius qui pro
tempore fuerit persona ecclesie memorate, ad eorundem prioris et monachorum
presentationem a diocesano loci admittendus. Qui omnia onera eiusdem ecclesie
ordinaria sustinebit; de extraordinariis vero utraque pars pro sua portione respondebit. Salvis in omnibus tam supra predicta portione monachorum quam super
aliis ad ipsam ecclesiam pertinentibus episcopalibus consuetudinibus et Linc'
ecclesie dignitate. Quod ut perpetuam optineat firmitatem, presenti scripto sigillum nostrum una cum sigillo predicti capituli nostri Linc' duximus apponendum.
Hiis testibus: Rogero decano, Galfrido precentore, Ricardo cancellario, Iohanne
subdecano, Reimundo Leirc', Ada Oxon' et Hugone Stowe archidiaconis, W.
Wellar' et Hugone Bathon' archidiaconis, magistris W. filio Fulconis, Roberto de
Gravel' et Gilberto de Scardeburg', Waltero Blundo, Rogero de Bristoll',
Stephano de Cicestr', Petro de Hungar', magistris Willelmo de Linc', Rogero de
Laccoc, Nicholao de Evesham' et Waltero de Well', Rogero de Bohun', Petro
Cheuremunt et Radulfo de Waravill', canonicis Linc'. Datum per manum Thome
de Fiskerton' capellani, canonici Linc', in capitulo Linc' apud Linc' xviii kalen-
das Septembris pontificatus nostri anno xiii.

a fidelibus *is inserted above the line.*

For Castle Acre's possessions in Fleet, see N. Neilson ed., *A Terrier of Fleet, Lincolnshire* (British Academy records of social and economic history 4, 1920), pp.
lxxiv, 42, 75, 80, 96, 117.

188. Abbey of La Couture

Grant in proprios usus, made with the assent of Roger the dean and the chapter of Lincoln, to the abbot and convent of St Peter, La Couture, Le Mans, of the church of Great Woolstone, saving a perpetual vicarage to be ordained according to the statutes of the Council of Oxford.   Lincoln, in chapter, 15 August 1222

> A = Northamptonshire RO, Stopford-Sackville archives, SS.608. Endorsed: Carta appropriationis de ecclesia et manerio de Wuolsinton' maioris in Anglia (s. xiii); 183 mm. x 109 mm. + 17 mm. On left-hand side, seal and counterseal of bp, green wax, on cords; on right-hand side, seal and counterseal of the Chapter of Lincoln, green wax, on cords.

Omnibus Cristi fidelibus ad quos presens scriptum pervenerit, Hugo Dei gratia Linc' episcopus salutem in domino. Noverit universitas vestra nos, de assensu Rogeri decani et capituli nostri Linc', dedisse et concessisse dilectis in Cristo filiis abbati et conventui sancti Petri de Cultura Cenomann' ecclesiam de Wulsiston' maiori habendam in perpetuum et in proprios usus possidendam cum terra eiusdem ville que est de libera elemosina eorum, et cum manso ad ipsam ecclesiam pertinente; salva vicaria perpetua per nos assignanda secundum statuta concilii nuper Oxon' celebrati, cum manso competente ad opus vicarii perpetui, ad eorundem abbatis et conventus presentationem a nobis et successoribus nostris admittendi et in eadem instituendi: qui eidem ecclesie in ordine sacerdotali personaliter deserviet et synodalia persolvet; salvis etiam in omnibus episcopalibus consuetudinibus et Linc' ecclesie dignitate. Quod ut perpetuam optineat firmitatem, presenti scripto sigillum nostrum una cum sigillo predicti nostri capituli Linc' duximus apponendum. Hiis testibus: Rogero decano, Galfrido precentore, Ricardo cancellario, Iohanne subdecano, Reymundo Leirc', Ada Oxon' et Hugone Stowe archidiaconis, Willelmo Wellar' et Hugone Bathon' archidiaconis, magistris Willelmo filio Fulconis, Roberto de Gravel' et Gilberto de Scardeburg', Waltero Blundo, Rogero de Bristoll', Stephano de Cicestr', Petro de Hungar', magistris Willelmo de Linc', Rogero de Laccoc, Nicholao de Evesham' et Waltero de Well', Rogero de Bohun', Petro Cheuremunt et Radulfo de Waravill', canonicis Linc'. Dat' per manum Thome de Fiskerton' capellani, canonici Linc', in capitulo Linc' apud Linc' octavodecimo kalendas Septembris pontificatus nostri anno tertio decimo.

> The reference to the Council of Oxford of 1222 is to canon 21 concerning perpetual vicarages and setting a minimum value of five marks (*Councils and Synods* ii (i) 112–13).

189. Eynsham abbey

Grant, made with the assent of Roger the dean and the chapter of Lincoln, to the abbot and convent of Eynsham of the church of Whitfield in proprios usus: saving a perpetual vicarage in accordance with the constitution of the provincial council held at Oxford by Archbishop Stephen [Langton] of Canterbury. The vicar shall pay synodal dues and the monks shall find hospitality for the archdeacon.
                                        Lincoln, in chapter, 25 November 1222

> A = LAO Lincoln D. & C. Dij/61/4/14 (this document cannot now be located at the LAO). The original was very extensively damaged and words in square brackets are supplied from B or else are conjectural. No seal had survived.

B = LAO Wells roll ix, m. 2.
Pd from A in *Reg. Ant.* iii no. 898; *Eynsham Cartulary* ii no. 713; from B in *RHW* ii 199.

Omnibus Cristi fidelibus ad quos presens scriptum pervenerit, Hugo Dei gratia L[inc' episcopus salutem in domino. Noverit universitas] vestra nos, de assensu Rogeri decani et capituli nostri Linc', dedisse et concess[isse dilectis in Cristo filiis abbati et conventui Eg]nesham' ecclesiam de Whitefeld' cum pertinentiis in proprios usus habendam et [in perpetuum possidendam, salva perpetua vicaria in] eadem e[cclesia], iuxta constitucionem concilii provincialis apud Oxon' [sub venerabili patre domino Stephano Cantuariensi archiepiscopo] tocius [Angiie primate] et sancte Romane ecclesie cardinale celebrati, per nos [ordinanda. Vicarius autem eiusdem ecclesie sinodalia solvet et] dicti monachi hospicium archidiaconi procurabunt salvis [in omnibus episcopalibus consuetudinibus et Lincolniensis] ecclesie dignitate. Quod ut perpetuam optineat firmitatem [presenti scripto sigillum nostrum una cum sigillo predicti] capituli nostri Lincolniensis duximus apponendum. Hiis testibus: Ro[gero decano, Galfrido precentore, Ricardo cancellario, Iohanne subdecano,] Roberto Huntingd' et Hugone Stowe archidi[aconis, magistris Willelmo filio Fulconis, Gileberto de Scardeburgh' et Ricardo de] Lindwod', Rogero de Bristoll', Roberto de W[assingeburg' et Stephano de Cicestr', Petro de Hunger', Willelmo de Avalon',] magistris Willelmo de Cant' et Amaurico de Bugged', [Petro de Bathon' et Petro de Cheuremunt, canonicis Linc'.] Dat' per manum Oliveri de Chedneto, clerici, in capitulo [Linc' apud Linc' septimo kalendas Decembris pontificatus nostri anno terciodecimo.]

> A marginal entry in *RHW* records: 'Hec nondum tradita est, sed est in scriniis domini episcopi'. This grant was ineffective and another appropriation and ordination of a vicarage was undertaken by Bp Robert Grosseteste, 29 July 1240 (*Eynsham Cartulary* i no. 235A). The Council of Oxford was held on 17 April 1222: canons 13–16 dealt specifically with parish clergy and vicarages (*Councils and Synods* ii (i) 110–11). Cf. LAO Lincoln D. & C. Dij/88/3/13b, a fragment of charter relating to the appropriation of Whitfield.

190. Northampton, priory of St Andrew

Grant, with the assent of the dean and the chapter of Lincoln, to the priory of St Andrew, Northampton, of an annual pension of four marks from the church of St Peter, Northampton, after the death of the present rector, master Robert of Bath. The priory will still continue to receive the annual pension of six marks which they are already accustomed to receive from the church.

Lincoln, in chapter, 25 November 1222

B = LAO Wells roll ix, m. 2. C = BL ms. Royal 11 B ix (cartulary of St Andrew, Northampton), fo. 37r. s. xiii ex.
Pd from B in *RHW* ii 198–9.

Hiis testibus: Rogero decano, Galfrido precentore, Ricardo cancellario, Iohanne subdecano,[a] Roberto Huntingd'[b] et Hugone Stowe archidiaconis, magistris Willelmo filio Fulconis, Gileberto de Scardeburg' et Ricardo de Lindwod',[c] Rogero de Bristoll', Roberto de Wassingeburg'[d] et Stephano de Cicestr', Petro de Hunger',[e] Willelmo de Avalon',[f] magistris Willelmo de Cant'[g] et Amaurico de

Bugend',[h] Petro de Bathon' et Petro de Cheuremunt, canonicis Linc'. Dat' per manum Oliveri de Chedney,[i] clerici, in capitulo Linc' apud Linc'[j] septimo kalendas Decembris pontificatus nostri anno tertiodecimo.

[a] subdiacono (sic) C.   [b] Huntend' C.   [c] Lindwode C.   [d] Wassingburg' C.
[e] Hung' C.   [f] Avalun' C.   [g] Cantuar' C.   [h] Buged' C.   [i] Chedneto C.   [j] Lincoln' C.

191.   Northampton, priory of St Andrew

A similar grant to the preceding one, except that the new annual pension of four marks is to be paid by master Robert of Bath, instead of taking effect after his death.   Lincoln, in chapter, 25 November 1222

> B = LAO Wells roll ix, m. 2.

Omnibus etc. Noverit universitas vestra nos, de assensu Rogeri decani et capituli nostri Linc', dedisse et concessisse dilectis in Cristo filiis priori et conventui sancti Andree Norhamt' quatuor marcas annuas de ecclesia sancti Petri Norhamt' per manum magistri Roberti de Bathon' rectoris eiusdem ecclesie et successorum suorum nomine perpetui beneficii in perpetuum percipiendas, una cum sex marcis annuis quas prius de eadem ecclesia percipere consueverunt: salvis in omnibus episcopalibus etc. Quod ut perpetuam etc. Hiis testibus, dat' ut supra in proxima carta.

> This entry was omitted in the printed edition. It should immediately follow the Whitfield entry in *RHW* ii 199 (i.e. no. 189 above).

192.   Leicester abbey

Institution of Ralph de Bleibuir', clerk, to the church of Syresham, on the presentation of the abbot and convent of Leicester, saving to the abbey their customary pension.   [20 December 1221 x 19 December 1222]

> B = LAO Wells roll ix, m. 2.
> Pd *RHW* ii 198.

Testibus et dat' ut supra in carta de Haliwell' in archidiaconatu Huntengd'.

> The institution is recorded in the institution roll among entries for the bp's twelfth pontifical year, 20 December 1220 x 19 December 1221 (ibid. 108). The Huntingdon archdeaconry charter roll has not survived; the charter referred to is likely to have been the letter of institution of Roger the clerk to Holywell church, recorded in the Huntingdon archdeaconry institution roll for the thirteenth pontifical year, 20 December 1221 x 19 December 1222 (ibid. iii 58).

193.   Northampton, priory of St Andrew

Similar charter to no. 148, recording the institution of Thomas of Fiskerton to the church of St Peter, Northampton.   [20 December 1221 x 19 December 1222]

> B = LAO Wells roll ix, m. 2 (no witnesses or date, placed among entries for the bp's thirteenth pontifical year). C = BL ms. Royal 11 B ix (cartulary of St Andrew, Northampton) fo. 34v. s. xiii ex.
> Pd from B in *RHW* ii 199.

*194.   Studley priory

Charter to the nuns of Studley about the church of Ilmer.
                                        [20 December 1221 x 19 December 1222]

> Mentioned in the list of churches, pensions and rents granted by Bp Hugh to the
> religious in LAO Wells roll xi, pd *RHW* iii 94, dated to the bp's thirteenth
> pontifical year. This lost document is clearly different from the Studley/Ilmer
> document of 1223 x 1225 (see no. 235 below).

*195.   Southwick church

*Settlement of a dispute between the prior of Huntingdon and William Avalon, pre-
bendary of Nassington in the cathedral church of Lincoln, over the church of
Southwick, which the latter has claimed as a chapel of his prebend, and the
former as in their patronage. The bishop adjudges the church to the prior and
convent of Huntingdon, and William and his successors as prebendaries of
Nassington are to receive ten shillings a year for ever from the church, in the
name of a perpetual benefice, payable in equal instalments at Easter and Michaelmas by the rector of Southwick.*   Buckden, 14 January 1223 [*or* 1222]

> Mention of original charter produced in a case between John Sheppey, prebendary
> of Nassington, and the prior of Huntingdon, Coram Rege, Michaelmas 9
> Richard II (1385), pd L.C. Hector & M.E. Hager eds., *Year Books of Richard
> II: 8–10 Richard II, 1385–1387* (Ames Foundation, 1987), pp. 57–8. The
> indented charter bore four seals: those of Bp Hugh, the chapter of Lincoln,
> the prior and convent of Huntingdon, and William Avalon. The date of the
> document is given as at Buckden, the 19th calends of February in the four-
> teenth pontifical year of the bp and the sixth year of King Edward I. The use
> of King Edward is clearly an error for Henry III, but even so the dates are not
> compatible: the fourteenth pontifical year would make it 14 January 1223,
> but 6 Henry III is 14 January 1222.

196.   Northampton, priory of St Andrew

*Institution of master Robert of Bath, clerk, to the church of St Peter, Northamp-
ton, on the presentation of the prior and convent of St Andrew, Northampton:
saving to the aforesaid prior and convent after the death of master Robert an
annual pension of four marks to be paid by the parsons of the church in perpetuity; together with the six marks a year which the priory are already accustomed to
receive. Robert shall pay this pension of six marks each year as long as he lives.*
                                                    Banbury, 23 January 1223

> B = LAO Wells roll ix, m. 2. C = BL ms. Royal 11 B ix (cartulary of St Andrew,
>   Northampton) fo. 30r–v. s. xiii ex. D = BL ms. Cotton Vespasian E xvii (car-
>   tulary of St Andrew, Northampton) fos. 293v–294r (276v–277r). s. xv med.
>   Pd from B in *RHW* ii 199–200.

Hiis testibus: magistro Rogero de Laccok'[a], Petro de Bathon' et Radulfo de
Warevill'[b], canonicis Linc', Willelmo de Winchec'[c], Ricardo de Oxon', Martino
de Eston', Philippo de Langeport'[d] et Iohanne de Bannebir'[e], clericis[f]. Dat' per
manum Oliveri de Chedn'[g], clerici, apud Bannebir' decimo kalendas Februarii
anno pontificatus nostri xiiii°.[i]

   [a] Laccok CD.   [b] Waraville CD.   [c] Wichesch' C; Wychesch' D.   [d] Langeport C;

Langeporth'D.   ^e Bannebury D.   ^f clerici C.   ^g Chedon' CD.   ^h Bannebyry D.
ⁱ quartodecimo C.

CD insert 'cum capellis de Upton' et Torp' et aliis' after the mention of St Peter's
church ('ad eandem ecclesiam') on line 3 of *RHW* ii 200. Cf. *acta* nos. 190–1 for
the provisions for a pension. Robert's institution is recorded ibid. 108, among
entries for the bp's twelfth pontifical year, 20 December 1220 x 19 December 1221.
The problem about the dating of letters of institution, discussed in the introduction,
is highlighted in this group of Northampton charters. In two documents of 25
November 1222 (nos. 190–1) Robert of Bath is already described as rector of St
Peter's, Northampton, but this present letter of institution is dated two months later.

197. Selby abbey

Institution of master William of Lincoln to the church of Stanford on Avon, on the
presentation of the abbot and convent of Selby.   Kilsby, 27 February 1223

  B = LAO Wells roll ix, m. 2.
  Pd *RHW* ii 200.

Hiis testibus: magistris Willelmo de Cantuar', Willelmo de Linc', Nicholao de
Evesham' et Rogero de Laccock' et Radulfo de Warevill', canonicis Linc',
Philippo de Langeport' et Iohanne de Bannebir', clericis. Dat' per manum Oliveri
de Chedn', clerici, <apud Cildesby> iii kalendas Martii pontificatus nostri anno
xiiii°.

  The institution is recorded in the institution roll among entries for the bp's eleventh
  pontifical year, 20 December 1219 x 19 December 1220 (ibid. 98).

198. Althorpe and Bottesford churches

Notification of an award made by the bishop and Robert archdeacon of Hunting-
don to settle a dispute between Adam rector of Althorpe and Oliver parson of
Bottesford about the tithes of that part of the village of Burringham, which is in
the fee of Ashby. Oliver had complained that Adam, wrongfully admitting the
parishioners dwelling in the aforesaid part of the village to burial and other sac-
raments of the church, withheld the oblations of the parishioners for the living
and the dead and the mortuaries, to the prejudice of the church of Bottesford. The
award is as follows: the small tithes and the garb tithes of the said part of the
village shall belong to the church of Bottesford, and the church of Althorpe shall
receive the other half of the garb tithes, and shall retain the oblations of the
parishioners dwelling in the said part and their mortuaries by admitting those
parishioners to burial and to other sacraments of the church. The particular
lands and tofts from which each of the two churches shall receive its half of the
garb tithes are described in detail and provision is made with respect of land
which may hereafter be brought into cultivation. The church of Bottesford shall
have all kinds of tithes and all parochial rights in respect of the land in Burring-
ham and Butterwick, which at the time of the award belongs to the fee of Nicholas
de Chavincurt. The award is approved by the two rectors and by the patrons of
the two churches.   Lincoln, in chapter, 12 March 1223

  A = LAO Lincoln D. & C. doct. Dij/67/1/15. Endt. Composicio inter personas de
      Botensford et de Aletorp. (s. xiii). This charter is indented and C Y R O G R

A P H V M is written across the indentations, upside down in relation to the rest of the handwriting. No surviving seal. Six slits for seal-tags. size: 311 mm x 165 mm.

B = BL ms. Cotton Nero D iii (St Leonard's cartulary, York), fos. 16v–17r. ss. xiv–xv. C = LAO Lincoln D. & C. doct. Dij/67/1/15a (s. xvi copy on paper). Pd from A in *Reg. Ant.*, ii, no. 513.

Omnibus Cristi fidelibus ad quos presens scriptum pervenerit, Hugo Dei gratia Linc' episcopus salutem in domino. Noverit universitas vestra quod cum inter Adam rectorem ecclesie de Althorp' actorem ex una parte et Oliverum personam ecclesie de Botlesford' parte rei fungentem ex altera, coram priore sancte Trinitatis Eboraci et coniudicibus suis, auctoritate litterarum domini pape Honorii tertii, questio verteretur super omnibus decimis de tota parte ville de Burringeham' que est de feodo de Askeby. Item cum dictus Oliverus prefatum Adam coram priore Hospitalis Linc' et coniudicibus suis ab eodem domino papa delegatis traxisset in causam super eo quod idem Adam omnes parrochianos habitantes in predicta parte ville de Burringeham' ad sepulturam et ad alia sacramenta ecclesiastica iniuste admittens, obblationes (*sic*) eorundem parrochianorum tam pro vivis quam pro mortuis et legata eorum in preiudicium ecclesie de Botlesford' retinuit, tandem supradictus Adam persona ecclesie de Althorp' et magister et fratres militie Templi in Anglia patroni unius medietatis eiusdem ecclesie et prior et fratres hospitalis Ebor' patroni alterius medietatis, item predictus Oliverus persona ecclesie de Botlesford' et prior et conventus de Thornholm', qui se dicebant esse patronos ipsius ecclesie, se sponte simpliciter et pure super omnibus premissis nostre et dilecti filii Roberti archidiaconi Huntingdon' subiecerunt ordinationi. Nos igitur super iure et possessione que tam ecclesia de Althorp' quam ecclesia de Botlesford in hiis habere videbantur, diligentem prius inquisitionem facientes per testes ab utraque parte productos iuratos et examinatos diligenter, ut predictarum ecclesiarum que a longis retro temporibus sepe sibi ad invicem pro premissis lites ingesserunt paci et tranquillitati de cetero provideatur, solum deum habentes pre oculis de consensu partium ita duximus ordinandum: videlicet, quod omnes minute decime totius predicte partis ville de Burringeham' que est de feodo de Askebi et medietas decime omnium garbarum eiusdem partis ad ecclesiam de Botlesford integre et pacifice in perpetuum pertinebunt. Ecclesia autem de Althorp' aliam medietatem decime omnium garbarum ipsius partis de Burringeham que est de feodo de Askeby in perpetuum percipiet et omnes oblationes omnium parrochianorum manentium in eadem parte de Burringeham' que est de predicto feodo de Askeby tam pro vivis quam pro mortuis et legata eorum perpetuo retinebit, omnes ipsos parrochianos ad sepulturam et ad alia sacramenta ecclesiastica admittendo. Et ne pro divisione garbarum facienda de predictis decimis lis inter prefatas ecclesias de Althorp' et de Botlesford aliquo tempore oriatur, totam terram quam homines tenuerunt in tota sepedicta parte ville de Burringeham', que est de feodo de Askeby tempore huius ordinationis, cum toftis adiacentibus in duas medietates equales dividi fecimus, assignantes ecclesie de Botlesford' omnes decimas garbarum de una medietate provenientes; ecclesie vero de Althorp' omnes decimas garbarum provenientes ex altera medietate in perpetuum percipiendas. Ecclesia igitur de Botlesford' percipiet in perpetuum omnes decimas garbarum de terris et toftis subscriptis: scilicet, de dimidia bovata terre Galfridi Blundi cum tofto suo, de dimidia bovata et quarta parte unius bovate terre Gilberti diaconi que fuit Ade Blundi cum tofto suo, de dimidia bovata terre Walteri filii Ranulfi cum tofto suo, de dimidia bovata terre Margarete filie Roberti filii Brand' cum tofto suo, de dimidia bovata terre Willelmi filii Gilberti cum tofto suo, de tertia parte unius bovate terre Willelmi filii Aylfled' cum tofto suo, de dimidia bovata terre Ranulfi filii Wybaldi cum tofto suo, de una bovata terre Willelmi filii Wacelini cum tofto suo, de uno tofto Matildis braciatricis, de dimida bovata terre Ricardi filii Higemund' cum tofto suo, de uno tofto Ade Kappescore et de uno tofto Hugonis fratris eius, de tertia parte unius bovate terre Arnaldi filii Aelicie cum tofto suo, de quarta parte unius bovate terre Ade filii Sigerich cum tofto suo. Ecclesia autem de Althorp' decimas garbarum habebit in perpetuum de terris et toftis subscriptis: scilicet, de una bovata et quarta parte unius bovate terre Iohannis filii Gocelini cum tofto suo, de una bovata terre Gwiot filii Rogeri cum tofto suo, de tertia parte unius bovate terre Geralini filii Gocelini cum tofto suo, de dimidia bovata terre Odonis filii Wiminan' et Thome fratris eius cum toftis suis, de tertia parte unius bovate terre Ade filii Gamellini cum tofto suo, de tertia parte unius bovate terre Willelmi Dust cum tofto suo, de dimidia bovata terre Hugonis ad Fled cum tofto suo, de tofto Thome fratris ipsius, de dimidia bovata terre Ade filii Cristiane cum tofto suo, de tertia parte unius bovate terre Ade filii Habfede cum tofto suo, de tertia parte unius bovate terre Hereberti fratris ipsius cum tofto suo, de tertia parte unius bovate terre Aelicie uxoris Walteri filii Berewaldi cum tofto suo, de uno tofto Gilberti diaconi. Si vero contigerit in posterum quod aliqua terra alia a premissis que tempore istius ordinationis fuit de feodo de Askeby apud Burringeham de novo excolatur, prefate ecclesie de Botlesford' et de Alethorp' omnes decimas garbarum illius terre quecumque illa sit inter se in perpetuum equaliter dimidiabunt, salvis in perpetuum ecclesie de Botlesford' omnibus minutis decimis inde contingentibus: salvis etiam nichilominus in perpetuum eidem ecclesie de Botlesford' omnimodis decimis cum toto iure parrochiali de tota terra in Burringeham' et in Butterwic', que tempore huius ordinationis fuit de feodo Nicholai de Chavincurt'. Quas quidem omnimodas decimas et quod totum ius parrochiale ipsa ecclesia de Botlesford' semper pacifice possidebit. Nos igitur hanc ordinationem a nobis et dicto archidiacono factam et a partibus approbatam, auctoritate episcopali de consensu Willelmi decani et capituli nostri Linc' confirmamus. Et in huius rei testimonium presenti scripto sigillum nostrum et sigillum predicti capituli nostri Linc' una cum sigillo prefati Roberti archidiaconi Huntingdon' coordinatoris nostri et sigillis omnium predictarum partium duximus apponenda. Hiis testibus: Willelmo decano, Galfrido precentore, Ricardo cancellario, Gilberto thesaurario, Iohanne subdecano, Roberto Huntingdon', Ada Oxon', Iohanne Bedeford' et Willelmo Stowe archidiaconis, Gilberto de Scardeburg', magistris Ricardo de Lindwode, Roberto de Gravel' et Stephano de Cicestr', Waltero Blundo, Rogero de Bristoll', Roberto de Wassingburg', magistro Willelmo de Linc', Petro de Hungar' et Willelmo de Avalon', magistris Willelmo de Cantuar', Nicholao de Evesham', Amaurico de Bugeden', Waltero de Well' et Roberto de Brincl', Radulfo de Waravill, Rogero de Bohun et Petro de Cheuremunt, canonicis Lincoln'. Dat' per manum Petri de Bathon', canonici Linc', in capitulo Lincoln' apud Lincoln' quarto idus Martii pontificatus nostri anno quartodecimo.

The parson of Bottesford was Oliver Chesney, an episcopal clerk and datary. He was instituted to the church in 20 December 1219 x 19 December 1220 (*RHW* i 213).

199. Althorpe and Bottesford churches

Notification that in the aforesaid award of the bishop and the archdeacon of Huntingdon, half of the garb tithes of that part of the village of Burringham, which is in the fee of Ashby, were assigned to the church of Althorpe. However, Adam the parson of Althorpe, with the consent of the patrons of the church, has granted the aforesaid tithes to Oliver, parson of Bottesford for his life, on payment of four shillings a year to the church of Althorpe. This arrangement is to cease on Oliver's death and the tithes are to be possessed by Althorpe church.

Lincoln, in chapter, 12 March 1223

B = BL ms. Cotton Nero D iii (St Leonard's cartulary, York), fo. 16v. ss. xiv–xv.

Omnibus Cristi fidelibus ad quos presens scriptum pervenerit, Hugo Dei gratia Linc' episcopus salutem in domino. Noverit universitas vestra quod cum nos et dilectus filius Robertus archidiaconus Huntyngdon' per ordinationem a nobis factam medietatem decime omnium garbarum de tota illa parte ville de Burringham que tunc fuit de feodo de Askeby, ecclesie de Alethorp' imperpetuum participiendam assignaremus, Adam tunc temporis persona ecclesie predicte de Alethorp', ad petitionem predicti Roberti archidiaconi et magistri Willelmi de Cantuar' canonici Linc', prefatas omnes decimas, de consensu magistri et fratrum militie Templi in Anglia patronorum unius medietatis dicte ecclesie de Alethorp' et prioris et fratrum hospitalis sancti Leonardi de Ebor' patronorum alterius medietatis eiusdem ecclesie, Olivero persone ecclesie de Botlesford' concessit et dimisit de ecclesia de Alethorp' integre, quamdiu idem Oliverus vixerit tenendas, sub annua firma quatuor solidorum ad festum sancti Michaelis eidem ecclesie de Alethorp' annuatim solvenda; ita quod ipsa ecclesia de Alethorp' et rectores eiusdem post decessum prefati Oliveri integre et plenarie et absque omni contradictione prefatas decimas imperpetuum percipient, cessante extunc perpetuo solutione predicte firme quatuor solidorum quam eadem ecclesia de Alethorp' pro predictis decimis percipere consuevit et ecclesia de Botlesford' de ipsa prestatione quatuor solidorum annuorum imperpetuum quieta. Nos igitur hanc concessionem sepedicto Oliver factam, de consensu Willelmi decani et capituli nostri Linc' auctoritate episcopali[a] confirmamus. Et in huius rei testimonium tam sigillum nostrum et sigillum capituli nostri Linc' quam sigilla supradicti Ade persone ecclesie de Alethorp' et prefati magistri militie Templi in Anglia patroni unius medietatis ecclesie predicte de Alethorp' et dictorum prioris et fratrum hospitalis sancti Leonardi de Ebor' patronorum alterius medietatis ipsius ecclesie de Alethorp', presenti scripto sunt appensa. Hiis testibus: Willelmo decano, Galfrido precentore, Ricardo cancellario, Gilberto thesaurario, Iohanne subdecano, Roberto Huntingdon', Ada Oxon', Iohanne Bedeford' et Willelmo Stowe archidiaconis, Gilberto de Scardeburg', magistris Ricardo de Lynwod', Roberto de Gravell' et Stephano de Cicestr', Waltero Blundo, Rogero de Bristoll', et Roberto de Wassyngburg, magistro Willelmo de Linc', Petro de Hungar' et Willelmo de Avalun[b], magistris Willelmo de Cantuar', Nicholao de Evesham, Amaurico de Buggeden', Waltero de Well et Roberto de Brincl', Radulpho de Warevill', Rogero de Bohum' et Petro de Cheuremunt, canonicis Linc'. Dat' per manum Petri de Bathon', canonici Linc', in capitulo Linc' apud Lincoln' iiij[c] Martii pontificatus nostri anno quartodecimo.

^a apiscopali B.   ^b Avasun B.   ^c *sic. there is no indication whether this should be* calends, ides *or* nones, *but having regard to actum no.198, it seems certain that* idus *should be inserted.*

200.   Coventry priory

Institution of Geoffrey de Fudeham , clerk, to the church of Checkendon, on the presentation of the prior and convent of Coventry.   Nettleham, 12 March 1223

> B = Buckinghamshire Record Office, Boarstall cartulary, Checkendon fo. 2r. s. xv
> med.
> Pd *Boarstall Cartulary* no. 6.

Hiis testibus: magistris Willelmo de Cantuaria, Willelmo de Lincoln', Nicholao de Seusham et Rogero de Lacok', Petro de Bathon' et Radulpho de Warevill', canonicis Lincoln', Willelmo de Wynchecombe, Philippo de Langeport et Iohanne de Bannebury, clericis. Data per manum Oliveri de Chedn', clerici, apud Netellam quarto idus Martii pontificatus nostri anno quartodecimo.

> Fudeham is given as Rudeham in the Lincoln institution rolls (*RHW* ii 7). Nicholas de Seusham is obviously an error for Evesham. The institution rolls indicate that the church was collated to Geoffrey by bp Hugh during his thirteenth pontifical year (20 December 1221 x 19 December 1222), after a vacancy of six months caused by a lawsuit between Geoffrey Marmiun and the prior of Coventry (see also *Boarstall Cartulary* no. 7).

201.   Northampton, abbey of St James

Grant, with the assent of William the dean and the chapter of Lincoln, to the abbot and convent of St James, Northampton of an annual pension of ten shillings from the church of Litchborough, in the name of a perpetual benefice. This pension shall be paid by John of Banbury, parson of the church, and his successors and is in addition to the previous pension of ten shillings a year which the abbot and convent are accustomed to receive. The increased pension is to be paid in two equal instalments each year, namely at Michaelmas and Easter.
[? Lincoln, in chapter, 12 March 1223]

> B = LAO Wells roll ix, m. 2.
> Pd *RHW* ii 200–1.

Testibus et dat' ut supra in carta de Burringham in archidiaconatu Stowe.

> The Stow archdeaconry charter roll has not survived, but it seems probable that the Burringham charter referred to can be identified with either no. 198 or no. 199.

*202.   Newnham priory

Letters addressed to William de Beauchamp enquiring about the right and possession of the church of Wootton by the canons of Newnham.   [c. 1223]

> Mentioned in William de Beauchamp's reply to the bp, *Newnham Cartulary* i no. 26.

> This, and the preceding document from William de Beauchamp to Archbp Stephen Langton, most probably dates from shortly before the bp's award relating to Wootton church, 19 October 1223 (see below, no. 208).

203.   Overstone church

Institution of master Humphrey de Millers, clerk, to the church of Overstone, on the presentation of William de Millers, knight.

Old Temple, London, 22 May 1223

B = LAO Wells roll ix, m. 2.
Pd *RHW* ii 201.

Hiis testibus: Willelmo archidiacono Wellen', Ada archidiacono Oxon', magistris Willelmo de Cantuar', Willelmo de Linc', Nicholao de Evesham, Amaurico de Buggeden', canonicis Linc'. Dat' per manum Oliveri de Chedn', clerici, apud Vetus Templum, Lond', xi kalendas Iunii pontificatus nostri anno xiiii°.

The institution is recorded in the institution roll among entries for the bp's twelfth pontifical year, 20 December 1221 x 19 December 1222 (ibid. 107–8).

204.   Launde priory

Institution of Martin the chaplain to the perpetual vicarage of Ashby St Ledgers, on the presentation of the prior and convent of Launde. The vicarage consists of the whole altarage of the church, the third part of the garb tithes of the demesnes of John of Cranford and Ledger de Dive, the garb tithes of one and a half virgates which Richard of Harrowden holds and the manse which the said prior and convent have of the gift of Hugh Heres (le Eyr). The vicar shall pay synodal dues and the prior and canons shall provide hospitality for the archdeacon.

Kilsby, 2 September 1223

B = LAO Wells roll ix, m. 2.
Pd *RHW* ii 201–2.

Hiis testibus: magistro Rogero de Laccock' et Radulfo de Warevill', canonicis Linc', Iohanne de Tanton' et Galfrido, cappellanis, Ricardo de Oxon', Philippo de Langeport et Iohanne de Bannebir', clericis. Dat' per manum Oliveri de Chedn', clerici, apud Kildesby iiii° nonas Septembris pontificatus nostri anno quartodecimo.

205.   Ridlington church

Institution of Edward of Westminster, subdeacon, to the church of Ridlington, on the presentation of William de Cantilupe, patron by virtue of the wardship of the land and heir of Thurstan de Montfort.   [24 September x 19 December 1223]

B = LAO Wells roll ix, m. 3 (among entries for the bp's fourteenth pontifical year).
Pd *RHW* ii 202.

Testibus et dat' ut in carta de Herdewic in archidiaconatu Buckingham'.

The institution is recorded in the institution roll and dated 24 September 1223 (ibid. 112). As has become apparent, the letter of institution was not always issued on the same day as the act of institution was performed. The bp's fourteenth pontifical year ended on 19 December 1223. The Buckingham archdeaconry charter roll has not survived; the charter in question is likely to have been the letter of institution of William Russel to the church of Hardwick, recorded in the Buckingham archdeaconry institution roll for 24 September 1223 (ibid. 62).

206. Brampton Ash chantry

Notification that Thomas the parson of the church of Brampton [Ash] and the prior and convent of St Neots, the patrons of the church, have consented that William de Insula, knight, and his heirs, shall have a chantry in a chapel to be erected in his curia *in Brampton, saving the rights of the mother church. William shall have the chapel built and he and his heirs shall pay for the chaplain serving there every day at their own expense. They shall not claim the patronage of the chapel, the appointment or removal of the chaplain, or any offerings and revenues of the chapel. William and his household* (familia) *shall attend the parish church on solemn festivals, as laid down in the charter of the parson and the patrons. The bishop confirms this arrangement.*   Buckden, 29 September 1223

> B = LAO Wells roll ix, m. 3.
> Pd *RHW* ii 202–3.

Hiis testibus: magistro Rogero de Laccock' et Radulfo de Warevill', canonicis Linc', Galfrido Scoto cappellano, Willelmo de Winch'cumb', Iohanne de Herlaua, Philippo de Langeport, Olivero de Chedn' et Iohanne de Bannebir', clericis. Dat' per manum Iohannis de Tanton', cappellani apud Buggeden' tertio kalendas Octobris pontificatus nostri anno xiiii.

*207. Henry of Dean and Henry of Buckworth

Notification to the royal justices that Henry of Dean and Henry of Buckworth are excommunicate.   [Michaelmas term 1223]

> Mention of letters patent in *CRR* xi no. 902, in a case between Gilbert, parson of Dean, and the two Henrys over a messuage and half a virgate of land in Dean, Michaelmas term 1223: 'et super hoc misit episcopus Lincolniensis literas suas patentes quod ipsi Henricus et Henricus propter manifestos excessus sunt excommunicati'. It is recorded in the entry that the two Henrys were subsequently absolved by Pandulph, the papal legate.

208. Newnham priory

Award in respect of Wootton church, made with the assent of William the dean and the chapter of Lincoln, and at the wish of the prior and convent of Newnham, patrons of the church. The priory shall have, in the name of a perpetual benefice, a mediety of the church of Wootton, except the altarage and the demesne messuage of the church, with the croft adjoining it. Martin of Easton, clerk, whom the bishop has instituted as parson, on the presentation of the prior and convent, shall have the other mediety and in addition the entire altarage and the aforementioned demesne messuage and croft, saving an annual pension of twenty shillings to be paid by Martin and his successors as parsons to the priory for half the altarage, namely ten shillings at the Michaelmas synod and ten at the Easter synod. Martin and his successors shall bear all ordinary and customary charges of the church, and if there are any extraordinary charges the prior and convent shall be responsible for their portion. All other lands, rents and possessions belonging to the church, whose possession is not yet established, shall be equally divided between the parsons of Wootton and the canons of Newnham.

Lincoln, in chapter, 19 October 1223

B = BL ms. Harl. 3656 (Newnham cartulary) fos. 57v–58r. s. xv in.
Pd *Newnham Cartulary* i no. 97.

Teste: W. decano, Galfrido precentore, Ricardo cancellario et aliis. Datum per manum Iohannis de Tanton' in capitulo Linc' apud Linc' xiiii° kalendas Novembris pontificatus nostri anno xiiii°.

209. Manton church

Institution of Helias of Berkhamsted, clerk, to the church of Manton, on the presentation of the queen.   Fingest, 4 November 1223

B = LAO Wells roll, m. 2.
Pd *RHW* ii 203.

Hiis testibus: magistris Rogero de Laccock', Willelmo de Cantuar' et Radulfo de Warevill', canonicis Linc', Galfrido Scoto cappellano, Olivero de Chedn', Willelmo de Winchecumb', Philippo de Langeport, Iohanne de Herlawe et Iohanne de Bannebir', clericis. Dat' per manum Iohannis de Tanton', cappellani, apud Tinghurst pridie nonas Novembris pontificatus nostri anno xiiii°.

210. Hugh de Chastillun

Notification to King Henry III stating that after examination the bishop has found that Hugh de Chastillun and Gunnora de Bray were lawfully married. Hugh de Chastillun, however, has appealed to the pope against the bishop's decision.   Banbury, 18 November 1223

B = LAO Wells roll ix, m. 2d (no witnesses).
Pd *RHW* ii 204; (transl.), C.J. Offer, *The Bishop's Register*, p. 213.

Dat' per manum Iohannis de Tanton', capellani, apud Bannebir' xiiii kalendas Decembris pontificatus nostri anno xiiii.

211. Launde priory

Institution of Peter nepos of Romanus, cardinal deacon of St Angelus, to the church of Wardley, with the consent of the prior and convent of Launde the patrons. The bishop had been obliged to pay Peter ten marks a year until he could be provided to an ecclesiastical benefice equivalent in value or better. Peter is to pay to the prior the customary annual pension of one mark.   Kilsby, 19 December 1223

B = LAO Wells roll ix, m. 3 (no witnesses).
Pd *RHW* ii 203–4.

Act' apud Kildeb' anno pontificatus nostri xiiii^mo. xiiii^mo kalendas Ianuarii *[inserted above entry]*.

A mandate for the induction of Peter's proctor into possession of the church is to be found in the institution roll among entries for the bp's fifteenth pontifical year, 20 December 1223 x December 1224 (ibid. 117).

212. Geddington church

Institution of Nicholas de Breauté, clerk, to the church of Geddington, on the presentation of King Henry III.   [20 December 1222 x 19 December 1223]

B = LAO Wells roll ix, m. 2.
Pd *RHW* ii 201.

Testibus et dat' ut in carta de Wilden' in archidiaconatu Bedeford'.

The institution is recorded in the Northampton archdeaconry institution roll among entries for the bp's fourteenth pontifical year, 20 December 1222 x 19 December 1223 (ibid. 110). The Bedford archdeaconry charter roll has not survived: the Wilden charter referred to is likely to have been the letter of institution of Nicholas de Breauté to that church which occurs in the Bedford archdeaconry institution roll under the bp's thirteenth pontifical year, 20 December 1221 x 19 December 1222 (ibid. iii 5). Nicholas was the brother of Fawkes de Breauté (ibid. i 92).

213. Aldwincle church

Institution of Robert de Lungeville, subdeacon, to the church of All Saints, Aldwincle, on the presentation of Henry of Aldwincle, knight.

Old Temple, London, 25 December 1223

B = LAO Wells roll ix, m. 4.
Pd *RHW* ii 205.

Hiis testibus: magistris Willelmo de Linc' et Rogero de Laccock' et Radulfo de Warevill', canonicis Linc', Galfrido Scoto cappellano, Willelmo de Winchecumb', Iohanne de Herl', Philippo de Langeport et Iohanne de Bannebir', clericis. Dat' per manum Iohannis de Tanton', cappellani, apud Vetus Templum, Lond', viii⁰ kalendas Ianuarii pontificatus nostri anno xv⁰.

The institution is recorded in the institution roll (ibid. 113).

214. Kislingbury church

Institution of Peter de Ruddehal, clerk, to the church of Kislingbury, on the presentation of Geoffrey de Armenteres, saving to Thomas the chaplain his perpetual vicarage. Thomas shall hold the church as long as he lives, paying to Peter the parson an annual pension of one hundred shillings.   Buckden, 4 January 1224

B = LAO Wells roll ix, m. 4.
Pd *RHW* ii 204.

Hiis testibus: Willelmo archidiacono Stowe, magistro Amaurico de Buged' et Rogero de Laccok, canonicis Linc', Willelmo de Winch', Ricardo de Oxon', Roberto de Dunelm' et Iohanne de Harl', clericis. Dat' per manum Iohannis de Tanton', capellani, apud Buged' pridie nonas Ianuarii pontificatus nostri anno xv⁰.

The institution is recorded in the institution roll and dated 18 November 1223 (ibid. 113). The surname of the incumbent is given there as Ruddeham.

215.   Peterborough abbey

Ordination, made with the assent of William the dean and the chapter of Lincoln, regarding Normanby church and the abbot and convent of Peterborough. The abbey, at each vacancy of the church, shall present a suitable clerk to the bishop and his successors for institution as parson. The latter shall pay to the abbey an annual pension of ten marks for the use of the almoner, in the name of a perpetual benefice, in four equal instalments at Michaelmas, Christmas, Easter, and St John the Baptist. The parson shall bear all ordinary charges of the church and both he and the abbey shall answer proportionally for extraordinary charges.
[28 January 1223 x 19 December 1224, ? April/May 1224]

> B = CUL, Peterborough D. & C. ms. 1 (Liber R. de Swaffham), fo. 108v (xciii v). s. xiii med.

Omnibus Cristi fidelibus ad quos presens scriptum pervenerit, Hugo Dei gratia Lincolniensis episcopus salutem in domino. Noverit universitas vestra quod cum dilecti filii abbas et conventus de Burgo ecclesiam de Normanneby tunc vacantem ratione quorundem instrumentorum que habebant in proprios usus exigissent possidendam, tandem ordinationi nostre se subiecerunt et omni iuri quod habere videbantur de habendo eam in proprios usus in perpetuum renuntiaverunt. Nos igitur, de assensu Willelmi decani et capituli nostri Lincol', de ea ita duximus ordinandum: videlicet, quod dicti abbas et conventus cum dictam ecclesiam vacare contigerit ad eam clericum idoneum nobis et successoribus nostris presentabunt ad eandem a nobis admittendum, et in ea canonice personam instituendum. Qui quidem solvet memoratis abbati et conventui decem marcas annuas ad opus elemosinarie sue, nomine perpetui beneficii, ad quatuor anni terminos, videlicet, ad festum sancti Michaelis duas marcas et dimidiam, ad Pasca duas marcas et dimidiam, ad Natale Domini duas marcas et dimidiam, et ad festum sancti Iohannis Baptiste duas marcas et dimidiam. Persona etiam omnia honera illius ecclesie ordinaria sustinebit; de extraordinariis autem utraque pars pro sua portione respondebit: salvis in omnibus episcopalibus consuetudinibus et Lincolniensis ecclesie dignitate. Quod ut perpetuam optineat firmitatem, sigillum nostrum una cum sigillo dicti capituli[a] nostri Lincolniensis presenti scripto duximus apponendum.[b] Hiis testibus.

[a] capelli *originally written* B, *with* el *dotted for deletion and* itu *interlined.*
[b] *apponendam* B.

William de Thornaco became dean of Lincoln after Roger of Rolleston, who died on 28 January 1223 (*Fasti Lincoln*, p. 10). The charter is mentioned at the time of the institution of William de Burgo (Peterborough) to the church of Normanby during the bp's fifteenth pontifical year, 20 December 1223 x 19 December 1224, possibly April/May 1224 (the entry is placed between entries dated 30 March and 16 May) (*RHW* i 220). The advowson had been disputed between Peterborough and the earl of Chester and Lincoln, and it is probable that the document was issued shortly before William de Burgo's institution.

216.   Northampton, abbey of St James

Institution of John of Banbury, clerk, to the church of Litchborough, on the presentation of the abbot and convent of St James, Northampton, saving to the abbey an annual pension of ten shillings which the bishop has granted to them, with the consent of William the dean and the chapter of Lincoln [no. 201]. This sum is to be paid by John the parson and his successors, together with the annual pension of ten shillings which the abbey is accustomed to receive from the church already.

Aylesbury, 1 July 1224

B = LAO Wells roll ix, m. 4.
Pd *RHW* ii 205.

Hiis testibus: Iohanne archidiacono Bedeford', Theodbaldo de Bosell', canonico Linc', Galfrido Scoto cappellano, magistro Ricardo de Windeleshor', Willelmo de Winch', Ricardo de Oxon', Iohanne de Herl' et Philippo de Langeport, clericis. Dat' per manum Iohannis de Tanton', cappellani, apud Eylesbir' kalendis Iulii pontificatus nostri anno quintodecimo.

The institution is recorded in the institution roll among entries for the bp's fourteenth pontifical year, 20 December 1222 x 19 December 1223 (ibid. 110–11). The actual grant of the pension referred to, with John of Banbury already described as incumbent, is dated 12 March 1223 (no. 201 above).

217. Bury St Edmunds abbey

Institution of John de Tumpeston, clerk, to the church of Warkton, on the presentation of the abbot of Bury St Edmunds. Elstow, 4 July 1224

B = LAO Wells roll ix, m. 4.
Pd *RHW* ii 205–6.

Testibus: Iohanne archidiacono Bedeford', Galfrido Scoto capellano, magistro Ricardo de Windleshor', Willelmo de Winchecumb', Ricardo de Oxon', Philippo de Langeport', Iohanne de Bannebir' et Iohanne de Herlau', clericis. Dat' per manum Iohannis de Tanton', capellani, apud Alnestow' quarto nonas Iulii anno pontificatus nostri xv°.

The institution is recorded in the institution roll (ibid. 116).

218. Rowney priory

Confirmation of the gift made by Guy de la Val and Gerard de Furnival, patrons of the church of Munden, to the church and the nuns of St John the Baptist, Rowney, of two portions of all the demesne tithes of the village of Munden: saving to the mother church its customary portion of the tithes from the same demesne.

Elstow, 10 July 1224

B = PRO E315/62 (? register of Sir John Fray) fo. 7r. s. xv med. C = ibid. fo. 7r (in an inspeximus of William the dean and the chapter of Lincoln).

Omnibus Cristi fidelibus ad quos presens scriptum pervenerit, Hugo Dei gratia Linc' episcopus salutem in domino. Cum pia vota fidelium pio sint favore prosequenda, nos divine pietatis intuitu donationem Widonis[a] de Lavall' et Gerardi de Furnivall' patronorum ecclesie de Munden' maiori successione[b] factam Deo et beate Marie et ecclesie sancti Iohannis Baptiste de Ruweneya et dilectis in Cristo filiabus monialibus ibidem Deo servientibus de duabus portionibus omnimodarum decimarum de dominico eiusdem ville de Munden' provenientium, prout in cartis eorundem Widonis[a] et Gerardi continetur, ratam habentes et gratam easdem decimas, de consensu^c dilecti filii Ricardi de Cernay rectoris dicte ecclesie de Munden', dictis monialibus episcopali confirmavimus auctoritate, salva matrici ecclesie portione decimarum quam ab antiquo de dicto dominico percipere consuevit: salvis etiam in omnibus episcopalibus consuetudinibus et Linc' ecclesie dignitate. Quod ut perpetuam optineat firmitatem, presenti scripto sigillum nostrum duximus apponendum. Hiis testibus: domino Iocelino Bathon' episcopo, Iohanne archidiacono Bedeford', Galfrido Scoto capellano, Willelmo de Winchecumb^d, magistro Ricardo de Wyndeshor', Ricardo de Oxon', Ricardo de Cernay persona ecclesie de Munden', Philippo de Langeporter', Iohanne de Banebyr' et Iohanne de Herlaw, clericis. Dat' per manum Iohannis de Taunton', capellani, apud Alnestow sexto idus Iulii pontificatus nostri anno quintodecimo.

^{a} Wydonis C. ^{b} successive C. ^{c} concensu B. ^{d} Wynchecumb C.

219. Bury St Edmunds abbey

Institution of Luke of Arthingworth, chaplain, to the church of Scaldwell, on the presentation of Hugh II, abbot of Bury St Edmunds.   Elstow, 23 July 1224

> B = LAO Wells roll ix, m. 4d (no witnesses).
> Pd *RHW* ii 206.

Dat' per manum Iohannis de Tanton', cappellani, apud Alnestowam x^{mo} kalendas Augusti anno pontificatus nostri xv^{mo}.

> The institution is recorded in the institution roll (ibid. 117). For a similar letter of institution, see below no. 224.

220. Thrapston bridge

Indulgence of ten days for all those who contribute alms towards the construction and repair of Thrapston bridge. This indulgence is to last for one year and no collectors are to be sent out to collect alms.   Elstow, 2 August 1224

> B = LAO Wells roll ix, m. 4d (no witnesses).
> Pd *RHW* ii 206–7.

Dat' per manum Iohannis de Tanton', capellani, apud Alnestow' iiii^{to} nonas Augusti anno pontificatus nostri xv^o.

> For a later indulgence for Thrapston bridge see below no. 256.

221. Breamore priory

Institution of master Thomas de Insula, clerk, to the perpetual vicarage of Brockhall, on the presentation of John Wak, parson of the church, with the consent of the prior and convent of Breamore, the patrons. Thomas shall hold the church as long as he lives, paying to John and his successors as parsons an annual pension of two marks.   Spaldwick, 27 August 1224

> B = LAO Wells roll ix, m. 4d (no witnesses).
> Pd *RHW* ii 207.

Dat' per manum Iohannis de Tanton', cappellani, apud Spaldewic vi kalendas Septembris pontificatus nostri anno quintodecimo.

The institution is recorded in the institution roll (ibid. 118). The marginal heading (*Littere Iohannis Wack'*) indicates that this letter of institution was intended for the rector (see below).

222. Breamore priory

Identical letter of institution of master Thomas de Insula to the perpetual vicarage of Brockhall.   Spaldwick, 27 August 1224

B = LAO Wells roll ix, m. 4d.
Pd *RHW* ii 207.

The marginal heading (*Littere prioris Brumor'*) indicates that another copy of the letter of institution was required by the patrons.

223. Crowland abbey

Institution of Ralph of Rippingale, clerk, to the church of Morbourne, on the presentation of the abbot and convent of Crowland.   Lyddington, 3 September 1224

B = Spalding Gentlemen's Society, Crowland cartulary fo. 196r, no. ii. s. xiv med.

Omnibus Cristi fidelibus ad quos presens scriptum pervenerit, Hugo Dei gratia Linc' episcopus salutem in domino. Noverit universitas vestra nos, ad presentationem dilectorum filiorum abbatis et conventus de Croiland' patronorum ecclesie de Morbourne, dilectum in Cristo filium Radulfum de Repinghale clericum ad eandem ecclesiam admisisse, ipsumque in ea canonice personam instituisse, salvis in omnibus episcopalibus consuetudinibus et Linc' ecclesie dignitate. Quod ut perpetuam obtineat firmitatem, presenti scripto sigillum nostrum duximus apponendum. Hiis testibus etc. Dat' per manum Iohannis de Tanton', capellani, apud Lidington' iii° nonas Septembris pontificatus nostri anno quintodecimo.

The institution is recorded in the Huntingdon archdeaconry institution roll (*RHW* iii 47).

224. Bury St Edmunds abbey

Institution of Luke of Arthingworth to the church of Scaldwell as in no. 219.
                                    Arthingworth, 13 September 1224

B = LAO Wells roll ix, m. 4.
Pd *RHW* ii 206.

Testibus: magistris Amaurico de Buked' et Rogero de Lakok' et Radulfo de Warevill', canonicis Lincolniensibus, W. de Winchecumb', magistro Ricardo de Windlesor', Ricardo de Oxon', Philippo de Langeporth' et Iohanne de Bannebir', clericis. Dat' per manum Iohannis de Tanton', cappellani, apud Ermingwurth' idibus Septembris anno pontificatus nostri xv°.

Besides the differences of date and witnesses between this letter of institution and that of 23 July 1224 (no. 219), the only other change is that the abbot of Bury is not mentioned by name in this document, whereas he is in the July letter.

225. Salisbury cathedral

Notification to the archdeacon of Northampton, his official and all deans, parsons, vicars and chaplains of the archdeaconry that, with the assent of William the dean and the chapter of Lincoln, the bishop has given permission to Bishop R(ichard) and the chapter of Salisbury to send collectors throughout the archdeaconry seeking contributions towards the fabric of the new cathedral at Salisbury. The bishop also grants an indulgence of twenty days to all those of the Lincoln diocese, and others whose diocesan bishops should approve, who shall contribute alms. This indulgence is to be valid for one year from the feast of St Luke [18 October] next. Banbury, 2 October 1224

B = LAO Wells roll ix, m. 4d (no witnesses).
Pd *RHW* ii 207–8.

Dat' per manum Iohannis de Tanton', cappellani, apud Bannebr' ii die Octobris pontificatus nostri anno xv^{mo}.

226. Nuneaton priory

Collation of the church of Claybrooke to master Laurence of Warwick, clerk, by authority of the Council, saving in future the right of presentation of the nuns of Nuneaton. Old Temple, London, 24 October 1224

A = BL Add. Ch. 47561 (slightly stained). Not endorsed: approx. 145 x 45mm.; seal missing, parchment tongue and tie torn away.

Omnibus Cristi fidelibus ad quos presens scriptum pervenerit, Hugo Dei gratia Linc' episcopus salutem in domino. Noverit universitas vestra [no]s ecclesiam de Cleibroc dilecto in Cristo filio magistro Laurentio de Warewic', clerico, autoritate concilii contulisse, ipsumque in ea canonice personam instituisse, salvo in posterum monialibus de Etton' eiusdem ecclesie patronis cum ipsam alias vacare contigerit iure suo presentandi ad eandem: salvis etiam in omnibus episcopalibus consuetudinibus et Linc' ecclesie dignitate. In huius autem rei testimonium presenti scripto sigillum nostrum duximus apponendum. Dat' per manum Iohannis de Tanton', capellani, canonici Linc', apud Vetus Templum Lond' nono kalendas Novembris pontificatus nostri anno quinto decimo.

The square brackets indicate a small hole in the document. The collation is recorded in the Leicester archdeaconry institution roll (*RHW* ii 293). The consent of the nuns was had to the collation. There had been a dispute over the patronage between the nuns and Arnulf de Bosco and Nicholas of Haversham.

Another version of the preceding collation.
Godstow, 6 December 1224

A = BL Add. Ch. 47562. Endorsed: Institucio magistri Laurentii de Warrwyk ad ecclesiam de Claybrok (s. xiii); approx. 150 x 47 + 13 mm.; seal missing, parchment tag (sealing method 1).

Omnibus Cristi fidelibus ad quos presens scriptum pervenerit, Hugo Dei gratia Linc' episcopus salutem in domino. Noverit universitas vestra nos ecclesiam de Cleibroc' dilecto in Cristo filio magistro Laurentio de Warewic', clerico, autoritate concilii contulisse, ipsumque in ea canonice personam instituisse, salvo dilectis in Cristo monialibus de Etton' eiusdem ecclesie patronis cum ipsam vacare contigerit iure suo presentandi ad eandem: salvis etiam in omnibus episcopalibus consuetudinibus et Linc' ecclesie dignitate. Quod ut perpetuam optineat firmitatem, presenti scripto sigillum nostrum duximus apponendum. Hiis testibus: magistro Willelmo de Linc', magistro Ricardo de Windlesores, Hugone de Welles, Willelmo de Winchecumb', Ricardo de Oxon', Philippo de Langeport et Roberto de Aketon', clericis. Data per manum Iohannis de Tanton', cappellani, canonici Linc', apud Godestowe octavo idus Decembris pontificatus nostri anno quinto decimo.

> Presumably one of these two preceding letters of collation was intended for master Laurence, the other for the nuns, although both of these documents come from the nuns' archives.

227. Salisbury cathedral, prebends of Shipton-under-Wychwood and Brixworth

Settlement by the bishop and his brother Jocelin, bishop of Bath, of a dispute between the bishop and chapter of Salisbury and Adam of Brimpton, knight, as to the right of collation to the churches of Shipton-under-Wychwood and Brixworth, prebends of Salisbury.   [20 December 1223 x 19 December 1224]

> B = Salisbury D. & C., Liber Evidentiarum C, fos. xlix r–v. s. xiii ex. C = Wiltshire RO, Salisbury Liber Evidentiarum B, fos. xlii–xliii. ss. xiv–xvi. D = Wiltshire RO, Salisbury Liber Ruber, no. 122. ss. xiv–xvi.
> Pd from B in *Salisbury Charters*, no. cxxv, pp. 102–5.

Omnibus Cristi fidelibus presens scriptum inspecturis, Iocelinus Bathon'[a] et Hugo Linc'[b] Dei gratia episcopi salutem in domino. Cum super ecclesiis de Schipton'[c] et de Brikeworth'[d] cum pertinentiis inter venerabilem fratrem Ricardum episcopum et capitulum Sar'[e] ex una parte et Adam de Brinton'[f] militem ex altera, questio verteretur, dicto episcopo asserente collationem dictarum ecclesiarum sicut ceterarum prebendarum in ecclesia sua Sar'[e] vacantium ad ipsum immediate de iure debere pertinere, prefato vero A. econtrario dicente dictarum ecclesiarum jus patronatus ad ipsum de iure debere spectare, tandem dictus episcopus et capitulum Sar'[e], item dictus A. pro se et heredibus suis, sponte et absolute, totum ius quod se in dictis ecclesiis habere contendabant, omni appellatione et subterfugio remotis, in nostrum transtulerunt ordinationem et provisionem; caventibus nobis dicto episcopo et capitulo Sar'[g] per literas suas patentes, et dicto A. milite pro se et pro heredibus suis juramento prestito hoc idem faciente, quod nostram imperpetuum ratam haberent et observarent ordinationem. Nos igitur habita diligenti deliberatione et tractatu, communicato quoque prudentum virorum consilio, volentes quieti partium prospicere, et materiam contentionis et iurgiorum inposterum amputare; attendentes insuper diligenter dictarum ecclesiarum fructuum et proventum sufficientiam et habundantiam ad duorum rectorum honestam sufficere sustentationem, ita duximus ordinandum: videlicet, quod omnibus redditibus, possessionibus, proventibus et aliis commoditatibus dictarum ecclesiarum cum pertinentiis in duas equales portiones distributis, utraque ecclesia, de consensu decani et capituli Linc'[i], de cetero imperpetuum[h] remaneat prebendalis, statuentes quod venerabili fratri R. Sar'[e] episcopo et successoribus suis ecclesia de Brikeworth' per nostram remaneat ordinationem cum pertinentiis et portionibus subscriptis et inferius eidem assignatis, ad quam ecclesiam cum pertinentiis dictus episcopus et successores sui tanquam veri patroni diocesano episcopo clericum presentabunt ydoneum ad curam animarum[j] personam instituendam. Ad ecclesiam vero de Schipt'[c] cum pertinentiis inferius scriptis et eidem assignatis, dictus miles et heredes eius tanquam veri patroni clericum eligent ydoneum, et illum episcopus Sar'[e] qui pro tempore fuerit Linc' episcopo et successoribus suis presentabit personam instituendam, qui sicut ceteri canonici Sar'[e] stallum habebit in choro et locum in capitulo cum communa. Estimatis autem per viros fidedignos et juratos redditibus, possessionibus, proventibus et ceteris commoditatibus dictarum ecclesiarum, facta est auctoritate nostra subscripta assignatio portionem, quas ad majorem certitudinem ceteris nominibus duximus exprimendas: videlicet sic, quod canonicus prebende[k] de Brikeworth' qui pro tempore fuerit, habebit totam ecclesiam de Brikeleworth'[l] cum omnibus pertinentiis suis in prebendam ; canonicus vero prebende de Schipt'[m] qui pro tempore fuerit, habebit in prebendam decimas garbarum proventium de villa de Shipt'[m] et Middilton'[n] et Langeleg'[o] et Felde et Adefelde[p] preter assarta et assartanda, et solvat[q] inde[r] canonico prebende de Brikeworth'[s] annuatim vii solidos et quatuor[t] denarios ad duos terminos anni[u], scilicet, ad Pascha medietatem et ad festum sancti Michaelis alteram[v] medietatem. Ad canonicum etiam de Schipt'[w] pertinebit totum altilagium[x] de Schipt'[y]. Dicti vero canonici totam terram pertinentem ad ecclesiam de Shipt'[m], scilicet, xx virgatas terre inter se equaliter divident, tam in dominico quam in tenentibus. Marcam autem annuam quam reddit capella de Swinbrok'[z] ecclesie de Schipt'[w] habebit[aa] canonicus de Brikelewth'[bb], cum emolumento quod sequi potest; marcam autem quam solvit capella de Eston' annuatim ecclesie de Schipt'[m] habebit canonicus de Shipt'[cc] similiter cum suo emolumento. Boscum autem pertinentem ad ecclesiam de Shipt'[m] et decimas provenientes ex assartis et assartandis in parochia de Shiptun'[dd], et decimas garbarum provenientes de villa de Linham equaliter inter se dividant. Omnes autem proventus capellarum de Fifhide[ee] et de Idebyr' equaliter inter se dividant, ita quod equaliter sustinent onera et percipiant[ff] emolumenta. Actiones autem, sique competant, in villa de Fifhide[gg] et de Ideb'[hh] cedant canonico de Brikeleworth'[s] Actiones vero, sique competant[ii], in villa de Middelton'[jj] et de Langelee[kk] cedant canonico de Shipt'[w]. Emolumentum vero actionum, sique competant, in villa de Linham equaliter inter se dividant. Ordinavimus insuper quod medietas terre de Uffecot' et redditus qui ad canonicum de Shipt'[ll] solebant pertinere, remaneant imperpetuum canonico de altera Brikeleworth'[r], et medietas canonico de Shipt'[m]. Ordinavimus, nihilominus, quod clericus qui pro tempore canonicus fuerit de Shipt'[m], cum assensu predicti A. militis et heredum suorum et predicti domini Sar'[e] et successorum suorum et capituli Sar'[e], presentet imperpetuum episcopo Linc'[b] et successoribus suis clericum ydoneum ad vicariam ecclesie de Schipt'[mm], qui de proventibus eiusdem ecclesie tantam percipiet portionem nomine vicarie que c.[nn] solidos valeat annuatim ad dandam ad firmam, qui ab episcopo admissus est et perpetuus vicarius institutus residentiam facere debebit in ecclesia de Shipt'[m]. Similiter canonicus de Brikeleworth'[s] qui pro tempore fuerit, cum assensu domini Sar'[e] et successorum suorum et capituli Sar'[e], presentet imperpetuum episcopo Linc'[b] et successoribus suis clericum, ydoneum ad vicariam ecclesie de Brikelewrth'[oo] qui de proventibus ecclesie eiusdem tantam percipiet portionem nomine vicarie que c.[nn] solidos valeat annuatim ad dandam ad firmam, qui ab episcopo admissus est et perpetuus vicarius institutus residentiam facere debebit in ecclesia de Brikel'. Omnes vero cartas vel instrumenta que habet et habuit dictus A.^{pp} miles et predecessores sui super dictis decimis cum pertinentiis resignavit^{qq} in manus dicti episcopi. Ordinavimus etiam quod si aliqua instrumenta penes dictum A. militem vel heredes suos, sive predictum episcopum vel successores suos, aut capitulum Sar'^{e} inventa fuerant, jam habita vel inposterum optinenda, que contra hanc^{rr} nostram ordinationem facere videantur, nullas vires habeant contra eam, quominus imperpetuum stabilis et firma permaneat, Et sciendum est^{ss} quod hec omnia ordinavimus, salvis in omnibus episcopis Linc' et ecclesie Linc' juribus et dignitatibus et consuetudinibus, quas habuerunt in predictis^{tt} ecclesiis de Brikeleworth'^{s} et Shiptunn'^{w} cum pertinentiis ante hanc nostram ordinationem. Et ad perpetuam huius nostre ordinationis firmitatem, tria sub eodem tenore confecta sunt instrumenta, quorum unum remanebit penes^{uu} dictum episcopum et successores suos, alterum penes capitulum Sar'^{e}, et tertium penes dictum A. militem et heredes suos, sigillis^{vv} nostris et predicti domini Sar'^{e} et capitulorum Linc' . Sar'^{e} et sepedicti A. munita. Et si forte aliqua per fraudem suppressa, vel per negligentiam omissa, vel per nimiam occupationem seu subreptitionem fuerint pretermissa, quominus suprascripta assignatio equaliter facta sit prout debet, vel fortasse erratum in aliquo, nobis correctionem reservamus.

^{a} Baton' D.　　^{b} Lincol' C.　　^{c} Scipton' D.　　^{d} Brikeleswrth' C.　　^{e} Sarr' D. ^{f} Brumpton' C.　　^{g} Sar' *omitted* C; Sarr' D.　　^{h} inperpetuum C.　　^{i} Lincoln' C. ^{j} curam animarum *omitted* C.　　^{k} prebende *omitted* D.　　^{l} Brikesworth' C; Brikeworth' D.　　^{m} Schipton　C; Schipt' D.　　^{n} Midilton' D.　　^{o} Langele C.　　^{p} Aldefeld' C.　　^{q}.absolvat D.　　^{r} tum BD.　　^{s} Brikelesworth' D.　　^{t} iiij CD.　　^{u} anni terminis C.　　^{v} aliam D.　　^{w} Schipton' CD.　　^{x} altelagium C.　　^{y} Schipt' C; Schipton' D. ^{z} Swinbroch C.　　^{aa} *insert* etiam C.　　^{bb} Brikeleswrth' C; Brikeleworth' D. ^{cc} Schipt' D; de Shipt' *omitted* C.　　^{dd} Schipt' C.　　^{ee} Fifhid' C; Fifide D.　　^{ff} percipient D.　　^{gg} Fyfhide D.　　^{hh} Idebir' C.　　^{ii} competent D.　　^{jj} Midelton' C; Midilton D.　　^{kk} Langel' C.　　^{ll} Schipt' CD.　　^{mm} Scipt' C; Schipt' D.　　^{nn} centum C. ^{oo} *Word misplaced before* ydoneum; Brikeleswort' D.　　^{pp} H. BD.　　^{qq} resignabit D. ^{rr} hanc *omitted* CD.　　^{ss} est *omitted* C.　　^{tt} dictis D.　　^{uu} penes *omitted* B.　　^{vv} sigillis nostris et *replaced by* sigilla nostra in C.

For the prebends of Shipton and Brixworth see *Fasti Salisbury* pp. 55–6, 97 which also mentions the date of this settlement. Richard Poore became bp of Salisbury in 1217 and in the fifteenth year of the Bp Hugh's pontificate, master Adam of Ashby was instituted to Brixworth 'secundum ordinationem domini Bathoniensis et domini Lincolniensis et de consensu eiusdem domini Sarrisburiensis et Ade de Brimton' militis, quondam ipsius ecclesie patroni' (*RHW* ii 116–17 and cf. 22). The bishop's fifteenth year was from 20 December 1223 to 19 December 1224.

228.　Breamore priory

Institution of master Thomas de Insula, clerk, to the perpetual vicarage of Brockhall [as in nos. 221–2].　　　　　　　　　　　　　　Buckden, 20 January 1225

B = LAO Wells roll ix, m. 4.
Pd *RHW* ii 208–9.

Hiis testibus: M. archidiacono Buckingh', W. archidiacono Well' et Radulfo de Waravill', canonico Linc', magistro Ricardo de Windlesores, Willelmo de Winchecumb', Ricardo de Oxon', Philippo de Langeport, Iohanne de Bannebir' et Roberto de Aketon', clericis. Dat' per manum Iohannis de Tanton' capellani, canonici Linc', apud Bukeden' xiii^mo kalendas Februarii pontificatus nostri anno sexto decimo.

See nos. 221–2 for similar letters of institution dated 27 August 1224.

229. Boscherville, abbey of St George

Institution of Bartholomew de Kanvill, chaplain, to the church of [Edith] Weston, on the presentation of the abbot and convent of St George, Boscherville.

Lincoln, 27 March 1225

B = LAO Wells roll ix, m. 4.
Pd *RHW* ii 209.

Hiis testibus: magistris Willelmo de Linc', Rogero de Lakok' et Amaurico de Buggeden' et Radulfo de Waravill', canonicis Linc', Willelmo de Winchecumb', Ricardo de Oxon', Philippo de Langeport', Iohanne de Banneb' et Roberto de Aketon', clericis. Dat' per manum Iohannis de Tanton' cappellani, canonici Linc', apud Linc' vi^to kalendas Aprilis anno pontificatus nostri xvi^mo.

The institution is recorded in the institution rolls among entries for the bp's fifteenth pontifical year, 20 December 1223 x 19 December 1224 (ibid. 119).

230. Thorney abbey

Institution of Robert son of Fulk of Nottingham, chaplain, to the perpetual vicarage of Yaxley, on the presentation of Nigel de Insula, parson of the church, made with the assent of the abbot and convent of Thorney, the patrons. He is to serve personally and shall hold the entire church in the name of his vicarage, paying to Nigel and his successors an annual pension of sixteen marks. He shall also bear all due and customary charges of the church.

Stanground, 3 April 1225

B = CUL ms. Add. 3020 (Thorney cartulary) fo. 72v (pars secunda, 32v) no. cxxiii. s. xiv in.

Omnibus Cristi fidelibus ad quos presens scriptum pervenerit, Hugo Dei gratia Linc' episcopus salutem in domino. Noverit universitas vestra nos, ad presentationem dilecti filii Nigelli de Insua^a persone ecclesie de Iakele, factam de asensu (*sic*) dilectorum nobis abbatis et conventus de Thorneie patronorum eiusdem, dilectum in Cristo filium Robertum filium Fulconis de Notingham capellanum ad perpetuam ipsius ecclesie vicariam admisisse ipsum que in ea canonice vicarium perpetuum instituisse, cum onere ministrandi personaliter^b in eadem; qui^c quidem totam ecclesiam illam cum pertinentiis nomine vicarie sue tenebit quoad vixerit; reddendo inde dicto Nigello et successoribus suis eiusdem ecclesie personis sexdecim marcas annuas nomine pensionis et omnia onera illius ecclesie debita et consueta sustinendo: salvis in omnibus episcopalibus consuetudinibus et Linc' ecclesie dignitate. Quod ut perpetuam optineat firmitatem, presenti scripto sigillum nostrum duximus apponendum. Hiis testibus: Willelmo archidiacono Well', magistris Willelmo^d de Gravel', Willelmo de Linc', Rogero de Lakok et Aumaurico de Longedon'^e et Radulfo de Waravill', canonicis Linc',

Willelmo de Winchecumb', Ricardo de Oxon', Philippo de Langeport', Iohanne de Bannebur' et Roberto de Akton', clericis. Dat' per manum Iohannis de Tanton' capellani, canonici Linc', apud Stangrund tertio nonas Aprilis pontificatus nostri anno sexto decimo.

> [a] *recte* Insula.   [b] *written in the margin.*   [c] quia *written originally, with final letter dotted for deletion.*   [d] *recte* Roberto.   [e] *recte* Bugedon'.

> The institution is recorded in the Huntingdon archdeaconry institution roll (*RHW* iii 48); see also no. 283 below. The rectory and the vicarage were consolidated by Bp Grosseteste on 29 June 1248 (*RRG* p. 295).

231. Hospitallers

Institution of William of Westwell, clerk, to the church of Cosgrove, on the presentation of brother Robert de Dive, prior of the Hospitallers in England.
                                         Old Temple, London, 11 April 1225

> B = LAO Wells roll ix, m. 4.
> Pd *RHW* ii 209–10.

Hiis testibus: Willelmo archidiacono Wellen', magistris Willelmo de Linc' et Rogero de Laccock', canonicis Linc', Willelmo de Winch'cumb', Ricardo de Oxon', Philippo de Langeport', Roberto de Aketon' et Iohanne de Bannebir', clericis. Dat' per manum Iohannis de Tanton' cappellani, canonici Linc', apud Vetus Templum, Lond', tertio idus Aprilis pontificatus nostri anno xvi°.

> The institution is recorded in the institution rolls (ibid. 121).

232. Daventry priory

Institution of master Adam of St Bridget to the church of Walgrave, on the presentation of the prior and convent of Daventry.   Fingest, 25 August 1225

> B = LAO Wells roll ix, m. 4.
> Pd *RHW* ii 210.

Hiis testibus: Willelmo archidiacono Wellens', magistro Rogero de Lakok' et Radulfo de Waravill', canonicis Linc', magistro Ricardo de Kant' cappellano, Willelmo de Winchecumb', Ricardo de Oxon', Philippo de Langeport, Iohanne de Bannebir' et Roberto de Aketon', clericis. Dat' per manum Iohannis de Tanton' capellani, canonici Linc', apud Tinghurst viii kalendas Septembris pontificatus nostri anno xvi°.

> The institution is noted in the institution rolls (ibid. 123). The church was vacant by the death of master Geoffrey of Dodford (see no. 92).

233. Alvingham priory

Institution of Peter of Lincoln, clerk, to two parts of the church of Stainton [-le- -Vale], on the presentation of the master of the order of Sempringham and the prior and convent of Alvingham.   Nettleham, 26 September 1225

> B = Oxford, Bodl. ms. Laud misc. 642 (Alvingham cartulary) fos. 143v–144r.
> s. xiii ex. C = ibid. fo. 4v (s. xiv insertion at the foot of the folio).

Omnibus Cristi fidelibus ad quos presens scriptum pervenerit[a], Hugo Dei gratia Linc' episcopus salutem in domino. Noverit universitas vestra nos, ad presentationem dilectorum filiorum magistri ordinis de Sempingham[b] et prioris et conventus de Al.[c] patronorum duarum partium ecclesie de Staintona[d], dilectum in Cristo filium Petrum de Linc' [fo. 144r] clericum ad easdem duas partes admisisse, ipsumque in eisdem canonice personam instituisse, salvis in omnibus episcopalibus consuetudinibus et Linc' ecclesie dignitate. Quod ut perpetuam optineat firmitatem, presenti scripto sigillum nostrum duximus apponendum. Hiis testibus[e]: I. precentore Linc', W. archidiacono Well', magistris Willelmo de Linc', Rogero de Lacok et Amaurico Buggeden' et Hugone de Well', canonicis Lincoln', magistris Willelmo de Beningwurth', Ricardo de Cant', capellanis et Ricardo de Wind<l>esoris, Willelmo de Winchecumb', Ricardo de Oxon', Philippo de Langeport', Iohanne de Bannebir' et Roberto de Aketon', clericis. Dat' per manum Radulfi de Warevil', canonici Linc', apud Nettelham' vi kalendas Octobris pontificatus nostri anno sextodecimo.

[a] C *has* Omnibus Christi etc.   [b] Semperingham C.   [c] Alvingham C.   [d] dingnitate C.   [e] B *ends here.*

The institution is recorded in the institution roll *(RHW* iii 141).

234. Lincoln cathedral

Grant, with the assent of the dean and chapter of Lincoln, to Peter of Kirmond of fifteen marks in the name of a prebend (Decem Librarum) of Lincoln, to be received by Peter from the render of the archdeaconry of Lincoln, until the bishop shall provide for him in the church of Lincoln. When this is done, the fifteen marks shall revert to the bishop.   Lincoln, in chapter, 28 September 1225

> A = LAO Lincoln D & C doct.Dij/55/3/3. Endt: De prebenda .xv. marcis (s. xiii). No surviving seal. Parchment tag for one seal and slit for another seal-tag Size:178 mm x 85 mm.
> Pd *Reg. Ant.* ii no. 352.

Omnibus Cristi fidelibus ad quos presens scriptum pervenerit, Hugo Dei gratia Linc' episcopus salutem in domino. Noverit universitas vestra nos, de assensu Willelmi decani et capituli nostri Linc', dedisse et concessisse dilecto in Cristo filio Petro de Cheueremunt quindecim marcas annuas, nomine prebende Linc', de redditu nostro de archidiaconatu Linc' per manum archidiaconi eiusdem loci annuatim percipiendas ad quatuor anni terminos: videlicet, ad Natale Domini quinquaginta solidos, ad Pascha quinquaginta solidos, ad Nativitatem beati Iohannis Baptiste quinquaginta solidos, et ad festum sancti Michaelis quinquaginta solidos: habendas et tenendas eidem Petro, donec illi in ecclesia nostra Linc' per nos vel successores nostros competenter provideatur. Statuentes de consilio predictorum decano et capituli ut cum ipsi P. fuerit sicut dictum est provisum extunc predicte quindecim marce tanquam ius nostrum et proprius redditus noster absque omni reclamatione et contradictione ad nos et successores nostros libere quiete revertantur. Quod ut firmitatem optineat, presenti scripto sigillum nostrum una cum sigillo predicti capituli nostri Linc' duximus apponendum. Hiis testibus: Willelmo decano, Iohanne precentore, Ricardo cancellario, Roberto Linc' et Willelmo Wellen' archidiaconis, Iohanne subdecano, magistro Roberto de Gravel', Gilberto de Scardeburg', Waltero Blundo, Rogero de Bristoll', magistro Stephano de Cicestr', Petro de Hunger', magistris Willelmo de Linc', Rogero de Laccock' et Amaurico de Buggeden', Rogero de Bohun' et Hugone de Well', canonicis Linc'. Dat' per manum Radulfi de Warevill', canonici Linc', in capitulo Linc' quarto kalendas Octobris anno pontificatus nostri sexto decimo.

The previous prebendary of Decem Librarum was master William, son of Fulk, archdeacon of Stow, ibid. no. 350; cf. *Fasti Lincoln*, pp. 65–6.

235. Studley priory

Appropriation of the church of Ilmer to the nuns of Studley and ordination of a perpetual vicarage.   [28 January 1223 x 26 September 1225]

B = abstract of a charter in Oxford, Bodl. ms. Twyne 24 (extracts from a lost cartulary of Studley) pp. 650–1. s. xvii in. This document is noted in J. Dunkin, *Oxfordshire: the history and antiquities of the Hundreds of Bullington and Ploughley* (2 vols., 1823) i 136.

Ibidem ordinatio vicariae ecclesiae de Hylmere ad coenobium sanctimonialium de Stodley pertinentis per Hugonem (scilicet Wallys) episcopum Lyncolniensem etc. Hiis testibus: Willelmo decano, Galfrido praecentore, Ricardo cancellario, Gilberto thesaurario, Iohanne subdecano, Roberto Linc', Philippo Huntyngdon, Ada Oxon', Matheo Buckyngham et Willelmo Stowe archidiaconis etc. Eam autem ecclesiam coenobio sanctimo[p. 651]nialium predictarum quaedam faemina Albritha filia David de Romenel necnon quidam Thomas filius Bernardi per chartas suas contulerunt ut in predicto libro videntur, scilicet, quam donationem Petrus[a] Blesensis Lyncolniensis episcopus tempore regis Iohannis suo chyrographo confirmavit [*EEA* 4 no. 292] ac deinde Hugo episcopus Lyncolniensis eius successor eam predictis sanctimonialibus appropriavit et postea[b] vicariam in eadem institutam, ecclesiam illam sanctimonialibus predictis possidendam tradidit, salva perpetua vicaria in eadem iuxta constitutionem concilii[c] provincialis apud Oxon' sub venerabili patre domino Stephano Cantuariensi archiepiscopo totius Angliae primate et sanctae Romanae ecclesiae cardinali celebrati, ut in charta <ipsius> Hugonis episcopi Lyncolniensis continetur etc.

[a] *recte* Willelmus.   [b] post B.   [c] consilii B.

Roger of Rolleston, William de Thornaco's predecessor as dean of Lincoln, died on 28 January 1223 and Geoffrey of Deeping had been succeeded as precentor of Lincoln by 26 September 1225. This charter is clearly not the Studley/Ilmer transaction noted in *RHW* iii 94 and dated to the bp's thirteenth pontifical year (20 December 1221 x 19 December 1222). The witnesses do not fit that date. Bp William of Blois's confirmation is *EEA* 4 no. 292. See also above, no. 194.

236. Harpole church

Institution of Walkelin of Northampton, clerk, to the church of Harpole, on the presentation of Robert de Salceto, knight.
                    [20 December 1224 x 19 December 1225]

B = LAO Wells roll ix, m. 4.
Pd *RHW* ii 208.

Testibus et dat' ut in carta de Holewell' in archidiaconatu Bedeford'.

While the Harpole entry in the Northampton charter roll occurs among entries for the bp's sixteenth pontifical year, 20 December 1224 x December 1225, the institution roll entry (ibid. 117) is placed in the previous pontifical year. The Bedford archdeaconry charter roll has not survived; the charter in question is likely to have been the letter of institution of Geoffrey de Berkinges to Holwell church, recorded in the Bedford archdeaconry institution roll for the sixteenth pontifical year, 20 December 1224 x 19 December 1225 (ibid. iii 11).

237. Sempringham priory

Institution of Geoffrey de Wulward, clerk, to the church of Hannington, on the presentation of the master, prior and convent of Sempringham.
　　　　　　　　　　　　　　　　[20 December 1224 x 19 December 1225]

B = LAO Wells roll ix, m. 4.
Pd *RHW* ii 208.

Testibus et dat' ut supra carta proxima.

For the date, see no. 236. While the charter roll places this entry in the sixteenth pontifical year of the bp, 20 December 1224 x 19 December 1225, the institution roll entry (ibid. 118) records it under the previous pontifical year.

238. Morcott church

Institution of Ralph of Senlis (Silva Nectis), clerk, to the church of Morcott, on the presentation of Simon of Senlis, patron by virtue of his wardship of the land and heir of Richard Arbalister (Balistarius).
　　　　　　　　　　　　　　　　[20 December 1224 x 19 December 1225]

B = LAO Wells roll ix, m. 4.
Pd *RHW* ii 210.

Testibus et dat' ut in carta de Brocton' in archidiaconatu Oxon'.

The institution is recorded in the institution roll, among entries for the bp's sixteenth pontifical year, 20 December 1224 x 19 December 1225 (ibid. 120). The Oxford archdeaconry charter roll has not survived; it is possible that the charter alluded to relates to the institution of Benedict de Raleg' to Broughton church, recorded in the Oxford archdeaconry institution roll under the bp's fifteenth pontifical year, 20 December 1223 x 19 December 1224 (ibid. 17).

239. Chacombe priory

Institution of Robert of Acton, clerk, to the church of Aston le Walls, on the presentation of the prior and convent of Chacombe, saving to the priory an annual pension of forty shillings.　　　　[20 December 1224 x 19 December 1225]

B = LAO Wells roll ix, m. 4.
Pd *RHW* ii 210.

Testibus et dat' ut in carta de Parva Karleton' in archidiaconatu Stouwe.

The institution is recorded in the institution rolls, among entries for the bp's sixteenth pontifical year, 20 December 1224 x 19 December 1225 (ibid. 123–4). The

Stow archdeaconry charter roll has not survived. It is probable that the charter alluded to was the letter of collation of a pension of ten shillings in the church of Little Carlton to William of Banbury, noted in the Stow archdeaconry institution roll for this pontifical year (ibid. i 222–3).

240.   Etton church

Institution of John de Stokes, clerk, to the church of Etton, on the presentation of Robert de Stokes, knight, saving the right of Richard the chaplain in the vicarage of the church.   [20 December 1224 x 19 December 1225]

> B = LAO Wells roll ix, m. 5.
> Pd *RHW* ii 211.

Testibus et dat' ut supra carta proxima.

> For the date, see no. 239. The institution is recorded in the institution rolls (ibid. 121).

241.   Launde priory

Institution of Ralph le Walais, clerk, to the church of Glaston, on the presentation of the prior and convent of Launde.   [20 December 1224 x 19 December 1225]

> B = LAO Wells roll ix, m. 5.
> Pd *RHW* ii 211.

Testibus et dat' ut supra carta proxima.

> For the date, see no. 240. The institution is recorded in the institution rolls (ibid. 123).

242.   Abington church

Institution of Peter of Irchester, clerk, to the church of Abington, on the presentation of Isabella de Lysuris.   [20 December 1224 x 19 December 1225]

> B = LAO Wells roll ix, m. 5.
> Pd *RHW* ii 211.

Testibus et dat' ut supra carta proxima.

> For the date, see no. 241. The institution is recorded in the institution rolls (ibid. 124–5), where it is noted that there had been an assize of darrein presentment between Isabella and Nicholas of Bassingbourn.

243.   Rockingham bridge

Indulgence (number of days not specified) for all those who shall contribute alms towards the construction and repair of Rockingham bridge as in no. 96. The collector is forbidden to collect alms anywhere except at the bridge itself.

Lyddington, 22 February 1226

> B = LAO Wells roll ix, m. 5d (no witnesses).
> Pd *RHW* ii 217–18.

Dat' per manum Radulfi de Warevill', canonici Linc', apud Lidinton' viii kalendas Martii pontificatus nostri anno septimodecimo.

See also later indulgences for the bridge issued in 1229 and 1230, below nos. 309, 328.

*244. John son of Stephen

Notification of the legitimacy of John son of Stephen. [Hilary term 1226]

Mention of letters patent in *CRR* xii no. 1691, in a case between John and William Sherreve and Agnes his wife over half a virgate of land in Muscott, Hilary term 1226.

245. Launde priory

Ordination touching the church of Weldon, made with the consent of the prior and convent of Launde, the patrons, who have half of the garb tithes and the land of the church for their own use, and with the consent of William the chaplain, parson of the other moiety. In future, William and his successors as parsons shall have the entire altarage, the tithes of the quarries, hedges and mills. The parson shall bear all ordinary, due and customary charges of the church and shall pay to the canons of Launde four marks a year. The canons shall answer proportionally for any extraordinary charges. William and his successors shall have at their own expense a chaplain who will minister continually with them in the priestly office in the church. Lincoln, in chapter, 20 March 1226

B = LAO Wells roll ix, m. 5.
Pd *RHW* ii 212–13.

Hiis testibus: W. decano, I. precentore, Ricardo cancellario, Iohanne subdecano, Roberto Linc' et W. Stouw' archidiaconis, magistris G. de Scardeburg', Waltero Blundo, Roberto de Gravel', Stephano <de> Cycest' et Theobaldo de Cant', Rogero de Bristoll' et Roberto de Wassingburn' capellanis, Willelmo de Avalon', magistris W. de Linc' et Amaurico de Buggeden', Roberto de Brincl' et Waltero de Well', Petro de Cheuermunt, Rogero de Bohun' et Willelmo de Winchecumbe, canonicis Linc'. Dat' per manum Radulfi de Waravill', canonici Linc', apud Linc' in capitulo tertio decimo kalendas Aprilis pontificatus nostri anno xvii^mo.

See also no. 253 below.

246. Stamford, St Michael's priory

Grant in proprios usus, made with the assent of William the dean and the chapter of Lincoln, to the nuns of St Michael outside Stamford, of two parts of the church of Corby, the gift of Matilda de Dive, Ascelina de Waterville and Hamo Pecche: saving to Hugh of Osbournby his portion during his lifetime, and saving also the perpetual vicarage of Hilary the chaplain, with a suitable manse. The nuns shall bear all episcopal and archidiaconal charges pertaining to the two parts. Lincoln, in chapter, 19 April 1226

B = lost cartulary of Stamford, St Michael's, fo. 6v. C = PRO E210/11323 (transcript, s. xv). D = Oxford, Bodl. ms. Dodsworth 59 (ex quibusdam antiquis rotulis in pergameno penes me Rogerum Dodsworth) p. 167. s. xvii.

Pd from B in *Mon. Angl.* iv 262, no. xiv; *PL* cliii col. 1118, no. ii; (transl.) F. Peck, *Tertia Academia Anglicana*, lib. viii, 8–9.

Omnibus Cristi fidelibus ad quos presens scriptum pervenerit, Hugo Dei gratia Linc' episcopus salutem in domino. Noverit universitas vestra nos, de assensu et voluntate dilectorum in Cristo filiorum Willelmi decani et capituli nostri Linc', dedisse et concessisse dilectis filiabus in Cristo monialibus sancti Michaelis extra burgum Stanford duas partes ecclesie de Corby, que de dono Matildis de Dyve et Hamonis Pecch' ad ipsarum monialium advocationem pertinent: habendas eisdem et in proprios usibus imperpetuum possidendas; salva Hugoni de Osberneby portione sua ibidem quoad vixerit et salva vicaria perpetua cum manso competente, quam Hilarius capellanus optinet de predictis portionibus sibi et successoribus suis dictarum portionum vicariis assignatis. Predicte autem moniales omnia onera episcopalia et archidiaconalia sepedictas duas partes contingentia sustinebunt; salvis etiam in omnibus episcopalibus consuetudinibus et Linc' ecclesie dignitate. Quod ut perpetuam optineat firmitatem, presentem cartam sigillo nostro una cum sigillo predicti capituli nostri duximus muniendum. Hiis testibus:[a] Willelmo decano, Iohanne precentore, Ricardo cancellario, Gileberto thesaurario, Roberto Linc' et Willelmo de Stouw archidiaconis, Iohanne subdecano, Rogero de Bristoll', Waltero Blundo, magistris Roberto de Gravel', Stephano de Cicestria et Theobaldo de Cantia, Hugone de Burgund', Willelmo de Aval', Roberto de Wassingburg' et Thoma de Northon, capellanis, et canonicis Linc', magistris Willelmo de Linc', Petro de Hungar', Willelmo de Winchecumb', Theobaldo de Bosell, magistris Roberto de [ ][b], [Dat' per manum *omitted*] Radulfi de Waravill', canonici Linc', in capitulo Lincoln' tertiodecimo kalendas Maii pontificatus nostri anno septimo decimo.

[a] *The witness list is taken from* D. BC *have abbreviated lists*: Hiis testibus: Willelmo decano, Iohanne precentore, Ricardo cancellario, Gileberto thesaurario et aliis C; B *has the first two witnesses only.* [b] *The surname here is difficult to decipher, as the initial letter has been altered.* Windaun' *is a possibility, although the episcopal clerk with the surname* 'Wendover' *is called Richard, not Robert. At this point Dodsworth clearly omits a line, since* Dat' per manum' *is omitted (and possibly other witnesses preceding it).*

The charters of Ascelina de Waterville and Matilda de Dive in respect of Corby church are *Mon. Angl.* iv 262, nos. x–xii.

247. Fineshade priory

Confirmation, made with the assent of William the dean and the chapter of Lincoln, Vitalis Engayne, the patron, and Simon the parson of the church of Laxton, of the site of the priory of Castle Hymel [Fineshade] together with all those possessions in the diocese of Lincoln given to the canons by Richard Engayne, the founder of the priory, and other benefactors: saving the right of the mother church of Laxton.   Fingest, 28 May 1226

A = PRO E326/1877 (stained, some holes, repaired). Endorsed: Carta Hugonis Linc' episcopi et capituli (s. xiii); Confirmacio domini Hugonis Linc'episcopi , de fundacione loci et de omnibus terris etc. (s. xiii); approx. 158 x 103 + 12 mm.; seals and tags missing; two slits for seal-tags, sealing (method 1).
B = LAO Wells roll ix, m. 5 (supplying words in square brackets).
Pd from B in *RHW* ii 213.

Omnibus Cristi fidelibus ad quos presens scriptum pervenerit, Hugo Dei gratia Linc' episcopus salutem in domino. Quia pia vota fidelium pio sunt favore prosequenda, nos, de assensu dilectorum filiorum Willelmi decani et capituli nostri Linc' et de assensu Vitalis Engayne patroni, Simone etiam persona ecclesie de Laxton' consenciente, locum fundacionis prioratus de Castro Imel cum omnibus que Ricardus Engayne predicti prioratus fundator Deo et sancte Marie et canonicis regularibus ibidem Deo servientibus et in perpetuum servituris, in liberam, puram et perpetuam elemosinam contulit, quieta prorsum ab omni seculari servitio et exactione. Omnia etiam terras, videlicet, redditus et tenementa in diocesi Linc' constituta ab aliis quibuscumque donatoribus et confirmatoribus dictis prioratui et canonicis in liberam, puram et perpetuam elemosinam collata, eisdem canonicis sicut ea ipsis iuste et rationabiliter concessa sunt et confirmata episcopali [confirmamus] autoritate; salvo iure predicte matricis ecclesie de Laxton' in omnibus et salvis in omnibus episcopalibus consuetudinibus et Linc' ecclesie dignitate. Quod ut perpetuam optineat firmitatem, presenti scripto sigillum nostrum una cum sigillo predicti capituli nostri Linc' duximus apponendum. Hiis testibus: Iohanne precentore Linc', Willelmo archidiacono Well', magistro Rogero de Lakok', Radulfo de Warevill' et Willelmo de Winchecumb', canonicis Linc', magistris Willelmo de Beningwurth' et Ricardo de Cant' capellanis, magistro Waltero de Cromba, Galfrido de Moris, Ricardo de Oxon', Philippo de Langeport', Iohanne de Bannebir' et Roberto de Aketon', clericis. Dat' per manum nostram apud Tinghurst quinto kalendas Iunii anno pontificatus nostri decimo [septimo].

> The priory of Fineshade or Castle Hymel was founded at some time before 1208. The 14th-century abstract of the priory's charters (Lambeth Palace, Court of Arches exhibits) notes this charter (fo. 10v): 'XLVᵃ continet confirmationem reverendi patris domini Hugonis Lincolniensis episcopi de fundatione domus de F. et de omnibus terris etc.'

248. Rocester abbey

Collation, by authority of the Council, of the church of Woodford [Halse] to master Thomas de Sanford, clerk, saving in future the right of the abbot and convent of Rocester.   Banbury, 7 June 1226

> B = LAO Wells roll ix, m. 5.
> Pd *RHW* ii 214.

Hiis testibus: Iohanne precentore Linc', Iohanne Bedeford' et Willelmo Well' archidiaconis, magistris Rogero de Lackok' et Amaurico de Bugeden' et Willelmo de Winchecumbe, canonicis Linc', magistris Willelmo de Beningwurth' et Ricardo de Cant' cappellanis, et magistro Waltero de Crumba, Galfrido de Moris, Ricardo de Oxon', Philippo de Langeport, Roberto de Aketon' et Iohanne de Bannebir', clericis. Dat' per manum Radulfi de Waravill', canonici Linc', apud Bannebir' septimo idus Iunii pontificatus nostri anno decimo septimo.

> The institution of master Thomas, on the presentation of the abbey of Rocester, is recorded in the institution roll, among entries for the bp's fifteenth pontifical year, 20 December 1223 x 19 December 1224 (ibid. 119). The obviously late date of this letter of institution makes for confusion, but there is evidence of subsequent reinstitution (after collation by lapse) on the presentation of the true patron (cf. nos. 270, 362n.).

249.   Luffield priory

Indulgence of ten days for all those who shall visit the monastery of Luffield on the Nativity of the Blessed Virgin Mary to pray and contribute alms. Other bishops may grant indulgences for Luffield, but not exceeding ten days. It is forbidden for a collector to collect alms anywhere outside the bounds of the monastery.   Chacombe, 11 June 1226

> B = LAO Wells roll ix, m. 5d.
> Pd *RHW* ii 220.

Dat' per manum nostram apud Chaucumb' iii idus Iunii pontificatus nostri anno xvii.

250.   Bretford bridge

Indulgence of seven days for all travellers who shall contribute towards the repair of Bretford bridge. This indulgence is to last for three years. No collectors are to be sent through the diocese to collect alms.   Kilsby, 21 June 1226

> B = LAO Wells roll ix, m. 5d (no witnesses).
> Pd *RHW* ii 219.

Dat' per manum nostram apud Kildeby xi kalendas Iulii anno pontificatus nostri decimo septimo.

> Bretford has not been positively identified. As this entry occurs on the Northampton archdeaconry charter roll, a location in Northamptonshire or Rutland would be expected. There is a Bretford just over the Northamptonshire border in Warwickshire.

251.   Northampton, abbey of St Mary de Prato

Institution of John of Eynsham, chaplain, to the perpetual vicarage of [Earl's] Barton, on the presentation of Ralph of Tynemouth, parson of the church, with the assent of the abbess and convent of St Mary de Prato, Northampton, the patrons. He is to serve personally. The vicarage consists of the entire altarage of the church with a suitable manse and one mark each year from the rent which Simon of Lavendon owes for the land he holds.   Arthingworth, 22 June 1226

> B = LAO Wells roll ix, m. 5.
> Pd *RHW* ii 214.

Hiis testibus: I. precentore Linc', W. archidiacono Well', et W. de Winchecumb', can(onicis) Linc', magistris Willelmo de Benigwurth' et Ricardo de Cant' cappellanis et magistro Waltero de Crumba, Ricardo de Oxon', Roberto de Dunholm' et I. de Bannebir', clericis. Dat' per manum nostram apud Erningewurth' x kalendas Iulii anno pontificatus nostri xvii^mo.

> The institution is recorded in the institution roll among entries for the bp's fourteenth pontifical year, 20 December 1222 x 19 December 1223 (ibid. 111).

252. York minster

Indulgence of thirteen days enjoined penance to all those who visit York Minster on the day of the commemoration of St William, archbishop of York, [8 June] or within eight days after that date. Newark, 5 July 1226

> B = BL ms. Cotton Claudius B iii (York Minster cartulary), f. 52r (p. 103). s. xiii ex.
> C = York D. & C. ms. L.2(1). Magnum Registrum Album, part II, f. 61r–v. s. xiv med.

Omnibus Cristi fidelibus ad quos presens scriptum pervenerit, Hugo Dei gratia Lincoln' episcopus salutem in domino. De misericordia Dei et gloriose Virginis Marie et beati Petri apostolorum principis necnon et beati Willelmi Ebor' ecclesie quondam archipresulis meritis confidentes omnibus Ebor' diocesis dum tamen eiusdem loci archiepiscopus id ratum habuerit, omnibus etiam nostre diocesis et aliis quorum diocesani ratam habuerint hanc nostram relaxationem ad dictam ecclesiam Ebor' in anniversario die depositionis beati Willelmi predicti, sexto videlicet idus Iunii vel infra octo dies sequentes, devotionis causa venientibus ᵃ⁻et de bonis sibi a Deo collatis elemosinas suas ibidem pie conferentibus, confessis et vere penitentibus⁻ᵃ, de iniuncta sibi penitentia tresdecim dies relaxamus; prohibentes ne cum hiis litteris patentibus nuntius aut predicator ad predictas elemosinas colligendas in episcopatum nostrum transmittatur. Dat' per manum nostram apud Newerk' iii nonas Iulii anno ab incarnatione domini mᵒ ccᵒ vicesimo sexto.

ᵃ⁻ᵃ *this entire clause is omitted* C.

253. Weldon church

Repetition of the ordination regarding Weldon church as far as it concerned the parson of the church [cf. no. 245]. Lyddington, 15 July 1226

> B = LAO Wells roll ix, m. 5.
> Pd *RHW* ii 214–15.

Hiis testibus: I. precentore Linc', W. archidiacono Well', magistris W. de Linc' et Rogero de Lakcok' et Willelmo de Winchelc', canonicis Linc', magistris W. de Beningwrd' et R. de Cant' capellanis, magistro Waltero de Cromb', Galfrido de Moris, Ricardo de Oxon', Philippo de Langeport', I. de Banneb' et Roberto de Aketon', clericis. Dat' per manum nostram apud Lidint' idibus Iulii pontificatus nostri anno xvii.

254. Cirencester abbey

Institution of John de Stanton, chaplain, to the perpetual vicarage of Brigstock ordained by authority of the Council, on the presentation of the abbot and convent of Cirencester. He is to serve personally. The vicarage consists of the entire altarage of the parish church and the chapel of Stanherne, all the demesne land of the church, with a suitable manse, and rent assessed at twenty-two shillings belonging to the church. The vicar shall pay synodal dues but the canons shall provide hospitality for the archdeacon. Lyddington, 22 July 1226

> B = LAO Wells roll ix, m. 5. C = Oxford, Bodl. ms. Dep. C392 (Cirencester cartulary), fos. 181r–182r (in a judgment of papal judges delegate in a suit

between the abbot of Cirencester and John, vicar of Brigstock, 17 September 1246). s. xiii med.
Pd from B in *RHW* ii 215; from C in *Cirencester Cartulary* ii no. 728.

Hiis testibus:[a] Iohanne precentore Linc', W. archidiacono Wellen', magistris R, de Laccock', N. de Evesh' et W. de Winchecumb', canonicis Linc', magistris W. de Benigworth' et R. de Cantia cappellanis, magistro W. de Cromb', Ricardo de Oxon', G. de Moris et I. de Bannebir', clericis. Dat' per manum Radulfi de Warevill', canonici Linc', apud Lidington' xi⁰ kalendas Augusti anno pontificatus nostri decimo septimo.

[a] Hiis testibus et cetera C.

255. Fineshade priory

Indulgence of twenty days for all those of the Lincoln diocese, and others whose diocesan bishops shall approve, who shall visit and contribute alms towards the construction of the monastery of Fineshade. This indulgence is to last for three years. It is forbidden for a collector to collect alms anywhere outside the bounds of the monastery. Lyddington, 26 July 1226

B = LAO Wells roll ix, m. 5d (no witnesses).
Pd *RHW* ii 219.

Dat' per manum R. de War' apud Lidingt' vii kalendas Augusti anno pontificatus nostri xvii.

256. Thrapston bridge

Indulgence of ten days for all those travellers who shall contribute alms towards the construction and repair of Thrapston bridge. This indulgence is to last for three years. It is forbidden for a collector to collect alms anywhere except at the bridge itself. Buckden, 31 July 1226

B = LAO Wells roll ix, m. 5d.
Pd *RHW* ii 219–20.

Dat' per manum Radulfi de Warevill', canonici Linc', apud Buggeden' pridie kalendas Augusti anno pontificatus nostri xvii.

For an earlier indulgence for Thrapston bridge, see nos. 13, 220.

257. Hereford, hospital of St Ethelbert

Indulgence of ten days to all those who contribute alms for the maintenance of the poor in the hospital founded near the [cathedral] church of St Ethelbert, Hereford, by the dean and chapter of Hereford, and for the construction of the hospital buildings. Old Temple, London, 18 October 1226

A = Hereford D. & C. document 2040. No medieval endorsement; approx. 157 x 70 mm.; seal missing, tongue and tie torn away.

Omnibus Cristi fidelibus ad quos presens scriptum pervenerit, H. Dei gratia Lincoln' episcopus salutem in domino. De misericordia Dei omnipotentis patris et filii et spiritus sancti et meritis beate virginis et omnium sanctorum confidentes, omnibus nostre diocesis et aliis quorum diocesani hanc nostram relaxationem ratam habuerint ad hospitale iuxta ecclesiam beati Adhelberti Herefordie per decanum et capitulum eiusdem loci factum venientibus, et ad sustentationem pauperum et domorum constructionem elemosinas suas ibidem pie conferentibus, confessis et vere penitentibus, de iniuncta sibi penitentia decem dies relaxamus: prohibentes ne nuntius vel predicator ad predictas elemosinas colligendas cum hiis litteris nostris patentibus in episcopatum nostrum transmittatur. Dat' per manum Radulfi de Waravill', canonici Linc', apud Vetus Templum London' quintodecimo kalendas Novembris anno pontificatus nostri decimo septimo. Valete.

> The hospital was founded c. 1225 by Elias of Bristol, canon of Hereford (see *EEA* 7 no. 344 and n. for further details).

258. Pickworth church

Institution of Ralph of Norwich, clerk, who has a dispensation from Pope Honorius [III], to the church of Pickworth, on the presentation of William de Gisneto.

Fingest, 31 October 1226

> B = LAO Wells roll ix, m. 5.
> Pd *RHW* ii 216.

Hiis testibus: Iohanne precentore, Willelmo de Winchecumb', canonic[o] Linc', magistris Willelmo de Benigwurth' et Ricardo de Cant' cappellanis, Ricardo de Oxon', Ricardo Mauclerc, Galfrido de Moris, Thoma de Askeby et Radulfo de Repinghal', clericis. Dat' per manum Radulfi de Waravill', canonici Linc', pridie kalendas Novembris pontificatus nostri anno decimoseptimo apud Tinghurst'.

> The institution is recorded in the institution roll (ibid. 151) and the dispensation from Honorius III is endorsed on the roll (ibid. 176–7).

259. Aynho bridge

Indulgence (number of days not specified) for all those who shall contribute alms towards the construction and repair of Aynho bridge. It is forbidden for a collector to collect alms anywhere except at the bridge itself.

Banbury, 10 November 1226

> B = LAO Wells roll ix, m. 5d (no witnesses).
> Pd *RHW* ii 220.

Dat' per manum Radulfi de Waravill' apud Bannebr' quarto idus Novembris pontificatus nostri anno decimo septimo.

> This indulgence is stated to be similar to one for Thrapston bridge issued during the bp's fifth pontifical year (no. 13). This latter document has not survived, unless it is a scribal error for the Thrapston indulgence issued 'anno decimo quinto' (no. 219).

260.   Merton priory

Mandate to the archdeacon of Northampton to induct master R(alph) de Derham into corporal possession of the church of Greatworth, to which he has been admitted on the presentation of the prior and convent of Merton. Gunnora de Kaynes has renounced her presentation.

[20 December 1225 x 19 December 1226]

B = BL ms. Cotton Cleopatra C vii (Merton register) fo. 100r (98r, 120r). s. xiii med.

H. Dei gratia episcopus Linc' archidiacono Norhamt' salutem. Quoniam dilectum filium magistrum R. de Derham ad presentationem prioris et conventus Meriton' ad ecclesiam de Grettewrhd' admisimus et Gunnora de Kaaines presentationem quam nobis fecit de predicto R. ad memoratam ecclesiam renuntiavit, mandamus vobis quatinus eundem R. in corporalem possessionem mittatis.

> Master Ralph was instituted to the church of Greatworth during the bp's seventeenth pontifical year, 20 December 1225 x 19 December 1226 (*RHW* ii 131). This document is mentioned in *The records of Merton priory in the county of Surrey*, ed. A.Heales (1898), p. 94, where the bp's name is wrongly given as Henry. The entry in the Merton register continues with a renunciation of presentation: 'Presentationem quam vobis fecimus de tali ad ecclesiam talem renuntiamus, concedentes et rogantes quatinus non obstante presentatione illa ydoneam personam admittatis et personam instituatis in eandem ad presentationem prioris et conventus de Meriton' ad ecclesiam memoratam. In huius rei testimonium presentibus litteris sigillum nostrum apposuimus.'

261.   Peterborough abbey

Institution of Richard of Stainsby, clerk, to the church of Peakirk on the presentation of the abbot and convent of Peterborough, saving to the abbey its customary pension.   [20 December 1225 x 19 December 1226]

> B = LAO Wells roll ix, m. 5 (under 17th pontifical year).
> Pd *RHW* ii 217.

Testibus et dat' sicut in carta de Grendon' in archidiaconatu Bukingham'.

> The Buckingham archdeaconry charter roll has not survived. The only Grendon Underwood entry in the Buckingham archdeaconry institution roll is the collation of the church to Robert Haldein of Banbury on 8 October 1224 (ibid. 65). See also no. 265 below.

262.   Newport Pagnell priory

Institution of Robert of Boddington, deacon, to the perpetual vicarage of Boddington, on the presentation of Roger the chaplain, rector of the church, with the assent of the prior and convent of Newport [Pagnell], patrons of two portions of the church. Robert is to minister personally. He shall hold for life that portion which his brother Hugh held, paying to Roger and his successors as parsons an annual pension of thirteen marks. He shall also bear all ordinary and customary burdens of the church.   [20 December 1225 x 19 December 1226]

> B = LAO Wells roll ix, m. 5.
> Pd *RHW* ii 211.

Testibus et dat' ut in carta de Stiveleya in archidiaconatu Buking'.

> While the Boddington entry in the Northampton charter roll occurs among entries
> for the bp's seventeenth pontifical year, 20 December 1225 x 19 December 1226,
> the institution roll entry (ibid. 125) is placed in the previous pontifical year. The
> Buckingham archdeaconry charter roll has not survived; the charter in question is
> likely to have been the letter of institution of Hubertinus de Conflencia to the
> church of Stukeley, recorded in the Buckingham archdeaconry institution roll for
> the bp's seventeenth pontifical year, 20 December 1225 x 19 December 1226 (ibid.
> 68).

263.   Titchmarsh church

Institution of Hugh de Sidenham, clerk, to the church of Titchmarsh, on the presentation of Ascelin de Sidenham.   [20 December 1225 x 19 December 1226]

> B = LAO Wells roll ix, m. 5.
> Pd *RHW* ii 215–16.

Hiis testibus: I. precentore Linc', W. archidiacono Wellens', magistris Rogero de
Lakk' et Willelmo de Winchecumb', canonicis Linc', magistris Willelmo de
Beningworth' et Ricardo de Cant' capellanis, magistris Waltero de Crumb',
Ricardo de Oxon', I. de Banneb', Philippo de Langeport et Galfrido de Moris,
clericis, anno pontificatus nostri xvii.

264.   Woodford church

*Institution of Robert son of Walter son of Robert, clerk, to a mediety of the church
of Woodford, on the presentation of B. de Ver, patron by virtue of his wardship of
the land and heir of William Maufe.*   [20 December 1225 x 19 December 1226]

> B = LAO Wells roll ix, m. 5.
> Pd *RHW* ii 216.

. . . sicut in rotulo inter cartas Hunting' anno pontificatus nostri xvii.

> The Huntingdon archdeaconry charter roll has not survived. The institution is
> recorded in the institution roll, where the incumbent's name is given as Robert son
> of Robert son of Walter (ibid. 128). The version in this present charter seems to be
> correct (see no. 289).

265.   Tansor church

*Confirmation of the institution of Richard of Stainsby to a mediety of the church
of Tansor, performed by Roger, late dean of Lincoln, by special mandate and with
the bishop's authority. The rector of the mediety shall pay an annual pension of
two and a half marks to the prebend of Nassington [in Lincoln cathedral].*
[20 December 1225 x 19 December 1226]

> B = LAO Wells roll ix, m. 5.
> Pd *RHW* ii 216–17.

Testibus et dat' ut in carta de Grendon' in archidiaconatu Bukingham'.

> The Buckingham archdeaconry charter roll has not survived; for the Grendon
> Underwood collation of 8 October 1224 see above, no. 261n. The entry in the

Northampton charter roll is placed among entries for the bp's seventeenth pontifical year, 20 December 1225 x 19 December 1226. Roger of Rolleston, dean of
Lincoln, died on 28 January 1223, so Stainsby's institution must obviously have
taken place before this date. There is no record of this institution in Bp Wells' surviving rolls. For Richard of Stainsby's institution to Peakirk see no. 260.

266. Crowland abbey

*Institution of Thomas Horn to the church of Gedney, on the presentation of the
abbot and convent of Crowland.*   [20 December 1225 x 19 December 1226]

>   B = Spalding Gentlemen's Society, Crowland cartulary fo. 108v, no. x. s. xiv med.
>   C = ibid., ms. 108/28 (Gedney charter roll). s. xiv med.

Omnibus Cristi fidelibus ad quos presens scriptum pervenerit, Hugo Dei gratia
Linc' episcopus salutem in domino. Noverit universitas vestra nos, ad presentationem dilectorum in Cristo filiorum abbatis et conventus Croiland' patronorum
ecclesie de Gedeneye, dilectum in Cristo filium Thomam Horn ad eanden ecclesiam admisisse, ipsumque in ea canonice personam instituisse: salvis in omnibus
episcopalibus consuetudinibus et Lincoln' ecclesie dignitate. Quod ut perpetuam
optineat firmitatem, presenti scripto sigillum nostrum duximus apponendum.
Hiis testibus etc.

>   The institution is recorded in *RHW* iii 144, among entries for the bp's seventeenth
>   pontifical year (20 December 1225 x 19 December 1226).

267. Canons Ashby priory

*Following upon a mandate of Pope Honorius III that master Guy de Aricio
should receive twenty marks sterling each year from the bishop's chamber
(camera) until he should be provided with a more profitable ecclesiastical benefice, the bishop has instituted him to the church of Moreton Pinkney, with the
assent of the patrons, the prior and convent of Canons Ashby.*
                                                    [20 December 1225 x 19 December 1226]

>   B = LAO Wells roll ix, m. 5 (no witnesses or dating clause, among entries for the
>   seventeenth pontifical year, and cross-reference to the now lost Oxford arch-
>   deaconry charter roll: 'ut in rotulo cartarum archidiaconatus Oxon' eiusdem
>   anni plene poterit inveniri').
>   Pd *RHW* ii 212.

268. Canons Ashby priory

*Following upon a mandate of Pope Honorius III that master Guy de Aricio
should be provided to an ecclesiastical benefice, the bishop had conferred upon
him the church of Moreton [Pinkney], on the presentation of the prior and
convent of Canons Ashby. The bishop now grants that the aforesaid prior and
convent may hold the same church at farm from master Guy for his lifetime. At his
death or cession the priory can claim no right or possession in the church by
reason of this farm, but are to hand over the church and the key of the church to
the archdeacon or the dean, as is customarily done with vacant benefices.
However, the priory's right of patronage and an annual rent of forty shillings
payable to them from the church are safeguarded. The prior and canons shall*

maintain the curia *of the parson with the houses, and shall not alienate any land which is of the demesne of the church. The priory shall provide a suitable chaplain to minister in the church as long as they hold it at farm. The chaplain shall be presented to the bishop and his successors before admission to be examined, and if found suitable to be admitted by episcopal mandate directed to the archdeacon. The chaplain shall have the whole altarage with a suitable dwelling near the church and he shall answer for archidiaconal hospitality and shall pay synodals.*   [20 December 1225 x 19 December 1226]

> B = LAO Wells roll ix, m. 5d (no witnesses or dating clause, among entries for the seventeenth pontifical year).
> Pd *RHW* ii 218.

> The institution is recorded ibid. 129. See also no. 267 above.

269. King Henry III

Assurance by S(tephen), archbishop of Canterbury, E(ustace), bishop of London, P(eter), bishop of Winchester, J(ocelin), bishop of Bath, H(ugh), bishop of Lincoln, R(ichard), bishop of Salisbury, R(alph), bishop of Chichester, W(alter), bishop of Carlisle, G(eoffrey), bishop of Ely and Thomas, bishop of Norwich, that they would work for the observance of the treaties between King Henry III and H(ugh) de Lusignan, count of La Marche and Angouleme and I(sabel) his wife (formerly queen of England), H(ugh), viscount of Thouars and William le Archevêque.   London, 20 December 1226

> B = PRO C66/35 (patent roll, 11 Henry III) m. 11d.
> Pd from B in *Foedera* 184; *CPR 1225–32*, pp. 152–3; *Acta Stephani Langton* no. 95; (calendar) *EEA* 9 no. 128.

270. Desborough church

Institution of master S[imon] of Missenden to the church of Desborough, on the presentation of William Burdun, patron by virtue of his wife, Agnes. The church had previously been collated to master Simon by authority of the Council.
                    Lyddington, 23 February 1227

> B = LAO Wells roll ix, m. 5.
> Pd *RHW* ii 220–1.

Hiis testibus: I. precentore Linc', M. de Pateshull', magistro R. de Lacok' et W. de Winchecomb', canonicis Lincoln', magistris W. de Benigwrd' et R. de Cant' capellanis, magistro R. de Windelesowr', R. de Oxon', R. Mauclerc', T. de Askeb' et G. de Moris, clericis. Dat' per manum R. de Warevill', canonici Linc', apud Lidinton' vii kalendas Martii pontificatus nostri anno xviii°.

> The collation is recorded in the institution roll, among entries for the bp's sixteenth pontifical year, 20 December 1224 x 19 December 1225 (ibid. 127).

271. Quarndon mill

Confirmation of the grant made by Roger of Rolleston, late dean of Lincoln, to his nepos, *William of Rolleston, of three parts of the mill of Quarndon for an annual payment each Michaelmas of twelve pence to the dean and his successors*

*for all service. It is stipulated that the right of William of Rolleston and his heirs
to sell the three parts of the mill shall be subject to the dean of Lincoln's right of
pre-emption.*   Lincoln, in chapter, 30 March 1227

> B = LAO Lincoln D. & C. A/1/7 (*Carte tangentes decanatum beate Marie Lincoln'*)
>   f. 53v, no. 152 (no witnesses). s. xiv med.
> Pd *Reg. Ant.* iii no. 754.

Dat' per manum Radulfi de Waravill', canonici Linc', in capitulo Lincoln' tertio
kalendas Aprilis anno pontificatus nostri decimo octavo.

> The original grant of Dean Roger of Rolleston (d. 1223) is *Reg. Ant.* ii no. 751, con-
> firmed by the chapter of Lincoln (no. 752) and subsequently by William de Thor-
> naco, Roger's successor as dean (no. 753).

272.   Peterborough abbey

*Institution of master Ralph of Colling[ham], clerk, to the church of Stanwick, on
the presentation of the abbot and convent of Peterborough.*
                                                            Bourne, 2 April 1227

> B = LAO Wells roll ix, m. 5.
> Pd *RHW* ii 221.

Hiis testibus: magistro A. de Bugged' et W. de Winchecumb', canonicis Linc',
magistris W. de Beningworth' et R. de Cant' cappellanis, Ricardo de Oxon', R.
Mauclerc', T. de Askeb' et G. de Moris, clericis. Dat' per manum R. de Waravill',
canonici Linc', apud Brunn' iiii° nonas Aprilis anno pontificatus nostri xviii.

> The institution is recorded in the institution roll, among entries for the bp's six-
> teenth pontifical year, 20 December 1224 x 19 December 1225 (ibid. 124).

273.   Northampton, abbey of St Mary de Prato

*Institution of Thomas of Gnosall, clerk, to the church of Broughton, on the pres-
entation of the abbess and convent of St Mary de Prato, Northampton.*
                                                            Fingest, 12 May 1227

> B = LAO Wells roll ix, m. 5.
> Pd *RHW* ii 221.

Testibus ut in carta Nicholai de Flora, persone de Beby in archidiaconatu Leic'.
Dat' per manum R. de Waravill', canonici Linc', apud Tingehurst' iiii idus Maii
anno pontificatus nostri xviii.

> The institution is recorded in the institution roll, among entries for the bp's eleventh
> pontifical year, 20 December 1219 x 19 December 1220 (ibid. 101). The Leicester
> archdeaconry charter roll has not survived; the institution of Nicholas to Beeby is
> recorded on the Leicester archdeaconry institution roll for the bp's eleventh pontifi-
> cal year, 20 December 1219 x 19 December 1220 (ibid. 280).

274.   Northampton, abbey of St James

*Institution of Robert de Schredecot, clerk, to the church of Cranford, on the pres-
entation of the abbot and convent of St James outside Northampton, and saving to
the abbey their customary pension.*   Fingest, 12 May 1227

B = LAO Wells roll ix, m. 5.
Pd *RHW* ii 221–2.

Testibus et dat' ut supra carta proxima [no. 273].

The institution is recorded on the ninth membrane of Wells roll x, *c.* 1217 x 1218 (ibid. i 65; cf. Smith, 'Rolls').

275. Northampton, abbey of St James

Institution of William of Northampton, chaplain, to the church of [Rothers]thorpe, on the presentation of the abbot and convent of St James, Northampton, and saving to the aforesaid abbey the portion which was granted and confirmed to them by the bishop and the chapter of Lincoln, in the name of a perpetual benefice. William is to serve personally. Kilsby, 28 June 1227

B = LAO Wells roll ix, m. 5.
Pd *RHW* ii 222.

Testibus: magistris Rogero de Lacok', Amaurico de Buggeden' et Willelmo de Winchecumb', canonicis Linc', magistris Willelmo de Beningwrd' et Ricardo de Cant' capellanis, magistro Ricardo de Windelesowr', Ricardo de Oxon', Galfrido de Moris et Thoma de Askeby, clericis. Dat' per manum nostram apud Kyldeby iiii kalendas Iulii anno pontificatus nostri xviii.

The institution is recorded in the institution roll (ibid. 135), where it is stated that William was formerly vicar of Duston. For the bp's grant to the abbey, mentioned in this charter, see no. 78.

276. Hospitallers

Institution of Richard of Worcester, clerk, to the church of Cosgrove, on the presentation of the prior and brethren of the Hospital in England.
Lyddington, 5 July 1227

B = LAO Wells roll ix, m. 6.
Pd *RHW* ii 222.

T(estibus): magistro A. de Buggeden' et Willelmo de Winch', canonicis Linc', magistris W. de Beningwrd' et R. de Cant' capellanis, R. de Oxon', I. de Bannebir' et T. de Askeby, clericis. Dat' per manum nostram apud Lidington' iii nonas Iulii anno pontificatus nostri xviii.

The institution is recorded in the institution rolls (ibid. 136), where it is noted that W. the previous incumbent (presumably William of Westwell, see no. 231) had become a Franciscan.

277. Richard, parson of Draughton

Notification that the church and all other property within the diocese belonging to Richard the chaplain, parson of Draughton, a crusader, have been taken under the bishop's protection. Lyddington, 10 July 1227

B = LAO Wells roll ix, m. 6d (no witnesses).
Pd *RHW* ii 224–5.

Dat' per manum R. de Warevill', canonici Linc', apud Lidington' vi idus Iulii anno pontificatus nostri xviii.

278. John of Banbury, rector of Litchborough

Similar notification placing the church and property of John of Banbury, rector of Litchborough, under the bishop's protection. [*c.* 10 July 1227]

> Mention of charter after the enrolment of no. 277: 'sub eadem forma scriptum est pro Iohanne de Bannebir' super ecclesia de Litcheberg' ', pd *RHW* ii 225.

279. North Ormsby priory

Confirmation for the priory of [North] Ormsby of all their lands, possessions, gifts, confirmations and tenements in Ormsby and Utterby, which they have been given by Ralph of Wyham, William his son, and Ralph his grandson.

Louth, 1 September 1227

> B = Oxford, Bodl. ms. Dodsworth 135 fo. 158v (copy of charter on fo. 16 of the lost cartulary of North Ormsby). s.xvii. C = ibid., fo. 143v (abbreviated version).

Universis sancte matris ecclesie filiis, Hugo Dei gratia Linc' episcopus[a] eternam[b] in domino salutem. Noveritis nos, divine caritatis intuitu, ad instantiam conventus utriusque sexus de Ormesby concessisse et presenti carta[c] confirmasse Deo et beate Marie et[d] conventui in puram et perpetuam elemosinam omnes terras, possessiones, donationes et confirmationes et omnia tenementa sine aliquo retenemento [f-]que habent in Ormesby et Uterby[g] de dono Radulfi de Wyhum et Willelmi filii sui et Radulfi filii dicti Willelmi, sicut carte eorum[h] plenius testantur,[-f] tam in terris arabilibus quam in pratis et paschuis, toftis et boscis et cum omnibus pertinentiis suis, libertatibus et aysiamentis infra villas[i] de Ormesby et Uterby et extra. Testibus[-f] etc. Dat' apud Ludam kalendis Septembris pontificatus nostri anno 18.

> [a] episcopus Lincolniensis C. [b] *word omitted* C. [c] nostra *inserted* C. [d] dicto *inserted* C. [e] et *inserted* C. [f-f] section *omitted* C. [g] Utterby C. [h] quam *written in* B *and then crossed out.* [i] villa B.

> For charters of Ralph of Wyham and his son William see *Gilbertine Charters* p. 40, nos. 2, 3.

280. Sulby abbey

Grant, with the assent of William the dean and the chapter of Lincoln, to the abbot and convent of Sulby of a pension of two marks a year from the church of Great Harrowden and the chapel of Little Harrowden, both in their patronage, in the name of a perpetual benefice. This arrangement is to take effect on the death or cession of master Richard of Kent, the present rector; until then, only one mark shall be paid to the abbey each year. Lincoln, 8 September 1227

> A = BL Add. Ch. 21999. No endorsement; approx. 185 x 127 + 15 mm.; fragment of episcopal seal (repaired) and capitular seal, brownish-white wax, on parchment tags, (method 1).
> B = LAO Wells roll ix, m. 6.
> Pd from B in *RHW* ii 222–3.

Omnibus Cristi fidelibus ad quos presens scriptum pervenerit, Hugo Dei gratia Lincoln' episcopus salutem in domino. Noverit universitas vestra nos, de assensu dilectorum filiorum Willelmi decani et capituli nostri Lincoln', concessisse et dedisse divine pietatis intuitu dilectis in Cristo filiis abbati et conventui de Suleby duas marcas annuas de ecclesia maioris Harewedun' et cappella minoris Harewedune, que de ipsorum advocatione sunt, post decessum vel cessionem magistri Ricardi de Cantia eiusdem ecclesie rectoris, per manum illius qui pro tempore in eadem ecclesia persona fuerit, nomine perpetui beneficii, annuatim percipiendas ad duos terminos: videlicet, ad festum omnium sanctorum unam marcam et ad Pascha unam marcam. Dictus autem magister Ricardus, quamdiu ipsam ecclesiam rexerit, tantum unam marcam annuam solvet abbati et conventui memoratis: salvis in omnibus episcopalibus consuetudinibus et Lincoln' ecclesie dignitate. Quod ut perpetuam optineat firmitatem, presenti scripto sigillum nostrum una cum sigillo predicti capituli nostri Lincoln' duximus apponendum. Hiis testibus: Willelmo decano, Roberto archidiacono Lincoln', Iohanne precentore et Ricardo cancellario, Willelmo Leycestr' et Willelmo Stouwe archidiaconis, Iohanne subdecano, Waltero Blundo, Rogero de Bristoll', magistris Roberto de Gravel', Theodbaldo de Cant' et Stephano de Cycestr', Roberto de Whassingburg', Galfrido Scoto et Thoma de Northon' cappellanis, magistro Willelmo de Lincoln', Waltero de Well' et Willelmo de Winchecumb' diaconis, magistro Amaurico de Buggeden', Petro de Cheuermont et Rogero de Boun subdiaconis, canonicis Lincoln'. Dat' per manum Radulfi de Waravill', canonici Lincoln', apud Lincoln' sexto idus Septembris anno pontificatus nostri decimo octavo.

There was a dispute over the advowson of this church between Sulby and Robert de Muschamp in Easter term 1227 (*CRR* xii no. 207), just before this grant was made.

*281. Huntingdon priory

Charter to the canons of Huntingdon about the domesne tithes of Abbotsley
[8 September 1227]

Mention of charter in the LAO Wells roll ix, m. 6 (no. 280 above), where the witness and dating clauses of the original are replaced in the copy by: testibus et dat' ut in carta canonicorum Huntingdon' super decimis dominici de Albodesl' in archidiaconatu Huntingdon', pd *RHW* ii 223.

Robert Grosseteste was rector of Abbotsley at this time (ibid. iii 48).

282. Wellingborough bridge

Indulgence of thirteen days for all those who contribute alms towards the construction and repair of the bridge at Wellingborough called Staples Bridge. This indulgence is to last for three years and the collector is forbidden to collect alms anywhere except at the bridge itself.   Spaldwick, 21 September 1227

B = LAO Wells roll ix, m. 6d (no witnesses).
Pd *RHW* ii 225.

Dat' per manum Radulfi de Waravill', canonici Linc', apud Spaldewic' xi° kalendas Octobris pontificatus nostri anno xviii°.

283. Thorney abbey

Institution of Thomas of Bath, chaplain, to the perpetual vicarage of Yaxley, on the presentation of Nigel de Insula, the rector, made with the assent of tbe abbot and convent of Thorney, the patrons. He is to serve personally and shall hold the entire church, paying to Nigel and his successors an annual pension of twenty marks, half at Easter and half at Michaelmas. He shall also pay two marks a year to the abbey in the name of Nigel and his successors.

Lyddington, 26 September 1227

> B = CUL ms. Add. 3020 (Thorney cartulary) fos. 72v–73r (pars secunda, 32v–33r) (in an inspeximus of Bp Robert Grosseteste (1235–53), the seal of Bp Hugh's original charter having broken). s. xiv in. C = ibid. ms. Add. 3021 (Thorney cartulary) fo. 431v (pars nona, xxxv). s. xiv in.

Omnibus Cristi fidelibus ad quos presens scriptum pervenerit, Hugo Dei gratia Linc' episcopus eternam in domino salutem. Noverit universitas vestra nos, ad presentationem dilecti filii Nigelli de Insula rectoris de Iakele[a], interveniente dilectorum in Cristo abbatis et conventus Thorneye[b] patronorum eiusdem assensu, dilectum in Cristo filium Thomam de Bathonia[c] capellanum ad ipsius ecclesie vicariam admisisse, ipsum<q>ue in ea perpetuum vicarium[d] instituisse cum honere[e] ministrandi personaliter in eadem; qui quidem totam illam ecclesiam cum omnibus suis pertinentiis tenebit quoad vixerit, reddendo inde <pre>dicto Nigello[f] et successoribus suis eiusdem ecclesie personis viginti[g] marcas annuas ad duos anni[h] terminos, videlicet ad Pascha decem[i] marcas et ad festum sancti Michaelis decem[i] marcas nomine pensionis; reddendo etiam nomine ipsius Nigelli[f] et successorum suorum ibidem duas marcas annuas ad predictos terminos abbati et conventui memoratis[k]: salvis in omnibus episcopalibus consuetudinibus et Lincoln' ecclesie dignitate. Quod ut perpetuam optineat firmitatem, presenti scripto sigillum nostrum duximus apponendum. Hiis testibus[l]: magistris Rogero de Lakok, Amaurico de Buggeden et Willelmo de Winchecumb', canonicis Lincoln', magistro Willelmo de Beningwrd' capellano, magistro Clemente Pigiun, Ricardo de Oxen', Galfrido de Moris et Thoma de Askebi, clericis. Dat' per manum Radulfi de Warevill', canonici Lincoln', apud Lidington' sexto[m] kalendas Octobris anno pontificatus nostri[n] decimo octavo.

[a] Iak' C. [b] Thorn' C. [c] Bathon' C. [d] vicarium perpetuum C. [e] onere C. [f] N. C. [g] xx C. [h] *omitted* C. [i] ii C. [k] *followed by the letter 's' dotted for deletion* C. [l] Hiis testibus etc. C. [m] vi C. [n] pontificatus nostri anno C.

See also no. 230.

284. Jocelin, bishop of Bath

Grant in free, pure and perpetual alms to Jocelin, bishop of Bath and his successors that they shall held the town of Axbridge, which is of the bishop of Lincoln's fee, quit of suit of the foreign hundred which the town used to owe to bishop Hugh and his heirs and likewise quit of half a mark due from the town each year and of all service and exactions.

Fingest, 7 November 1227

> B = Wells D. & C. Liber Albus II, fo. 342r. s.xvi in. C = ibid., fos. 350v–351r. Pd (calendar), *HMC Wells* i 471.

Omnibus Cristi fidelibus ad quos presens scriptum pervenerit, Hugo Dei gratia Lincoln' episcopus salutem in domino. Sciatis nos concessisse venerabili fratri[a] Ioscelino Bathon' episcopo et successoribus suis imperpetuum quod habeant et teneant villam de Axebrugg'[b] cum omnibus pertinentiis suis, que est de feodo nostro, in liberam, puram et perpetuam elemosynam, quietam de sequela forinseci hundredi quam eadem villa nobis et heredibus nostris debebat et similiter de dimidia marca que inde nobis debebatur annuatim et ab omni servitio et exactione seculari cum omnibus libertatibus quas alia maneria sua habent. Quod ut perpetuam optineat firmitatem, presenti scripto sigillum nostrum duximus apponendum. Hiis testibus: magistris Rogero de Lacok', Amaurico de Buggeden' et Willelmo de Winchecumb', canonicis Lincolniens', Rogero capellano, magistro Ada de Clenefeud'[c], Giliberto[d] de Tanton' et Roberto de Monte Sorelli,[e] canonicis Wellen', Stephano camerario, Thoma de Hautevill', Willelmo de Stok', Philippo de Wik'[f] Petro de Cotingtun'[g], Waltero de[h] Abbodestun'[i] Iohanne camerario et Rogero de Waleis[j]. Dat' per manum Radulfi de Waravill', canonici Lincoln', apud Tinghurst[k] septimo idus Novembris pontificatus nostri anno decimo octavo.

[a] C *adds* nostro.   [b] Axebrig' C.   [c] Clenefeud C.   [d] Gilberto C.   [e] Serello C.
[f] Wych' C.   [g] Cotington' C.   [h] *omitted* C.   [i] Abbedestun' C.   [j] Waleys C.
[k] Thinghurst' C.

This was the charter inspected and confirmed (but not recited) by King Henry III on 9 May 1228 and 15 May 1229 (*Cal. Ch. R.* i 75, 104; cf. also *Medieval Deeds of Bath* ii no. 298/5).

285. Cransley church

Institution of Ralph of Cransley, clerk, to the church of Cransley, on the presentation of Hugh of Cransley.   [20 December 1226 x 19 December 1227]

B = LAO Wells roll ix, m. 6 (among entries for the bp's eighteenth pontifical year). Pd *RHW* ii 223.

Testibus et dat' ut in carta Godefridi vicarii de Brocton' in archidiaconatu Stowe.

The institution is recorded in the institution rolls, among entries for the bp's eighteenth pontifical year, 20 December 1226 x 19 December 1227 (ibid. 136). The Stow archdeaconry charter roll has not survived; the institution of Godfrey the chaplain to the vicarage of Brant Broughton is recorded in the general institution roll for *c.* 1218 (ibid. i 118, cf. Smith 'Rolls').

286. Pilton church

Letter to the dean of Cambridge and his fellow judges about the institution of Stephen the chaplain to the church of Pilton and the removal of Walter the clerk, who had been presented to the same. When custody of the church was given to Walter, at the instance of the archdeacon of Northampton and others four years ago, it was stipulated that meanwhile he should further his knowledge and then appear before the bishop for examination as to his suitability and learning and then to be ordained and admitted. He did not appear when summoned on many occasions but later he was examined twice at Leicester and then at Peterborough by trustworthy persons who found him unsatisfactory. Accordingly, he was

removed and the patron was asked to make another presentation. Stephen the
chaplain was afterwards admitted and instituted.

[20 December 1226 x 19 December 1227]

> B = LAO Wells roll ix, m. 5d (no witnesses or date) (among entries for the bp's
> eighteenth pontifical year).
> Pd *RHW* ii 224.

> Stephen of Luffenham was instituted to Pilton in the sixteenth pontifical year of the
> bishop (20 December 1224 x 19 December 1225). Walter was the brother of the
> patron of the church, Bartholomew of Pilton, (ibid. 126).

287.   Daventry priory

Institution of Ralph of Gnosall, clerk, to the church of Thorpe [Mandeville], on
the presentation of the prior and convent of Daventry, saving to R[obert], arch-
deacon of Northampton, his vicarage. The archdeacon shall hold the church for
life, paying a pension of two shillings a year to Ralph and his successors as
parsons.   [20 December 1226 x 19 December 1227]

> B = LAO Wells roll ix, m. 6 (among entries for the bp's eighteenth pontifical year).
> Pd *RHW* ii 223.

Testibus et dat' ut in carta Nicholai de Henred' in archidiaconatu Oxon'.

> The institution is recorded in the institution roll, among entries for the bp's eight-
> eenth pontifical year, 20 December 1226 x 19 December 1227 (ibid., 139). The
> Oxford archdeaconry charter roll has not survived, but the reference is probably to
> the letter of institution of Nicholas de Henred to the church of Nuneham Courtenay
> (ibid. 26).

288.   Hanging Houghton

Collation for life to Stephen of Axbridge, clerk, of two parts of the garb tithes of
the demesne of Philip Bosce in [Hanging] Houghton, after a long vacancy
caused by the dispute between Philip and William de Wand, rector of Lamport,
over the tithes. Stephen can let these tithes at farm to the rector of Lamport for
one mark a year, payable at Michaelmas. The future right of the successful claim-
ant to these tithes is safeguarded.   Buckden, 4 January 1228

> B = LAO Wells roll ix, m. 5 (among entries for the bp's eighteenth pontifical year).
> Pd *RHW* ii 225–6.

Hiis testibus: magistro R. de Lacok' et Willelmo de Winchecumb', canonicis
Linc', magistris W. de Beningwrth' et R. de Cant', capellanis, magistris
Clemente Pigiun et Ricardo de Windelesour', R. de Oxon', G. de Moris, Thoma
de Askeby, clericis. Dat' per manum nostram apud Bugden' ii nonas Ianuarii anno
pontificatus nostri decimonono.

> The collation is recorded in the institution roll among entries for the bp's eighteenth
> pontifical year, 20 December 1226 x 19 December 1227 (ibid. 157).

289. Woodford church

Institution of Alexander of Elmham, chaplain, to the vicarage of a mediety of the church of Woodford ordained by the bishop, on the presentation of Robert son of Walter son of Robert, parson of the mediety, with the consent of R. de Ver, patron by virtue of his wardship of the land and heir of William Maufe. The vicar is to serve personally and shall hold the mediety for life, paying an annual pension of one hundred shillings to Robert and his successors as parsons, half at Michaelmas and half at Easter. Buckden, 4 January 1228

> B = LAO Wells roll ix, m. 6 (among entries for the bp's eighteenth pontifical year). Pd *RHW* ii 226.

Testibus et dat' ut in proxima carta supra [no. 288].

> The institution is recorded in the institution roll among entries for the bp's seventeenth pontifical year, 20 December 1225 x 19 December 1226 (ibid. 128).

290. Thomas of Morton

Notification to King Henry III that Thomas de Morton, chaplain, had sufficiently purged himself in the ecclesiastical court of the crime of homicide, of which he was accused before the justices itinerant in the county of Buckingham.
[1228, before 27 February]

> Mention of letters in the mandate of the king to the sheriffs of Buckinghamshire giving Thomas full seisin of the land in Morton, which had been taken into the king's hands, 27 February 1228, pd *Close Rolls 1227–31*, p. 24. Cf. *Bucks Eyre Roll* no. 596: Thomas the chaplain of Morton amerced for default.

291. Daventry priory

Indulgence of thirteen days for all those of the Lincoln diocese, and others whose diocesan bishops shall approve, who shall visit and contribute alms to the monastery of St. Augustine, Daventry. This indulgence is to last for three years. It is forbidden for a collector to collect alms anywhere outside the bounds of the monastery. Kilsby, 11 July 1228

> B = LAO Wells roll ix, m. 6d.
> Pd *RHW* ii 228.

Dat' per manum Radulfi de Waravill', canonici Linc', apud Kildeby v° idus Iulii anno pontificatus nostri xix°.

292. Compton Basset church

Settlement made by the bishop and his brother, Bishop Jocelin of Bath, following a dispute between Alan Basset and the prior and canons of Bicester over the church of Compton [Basset]. The bishop of Salisbury is to have the patronage of the church, and the portions of the parson and the priory of Bicester are defined.
[c. 1220 x 22 July 1228]

> A = BL Add. Ch. 10596 (slight staining). Endorsed: Cumton' Basset (s. xiv); I. Aumberl' (s. xiv, probably to be identified with John of Amberley, s. xiv in.,

see C.R. Cheney, *Notaries Public in England* (Oxford 1972) 113); R. Wich-
ford (s. xiv); approx. 293 x 108 + 22 mm.; six slits for seal strings, 3 seals
survive on strings, viz. (seal 2) Bp Jocelin of Bath, counterseal, green wax
(very good specimen, slightly repaired); (seal 3) Bp Richard of Salisbury,
counterseal, green wax (repaired at base); (seal 6) Alan Basset, round, green
wax, heraldic device, legend 'SIGILLVM ALANI BASSET', no counterseal.
The document is ruled for writing.
B = Salisbury D. & C. Liber Evidentiarum C fos. cviii v–cix r, no. 339. s. xiii ex. C
= ibid. no.462 (s.xiv copy sewn into the register). D = Wiltshire RO, Salisbury Liber Evidentiarum B fos. lxxxv v–lxxxvi r, no. 337. ss. xiv–xv. E =
ibid. fos. cxxxvii v–cxxxviii r, no. 444. F = ibid. Liber Ruber fos. 75v–76r,
no. 337. ss. xiv–xv.
Pd from A in Kennett, *Parochial Antiquities* i 287–8; B etc. in *Salisbury Charters*
no. cxxvi.

Omnibus Cristi fidelibus ad quos presens scriptum pervenerit, Hugo Lincoln' et
Ioscelinus Bathon' Dei gratia episcopi salutem in domino. Noveritis quod cum
controversia mota esset inter nobilem virum Alanum Basset et priorem et canonicos de Berencestr' super ecclesia de Cumton' tam dictus Alanus quam prior et
canonici insuper et venerabilis frater dominus Ricardus Sar' episcopus et Willelmus decanus et capitulum Sar' in nos consenserunt et ordinationi nostre pure et
absolute se subiecerunt, ratum et gratum habituri quicquid de dicta ecclesia et
eius proventibus ordinaremus. Nos itaque habita deliberatione et requisito pru-
dentum virorum consilio de predicta ecclesia de Cumton' et eius proventibus
ordinavimus in hunc modum: videlicet, quod predictus episcopus Sar' et eius successores habebunt inperpetuum advocationem predicte ecclesie de Cumton' cum
omni iure ad advocationem eiusdem ecclesie pertinente, ita quidem quod prefatus episcopus Sar' et successores sui conferent inperpetuum cui voluerint idonee
persone tertiam partem decimarum garbarum totius parrochie de Cumton' et
omnes minutas decimas que de iure debentur eidem ecclesie; et omnes obventiones altaris et cimiterii predicte ecclesie, et totam terram et curiam que fuit
persone illius ecclesie cum omnibus libertatibus et liberis consuetudinibus ad
predictam ecclesiam et terram illius pertinentibus; preter duas partes decimarum
garbarum predicte parochie et croftam que iacet iuxta curiam persone et unam
acram prati vicinam eidem crofte. Quas duas partes decimarum garbarum et
croftam et acram prati integre habebunt inperpetuum dicti prior et canonici,
nomine perpetui beneficii, absque omni onere ordinario; extra ordinariis oneribus inter personam qui pro tempore fuerit et priorem et canonicos predictos pro
rata partiendis. De consensu etiam dicti prioris et canonicorum providimus quod
de terra que fuit persone persona qui pro tempore fuerit decimas non dabit.
Siquid vero in hac ordinatione nostra obscurum fuerit vel minus plene declara-
tum, illud de consensu partium nobis reservavimus declarandum. Hanc autem
ordinationem nostram partibus recitavimus et ipsa ab eis gratanter fuerit accep-
tata. In cuius rei robur et testimonium tam sigillis nostris quam sigillis memorati
episcopi Sar' et capituli et predictorum Alani et prioris et canonicorum fecimus
presens scriptum communiri. Valete.

William became dean of Salisbury in 1220 and Bp Richard Poore of Salisbury was
translated to Durham in 1228, receiving the temporalities of the latter see on 22
July.

293. Newbold chantry

Grant that Ralph de Normanville and Alice his wife may have a chantry in their curia of Newbold for their lifetime, the nuns of Catesby, patrons of the church of Catesby, and John of Hellidon, vicar of Catesby, having given their consent. The details of the arrangement and particular safeguards for the mother church are described. Lyddington, 22 July 1228

> B = PRO E326/10338 (in an undated inspeximus by A. the prioress and convent of Catesby, s. xiii in.). C = LAO Wells roll ix, m. 6d (some slight differences and more abbreviated). No relevant endorsements.
> Pd from C in *RHW* ii 228–9.

Omnibus Cristi fidelibus ad quos presentes littere pervenerint, Hugo Dei gratia Linc' episcopus eternam in domino salutem.[a] Noverit universitas vestra quod cum dilectus in Cristo Radulfus de Normanvill' confirmasset dilectis in Cristo priorisse et monialibus de Catesby[b] dimidiam marcam [c-]in villa de Hotheby[-c] percipiendam inperpetuum, de qua Alicia[d] uxor eius dederat eisdem in libera viduitate sua sex solidos, uno obulo minus, et postea octo denarios et obulum [e-]in molendino suo de Neubot,[-e] prout carte dictorum Radulfi[f] et Alicie[d] penes dictas moniales residentes plenius testantur, nos ad petitionem eorum, interveniente consensu dictarum monialium, patronarum ecclesie de Catesby,[b] et Iohannis de Helidene[g] capellani, eiusdem ecclesie vicarii, capellam eis in curia sua de Neubot[h] et cantariam per capellanum proprium sumptibus eorundem ministraturum in ea, quotiens ambo vel alter illorum moram fecerit ibidem, concessimus sub hac forma: videlicet, quod capellanus autoritate[j] nostra de consensu monialium et vicarii de Catesby[k] in predicta capella ministraturus eisdem corporaliter prestabit iuramentum quod iura matricis ecclesie, quantum in ipso est, in omnibus conservabit illesa, et quod nullum parochianum suum ad confessionem vel[l] divinorum celebrationem in ipsa capella sine licentia sua recipiet, nec aliquod ius ecclesiasticum eis inpendet,[m] neque legatum vel privatum denarium aut quemcunque proventum recipiet ab eisdem; oblationes etiam omnimodas a quibuscunque factas in dicta capella supradictis vicario et monialibus sub debito iuramenti prestiti fideliter et sine diminutione restituet. Predicti[n] quoque[o] Radulfus[f] et Alicia[d] cum tota familia sua subiecti erunt[p] matrici ecclesie de Catesby[b] in omnibus iure parrochiali[q] et omnia iura ecclesiastica persolvent ei tanquam parrochiani[r] et sacramentalia percipient ab eadem, hoc solum illis concesso quod liceat eis cantariam predicto modo in predicta capella optinere. In precipuis vero solempnitatibus[a] subscriptis tam dicti Radulfus[f] et Alicia,[d] si presentes fuerint ibidem, quam tota familia sua, predictam matricem ecclesiam[t] cum oblationibus debitis et consuetis singulis annis visitabunt, scilicet die Natalis Domini, die Purificationis beate Marie, die Pasche, die Pentecost'[u], et die sollempnitatis ecclesie. Si autem contra hanc formam per predictos R. et Aliciam[d] vel per capellanum qui pro tempore in predicta capella ministrabit, matrix ecclesia[v] dampnificata fuerit in aliquo, ex tunc ad questionem[w] dictarum monialium vel vicarii per archidiaconum [x-]loci vel per decanum[-x] interdicetur capella memorata, donec de dampno ipsi ecclesie plene fuerit satisfactum. Post decessum autem [y-]dictorum Radulfi et Alicie[-y] predicta capella a divinorum celebratione cessabit inperpetuum, hac huius nostre concessionis gratia tunc penitus expirante, salvis in omnibus[z] episcopalibus consuetudinibus et Linc' ecclesie dignitate.[aa] In huius rei testimonium presentibus litteris sigillum nostrum duximus apponendum. Dat' per manum Radulfi de War', canonici Linc', apud Lidinton' xi kalendas Augusti pontificatus nostri anno decimonono.

[a] Omnibus etc. C. [b] Katteby C. [c–c] annuam de molendino de Houteb' C. [d] A. C. [e–e] *omitted* C. [f] R. C. [g] Haliden'C. [h] Neubo C. [i] eorum C. [j] auctoritate C. [k] Catteby C. [l] ad *inserted* C. [m] illi impendet C. [n] Predictus B. [o] vero C. [p] erunt subiecti C. [q] parochiali C. [r] parochiani C. [s] sollempnitatibus C. [t] suam *inserted* C. [u] Penthec'C. [v] *omitted* B. [w] conquestionem C. [x–x] vel decanum loci C. [y–y] dicte A. C. [z] C *adds* etc. [aa] B *ends here.*

Prioress Amice of Catesby occurs in 1226 (PRO, Notts F., CP25/1/182/4, no. 88) and the next recorded prioress was appointed by Bp Grosseteste June 1244 x June 1245 (*RRG*, p. 222).

294. Sulby abbey

Similar indulgence of thirteen days as in no. 291 for the monastery of Sulby.
Lyddington, 24 July 1228

B = LAO Wells roll ix, m. 6d.
Pd *RHW* ii 228.

Dat' per manum Radulfi de Waravill', canonici Linc', apud Lidingt' ix° kalendas Augusti pontificatus nostri xix°.

For a later indulgence for Sulby abbey see below no. 341.

295. Launde priory

Institution of John of Rothwell, clerk, to the church of [Little] Bowden, on the presentation of the prior and convent of Launde, saving to Henry the chaplain his vicarage. The vicar shall hold the church for life, paying to John the parson and his successors an annual pension of twenty shillings. Buckden, 5 October 1228

B = LAO Wells roll ix, m. 6.
Pd *RHW* ii 227.

Testibus: magistris W. de Beningworth', cappellano, A. de Bugged' et W. de Winchecumb', canonicis Linc', magistris R. Devon', Clemente Pigiun et A. de Arundell', Ricardo de Oxon', G. de Moris et Thoma de Ask'by, clericis. Dat' per manum R. de Waravill', canonici Lincoln', apud Bugged' iii nonas Octobris pontificatus nostri anno xix°.

The institution is recorded in the institution roll among entries for the bp's fifteenth pontifical year, 20 December 1223 x 19 December 1224 (ibid. 118).

296. Hospitallers

Institution of Ralph of Cirencester, clerk, to the church of Holcot, on the presentation of brother R(obert) de Dive, prior of the Hospitallers in England, saving to the prior and brethren their pension if it shall be proved to be customary.
[20 December 1227 x 19 December 1228]

B = LAO Wells roll ix, m. 6.
Pd *RHW* ii 226.

Testibus et dat' ut in carta de Duningeton' in archidiaconatu Leicestr'.

This letter of institution is entered in the charter roll for the bp's nineteenth pontifical year (20 December 1227 x 19 December 1228) but the institution is recorded in the institution roll among entries for the bp's seventeenth pontifical year, 20 December 1225 x 19 December 1226 (ibid. 131). The Leicester archdeaconry charter roll has not survived; the reference may just possibly refer to the institution of Richard of Stainsby to the church of Castle Donington, recorded under the bp's eighteenth pontifical year, 20 December 1226 x 19 December 1227 (ibid. 305).

297.   Bury St Edmunds abbey

Institution of master Alexander of St Edmund, clerk, to the church of Warkton, on the presentation of the abbot of Bury St Edmunds.
[20 December 1227 x 19 December 1228]

B = LAO Wells roll ix, m. 6.
Pd *RHW* ii 226–7.

Testibus et dat' ut supra carta proxima [no. 296].

This letter of institution is entered in the charter roll for the bp's nineteenth pontifical year (20 December 1227 x 19 December 1228) but the institution is recorded in the institution roll among entries for the bp's eighteenth pontifical year, 20 December 1226 x 19 December 1227 (ibid. 140).

298.   Lenton priory

Institution of master William of Lichfield, clerk, to the church of Harlestone, on the presentation of the prior and convent of Lenton.
[20 December 1227 x 19 December 1228]

B = LAO Wells roll ix, m.6.
Pd *RHW* ii 227.

Testibus et dat' ut supra carta proxima [no. 297].

This letter of institution is entered in the charter roll for the bp's nineteenth pontifical year (20 December 1227 x 19 December 1228) but the institution is recorded in the institution roll among entries for the bp's eighteenth pontifical year, 20 December 1226 x 19 December 1227 (ibid. 139).

299.   Creaton church

Institution of William of Creaton, clerk, to the church of Creaton on the presentation of Hugh of Whiston, patron by virtue of his wife, Sara.
[20 December 1227 x 19 December 1228]

B = LAO Wells roll ix, m. 6.
Pd *RHW* ii 227.

Testibus et dat' ut in carta de Wiketoft in archidiaconatu Lincoln'.

The institution is recorded in the institution roll among entries for the bp's seventeenth pontifical year, 20 December 1225 x 19 December 1226 (ibid. 132), but this charter roll entry is placed in the bp's nineteenth pontifical year, 20 December 1227 x 19 December 1228. There had been an assize of darrein presentment over the advowson in Hilary term 1226 (*CRR* xii nos. 1733, 1883, 2136), so presumably the actual institution took place in 1226, between Hilary and 19 December. The Lincoln archdeaconry charter roll has not survived; the charter referred to was possibly the letter of institution of Roger of Caen to the church of Wigtoft; his institution is recorded in the bp's eighteenth pontifical year, 20 December 1226 x 19 December 1227 (*RHW* iii 152–3).

300. Peterborough abbey

Institution of Geoffrey de Moris, clerk, to the church of Warmington, on the presentation of the abbot and convent of Peterborough.

Spaldwick, 30 December 1228

B = LAO Wells roll ix, m. 6.
Pd *RHW* ii 229–30.

Testibus: magistris W. de Beningworth' capellano, A. de Bugged', W. de Winch' et R. de Oxon', canonicis Linc', Warino capellano, magistris R. Devon', C. Pighyon', A. de Arundell', Thoma de Gedden', R. Mauclerc' et Thoma de Askeb', clericis. Dat' per manum R. de Waravill', canonici Linc', apud Spaldewic iii kalendas Ianuarii anno pontificatus nostri xx°.

The institution is recorded in the institution roll among entries for the bp's nineteenth pontifical year, 20 December 1227 x 19 December 1228 (ibid. 141). Geoffrey de Moris was an episcopal clerk.

301. Beauvais, abbey of St Lucien

Institution of Simon of Northampton, clerk, to the chapel of Plumpton, on the presentation of Nicholas, prior of Weedon [Lois], proctor of the patrons, the abbot and convent of St Lucien, Beauvais. Spaldwick, 30 December 1228

B = LAO Wells roll ix, m. 6.
Pd *RHW* ii 230.

Testibus et dat' ut supra in proxima [no. 300].

The institution is recorded in the institution roll among entries for the bp's nineteenth pontifical year, 20 December 1227 x 19 December 1228 (ibid. 143).

302. Nostell priory

Inspeximus and confirmation of a charter of Ralph Chesney [Chenedud], son of Ralph Chesney, dated 3 March 1229, concerning the renunciation of his appeal (along with that of Elias his uncle) before the official of the archdeacon of Buckingham against the prior and canons of St Oswald, Nostell, over the advowsons of the churches of Cheddington, [King's] Langley and Charwelton, and quitclaiming all right in these advowsons. [? c. 3 March 1229]

B = BL ms. Cotton Vespasian E xix (Nostell cartulary), fo. 112v, no. xii. s. xiii ex.

Omnibus Cristi fidelibus presentes litteras visuris vel audituris, H. Dei gratia Lincoln' episcopus salutem in domino. Noverit universitas vestra nos litteras domini Radulfi Chedned' sub hac forma recepisse: Venerabili in Cristo patri et domino suo specialissimo H. Dei gratia episcopo Linc', Radulfus Chenedud filius Radulfi Chenedud salutem eternam in domino. Noverit paternitas vestra quod nos, inspectis et recognitis instrumentis prioris et canonicorum sancti Osuu-aldi de Nostl' super advocationibus ecclesiarum de Chedend', Langel', et Cher-weltona, appellationi a procuratore nostro nomino nostro Elie Chedned' avunculi nostri coram officiali archidiaconi Bukinham interposite renuntiamus et omne ius quod habuimus vel habere sperabamus in dictis advocationibus remittimus et quietum clamamus. Et siquid decetero a nobis vel heredibus nostris contra con-firmationem nostram acceptum fuerit irritum sit et inane. Huius autem nostre paternitati signamus ne presentationes clericorum ad dictas ecclesias a dictis priore et canonicis facere vel inposterum faciende possint occasione aliqua impe-diri. In huius autem rei testimonium, presentibus litteris sigillum nostrum dignum duximus apponere. Act' apud Langel' die sabbati post diem cinerum proxima anno regni regis Henrici filii regis Iohannis xiiiº. Ne autem hec impos-terum alicui in dubium venire possit ad instantiam prioris et conventus sancti Osuualdi de Nostl' presentibus litteris sigillum nostrum apposuimus. Valete in domino.

> For the subsequent institution to Cheddington during the course of this pontifical year see no. 314 below. For the original gift of these three churches to Nostell by Simon de Chesney and Adeliza his mother c. 1114 x 1130 see *EEA* 1 no. 202 & n.

303. Newton Longville priory

Confirmation, with the assent of William the dean and the chapter of Lincoln, for the prior and convent of Newton Longville of an annual pension of three marks from the church of Horwood, which is of their patronage: namely one mark newly granted together with the two marks which they have received for some time. This pension is to be paid by the rector of the church, Richard de Tanet, and his suc-cessors. The rector shall bear all ordinary charges of the church and the priory shall answer proportionally for any extraordinary charges that may arise.

Lincoln, in chapter, 2 April 1229

> A = Oxford, New Coll. Mun., Newington Longeville deed 101. Endorsed: carta monachorum de Longavill' super iii[bus] marcis de ecclesia de Horwud' (s. xiii); pro pensione de Horewode (s. xiv); de pensione xl s. ecclesie ibidem (s. xv); I. de F.; approx. 182 x 136 + 18 mm.; episcopal seal (chipped in centre and round the edges), brownish-white wax, on parchment tag (method 2), counterseal; also fragment of capitular seal (centre only) on parchment tag (method 2).
> Pd from A in *Newington Longeville Charters* no. 26.

Omnibus Cristi fidelibus ad quos presens scriptum pervenerit, Hugo Dei gratia Lincoln' episcopus salutem in domino. Noverit universitas vestra nos, de assensu dilectorum filiorum Willelmi decani et capituli nostri Lincoln', concessisse, dedisse et hac presenti carta nostra confirmasse, divine pietatis intuitu, dilectis filiis priori et conventui de Longa villa tres marcas annuas de ecclesia de Horwode, que de eorum advocatione est, scilicet: unam marcam ipsis per nos de novo concessam, et duas marcas quas aliquamdiu habuerunt de eadem per manum Ricardi de Tanet capellani eiusdem ecclesie rectoris et successorum suorum qui pro tempore fuerint annuatim, nomine perpetui beneficii, percipien-das, in duobus anni terminis: videlicet, viginti solidos in festo sancti Martini et viginti solidos in festo Pentechost'. Dictus autem Ricardus et successores sui ecclesie memorate rectores omnia onera illius ecclesie ordinaria debita et consueta sustinebunt. Et si forte quid extraordinarium emerserit, dicti prior et conventus inde pro portione sua respondebunt: salvis in omnibus episcopalibus consuetudinibus et Lincoln' ecclesie dignitate. Quod ut perpetuam optineat firmitatem, presenti scripto sigillum nostrum una cum sigillo predicti capituli nostri Lincoln' duximus apponendum. Hiis testibus: Willelmo decano, Roberto archidiacono Lincoln', Iohanne precentore, Waltero thesaurario et Iohanne subdecano, Willelmo archidiacono Stouwe, Waltero Blundo, Willelmo de Avalon, magistris Roberto de Gravel', Stephano de Cicestr', Willelmo de Beningworth', Theodbaldo et Ricardo de Cant', Galfrido Scoto et Thoma de Norton' capellanis, magistris Willelmo de Lincoln' et Waltero de Well', Radulfo de Waravill' et Willelmo de Winchecumb' diaconis, magistro Amaurico de Buggeden' et Ricardo de Oxon' subdiaconis, canonicis Lincoln'. Dat' per manum nostram in capitulo Lincoln' quarto nonas Aprilis pontificatus nostri anno vicesimo.

> Richard de Tan(et), the rector, had been instituted during the bp's nineteenth pontifical year (20 December 1227 x 19 December 1228), the two medieties of the church having been united on this occasion, with the consent of the priory (*RHW* ii 73).

304. Hockliffe hospital

Grant, made with the assent of W[illiam] the dean and the chapter of Lincoln, to brother Thorald, master of the hospital of poor persons in the parish of Hockliffe and his successors, with the consent of Thomas the chaplain, rector of Hockliffe, to whom the patronage belongs, that they may have a chantry in their chapel, and burial at it for themselves only, saving the right of the neighbouring churches and of the mother church of Hockliffe.   Lincoln, in chapter, 2 April 1229

> A = LAO Lincoln D. & C. Dij/72/3/1(slightly damaged in parts. Words in square brackets are supplied conjecturally). Endorsed: Carta fratrum de Hocliua . super sepultura sua ibidem (s. xiii); Nota (s. xiv); approx. 178 x 152 + 16 mm.; no surviving seals, two slits for seal-tags (method 1).
> Pd *Reg. Ant.* iii no. 644, where tbe charter is incorrectly dated to 1230.

Omnibus Cristi fidelibus ad quos presens scriptum pervenerit, Hugo Dei gratia Lincoln' episcopus eternam in domino salutem. Noverit universitas vestra nos, de assensu dilectorum filiorum W. decani et capituli nostri Lincoln', concessisse divine pietatis intuitu dilectis filiis fratri Thuroldo magistro hospitalis pauperum in parrochia de Hoclive erecti et successoribus suis canonice per nos et successores nostros instituendis et fratribus ibidem deo servientibus et servituris imperpetuum, Thome etiam capellani rectoris ecclesie de Hoclive cuius ad predictos magistrum et fratres patronatus pertinet interveniente consensu, quod in capella sua infra septa ipsius hospitalis erecta cantariam habeant et apud eam sibi tantum qui habitum ibi religionis gestaverint sepulturam: salvo iure tam vicinarum ecclesiarum quam dicte matricis ecclesie de Hoclive in servientibus et aliis a premissis apud ipsum hospitale decedentibus et generaliter in omnibus et per omnia. Pro quo quidem iure sicut dictum est indempni conservando, magister loci qui pro tempore fuerit presente prefate matricis ecclesie rectore vel assignato suo [coram] archidiacono loci corporaliter pro se et fratribus suis in pleno capitulo prestabit sacramentum cum ipsius hospitalis receperit [ad]ministrationem. Iurabit etiam quod in preiudicium iuris ecclesie nostre Lincoln' aut nostri vel successorum nostrorum sepedicte matricis ecclesie vel vicinarum ecclesiarum nichil umquam attemptabit, impetrabit aut procurabit vel quantum in ipso est permittet impetrari. Et si aliqua forte contra premissa fuerint impetrata, quod numquam per se vel per alium utetur impetratis. Hec autem supradicta concessimus: salvis in omnibus episcopalibus consuetudinibus et Lincoln' ecclesie dignitate. Quod ut perpetuam optineat firmitatem, presenti scripto sigillum nostrum una cum sigillo predicti capituli nostri Lincoln' duximus apponendum. Hiis testibus: Willelmo decano, Roberto archidiacono Lincoln', Iohanne precentore, Waltero thesaurario et Iohanne subdecano, Willelmo archidiacono Stowe, Waltero Blundo, Willelmo de Avalon', magistris Roberto de Gravel', Stephano de Cicestr', Willelmo de Beningewrd', Theobaldo et Ricardo de Cantia, Thoma de Northon' et Galfrido Scoto capellanis, magistris Willelmo de Lincoln' et Waltero de Well', Radulfo de Waravill' et Willelmo de Winchecumb' diaconis, magistro Amaurico de Buggeden' et Ricardo de Oxon' subdiaconis, canonicis Lincoln'. Dat' per manum nostram in capitulo Lincoln' quarto nonas Aprilis pontificatus nostri anno vicesimo.

> The hospital of St John the Baptist, Hockliffe, was founded some time before 1219 (see above no. 108), some years earlier than the approximate date given in *KH*.

305.　Stonely hospital

Grant, made with the assent of William the dean and the chapter of Lincoln, to William, master of the hospital of Stonely in the parish of Kimbolton and his successors, with the consent of the rector of Kimbolton, that they may have a chantry in their chapel, and burial at it for themselves only, saving the right of the neighbouring churches and the mother church of Kimbolton.

[20 December 1228 x 19 December 1231, ? 2 April 1229]

> A – PRO E210/3084 (badly damaged, charred on the right hand side, repaired. All words in squarebrackets have been supplied conjecturally but with special reference to a similar actum, no. 304). Endorsed: Carta fratrum de Stonleya super sepultura sua ibidem (s. xiii); approx. 165 (surviving portion) x 133 + 16 mm.; seal and tag missing, slit for seal-tag, sealing method 1.

Omnibus Cristi fidelibus ad quos presens scriptum pervenerit, Hugo Dei gratia [Lincolniensis episcopus salutem in domino. Noverit uni]versitas vestra nos, de assensu dilectorum filiorum Willelmi decani et capituli nostri Lincoln', c[oncessisse divine pietatis intuitu dilectis filiis] Willelmo magistro hospitalis de Stoenl[e]gh' in parrochia de Kenebaulton' co[nstructi, et successoribus suis canonice per nos et] successores nostros instituendis, et fratribus ibidem Deo servientibus et servituris super [.............. rectoris] ecclesie de Kenebaulton' assensu, quod ad capellam suam infra septa ipsius hospit[alis erecta cantariam habeant et apud eam sibi tantum qui habitum] ibi religionis gestaverint sepulturam: salvo iure tam vicinarum ecclesiaruin quam dicte [matricis ecclesie de Kenebaulton inser]vientibus et aliis a premissis apud ipsum hospitale decedentibus et generaliter in omnibus et p[er omnia. Pro quo quidem iure sicut dictum est] indempni conservando, magister eiusdem loci qui pro tempore fuerit presente prefate ma[tricis ecclesie rectore co]ram archidiacono loci corporaliter pro se et fratribus suis in pleno capitulo prestabit sacramentum, [cum ipsius hospitalis recepe]rit

administrationem. Iurabit etiam quod in preiudicium iuris ecclesie nostre Lincolniensis, nostri vel successorum nostrorum sepedicte [matricis ecclesie vel
vi]cinarum ecclesiarum nichil unquam attemptabit, impetrabit aut procurabit vel
quantum in ipso est permittet impetrari. [Et si aliqua forte con]tra premissa
fuerint impetrata, quod nunquam per se vel per alium utetur impetratis. Hec
autem supradicta concessimus: [salvis in omnibus] episcopalibus consuetudinibus et Lincoln' ecclesie dignitate. Quod ut perpetuam optineat firmitatem, presenti scripto [sigillum nostrum una] cum sigillo predicti capituli nostri Lincoln'
duximus apponendum. Hiis testibus: Willelmo decano, Roberto archidiacono
Lincoln', [Iohanne pre]centore, Waltero thesaurario et Iohanne subdecano, Willelmo archidiacono Stouwe, Waltero Blundo, Willelmo de Aval[on'], m[agistris
Roberto de Gra]vel', Stephano de Cicestr', Willelmo de Bening[wor]th', Theodbaldo et Ricardo de Cant', Galfrido Scoto et Thoma de No[rton', magist]ris Willelmo de Lincoln' et Waltero de W[el]l', Radulfo de Waravill' et Willelmo de
Winchecumb', diaconis, mag[istro Amaurico de Bug]geden' et Ricardo de
Oxon', subdiaconis, canonicis Lincoln'. Dat' per manum nostram in capitulo Lincoln' quarto [...........] pontificatus nostri vicesi[mo ...?].

> The remarkable similarity between this *actum* and the Hockliffe hospital document
> (no. 302 above), the same witnesses, the same handwriting and part of the dating
> clause, would perhaps suggest that they were issued on the same occasion and
> indeed 'nonas Aprilis' would certainly fit into the damaged portion of the date. At
> any rate the charter must be dated between 20 December 1228 (the beginning of the
> bp's twentieth pontifical year) and 19 December 1231, by which time Amaury of
> Buckden had become archdn of Bedford. This document adds a little to our scanty
> knowledge of the Augustinian priory of Stonely, which presumably started its exis-
> tence as a hospital, if the recipient of this grant can be equated with the later house.
> Leland says the house was founded about 1180 by William de Mandeville, earl of
> Essex, but there is no further authority for this statement (*VCH Hunts.* i 395–6).

306. Stephen the almoner

*Grant, with the assent of the dean and chapter of Lincoln, to Stephen the almoner
and Amabel his wife, daughter of Lauretta, of a messuage with four bovates of
land in Nettleham which Ulf formerly held; and two bovates in Stow to hold to
Stephen and Amabel and their heirs of the bishop for a yearly render of one
pound of cummin. Stephen and Amabel shall warrant the four bovates in Nettleham to the bishop. If after Stephen's death, Amabel or her heirs lay claim to the
four bovates in Nettleham, it shall be lawful for the bishop to take into his hands
the two bovates in Stow; and before they shall implead the bishop they shall
return the forty shillings which he paid them in order to effect an agreement.*

Lincoln, in chapter, 16 April 1229

> A = LAO Lincoln Dean & Chapter Dij/84/2/17. No surviving seal; two slits for
> seal-tags. Endts: Netelhum °v. (s. xiii); Contra Stephanum elemosinarium et
> Amabiliam Neth' (s. xiii). Size: 158 mm x 198 mm. Indented: there is evi-
> dence that CYROGRAFUM was written across the indentation (A, F and M
> can be seen). The document is very badly damaged, a portion about 110 mm.
> x 50 mm. having been eaten away at the top of the document, leaving only a
> small fragment at the top right. Further down the document there are slits and
> holes. Turn-up for sealing with two slits. Seals and tags missing.
> Pd *Reg. Ant.* ii no. 618.

....
................................t universitas vestra nos, de assensu ....
.............................phano Elemosinario et Amabile filie ....
....quondam tenuit ibidem cum toftis
....et omnibus ad dictas quatuor bovatas et tof ....
.........Netelham et ....bus: videlicet quas dictus Stephanis et Amabil .... sua
clamabant esse ius et heredita ....ve, duas bovatas terre in Stowe, videlicet,
illam bovatam quam Alanus Buk' ....cum tofto in Westgate quod
iacet inter toftum prioris sancti Leonardi de Torkes' et toftum Rogeri Thurstan',
et aliam bovatam que .... as Virgil' tenuit cum tofto in Estgate, quod
iacet inter toftum Roberti filii Wlfward' et toftum Ricardi Richegod': habend' et
tenend' ipsis Stephano et Amabilie uxori sue et heredibus suis qui de eis proces-
serint integre et quiete, libere et pacifice, cum omnibus pertinentiis suis,de nobis
et successoribus nostris iure hereditario imperpetuum: reddendo inde nobis et
successoribus nostris annuatim unam libram cimini in Nativitate beate Marie
Virginis pro omni servitio et consuetudine ad dictam terram pertinente. Qui
dictas quatuor bovatas apud Netelham cum omnibus pertinentiis suis supradictis
nobis et successoribus suis warantizabunt inperpetuum contra omnes homines.
Adiectum est insuper quod si dicta Amabilia mulier vel heredes sui post decessum dicti Stephani ius exegerint vel clamium posuerunt in predictis quatuor
bovatis terre et toftis in Netelham vel aliquibus pertinentiis suis contra nos vel
successores nostros licebit nobis et successoribus nostris ex tunc cum voluerimus
sine contradictione qualibet in manus nostras saisire predictas duas bovatas de
Stowe cum toftis predictis et omnibus pertinentiis suis tanquam ius nostrum et
ecclesie nostre, et ab eis per clamium suum sic forisfactum et reddent nobis vel
successoribus nostris ante quam nos vel ipsos inde implacitent quadraginta
solidos quos eis pacavimus pre manibus. Et hec omnia bona fide et sine dolo et
malo ingenio firmiter imperpetuum tenenda, iuraverint d[icti] Stephanus et
Amabilia uxor sua pro se et heredibus suis in capitulo Lincoln' et postmodum in
pleno ....um . Ad perpetuam igitur omnium predictorum firmitatem, factum est hoc scriptum inter nos et predictum Stephanum et Amabiliam in
modum cyrographi et parti que residet penes nos et capitulum nostrum apposita
sunt [sig]illa ipsius Stephani et Amabilie uxoris sue: parti vero dictis Stephano et
Amabilie remanenti appositum est sigillum nostrum et sigillum capituli nostri.
Hiis testibus: Radulfo filio Reginaldi tunc vicecomite Lincoln', Iohanne fratre
suo, Gilberto de Treilly tunc senescallo nostro, Galfrido serviente nostro de
Stowa, Eustachio serviente nostro de Netelhum', Herberto camerario et Anketino
de Stowa, Willelmo de Rolleston', Rogero de Latun, Roberto Wale, Nicholao de
Marton', Galfrido Bernard', Willelmo de Burton', Rogero Marescallo, Rogero
Walensi, et aliis. Actum in capitulo Lincoln' sextodecimo kalendas Maii pontifi-
catus nostri anno vicesimo.

> The sense of this document was supplied by Canon Foster after examining other
> relevant documents.

307. Peterborough abbey

*Institution of master William of Scotter, clerk, to the church of Kettering, on the
presentation of the abbot and convent of Peterborough.*

Lyddington, 9 August 1229

B = LAO Wells roll ix, m. 6.
Pd *RHW* ii 231.

Testibus: magistris Willelmo de Beningworth' capellano, et Ricardo de Wendoure, Willelmo de Winchec' et Ricardo de Oxon', canonicis Linc', magistris Ricardo Devon' et Alardo de Arundell', Stephano de Castell' et Galfrido de Moris, clericis. Dat' per manum Radulfi de Waravill', canonici Linc', apud Lidingt' v idus Augusti pontificatus nostri anno xx.

> The institution is recorded in the institution roll among entries for the bp's twentieth pontifical year, 20 December 1228 x 19 December 1229 (ibid. 147). The entry notes that a customary pension is payable to the sacrist of Peterborough abbey. Master William of Scotter occurs in Peterborough documents – presumably as a clerk of the abbot – in 1216, 1214 x 1222 and 1212 x 1228 (*Carte Nativorum*, no. 517 & n.).

308. Cottesmore church

Institution of Robert of Hertford, chaplain, to the perpetual vicarage of Cottesmore, on the presentation of John of Ecton, the parson, with the assent of the patron, William Mauduit, the king's chamberlain. He is to serve personally. The vicarage consists of the entire altarage, the garb tithes of the whole demesne of the parson, the small tithes of the fodder of his animals, the tithes of hay of Wenton, and one virgate of land assigned to the vicar in Cottesmore from land belonging to the church, which lies in parcels between the lands of Henry son of the parson, William Coleville and Thomas Pere. The vicar shall have for the manse a certain copse beside the cemetery on the east side and beside the curia *of the parson, and the small meadow lying below and the rent of the manse which Ralph holds. The vicar shall pay synodal dues and the parson shall provide hospitality for the archdeacon.* Cottingham, 16 August 1229

B = LAO Wells roll ix, m. 6.
Pd *RHW* ii 232.

Testibus: magistris W. de Beningword' et Amaurico de Bugged' et aliis ut supra in carta proxima [no. 310], excepto Warino capellano. Dat' per manum R. de War', canonici Linc', apud Cotingeham xvii° kalendas Septembris pontificatus nostri anno xx°.

> The institution is recorded in the institution roll among entries for the bp's nineteenth pontifical year, 20 December 1227 x 19 December 1228 (ibid. 144). William III Mauduit succeeded his father Robert in 1222 and died in 1257 (Sanders, *Feudal Baronies*, pp. 50–1).

309. Rockingham bridge

Indulgence for Rockingham bridge as in no. 243. Lyddington, 16 August 1229

B = LAO Wells roll ix, m. 6d (no witnesses).
Pd *RHW* ii 233.

Dat' per manum Radulfi de Waravill', canonici Lincoln', apud Lidington' xvii kalendas Septembris pontificatus nostri anno vicesimo.

310. Northampton, priory of St Andrew

Institution of Adam of Barby, chaplain, to the chapel of Stuchbury, on the presentation of the prior and convent of St Andrew, Northampton. He is to serve personally.   Kilsby, 25 August 1229

B = LAO Wells roll ix, m. 6.
Pd *RHW* ii 231.

Testibus: magistris W. de Beningworth', capellano, et R. de Wendour', W. de Winchecumb' et R. de Oxon', canonicis Linc', Warino capellano, magistro Alardo de Arundell', Thoma de Askeb', S. de Castell' et G. de Moris, clericis. Dat' per manum nostram apud Kildesb' viii kalendas Septembris pontificatus nostri anno xx⁰.

The institution is recorded in the institution roll among entries for the bp's nineteenth pontifical year, 20 December 1227 x 19 December 1228 (ibid. 142).

311. Leicester abbey

Institution of William Katin, chaplain, to the vicarage of Brackley, on the presentation of the abbot and convent of Leicester. He is to serve personally. The vicarage consists of a third part of the garb tithes of Brackley and of Halso and half of the altarage, with a manse assigned to the vicar. It also consists of two parts of the garb tithes of eight virgates of land in the field of Evenley, the tithes of two virgates in Little Whitfield with the curia *of Th[omas] de Ermenters and the tithes of hay and of the mill.*   Kilsby, 31 August 1229

B = LAO Wells roll ix, m. 6.
Pd *RHW* ii 232.

Testibus ut supra in carta de Stuteb' [no. 310]. Dat' per manum R. de War', canonici L[incolniensis], apud Kildeb' II kalendas Septembris etc.

Tbe institution is recorded in the institution roll among entries for the bp's nineteenth pontifical year, 20 December 1227 x 19 December 1228 (ibid. 141).

312. Peterborough abbey

Institution of William of Watford, chaplain, to the perpetual vicarage of St John the Baptist, Peterborough, on the presentation of the abbot and convent of Peterborough. The vicarage consists of the third part of the tithes of wool, flax, lambs, piglets, chickens, calves and geese, the third part of the tithes of merchandise, the third part of all candles offered, half of all mass-pennies except at Thorpe where the vicar shall have all of them, the third part of all other oblations, except bread and relish (companagium) *and the tithe of milk and gardens which the vicar shall receive in their entirety. The sacrist shall receive all wax-scot and all oblations at mass and first testament. The vicarage also consists of twenty-three acres of arable land with a suitable manse for the vicar and a daily corrody of one monk to be taken either at the abbot's table or at the manse. The abbey shall bear all charges of the church except the parochial charge.*
     [20 December 1228 x 19 December 1229]

B = LAO Wells roll ix, m. 6. C = CUL, Peterborough D. & C. ms. 1 (Liber R. de

Swaffham), fos. 108v–109r (xciii v–xciv r) (witnesses and date omitted). s. xiii med.
Pd from B in *RHW* ii 230–1.

Testibus et dat' ut in carta de Wudeetton' in archidiaconatu Oxon'.

The charter roll entry is placed under the bp's twentieth pontifical year (20 December 1228 x 19 December 1229); the institution roll is recorded under the sixteenth pontifical year (20 December 1224 x 19 December 1225) (ibid. 126). The Oxford charter roll mentioned in the dating clause is now missing; the Woodeaton charter referred to was probably the letter of institution of Walter of St Edmund to the church of Woodeaton in the bp's nineteenth pontifical year, 20 December 1227 x 19 December 1228 (ibid. 30).

313. Spalding priory

Institution of William the chaplain to the perpetual vicarage of Spalding, on the presentation of the prior and convent of Spalding. The endowments of the vicarage are described.   [20 December 1228 x 19 December 1229]

B = BL ms. Add. 35296 (Spalding cartulary) fos. 284v–285r (56v–57r). s. xiv in.

Universis sancte matris ecciesie filiis ad quos presens scriptum pervenerit, H. Dei gratia Linc' episcopus salutem in domino. Noverit universitas vestra nos, ad presentationem prioris et conventus de Spalding' patronorum ecclesie de Spalding', dilectum in Cristo filium Willelmum capellanum[a] ad perpetuam eiusdem ecclesie de Spald' vicariam admisisse, et ipsum in eadem vicarium perpetuum instituisse. Consistit autem eadem vicaria in exhibitione capellani que debet accipere panem monachalem et cervisiam[b] cum generali de coquina et ad palefridum suum necessaria in avena et foragine. Consistit etiam vicaria in decimationibus operariorum et omnium mercatorum ville de Spalding' cum legatis capellano[c] debitis et visitationibus infirmorum cum denariis missalibus et denariis cum pane benedicto oblatis et caseis ad Pentecost' et gallinis ad Natale predicte ecclesie de Spald' debitis; salvis in omnibus episcopalibus consuetudinibus et Linc' ecclesie dignitate. Et ut hec institutio nostra perpetuam optineat firmitatem, eam presenti scripto et sigilli nostri duximus appositione confirmandum. Testibus etc.

[a] *The scribe of* B *has inserted an extra minim in this word.*   [b] c- *originally written at the beginning and altered to* s; *also an extra minim inserted in this word.*
[c] capelpellano B.

William of Alkborough was instituted to Spalding vicarage in the course of the bp's twentieth pontifical year, 20 December 1228 x 19 December 1229 (*RHW* iii 167).

314. Nostell priory

Institution of master Berard, papal scribe, to the church of Cheddington, on the presentation of the prior and convent of St Oswald, Nostell.
[20 December 1228 x 19 December 1229]

B = BL ms. Cotton Vespasian E xix (Nostell cartulary), fo. 112v, no. xi. s. xiii ex.

Omnibus Cristi fidelibus ad quos presens scriptum pervenerit, Hugo Dei gratia Linc' episcopus salutem in domino. Noverit universitas vestra nos, ad presentationem prioris et conventus sancti Osuualdi de Nostl' patronorum ecclesie de

Chetindon', dilectum in Cristo filium magistrum Berardum domini pape scriptorem ad eandem ecclesiam de Chetind' admisisse, ipsumque in ea canonice personam instituisse: salvis in omnibus episcopalibus consuetudinibus et Lincol' ecclesie dignitate. Quod ut perpetuam optineat firmitatem, presenti scripto sigillum nostrum duximus apponendum. Hiis testibus etc.

> The Buckingham archdeaconry institution roll records the institution of master Berard among the entries for the bp's twentieth pontifical year, 20 December 1228 x 19 December 1229 (*RHW* ii 76). The entry also states that Ralph and Helias de Chaendoit had renounced their appeal over the advowson of the church (see no. 302 above). For master Berard (de Setia) see *Letters of Guala* no. 65n.

315. Agnes Hayford, nun of Catesby

Notification to the archbishop of Canterbury that Agnes daughter of Richard of Hayford, having worn the religious habit at the priory of Catesby for over two years, has fled the monastery and has resumed a worldly life. After several monitions to return to her religious house, which have been unheeded, the bishop has excommunicated her. [10 June x 19 December 1229]

> B = LAO Wells roll ix, m. 6d (no witnesses or dating clause).
> Pd *RHW* ii 235.

> This entry is placed among the bp's acts for his twentieth pontifical year, 20 December 1228 x 19 December 1229. Archbp Stephen Langton died on 9 July 1228 and his successor, Richard Grant, was not consecrated until 10 June 1229. This signification was clearly addressed to the latter.

316. Agnes Hayford, nun of Catesby

A similar notification about this apostate nun of Catesby addressed to the sheriff of Northamptonshire. [10 June x 19 December 1229]

> B = LAO Wells roll ix, m. 6d (no witnesses or dating clause).
> Pd *RHW* ii 233.

> For the date see above. See also F.D. Logan, *Excommunication and the Secular Arm in medieval England* (Toronto, 1968).

*317. Agnes daughter of Richard of Hayford

Notification to the royal justices that Agnes daughter of Richard of Hayford is excommunicate. [Hilary term, 1230]

> Mention of letters patent in *CRR* xiii no. 2683, in a case between Agnes and the bp of Lincoln and Matthew le Sauser over a plea of land, Northamptonshire, Hilary term 1230: 'quia dominus episcopus mandavit per literas suas quod ipsa est excommunicata'.

318. Desborough church

Institution of master Roger de Bissopeslegh, clerk, to the church of Desborough, of the presentation of William Burdun, the patron. Kilsby, 26 January 1230

> B = LAO Wells roll ix, m. 6.
> Pd *RHW* ii 233–4.

Testibus: magistro W. de Beningworth' et Warino de Kyrketon' capellanis, magis-tris Amaurico de Buged' et Ricardo de Wendour', W. de Winch' et R. de Oxon', canonicis Linc', magistris Ricardo Devon' et A. de Arundell', Thoma de Askeby et S. de Castell', clericis. Dat' per manum nostram apud Kildeby vii° kalendas Februarii anno pontificatus nostri xxi°.

The institution is recorded in the institution roll (ibid. 152).

319. Kilsby church

Grant, to the church of St Andrew, Kilsby, and the parsons of the church for the time being, of the tithe of the bishop's windmill in the village.

Kilsby, 15 February 1230

B = LAO Wells roll ix, m. 7d.
Pd *RHW* ii 237.

Testibus: magistro W. de Beningword' et Warino de Kirket' capellanis, magistris A. de Bugeden' et Ricardo de Wendour', W. de Winch' et Ricardo de Oxon', canonicis Lincoln', magistris R. Devon' et Alardo de Arundell', G. de Moris, S. de Castello et Thoma de Askeby, clericis. Dat' per manum R. de Warr', canonici Linc', apud Kildeby xv kalendas Martii pontificatus nostri anno xxi°.

320. Lenton priory

Grant in proprios usus, with the consent of William the dean and the chapter of Lincoln, to the prior and convent of Lenton, in the name of a perpetual benefice, of the garb tithes and tithes of hay of the church of Rushden, which is of their patronage, except the tithes of thirteen virgates of land (named below). The remaining portion belongs to the parson of the church. The parsonage consists of the entire altarage and all small tithes belonging to the church and obventions, together with the manse which belonged to Hawisia Temprenoise, and half a virgate of land which William Bunch previously chaplain there held, free from all secular exactions and quit from the payment of tithes. It also consists of the annual pension of seven shillings and eightpence from the Hospital of St James in the same parish and twenty pence from the toft of Arnold le Tippere and the garb tithes and tithes of hay of thirteen virgates of land (namely: half a virgate of Edward le Newebonde, half a virgate of Battehull', half a virgate of Hugh the shepherd, half a virgate of Roger the chaplain, half a virgate of Warin son of Robert, half a virgate of Thurstan son of Wlmar, half a virgate of Nicholas son of Robert, half a virgate of Richard son of Warin, half a virgate of Warin the squire (armiger), half a virgate of Richard Long, half a virgate of Hugh son of Osbert, half a virgate of Peter Attelane and Seled Bagge, half a virgate of William Hoppe-sort, half a virgate of Henry ad portam, half a virgate of Matilda Suetis and Roger Lydy, half a virgate of Roger Laweite, half a virgate of William Finch, half a virgate of Richard Hunein, half a virgate of Richard Gnottere, half a virgate of Walter Fader, half a virgate of Simon Peck and Edward son of Roger, half a virgate of William son of Edric, half a virgate of Acer son of William, half a virgate of Samson, and one virgate of Fulk). The parson shall bear all ordinary charges of the church and shall serve personally in the church.

Lincoln, in chapter, 9 April 1230

B = LAO Wells roll ix, mm. 6–7.
Pd *RHW* ii 234–5.

Hiis testibus: Willelmo decano, Roberto archidiacono, Iohanne precentore, Willelmo cancellario, Waltero thesaurario et Iohanne subdecano Linc', I. Bedef', G. Hunted' et R. Leic' archidiaconis, Waltero Blundo et Willelmo de Avalon, magistris Roberto de Gravel', Stephano de Cicestr', Willelmo de Beningwrth', Theobaldo et Ricardo de Cant', Thomas sacrista et Warino de Kirket' capellanis, Willelmo de Lincoln' et Waltero de Well', Petro de Hungar', Radulfo de Waravill' et Willelmo de Winchecumb' diaconis, Theobaldo de Bosell' et Rogero de Bohum, magistris Amaurico de Bugged' et Ricardo de Wendour' et Ricardo de Oxon' subdiaconis, canonicis Linc'. Dat' per manum nostram in capitulo Linc' quinto idus Aprilis pontificatus nostri anno xxi°.

The institution roll record of the institution of Thomas of Northampton to this church in this twenty-first pontifical year (20 December 1229 x 19 December 1230), together with a description of the parsonage is ibid. 152–3. In this entry Hervey *ad portam* is given in place of Henry *ad portam*.

321. Clipston church

Institution of Osbert of London, clerk, to two parts of the church of Clipston on the presentation of J(ohn) the constable of Chester. Thurning, 7 June 1230

B = LAO Wells roll ix, m. 7.
Pd *RHW* ii 237.

T(estibus): magistris W. de Ben', A. de Bug' etc. ut supra in carta de Karleton' anno xxi° [no. 323], apposito hic magistro R. Devon'. Dat' per manum R. de Warr', canonici Lincoln', apud Tunrigg' vii° idus Iunii pontificatus nostri anni xxi°.

The institution is recorded in the institution roll among entries for the bp's twentieth pontifical year, 20 December 1228 x 19 December 1229 (ibid. 150).

*322. William son of Geoffrey son of John

Notification that William son of Geoffrey son of John had quitclaimed to the bishop and his successors and to the church of Lincoln, all right and claim in a mill called Shirefesmilne *to the east of Sleaford, a toft in Old Sleaford which William le Cumber once held; one bovate of land in Sleaford which Alan of Navenby holds; one bovate of land in Sleaford which Hugh Kemus holds; and one bovate of land in Holdingham which Reginald Popiclan holds. The bishop has given him ten marks.* [Trinity term 1230]

Mention of a charter in *CRR* xiv no. 5, Trinity term 1230: 'et pro hac recognitione etc. idem episcopus dedit ei x. marcas coram justiciariis in banco et fecit ei cartam suam que hoc testantur'.

323. East Carlton church

Institution of John de Burgo, clerk, to the church of [East] Carlton, on the presentation of Ralph son of Reginald. Lyddington, 5 September 1230

B = LAO Wells roll ix, m. 7.
Pd *RHW* ii 235–6.

Testibus: magistris W. de Beningewrd' capellano, Amaurico de Buged' et Ricardo de Wendour', W. de Winch', Ricardo de Oxon' et Thoma de Askeby, canonicis Lincoln', magistro Alardo de Arundell', G. de Moris et Stephano de Castell', clericis. Dat' per manum R. de War', canonici Lincoln', apud Lidington' nonis Septembris pontificatus nostri anno xxi°.

The institution is recorded in the institution roll (ibid. 155).

324.   Collyweston church

Institution of John of [Colly]weston, clerk, to the church of Collyweston, on the presentation of Peter of [Colly]weston, knight.   Lyddington, 5 September 1230

B = LAO Wells roll ix, m. 7.
Pd *RHW* ii 236.

Testibus et dat' ut supra in proxima [no. 323].

The institution is recorded in the institution roll among entries for the bp's twentieth pontifical year, 20 December 1228 x 19 December 1229 (ibid. 150–1).

325.   Islip church

Institution of Walter of Warmington, clerk, to the church of Islip, on the presentation of Gervase son of Richard.   Lyddington, 5 September 1230

B = LAO Wells roll ix, m. 7.
Pd *RHW* ii 236.

Testibus et dat' ut supra in secunda [no. 323].

The institution is recorded in the institution roll arnong entries for the bp's twentieth pontifical year, 20 December 1228 x 19 December 1229 (ibid. 151).

326.   Northampton, priory of St Andrew

Institution of master William Poeta, chaplain, to the perpetual vicarage of St Giles, Northampton, on the presentation of the prior and convent of St Andrew, Northampton. He is to serve personally and shall hold the church in the name of his vicarage, paying to the prior ten marks a year, which sum they are accustomed to receive.   Lyddington, 5 September 1230

B = LAO Wells roll ix, m. 7.
Pd *RHW* ii 236.

Testibus et dat' ut supra in tertia [no. 323].

The institution is recorded in the institution roll among entries for the bp's twentieth pontifical year, 20 December 1228 x 19 December 1229 (ibid. 152).

327.   Beauvais, abbey of St Lucien

Institution of John of Towcester, chaplain, to the vicarage of Weedon Lois [Pinkney], ordained by authority of the Council, on the presentation of the prior of Weedon Lois, general proctor of the abbot and convent of St Lucien, Beauvais. John is to serve personally. The vicarage consists of the entire altarage except mortuaries ('first legacy') and the garb tithes of twelve virgates of land. The vicar shall pay synodal dues only.   Lyddington, 5 September 1230

B = LAO Wells roll ix, m. 7.
Pd *RHW* ii 236–7.

Testibus et dat' ut supra in quarta [no. 323].

The institution is recorded in the institution roll (ibid. 153–4). There are significant differences in the description of the vicarage in the institution roll entry. The prior of Weedon is named as Nicholas.

328.   Rockingham bridge

Indulgence of thirteen days to all those who contribute alms for the construction and repair of Rockingham bridge. This indulgence is to last for three years. The collector is forbidden to collect alms anywhere except in the parish of Rockingham itself.   Gretton, 10 September 1230

B = LAO Wells roll ix, m. 7d (no witnesses).
Pd *RHW* ii 238.

Dat' per manum R. de Warr', canonici Linc', apud Gretton' iiii idus Septembris pontificatus nostri anno xxi°.

For earlier indulgences for Rockingham bridge, see nos. 96, 243, 309.

329.   Missenden abbey

Institution of Hugh le Waleys, clerk, to the church of Aldbury, on the presentation of the abbot and convent of Missenden.   Fingest, 18 November 1230

B = BL ms. Harl. 3688 (Missenden cartulary) fo. 159r. s. xiv in.
Pd *Missenden Cartulary* iii no. 800.

Hiis testibus: magistris Willelmo de Benningwurth' capellano, Amaurico de Buggeden' et Ricardo de Wendovere, Willelmo de Wynchecumbe, Ricardo de Oxonia et Thoma de Askeby, canonicis Lincol', magistro Alardo de Arundel, Galfrido de Moris et Stephano de Castell', clericis. Dat' per manum nostram apud Tyngehurst xiiii kalendas Decembris pontificatus nostri anno xxi.

There is no record of this institution at Lincoln, since the Huntingdon archdeaconry institution roll has perished after Bp Hugh's eighteenth pontifical year (20 December 1226 x 19 December 1227).

330.   Studley priory

Grant, with the assent of William the dean and the chapter of Lincoln, to the nuns of Studley of certain tithes (described in detail) in the church of Beckley, which is of their patronage, to be collected by their own servants and applied to their

common use, in the name of a perpetual benefice, together with the small tithes of
their curia, *namely tithes in Horton and Esses.*   Milton, 28 November 1230

> A = LAO Lincoln D. & C. Dij/67/2/4. Endts: Carta de Stodl' in decimis .x^{cem} ......
> in parochia de Beckel' (s. xiii); Decime in parochia de Beckeleye concesse
> monialibus de Stodley (s. xiv); vij. Notary's mark with the initials J.R. A
> small part of the charter is damaged. Words in square brackets have been
> supplied conjecturally. No surviving seal. Two slits for seal-tags. Size: 203
> mm x 98 mm.
> Pd *Reg. Ant.* iii no. 931.

Omnibus Cristi fidelibus ad quos presens scriptum pervenerit, Hugo Dei gratia
[Lincolniensis episcopus salu]tem in domino. Noverit universitas vestra nos,
intuitu Dei de assensu et voluntate dilectorum filiorum Willelmi decani et capituli nostri Linc', concessi[sse et dedisse] et hac presenti carta nostra confirmasse
dilectis in Cristo filiis monialibus de Stodleg' decimas subscriptas in parochia
ecclesie de Beckel', que de earum advocatione est, per proprios servientes suos
colligendas et in communes usus earum, nomine beneficii perpetui, converten-
das, simul cum minutis decimis de curia earundem: scilicet, decimas garbarum
quinque hydarum terre de feodo dominorum de Sancto Walerico in villa de
Horton' cum decimis feni spectantibus ad easdem quinque hydas; item decimas
tertie ga[rbe] duaram hydarum de dominicis que fuerunt Roberti de Bosco et
Iohannis filii Alexandri in villa de Esses cum decimis feni spectantibus ad
easdem suas hydas; item omnes decimas garbarum unius carucate terre quam
dicte moniales hactenus excoluerunt de assartis in eadem villa de Esses; ita quod
si dicte moniales decetero aliquod novum assartum in parochia predicta redegerint in culturam, solvant inde decimas ecclesie memorate: salvis in omnibus episcopalibus consuetudinibus et Lincoln' ecclesie dignitate. Quod ut perpetuam
optineat firmitatem, presenti scripto sigillum nostrum una cum sigillo predicti
capituli nostri duximus apponendum. Hiis testibus: magistris Willelmo de
Beningwrd', Amaurico de Bugeden' et Ricardo de Wendover', Willelmo de
Wynchecumb', Ricardo de Oxon' et Thoma de Askeby, canonicis Linc', Roberto
de Bollesover' capellano, magistro A. de Arundell' et Galfrido de Morys, clericis.
Actum apud Middelton' quarto kalendas Decembris pontificatus nostri anno
vicesimo primo.

> The advowson of the church was subsequently transferred by the prioress and
> convent of Studley to Bp Richard Gravesend of Lincoln (1258–79) (*Reg. Ant.* iii
> nos. 932–3).

331. Bradenstoke priory

Institution of Reginald the chaplain to the perpetual vicarage of [North] Aston,
on the presentation of the prior and convent of Bradenstoke. He is to serve per-
sonally. The vicarage consists of the whole altarage, the manse and the houses
belonging to the church, and six acres of land lying near Chaldewell in the east
field and half the tithes of Nethercote from the land of William Bufyn and Arnold
of Nethercote, and the tithes of two mills of Simon Gambon. The vicar is to find a
clerk and adequate lights in the church and he shall only pay synodal dues.
Dorchester, 1 December 1230

B = BL ms. Cotton Vitellius A xi (Bradenstoke cartulary) fo. 146v (143v). s. xiv
med. C = BL ms. Stowe 925 (Bradenstoke cartulary) fo. 29v, no. xi. ss.
xiv–xv.
Pd (calendar) from C in *Bradenstoke Cartulary* no. 11.

Omnibus Cristi fidelibus ad quos presens scriptum pervenerit, Hugo Dei gratia
Lincoln'[a] episcopus salutem in domino sempiternam. Noverit universitas vestra
nos, ad presentationem dilectorum in Cristo prioris et conventus de Brad-
enestok'[b], patronorum ecclesie de Northeston'[c], dilectum in Cristo filium
Reginaldum capellanum ad perpetuam ipsius ecclesie vicariam admisisse, ipsumque in ea vicarium perpetuum instituisse cum onere ministrandi personaliter in
eadem. Consistit autem ipsa vicaria in toto alteragio et in manso et domibus ad
ipsam ecclesiam pertinentibus, cum sex acris terre iacentibus iuxta Caldewelle[d]
in campo orientali et in medietate decimarum de Nedecot'[e] de terra Willelmi
Bufyn'[f] et Arnaldi de Nedecote[g] et decimis molendinorum duorum[h] Simonis
Gambon.[i] Et inveniet vicarius clericum et luminaria competentia in ecclesia et
solvet tantum sinodalia, salvis in omnibus episcopalibus consuetudinibus 'et'
Lincoln'[a] ecclesie dignitate. Quod ut perpetuam optineat firmitatem, presenti
scripto sigillum nostrum duximus apponendum. Hiis testibus: magistris Willelmo de Bennieword' et Ricardo de Wendour', Willelmo de Wynchecombe.[j]
Data per manum nostram apud Dorkecestr' kalendis Decembris pontificatus
nostri anno xxi[mo] etc.[k]

[a] Lyncoln' C.   [b] Bradenestoke C.   [c] Northaston' C.   [d] Chaldewell'C.   [e] Nethercote C.   [f] Buffyn C.   [g] Nedercot' C.   [h] duorum molendinorum C.   [i] Gaumbon
C.   [j] Wynchecoumbe C.   [k] *omitted* C.

The institution is recorded in the Oxford archdeaconry institution roll among
entries for the bp's eighteenth pontifical year, 20 December 1226 x 19 December
1227 (*RHW* ii 25–6).

332. Newnham priory

*Institution of William of Bedford, chaplain, to the perpetual vicarage of Stagsden,
on the presentation of the prior and convent of Newnham. He is to serve personally. The vicarage consists of the entire altarage of the church and all the small
tithes except wool and lambs, with a suitable manse assigned to the vicar. A
pension of two marks shall be paid by the vicar each year to the prior and
convent, who shall bear all the burdens of the church.*

[20 December 1229 x 19 December 1230]

B = BL ms. Harl. 3656 (Newnham cartulary) fos. 61v–62r (witnesses and date
omitted). s. xv in.
Pd *Newnham Cartulary* i no. 107 (dated incorrectly).

The institution of William of Bedford is recorded in the institution roll among
entries for the bp's twenty-first pontifical year, 20 December 1229 x 19 December
1230 (*RHW* iii 24–5).

333.   Osney abbey

? Confirmation for the canons of Osney of the church of St George in Oxford Castle and all its possessions.   [20 December 1229 x 19 December 1230]

> A = LAO Lincoln D. & C. A/2/18 no. 29 (fragment of the left-hand bottom corner of a charter, 70 mm. x 50 mm., in a hand of the first half of the thirteenth century).

Only portions of six lines of this document remain, viz:
> Clopham . Dukelinton'. in Wa....
> mas unius hyde . in Baldindon' d...
> ecclesia et canonici memorati de Osen'...
> habeant et possideant imperpetuum . salvis in omnibus ...
> sigillum nostrum una cum sigillo capituli nostri feci...
> ....mo primo.

From even this fragment it is possible to attempt a reconstruction of the whole document. Firstly, it is clear from the corroboration clause that the document has been issued in the name of a bishop, with the approval of his cathedral chapter, who likewise affixed their seal to it. 'Habeant and possideant imperpetuum' preceded by a list of possessions and the name of a religious house strongly suggests a general confirmation of possessions. The fragment of dating-clause on the last line is very probably part of the bp's pontifical year clearly 'vicesimo primo' or a higher number. If we assume that Osney abbey is receiving this confirmation, as seems likely, from its diocesan, the bp of Lincoln, then Hugh of Wells appears to be the strongest candidate. In the thirteenth century only two bps of Lincoln ruled the see for twenty-one years or over – Hugh of Wells and Richard Gravesend (1258–79). Two facts rule out the latter in a fairly convincing way: firstly, the handwriting is too early in style for the twenty-first year of the bp (1278–9), and secondly, as will be seen shortly, Bp Gravesend issued a confirmation on these same lines for Osney on 23 June 1259 (*Oseney Cartulary* iv no. 33). All these reasons lead me to the conclusion that we have here a small fragment of a charter of confirmation for Osney abbey issued by Bp Hugh in his twenty-first pontifical year (20 December 1229 x 19 December 1230). Fortunately the occurrence of the place-names, Clopham, Ducklington and Baldon in the fragment aids the identification of the confirmation. All these possessions once belonged to the church of St George in Oxford Castle granted to Osney in 1149 (*EEA* 1 no. 208). It seems very likely that the wording of this fragmentary charter was used in Bp Gravesend's 1259 confirmation (there are great similarities). No confirmatory charter of Bp Hugh was entered in the Osney cartulary and the existence of this fragment at Lincoln might possibly imply that the document was for some reason never issued.

334.   Hargrave church

Institution of Henry de Rand, clerk, to the church of Hargrave, on the presentation of Richard of Desborough, patron by virtue of his wardship of the land and heir of Amice de Costentin, his late wife.   Fingest, 29 March 1231

> B = LAO Wells roll ix, m. 7.
> Pd *RHW* ii 238.

Hiis testibus: magistris W. de Beningworth', Amaurico de Bugged' et Ricardo de Wendour', Willelmo de Winchecumb' et Thoma de Askeby, canonicis Linc', Roberto de Bolesour', capellano, magistris Waltero de Wermen' et Alardo de

Arund', Iohanne de Crakeh', Iohanne de Burg', G. de Moris et Stephano de Castell', clericis. Dat' per manum nostram apud Tinghurst iiii° kalendas Aprilis pontificatus nostri anno vicesimo secundo.

> The institution is recorded in the institution roll among entries for the bp's twentieth pontifical year, 20 December 1228 x 19 December 1229 (ibid. 151). There had been a dispute in the king's court at Westminster in Hilary term 1229 between Richard and the prior of the Hospitallers in England over the advowson, the prior acting on behalf of John Bauzan, a minor. Richard had established his claim through his late wife Amice (*CRR* xiii no. 1495).

335. Lyndon church

Institution of master Stephen of Sandwich, clerk, to the church of Lyndon, on the presentation of Alan of Lyndon.   Fingest, 1 April 1231

> B = LAO Wells roll ix, m. 7.
> Pd *RHW* ii 239.

Testibus ut supra in carta de Haregrave [no. 334], apposito hic Ricardo de Oxon'. Dat' per manum nostram apud Tinghurst' kalendis Aprilis pontificatus nostri anno xxii°.

> The institution is recorded in the institution roll among entries for the bp's twenty-first pontifical year, 20 December 1229 x 19 December 1230 (ibid. 158).

336. Church Brampton church

Institution of Robert Passelewe, clerk, to the church of [Church] Brampton, on the presentation of Thomas Picot.   Old Temple, London, 13 April 1231

> B = LAO Wells roll ix, m. 7.
> Pd *RHW* ii 238–9.

Testibus ut in carta Ricardi de Burg' super ecclesia de Sadingt' in comitatu Leirc' anno xxii°. Dat' per manum R. de Warravill', canonici Linc', apud Vetus Templum London' idibus Aprilis pontificatus nostri anno xxii° .

> The Leicester archdeaconry charter roll has not survived. The institution is recorded in the institution roll among entries for the bp's twenty-first pontifical year, 20 December 1229 x 19 December 1230 (ibid. 154–5). The Saddington charter referred to is no. 337 below, a copy of which has chanced to survive in the Easby cartulary.

337. Easby abbey

Institution of Richard de Burgo, clerk, to the church of Saddington, on the presentation of the abbot and convent of St Agatha's, Richmond alias Easby.
Old Temple, London, 13 April 1231

> B = BL ms. Egerton 2827 (Easby cartulary) fo. 303r. s. xiii ex.

Omnibus etc., Hugo Dei gratia Lyncoln' episcopus salutem. Noveritis nos, ad presentationem abbatis et conventus sancte Agathe, Richem', patronorum ecclesie de Sadyngt', dilectum in Cristo filium Ricardum de Burgo clericum ad eandem ecclesiam admisisse, ipsumque in ea canonice personam instituisse, salvis in omnibus episcopalibus consuetudinibus et Lincoln' ecclesie dignitate. Quod ut perpetuam optineat firmitatem, presenti scripto sigillum nostrum duximus apponendum.

The institution is recorded in the institution roll (*RHW* ii 313). For the date of this letter of institution see the reference to the witness list in the preceding *actum*.

338. Wadenhoe church

Institution of Henry de Len, clerk, to the church of Wadenhoe, on the presentation of Henry de Ver.   21 May 1231

B = LAO Wells roll ix, m. 7.
Pd *RHW* ii 239.

Hiis testibus: Roberto Linc', Iohanne Bedef' et G. Huntingd' archidiaconis, magistris W. de Beningewr' capellano, A. de Bugeden' et R. de Wendour', W. de Winch', R. de Oxon' et Thoma de Ask', canonicis Linc', Roberto de Bolesoure capellano, magistro Alardo de Arundel, G. de Moris et S. de Castell', clericis. Dat' per manum R. de War', canonici Linc', xii kalendas Iunii pontificatus nostri anno xxii°.

The institution is recorded in the institution roll among entries for the bp's seventeenth pontifical year, 20 December 1225 x 19 December 1226 (ibid. 127).

339. Bradden church

Institution of Reginald of Allington, clerk, to the church of Bradden, on the presentation of William de Gymeges.   Spaldwick, 29 May 1231

B = LAO Wells roll ix, m. 7.
Pd *RHW* ii 242.

Hiis testibus: magistris Amaurico de Bugged', R. de Wendour', W. de Winchecumb', R. de Oxon', Thoma de Askeb', canonicis Lincoln', R. de Bollesour' capellano, magistris W. de Werministr' et A. de Arund', G. de Moris, I. de Burgo et Stephano de Castell', clericis. Dat' per manum R. de Warravill', canonici Lincoln', apud Spaldewic' iiii kalendas Iunii pontificatus nostri anno xxii.

The institution is recorded in the institution roll among entries for the bp's twenty-first pontifical year, 20 December 1229 x 19 December 1230 (ibid. 156). William had recovered the patronage in the king's court against Walter of Bradden.

340. Whiston church

Institution of William of Whiston, clerk, to the church of Whiston, on the presentation of William of Whiston, knight.   Lyddington, 19 June 1231

B = LAO Wells roll ix, m. 7.
Pd *RHW* ii 240.

Hiis testibus: magistris W. de Beningword', A. de Bugged' et R. de Wendour', W. de Winch', R. de Ox' et Thoma de Ask', canonicis Linc', magistris W. de Wermen' et A. de Arund', Iohanne de Crak' et S. de Cast', clericis. Dat' per manum nostram apud Lidint' xiii° kalendas Iulii pontificatus nostri anno xxii°.

The institution is recorded in the institution roll among entries for the bp's twenty-first pontifical year, 20 December 1229 x 19 December 1230 (ibid. 155).

341. Sulby abbey

Similar indulgence for the monastery of Sulby as in no. 294 with the additional
clause that other bishops could grant indulgences if they so wished.
                                                    Arthingworth, 31 July 1231

> B = LAO Wells roll ix, m. 7d.
> Pd *RHW* ii 243.

Dat' apud Erningword' per manum R. de Warr', canonici Linc', ii kalendas
Augusti pontificatus nostri anno xxii°.

342. Northampton, priory of St Andrew

Institution of Robert de Kolebois, chaplain, to the perpetual vicarage of All
Saints, Northampton, on the presentation of the prior and convent of St Andrew,
Northampton. He is to serve personally. The vicarage consists of the corrody of a
monk in the refectory or in the prior's chamber or wherever the vicar desires. The
vicar's servant shall have a corrody too, such as one of the main servants of the
priory has. The vicar shall have thirty shillings a year for a stipend and an offer-
ing at the four principal feasts, namely sixpence at each feast; also half of the
*mortuaries (*secundus legatus*) and on Sunday the remainder of the consecrated*
bread. When a mass or a marriage is celebrated in the church he shall receive
one penny. The monks shall bear all the charges of the church and shall find two
secular chaplains to assist the vicar, with clerks for the chaplains. They shall also
provide a suitable manse for the vicar. The vicar, chaplains and clerks shall swear
an oath of fealty to the priory in regard to temporal matters.
                                                    Arthingworth, 1 August 1231

> B = LAO Wells roll ix, m. 7.
> Pd *RHW* ii 241.

Hiis testibus: magistris Amaurico de Bugged' et Ricardo de Wendour', Willelmo
de Winchecumb' et Ricardo de Oxon', canonicis Lincoln', Roberto de Bollesour'
capellano, magistris Waltero de Wermen' et A. de Arundell', I. de Burgo, S. de
Càstell' et G. de Moris, clericis. Dat' per manum Radulfi de Warravill', canonici
Linc', apud Ernigworth' kalendis Augusti pontificatus nostri anno vicesimo
secundo.

> The institution is recorded in the institution roll among entries for the bp's twentieth
> pontifical year, 20 December 1228 x 19 December 1229 (ibid. 148). See also no.
> 206.

343. St Neots priory

Confirmation, with the assent of the prior and convent of St Neots, the patrons of
the church of Brampton [Ash], of exchanges made between William son of
William de Insula and Thomas, rector of the church of St Mary, Brampton [Ash].
The bishop has inspected (but not recited) two charters of William. By the first,
William granted to the church of St Mary, Brampton [Ash], and to Thomas the

rector and his successors, all his wood called Lauedibradegates *and one selion at* Le Pottes, *which Griffin held (lying between the land of William Briselanc' and of Simon de Naveby), in exchange for a certain wood called* Le Holes *belonging to* Brampton [Ash] *church. By the second charter, William granted Thomas the rector of St Mary, Brampton [Ash] all his thicket* (riffletum) *which he had in* Holegate *on the south side of the ditch, and the thicket he had at* Fildegate, *lying between the thicket of Henry son of Richard and that which Thomas the rector had from William in* Holegate *(containing twenty-five perches in length and fifteen perches in width, measured according to the king's perch of twenty-five feet), in exchange for the thicket which the aforesaid Thomas has in* Le Nabbe *in the fields of Brampton [Ash] and in exchange also for the thicket Thomas has in* Holegate, *lying between* Derobueshille *and the thicket of W[illiam] de Insula and extending up to William's ditch on the south.*   Lyddington, 3 August 1231

> B = LAO Wells roll ix, m. 7d.
> Pd *RHW* ii 243–4.

Hiis testibus: magistris A. de Bugged' et R. de Wendour', W. de Winch' et R. de Oxon', canonicis Linc', magistris W. de Wermenistr' et A. de Arundell', G. de Moris, I. de Burg' et S. de Castell', clericis. Dat' per manum R. de Warravill', canonici Linc', apud Lidington' iii nonas Augusti pontificatus nostri anno xxii.

> For the king's perch, see R.D. Connor, *The Weights and Measures of England* (Science Museum, London, 1987), pp. 45–6.

344. Peterborough abbey

Statutes made by the bishop after his visitation of Peterborough abbey.
11 August 1231

> B = CUL, Peterborough D. & C. ms. 1, fo. 109r–v. rubric: Statuta H. Lincoln' epis-
> copi per visitationem factam per eodem episcopo (*sic*) apud Burg'. s. xiii
> med.

Visitatio facta per dominum Lincol' Hugonem secundum apud Burgum in capitulo anno domini milesimo ducentesimo tricesimo primo[a] in crastino sancti Laurentii, presentibus dominis Lincol' et Leicestrie archidiaconis, magistris Willelmo de Beninguurthe capellano et Amauro de Buggeden' et aliis eiusdem domini episcopi clericis, videlicet, quod de communi abbatis et conventus ibidem assensu predicti domini Lincol' auctoritate interveniente, provisum fuit sub pena excommunicationis quod capitula subscripta inviolabiliter observarentur:
• In primis de obedientiariis pertinentibus ad conventum preficiendis per abbatem de consilio partis sanioris conventus et de eisdem simili modo amovendis et hoc fiat ex caritate.
• De beneficiis ecclesiasticis conferendis per abbatem et de assensu conventus et ut conventus de facili suum ad id inclinat assensum dum modo puritas fuerit in collatione et persona idonea.
• Ne abbas mutuo accipiat denarios a Iudeis sub usura vel a Cristianis usurariis cum aliqua pene adiectione sine assensu conventus nec unquam obliget monasterium vel bona monasterii mobilia[b] seu inmobilia in tali casu.
• De auxiliis de Pilesgate per abbatem et conventum ad turrim ecclesie construendam vel ad refectorium reedificandum prout abbas melius voluerit.

• Ut sacrista habeat sicut habere consuevit equos et omnia alia cum corporibus militum defunctorum, hoc adiecto [fo. 109v] moderamine. Quod si aliquis equs (*sic*) militis defuncti excedat pretium quatuor marcarum cedat in usus abbatis. Arma vero seu pretium armorum reponantur in tuto loco per abbatem de conscientia conventus ad defensionem patrie et pacis ecclesie tuitionem et de pretio armorum emendentur vel sustenturetur (*sic*) arma vel alia emi aut ad usus predictos.

• Ut sacrista unicam per annum ex debito moderatam faciat abbati procurationem apud Pilesgate cum ad hoc ab abbate fuerit premunitus.

• Ipse nichilominus et omnes alii obedientiarii de rebus pertinentibus ad obedientias suas tam infra septa monasterii quam extra omnem honorem et reverentiam et solatium cum requisiti fuerint abbati exhibebunt humiliter et devote.

• Item provisum est quod si aliquis obedientiarius aliam ecclesiasticam personam vel secularem voluerit convenire super rebus mobilibus vel inmobilibus aliquibus ad suam obedientiam adquirendis vel revocandis sumptibus suis, hoc faciat quatenus[c] ad hoc suffecerit et hoc numquam aggrediatur nisi de consilio abbatis et conscientia conventus, si non conveniatur super huiusmodi rebus de quibus dictum est sustineat abbas onera litis nisi obedientia ipsa ad hoc sibi sufficiat. De celararia in speciale sit quod quotienscumque in huiusmodi casu dubitetur utrum sibi sufficiat an non ad onera litis, an expensas illud per abbatem et conventum discutiatur et si insufficientia eiusdem manifeste appareat abbas tunc demum ministret expensas.

• Ut camerarius sine difficultate et dilatione ad terminos statutos in cartis abbatum percipiat redditum ad camerariam[d] pertinentem.

• Ut abbas habeat plenam potestatem et auctoritatem tam in temporalibus quam in spiritualibus secundum statuta regule beati Benedicti et ut universi et singuli obedientiarii sicut dictum est et alii honorem et reverentiam debitam et devotam ei exhibeant obedientiam et abbas vice versa illos in omnibus fraterna caritate pertractet secundum statuta eiusdem regule.

• Nec aliquid arduum umquam attemptet sine consilio totius conventus vel partis sanioris quorum consilium semper in huiusmodi preferat consiliis secularium.

In predictorum igitur testimonium, predicti dominus episcopus abbas et conventus presenti scripto sigilla sua apposuerunt.

[a] uno *originally written and* primo *interlined.*   [b] monachis *originally written, with* nachis *dotted for deletion and* bilia *interlined.*   [c] quatinus *originally written and* i *dotted for deletion and* e *interlined.*   [d] ar *interlined.*

345. Oakham and Hambleton churches

Notification by the bishop and William the dean and the chapter of Lincoln that they have agreed, by way of compromise, that Robert archdeacon of Lincoln, John archdeacon of Bedford, Richard prior of Hurley and master William de Lyra shall ordain and dispose of the churches of Oakham and Hambleton and that they will ratify what they ordain. There was a suit between the bishop and the abbey of Westminster over these churches.   [Before September 1231]

A

(Lincoln version)

A = LAO Lincoln D. & C. Dij/89/1/12. Endts: De Hameldon' ecclesia (hand of John de Schalby) Okham et Hameldon' (s. xiii ex.). No surviving seals. Two strips for seal and riband. Size: 170 mm x 63 mm
B = LAO Lincoln D. & C. A/1/6 (Registrum), no. 334.
Pd from A in *Reg. Ant.* iii no. 1008.

Omnibus Cristi fidelibus presens scriptum inspecturis, Hugo Dei gratia Lincoln' episcopus, Willelmus decanus Lincoln' ecclesie et eiusdem loci capitulum, salutem in domino. Noverit universitas vestra nos consensisse et compromisisse in viros venerabiles Robertum Lincoln' et Iohannem Bedeford' archidiaconos et in dominum Ricardum priorem de Hurl' et magistrum Willelmum de Lyra, ut ipsi, invocata Spiritus Sancti gratia tantum Deum pre oculis habentes, ordinent et disponant ad honorem ecclesie Lincoln' et nostrum, ad honorem etiam ecclesie abbatis et conventus Westmonasterii de subscriptis ecclesiis in Lincoln' diocesi constitutis: videlicet, de ecclesia de Okham' cum pertinentiis, de ecclesia de Hameledon' cum pertinentiis, ut quicquid dicti ordinatores vel tres ex ipsis de ecclesiis prenominatis duxerint ordinandum, ratum et stabile perseveret a nobis irrefragabiliter acceptandum. In cuius rei testimonium presenti scripto sigilla nostra duximus apponenda.

B

(Westminster version)

A = Westminster abbey mun. 20622. Endt: Compromissio ordinationis ecclesie de Ocham (s. xiii). Seal of bishop, fragment on first parchment tongue, white wax repaired. Fragment of Chapter seal on second tongue – white wax, ribands remain. Size: 177 mm x 57 mm (left-hand side) – 40 mm (right hand side).
B = BL ms. Cotton Faustina A iii (Westminster abbey cartulary) fos. 266v–267r.
Pd from B in *Mon. Angl.* i 311a.

Omnibus Cristi fidelibus ad quos presens scriptum pervenerit, Hugo Dei gratia Lincoln' episcopus, Willelmus Lincoln' ecclesie decanus et eiusdem loci capitulum, salutem in domino. Noverit universitas vestra nos consensisse et compromisisse in dilectos nobis Robertum Lincoln' et Iohannem Bedeford' archidiaconos et in dominum Ricardum priorem de Hurnle et magistrum Willelmum de Lyra, ut ipsi, invocata Spiritus Sancti gratia tantum Deum pre oculis habentes, ordinent et disponant ad honorem ecclesie Lincoln' et nostrum, ad honorem etiam ecclesie Westmonasterii abbatis et conventus eiusdem loci, de subscriptis ecclesiis in diocesi Lincoln' constitutis: videlicet, de ecclesia de Ocham cum pertinentiis, de ecclesia de Hameldon' cum pertinentiis, ut quicquid ordinatores predicti vel tres ex ipsis de ecclesiis prenominatis duxerint ordinandum, ratum et stabile perseveret a nobis irrefragabiliter acceptandum. In cuius rei testimonium presenti scripto sigilla nostra duximus apponenda. Valete.

The decision of the above mentioned papal judges delegate is dated September 1231 (*Reg. Ant.* ii no. 374) *Lincoln versions*: A = LAO Lincoln D. & C. Dij/89/1/16; BCD = A/1/5, nos. 232 & 946 & A/1/6, no. 336): *Westminster versions*: A = Westminster abbey mun. 20619; B = BL ms. Cotton Faustina A iii, fos. 264r–265v).

The actual settlement made by the archdeacons of Lincoln and Bedford, the prior of Hurley and master William de Lyra was issued in September 1231 (*Reg. Ant.* ii no. 374). The abbey had claimed a pension of twenty pounds from the churches, with a procuration of two days a year, and also the appropriation of the church of Oakham. By the settlement, after the cession or death of Gilbert Marshal the then rector of Oakham, the abbey were to have all the fruits and issues of the church of Oakham and the chapels of Langham, Egleton, Brooke and Gunthorpe, with the village of Thorpe by the Water, in the name of a perpetual benefice, together with the manse which is on the west side of the church of Oakham, with the lands, homages, and rents belonging to the said church and chapels, except the rector's portion. The rector was to be presented to the diocesan bishop by the abbey. Bp Hugh shall ordain as he thinks fit with respect to the church of Hambleton and its advowson, and a pension of twenty shillings from the church of St Peter, Stamford, and the chapel of Braunston. The abbey, when they hear of the bp's death, are to perform the service of the dead for him as for an abbot of Westminster, and shall feed one hundred poor people; and they shall observe his anniversary, making a special memorial for him and for deceased canons of Lincoln and benefactors of that church.

346. Rochester cathedral priory

Confirmation, made with the consent of William the dean and the chapter of Lincoln, for the prior and monks of the conventual church of St Andrew, Rochester, of the church of Haddenham and its chapels of Cuddington and Kingsey, which the bishop has discovered by inquisition the monks have possessed of old, saving perpetual vicarages (one in the church of Haddenham, the other in the chapel of Kingsey) ordained by the bishop with the assent of the prior and convent. The prior and convent shall present chaplains or clerks to the bishop and his successors for institution whenever there is a vacancy. These clerks are to be ordained to priest's orders within a year and are to minister in person. The endowments of the vicarage of Haddenham are described [as in no. 91 above]. The vicarage of Kingsey consists of the entire altarage of the chapel, a virgate of land with a meadow and manse, a croft outside the enclosure of the manse, and the tithes of hay of the village of Kingsey. The monks shall be responsible for the repair of the chancels of the church and the chapels, and shall bear all episcopal and archidiaconal charges for the chapel of Kingsey, and all extraordinary charges for the mother church and the chapels in proportion.

Lincoln, in chapter, 9 September 1231

B = BL ms. Cotton Domitian A x (Rochester cartulary) fos. 205v–206r (203v–204r). s. xiii in. C = LAO Lincoln Ep. Reg. VI (register of Bp Thomas Bek 1342–7), fo. 101r (in an inspeximus of Bp Bek 22 June 1345).
Pd from B in *Reg. Roff.* 386–7.

Omnibus Cristi fidelibus ad quos presens scriptum pervenerit, Hugo Dei gratia Lincoln' episcopus salutem in domino. Noverit universitas vestra quod nos, pia vota fidelium pio volentes favore prosequi, de consensu et voluntate dilectorum filiorum Willelmi decani et capituli nostri Lincoln', intuitu Dei concessimus et auctoritate episcopali confirmavimus conventuali ecclesie sancti Andree de Roff',[a] priori et monachis ibidem Deo servientibus et servituris in perpetuum, ecclesiam de Hedreham[b] cum capellis suis de Codington' et Kingeseya,[c] quas ab antiquo continue et pacifice sicut per inquisitionem inde factam accepimus dicti monachi possiderunt et^d de quibus in eorum autenticis plenius est expressum: salvis ibi vicariis perpetuis, una, scilicet, in ecclesia de Hedreham^b et alia in capella de Kingeseya,^{c} de dictorum prioris et conventus assensu, per nos ordinatis ut inferius; ad quas quotiens vacaverint dicti prior et conventus capellanos ydoneos vel clericos qui infra annum in sacerdotes possint promoveri nobis et successoribus nostris a nobis instituendos et ibidem in officio sacerdotali ministraturos personaliter ut moris est presentabunt. Consistit autem vicaria de Hedreham in toto altelagio^e ipsius ecclesie et tota capella de Codington', ^{f}-exceptis minutis decimis de dominico monachorum et in una virgata terre cum manso ad eam spectante in villa de Codington' et in tota decima garbarum trium hidarum terre de feudo Ricardi iunioris in villa de Hedreham^b et in uno manso cum domibus Willelmi quondam capellani eiusdem ville et tota curia ad eundem mansum spectantibus.^{g} Tertiam vero garbam decimarum totius ville de Codington'-^{f}, ipsi vicarie prius deputatam in usus predictorum prioris et conventus decrevimus convertendam; et inveniet vicarius capellanum idoneum capelle de Codington' deservientem, et alia onera eiusdem ecclesie et capelle ordinaria debita et consueta sustinebit. Vicaria vero de Kingeseya^c consistit in toto altelagio^e ipsius capelle et una virgata terre cum prato et manso competenter edificato et una crofta extra septa dicti mansi pertinentibus ad capellam ipsam et in decimis feni de eadem villa de Kingeseya^c provenientibus. Monachi Roffen', qui ad reparationem cancellorum tam matricis ecclesie quam capellarum predictarum tenentur, omnia onera episcopalia et archidiaconalia pro dicta capella de Kingeseya^c sustinebunt, et de oneribus extraordinariis sepedictam matricem ecclesiam de Hedreham^b et capellas memoratas contingentibus cum emerserint pro portionibus suis respondebunt: salvis in omnibus episcopalibus consuetudinibus et Lincoln' ecclesie dignitate. Quod ut perpetuam obtineat firmitatem, presenti scripto sigillum nostrum una cum sigillo predicti capituli nostri duximus apponendum. Hiis testibus: Willelmo decano, Roberto archidiacono, Iohanne precentore, Willelmo cancellario, Waltero thesaurario et Iohanne subdecano Lincoln', Roberto Leircestr',^{h} Willelmo Stouwe,^{i} Iohanne Bedeford', Matheo Bukingham',^{j} Ada Oxon', Gilberto Huntigd'^{k} archidiaconis, Willelmo de Avalun, magistris Stephano de [fo. 204r] Cicestr', Roberto de Gravel',^{l}Willelmo de Beningworth',^{m} Theodbaldo^n et Ricardo de Cantia, Galfrido Scoto, Thoma de Norton', Warino de Kirketon',^{o} capellanis, magistris Willelmo de Lincoln', Roberto de Brind'^{p} et Waltero de Well',^{q} Radulfo de Waravill',^{r} Petro de Hungar' et Willelmo de Winchecumb',^{s} diaconis, Theodbaldo^n de Bosell', magistris Amaurico de Bugged' et Ricardo de Wendour',^{t} Ricardo de Oxon' et Thoma de Askeb',^{u} subdiaconis, canonicis Lincoln'. Datum per manum nostram in capitulo Lincoln' quinto idus Septembris pontificatus nostri anno vicesimo secundo.

^{a} Roffa C. ^{b} Hadenham C. ^{c} Kyngeseya C. ^{d} et *omitted* C. ^{e} alteragio C.
$^{f-f}$ *inserted in the margin* B. ^{g} spectante C. ^{h} Leyrecestr' C. up6 i Stowe C.
^{j} Buckyngham C. up6 k Huntingdon' C. ^{l} Gravele C. ^{m} Benyngworth' C.
^{n} Theobaldo C. ^{o} Kyrketon' C. ^{p} *sic, recte* Brincl'; Bryncl' C. ^{q} Welle C.
^{r} Warravil' C. ^{s} Wynchecumb' C. ^{t} Wendoure C. ^{u} Alkeb' (*sic*) C.

It is probable that this is the charter alluded to in the Kingsey entry on the Buckingham institution roll 20 December 1231 x 19 December 1232 (*RHW* ii 84): *Consistit autem ipsa vicaria ut in rotulo cartarum anni xxii*. The Buckingham archdeaconry charter roll is lost. It is just conceivable that a very small fragment of a charter of Bp Hugh surviving in the Lincoln dean and chapter muniments (Dij/73/1/38 – size:

133 mm. x 75 mm. approx.) relates to this confirmation. The charter is so badly damaged that it would be pointless to transcribe what little of it remains. Suffice it to say it mentions Haddenham and the chapels of Cuddington and Kingsey but nothing more is discernible and no trace of the date has survived.

347. Northampton, priory of St Andrew

Letter to the abbot of Crowland and his fellow judges delegate in connection with the case being heard before them between the prior and convent of St Andrew, Northampton, and Henry, vicar of the church of St Mary by Northampton Castle. The priory are claiming a further pension from Henry. Since new pensions should not be granted nor old ones increased without the diocesan's assent, the bishop is appealing to Rome. Nettleham, 12 September 1231

B = LAO Wells roll ix, m. 7d (no witnesses).
Pd *RHW* ii 244.

Dat' per manum Radulfi de Warrav' apud Netelham ii idus Septembris pontificatus nostri anno xxii.

*348. Oakham and Hambleton churches

Letters to the abbot of Chertsey and his fellow judges withdrawing the appeal he had made to the pope against their decision relating to the churches of Oakham and Hambleton. [*c.* September 1231]

Mention of letters in LAO Wells roll ix, m. 7d, as being entered in the memoranda roll (now lost) for the bp's twenty second pontifical year (20 December 1230–19 December 1231).
Pd *RHW* ii 244.

For the date see no. 345.

349. Peterborough abbey

Institution of William de Burgo [Peterborough], clerk, to the church of Peakirk, on the presentation of the abbot and convent of Peterborough. Louth, 14 October 1231

B = LAO Wells roll ix, m. 7.
Pd *RHW* ii 241–2.

Hiis testibus: magistro Amaurico de Bugged', W. de Winch', R. de Ox' et Thoma de Ask', canonicis Linc', magistro A. de Arund', I. de Burg', I. de Crakeh' et S. de Castello, clericis. Dat' apud Lud' per manum R. de Warr', canonici Linc', pridie idus Octobris pontificatus nostri anno vicesimo secundo.

The institution is recorded in the institution roll (ibid. 160).

350. Nostell priory

Institution of Philip de Land', clerk, to the church of Charwelton, on the presentation of the prior and convent of St Oswald, Nostell. Louth, 14 October 1231

B = LAO Wells roll ix, m. 7.
Pd *RHW* ii 242.

Testibus et dat' ut supra in carta proxima [no. 349].

> The institution is recorded in the institution roll among entries for the bp's twenty-first pontifical year, 20 December 1229 x 19 December 1230 (ibid. 155–6). The incumbent's narne is given as Philip de Wauda.

351. Lilford church

Institution of David of Haddington, clerk, to the church of Lilford, on the presentation of Walter Olifard.   Louth, 14 October 1231

> B = LAO Wells roll ix, m. 7.
> Pd *RHW* ii 242.

Testibus et dat' ut supra in carta proxima [no. 350].

> The institution is recorded in the institution roll among entries for the bp's twentieth pontifical year, 20 December 1228 x 19 December 1229 (ibid. 150).

352. Northampton archdeaconry

Notification to all the clergy of the archdeaconry of Northampton that the bishop has appointed William, dean of Arthingworth, and Philip of Sydenham, chaplain, as his sequestrators in the archdeaconry during pleasure.
[20 December 1230 x 19 December1231]

> B = LAO Wells roll ix, m. 7d (witnesses and date omitted).
> Pd *RHW* ii 245.

> The entry is placed under the bp's twenty-second pontifical year, 20 December 1230 x 19 December 1231. The term 'sequestrator' is not actually used in the text. The bp appoints them *procuratores nostros . . . ad recipiendum, colligendum et custodiendum . . . sequestra nostra de archidiaconatu Norh't.*

353. Coventry priory

Institution of Reginald de Haltsted, clerk, to the church of Winwick, on the presentation of the prior and convent of Coventry.
[20 December 1230 x 19 December 1231]

> B = LAO Wells roll ix, m. 7.
> Pd *RHW* ii 240.

Testibus et dat' ut in carta Roberti de Segrave super ecclesia de Wigint' in archidiaconatu Oxon' anno xxii°.

> The institution is recorded ibid. 155, among entries for the bp's twenty-first pontifical year, 20 December 1229 x 19 December 1230. The letter of institution apparently dates from the following year. The Oxford archdeaconry charter roll has not survived; the charter alluded to is likely to have been the letter of institution of Robert de Segrave to the church of Wigginton, entered in the Oxford archdeaconry institution roll under the bp's twenty-second pontifical year (ibid. 34–5).

354.   Northampton, abbey of St Mary de Prato

Institution of Robert of Wilton, clerk, to the church of [Earl's] Barton, on the presentation of the abbess and convent of St Mary de Prato, Northampton, saving to the abbey two marks a year, in the name of a perpetual benefice, and saving to John of Eynsham, chaplain, his perpetual vicarage.

[20 December 1230 x 19 December 1231]

B = LAO Wells roll ix, m. 7.
Pd *RHW* ii 240.

Testibus et dat' ut supra in carta proxima [no. 353].

The institution is recorded in the institution roll (ibid. 159).

355.   Hospitallers

Notification that the prior and brethren of the Hospitallers in England have brought an action before the bishop claiming five marks from the church of Holcott, in their patronage, but they have failed to prove their claim. The bishop, with the consent of W(illiam) the dean and the chapter of Lincoln, grants to them an annual pension of forty shillings from the aforesaid church, in the name of a perpetual benefice. It is to be paid by Ralph of Cirencester, the rector of the church, and his successors, in two instalments each year, namely, twenty shillings at Martinmas and twenty at Whitsun.

[20 December 1230 x 19 December 1231]

B = LAO Wells roll ix, m. 7d.
Pd *RHW* ii 245.

Testibus et dat' ut in carta de Ellesham' et de Torkeseia de ecclesiis de Kynereby et de Snarteford' et de Wykingeb' in archidiaconatu Lincoln'.

The Lincoln archdeaconry charter roll has not survived. There was an institution to Kingerby recorded in the Lincoln archdeaconry institution roll for the bp's twenty-second pontifical year, 20 December 1230 x 19 December 1231 (ibid. iii 192), but nothing for Wickenby; an institution to Snarford in the same year is recorded in the Stow archdeaconry institution roll (ibid. i 233). For Ralph of Cirencester's institution to Holcott see no. 296.

356.   Peterborough abbey

Institution of Martin of St Ives, clerk, to the church of Clopton, on the presentation of the abbot and convent of Peterborough.

[20 December 1230 x 19 December 1231]

B = LAO Wells roll ix, m. 7.
Pd *RHW* ii 239–40.

Testibus et dat' ut in carta de Stanlak' in archidiaconatu Oxon'.

In the Northampton charter roll this entry is placed under the bp's twenty-second pontifical year (20 December 1230 x 19 December 1231); in the institution roll it is recorded among entries for the twenty-first pontifical year, 20 December 1229 x 19 December 1230 (ibid. 156). The Oxford archdeaconry charter roll has not survived and the only Stanlake entry in the institution roll is the institution of John de

Limesey to the church during the bp's nineteenth pontifical year, 20 December
1227 x 19 December 1228 (ibid. 28).

357. Studley priory

Notification that the nuns of Studley had recovered seisin of the presentation to
the church of Beckley against the king and the master of the Templars in England.
At the petition of the king and of R[ichard], count of Poitou and earl of Cornwall,
and other nobles, the bishop has granted the church in proprios usus *to the nuns*
to alleviate their need, assigning to the nuns ten marks worth in certain portions
of the church (noted in detail) and the small tithes of their curia. *The bishop had*
admitted and instituted as parson of the church Nicholas de Anna, clerk, on the
presentation of the nuns.   [20 December 1230 x 19 December 1231]

   B = Oxfordshire Archives, ms. d.d. Henderson c. 9 (copies of Studley priory char-
      ters), fo. 25r–v. s. xvii.

Omnibus Cristi fidelibus ad quos presens scriptum pervenerit, Hugo Dei gratia
Linc' episcopus salutem in domino. Noveritis quod cum moniales de Stodleia seisinam presentationis ad ecclesiam de Beckley versus dominum regem et magistrum milicie Templi in Anglia recuperassent, prout idem dominus rex nobis
significavit, nos, ad petitionem ipsius domini regis, nobilis viri R. comitis Pictav'
et Cornub' et aliorum nobilium et magnatum complurium, ecclesiam ipsam
monialibus ipsis in propriis usibus ad allevationem ipsorum inopie confirmari
postulantium, ut eorum interventionem in parte saltem sortiretur effectum, de
consensu et consilio dilectorum filiorum Willelmi decani et capituli nostri Lincoln', decem marcatas in certis portionibus notatis inferius de eadem ecclesia
monialibus ipsis simul cum minutis decimis de curia earundem assignavimus et
episcopali confirmavimus auctoritate. Que quidem moniales tunc demum ad
ecclesiam antedictam, salvis portionibus predictis concessis si pro nobis ut
dictum est et confirmatis, dilectum in Cristo filium Nicholaum de Anna,
clericum, nobis presentaverunt, quem prout decuit liberaliter[a] admisimus et sub
forma predicta personam instituimus in eadem, iniungentis instituto sub debito
iuramenti nobis prestiti ne memoratis monialibus in assignationis et confirmationis preiudicium molestie quacumque inferat[b] aut gravaminis, eodem in id
expresse consentiente. Sunt autem he[e] omnes decime garbarum quinque
hidarum terre de feodo dominorum de sancto Walerico in villa de Harton' cum
decimis feni spectantibus ad easdem quinque hidas; item decime terre garbe
duarum hidarum de dominicis que fuerunt Roberti de Bosco et Iohannis filii[c]
Alexandri in villa de Esses cum decimis feni spectantibus ad easdem duas hidas;
item omnes decime garbarum unius carrucate terre quam dicte moniales hactenus excoluerunt de assartis in eadem villa de Esses; ita quod si dicte moniales de
cetero aliquod novum assartum in parochia predicta redegerint [fo. 25v] in culturam, solvant inde decimas ecclesie memorate. Hec autem ad dictarum monialium
instantiam universitatis vestre presentibus intimamus ut per ea de ipsarum iure
nobis plenius constare debeat et de dicti negotii processus coram nobis habenti
veritate.

   [a] libalt' B.   [b] inferretant B. *The institution roll entry (see note) reads at this point*:
dictis monialibus super portionibus predictis molestiam contra ordinationem et

assignationem predictam nequaquam inferat aut gravamen, eodem in id consentiente.   ^c filium B.

The institution of Nicholas de Anna is noted in the Oxford archdeaconry institution roll among entries of the bp's twenty-second pontifical year (20 December 1230 x 19 December 1231) (*RHW* ii 33–4). The entry mentions that the details of the portions etc. (presumably a copy of this charter) were entered on the (now lost) Oxford archdeaconry charter roll and the bp's memoranda roll (also lost); cf. J. Dunkin, *Oxfordshire: the history and antiquities of the Hundreds of Bullington and Ploughley* (2 vols., 1823) i 135–6. For the assize of darrein presentment see *CRR* xiv no. 495.

358.   Master Alexander of Michaelstow

Dispensation, pursuant to letters (recited in full) of Pope Gregory IX, dated at the Lateran, 16 March 1231, to master Alexander of Michaelstow, subdeacon, to proceed to holy orders and to receive a benefice, notwithstanding a defect of birth in that he is the son of a subdeacon. He shall not be promoted to the episcopal dignity without special licence of the pope. This dispensation was issued by the bishop on the testimony of H., bishop of Ely, Walter, treasurer of Lincoln, John then archdeacon of Bedford, and others.   Buckden, 27 December 1231

>B = LAO Wells roll ix, m. 8d.
>Pd *RHW* ii 254–5.

Dat' apud Bugged' per manum Radulfi de Warr', canonici Linc', vi kalendas Ianuarii pontificatus nostri anno xxiii°.

>John de Houton, archdn of Bedford, became archdn of Northampton at the end of 1231(see no. 359 below).

359.   Greens Norton church

Institution of master Philip of St David, clerk, to the church of [Greens] Norton, on the presentation of John Marshal.   Buckden, 27 December 1231

>B = LAO Wells roll ix, m. 8.
>Pd *RHW* ii 246–7.

Hiis testibus: Iohanne Norh't, G. Hunt' et Amaurico Bedef' archidiaconis, Willelmo subdecano, R. de Bolesour' capellano, magistris W. de Wermen' et R. de Wend', Willelmo de Winch', R. de Ox' et Thoma de Ask', canonicis Linc'. Dat' apud Bugged' per manum Radulfi de Warr', canonici Linc', vi kalendas Ianuarii pontificatus nostri anno xxiii°.

>The institution is recorded in the institution roll among entries for the bp's twenty-second pontifical year, 20 December 1230 x 19 December 1231 (ibid. 162).

360.   Polebrook chantry

Inspeximus of a charter of Robert le Flemeng, patron and parson of the church of Polebrook, granting to Ralph son of Reginald and his heirs the right to have a chapel and chantry in Polebrook: saving the rights of the mother church.
                                                Buckden, 5 January 1232

A = Boughton House, Buccleuch muns. B.1.470. (from photograph only). No
endorsement seen; approx. 215 x 165 + 12 mm.; seal missing, parchment tag
for sealing (method 1).
B = LAO Wells roll ix, m. 8d.
Pd from B in *RHW* ii 255–6.

Universis sancte matris ecclesie filiis presens scriptum visuris vel audituris,
Hugo Dei gratia Lincoln' episcopus salutem in domino sempiternam. Inspeximus
cartam dilecti filii Roberti le Flemeng patroni et persone ecclesie de Pokebroc in
hec verba: Omnibus Cristi fidelibus ad quos presens scriptum pervenerit, Robertus le Flemeng patronus et persona ecclesie de Pokebroc salutem in domino.
Noveritis me quantum ad patronum et personam ecclesie de Pokebroc pertinet
concessisse et quantum in me est presenti carta mea confirmasse pro me et
heredibus et successoribus meis quod dilectus mihi in Cristo Radulfus filius
Reginaldi habeat capellam et cantariam in eadem in curia sua de Pokebroc sibi et
heredibus ac successoribus ipsius Radulfi et hospitibus suis ac domestice familie
sue, servata tamen in omnibus indempnitate matricis ecclesie mee predicte tam
in oblationibus et obventionibus omnimodis quam in decimis maioribus et mino-
ribus eidem ecclesie matrici persolvendis imperpetuum, ita quidem quod tam
dictus Radulfus, heredes et successores sui quam capellanus qui sumptibus
ipsorum in dicta capella pro tempore ministrabit, antequam ab archidiacono loci
admittatur, iurabunt coram eo quod nichil impetrabunt in preiudicium iuris matricis ecclesie supradicte vel vicinarum ecclesiarum occasione dicte capelle et can-
tarie sibi concesse in eadem, nec impetrari procurabunt aut quantum in ipsis est
sustinebunt procurari, et si contra predicta fuerit impetratum non utentur impetratis. Omnes quoque heredes et successores ipsius Radulfi, cum legittime fuerint
etatis et custodes eorum cum infra etatem fuerint, similem prestabunt securitatem in initio sue possessionis. Capellanus insuper iurabit inspectis sacrosanctis
quod nullum parochianum predicte matricis ecclesie mee vel alterius ad confessionem vel aliquod sacramentum ecclesiasticum recipiet, nec aliquos ius ecclesiasticum alicui impendet, nisi in articulo necessitatis; immo quod matricem
ecclesiam supradictam in oblationibus ibidem quomodocumque provenientibus
et alias ecclesias in huiusmodi et omnibus aliis quantum in ipso est conservabit
indempnes. Sepedictus vero Radulfus et heredes ac successores sui et eorum
familia predicta iure parrochiali in omnibus ecclesie matrici predicte tanquam
parrochiani subiecti erunt, hoc solum excepto quod non cogentur in ea divina
audire vel ipsam cum oblationibus visitare, nisi diebus subscriptis: scilicet,
diebus Natalis Domini, Purificationis, Pasche, Pentecost' et Omnium Sanctorum.
Et si forte quod absit per ipsum capellanum vel predictos Radulfum aut heredes
vel successores ipsius predicta matrix ecclesia dampnificata fuerit in aliquo
premissorum et de hoc canonice constiterit; extunc dicta capella cessabit a
divinis donec ecclesie matrici supradicte competenter fuerit satisfactum. In huius
igitur concessionis mee et confirmationis quantum ad me et heredes ac successores meos pertinet perpetuum robur et testimonium, presenti scripto sigillum
meum apposui. Hiis testibus: Roberto de Bolesour' capellano, magistro Ricardo
de Wendour', Ricardo de Oxon' et Thoma de Askeby, canonicis Linc', magistro
Alardo de Arund', Galfrido de Moris, Iohanne de Crakeh', Stephano de Castello,
Roberto de Bernewell' et Reginaldo de Ailingt', clericis, Baldewino de Ver,
Roberto filio suo, militibus, Iohanne de Ailingt', Andrea filio Reginaldi et
Roberto filio Walteri de Pokebroc, liberis hominibus. Nos autem prenotatam

dicti Roberti le Flemeng concessionem ratam habentes et gratam, eam episcopali confirmamus auctoritate: salvis in omnibus episcopalibus consuetudinibus et Linc' ecclesie dignitate. Quod ut perpetuam optineat firmitatem, presenti scripto sigillum nostrum duximus apponendum. Hiis testibus: domino Ioscelino Bathon' episcopo, Willelmo subdecano, Roberto de Bolesour' capellano, magistro Ricardo de Wendour', Willelmo de Winchecumb', Ricardo de Oxon' et Thoma de Askeby, canonicis Linc', magistro Alardo de Arund', Iohanne de Crakeh', G. de Moris, I. de Burgo et S. de Castell', clericis. Dat' per manum Radulfi de Warravill', canonici Lincoln', apud Buggeden' nonis Ianuarii pontificatus nostri anno vicesimo tertio.

361. Helpston church

Institution of Geoffrey of Helpston, chaplain, to the perpetual vicarage of Helpston, on the presentation of Walter de Burgo, parson of the church, made with the assent of Roger son of Pain, the patron. The vicar is to serve personally and shall hold the church for life paying to Walter and his successors as parson an annual pension of four marks: namely, two marks at Easter and two at Michaelmas. The vicar shall bear all the ordinary and customary burdens of the church.

Broughton (?), 13 January 1232

B = LAO Wells roll ix, m. 7.
Pd *RHW* ii 245–6.

Hiis testibus: Roberto de Bollesour' capellano, magistris R. de Wendour' et W. de Werministr', W. de Winchecumb', R. de Oxon' et Thoma de Askeb', magistro A. de Arundell', R. Mauclerc et S. de Castell', clericis. Dat' apud Brocton' per manum R. de Warr', canonici Linc', idibus Ianuarii pontificatus nostri anno xxiii.

The institution is recorded in the institution roll among entries for the bp's twenty-second pontifical year, 20 December 1230 x 19 December 1231 (ibid. 161).

362. Sulby abbey

Institution of master Richard of Kent, chaplain, to the church of Great Harrowden, on the presentation of the abbot and convent of Sulby, saving to the abbey one mark a year to be paid by master Richard, in the name of a perpetual benefice.

Spaldwick, 6 February 1232

B = LAO Wells roll ix, m. 8.
Pd *RHW* ii 246.

Hiis testibus: Warino de Kirket' et Roberto de Bollesour', capellanis, magistro R. de Wendour' et W. de Winch', canonicis Linc', magistro Alardo de Arund', G. de Moris et S. de Castell', clericis. Dat' per manum R. de Warr', canonici Linc', apud Spald' viii idus Februarii anno pontificatus nostri xxiii.

The institution is recorded in the institution roll among entries for the bp's eighteenth pontifical year, 20 December 1226 x 19 December 1227 (ibid. 136–7). The church had originally been collated to master Richard by authority of the Council and afterwards he was presented by the abbey of Sulby. He occurs as rector on 8 September 1227 [no. 280].

363. Northampton, All Saints church

Indulgence of twenty days for all those who shall contribute alms towards the construction and repair of All Saints church, Northampton. This indulgence is to last for three years. Other bishops may grant indulgences for the church if they wish. It is forbidden for a collector to travel through the diocese collecting alms.

Northampton, 14 February 1232

> B= LAO Wells roll ix, m. 8d (no witnesses).
> Pd *RHW* ii 253–4.

Dat' per manum Radulfi de Warr', canonici Linc', apud Norh't xvi kalendas Martii pontificatus nostri anno xxiii°.

*364. Abington church

Similar indulgence for thirteen days for all those who shall contribute alms to the church of St Peter, Abington.   [20 December 1231 x 19 December 1232]

> Mention of indulgence in the Northampton archdeaconry charter roll of Bp Hugh among entries for his twenty-third pontifical year.
> Pd *RHW* ii 254.

> It is not clear from the brief entry whether this indulgence was granted on the same day as the All Saints, Northampton, indulgence [no. 363].

365. Northampton, abbey of St James

Institution of Thomas Sparhauek, chaplain, to the vicarage of Weekley, on the presentation of the abbot and convent of St James, Northampton. He is to serve personally. The vicarage consists of the entire altarage of the church with a suitable manse. The vicar shall pay synodal dues only and the aforesaid canons shall bear all the ordinary and customary burdens of the church.

Kilsby, 26 February 1232

> B = LAO Wells roll ix, m. 8.
> Pd *RHW* ii 247.

Hiis testibus: Warino de Kirket' et Roberto de Bolesour', capellanis, W. de Winch', R. de Ox' et Thoma de Ask', canonicis Linc', magistro Alardo de Arund', Iohanne de Crakehal' et Stephano de Cast', clericis. Dat' per manum Radulfi de Warr', canonici Linc', apud Kildeby quinto kalendas Martii pontificatus nostri anno xxiii°.

> The institution is recorded in the institution roll among entries for the bp's nineteenth pontifical year, 20 December 1227 x 19 December 1228 (ibid. 144).

366. Beauvais, abbey of St Lucien

Institution of John of Towcester, chaplain, to the vicarage of Weedon [Pinkney], on the presentation of Nicholas, prior of Weedon, general proctor in England of the abbot and convent of St Lucien, Beauvais, the patrons. He is to serve personally. The vicarage consists of the garb tithes of twelve and a half virgates of land with a suitable manse and a quarter of the entire altarage, except for the small tithes of the curia *of the lord, offerings at the relics in Weedon church, and candles on the day of the purification of the Virgin.* Kilsby, 26 February 1232

B = LAO Wells roll ix, m. 8.
Pd *RHW* ii 247.

Testibus et dat' ut supra in carta proxima [no. 365].

367. Chacombe priory

Institution of Roger, the chaplain of Banbury Castle, to the church of Boddington, on the presentation of the prior and convent of Chacombe, patrons of one mediety of the church (the other mediety was afterwards collated to him by authority of the Council), saving to the canons their annual pension of one mark which the bishop and chapter of Lincoln have granted to them, and saving also in future the right of patronage of the other mediety, and saving the vicarage of Robert of Boddington, chaplain. Robert shall hold the vicarage for his lifetime, namely all that portion which Hugh his brother held, paying to Roger and his successors as parsons an annual pension of thirteen marks. He shall also bear all ordinary charges of the church. Banbury, 29 February 1232

B = LAO Wells roll ix, m. 8.
Pd *RHW* ii 248.

Testibus: Warino de Kirketon' et R. de Bollesour', capellanis, magistro R. de Wendour', W. de Winch' et R. de Oxon', canonicis L[incolniensibus], magistro A. de Arundell', I. de Crackal' et S. de Castell', clericis. Dat' per manum nostram apud Bannebir' ii kalendas Martii pontificatus nostri anno xxiiiº.

Roger was instituted to one mediety of the church *c.* 1217 (ibid. i 53, cf. Smith, 'Rolls'); he was certainly incumbent by 28 December 1217 (see no. 67). The other mediety was collated to him 20 December 1218 x 19 December 1219 (ibid. 151). Robert of Boddington was instituted to the vicarage 20 December 1224 x 19 December 1225 or 20 December 1225 x 19 December 1226 (see no. 262 and note).

368. Sibyl de Saucey

Acknowledgement that Sibyl de Saucey, widow of Richard of Williamscote, has paid fifty silver marks to Bishop Hugh for the custody of Thomas her son and heir and of the land of her late husband, which is of the bishop's fee, in accordance with the chirograph made between her and the bishop.
Banbury, 5 March 1232

B = LAO Wells roll ix, m. 8d (no witnesses).
Pd *RHW* ii 254.

Dat' per manum nostram apud Bannebir' iii nonas Martii pontificatus nostri anno xxiiiº.

369. Snelshall priory

Confirmation of the grant made by the abbot and convent of Lavendon to the prior and monks of Snelshall of the chapel of Tattenhoe with all appurtenances and the remission of an annual pension of one mark, which the monks were accustomed to pay to the canons of Lavendon.   Fingest, 1 April 1232

> B = BL ms. Add. 37068 (Snelshall cartulary) fo. 72v (23v). s. xiii ex. C = ibid., fo. 2r. ss. xiii/xiv. D = ibid., fo. 11r.
> Pd (calendar) from B in *Snelshall Cartulary* no. 39; from CD ibid., nos. 6, 204.

Omnibus Cristi fidelibus ad quos presens scriptum pervenerit, Hugo Dei gratia Lincol' episcopus salutem in domino. Noverit universitas vestra quod nos concessionem et donationem dilectorum filiorum abbatis et conventus de Lavend'[a] factam dilectis filiis priori et monachis de Snelleshale de capella de Tathenho[b] cum omnibus eius pertinentiis et de remissione unius marce annue quam dicti monachi pro loco in quo monasterium eorum situm est dictis canonicis de Lavend'[a] reddere consueverunt, prout in carta inter eosdem canonicos et monachos inde[c] facta plenius continetur, ratam habentes et gratam eandem episcopali confirmamus auctoritate: salvis in omnibus episcopalibus consuetudinibus et Lincoln' ecclesie dignitate. Quod ut perpetuam optineat firmitatem, presenti scripto sigillum nostrum duximus apponendum. Hiis testibus: Iohanne archidiacono Norhamton[d], Warino de Kirketon'[e] capellano, magistris[f] Waltero de Wermenistr[g] et Ricardo de Wendour'[h], Willelmo de Winchecumb''et Ricardo de Oxon', canonicis Lincol', Philippo de Sideham capellano et Stephano de Castell' clerico. Datum per manum nostram apud Tingherst kalendis Aprilis pontificatus nostri anno vicesimo tertio.

[a] Lavenden' C; Lavendene D.   [b] Tateho D.   [c] *omitted* BC   [d] Northampt' D.
[e] Kyrketon' C.   [f] magistro BC.   [g] Vermenistr' C.   [h] BC *end here with* et aliis.

> Snelshall was originally a Premonstratensian cell of Lavendon abbey but later (1203 x 1219) became Benedictine. For the Lavendon grant see *Snelshall Cartulary*, no. 5; Colvin, *White Canons*, pp. 83–5.

370. Armston hospital

Confirmation of the arrangements made between Ralph de Trubleville (Turberville) and Alice his wife, on the one hand, and Robert le Flemeng, patron and parson of the church of Polebrook on the other. Ralph and Alice have founded a hospital with a chapel at Armston, which is in the parish of Polebrook. A chaplain shall serve the chapel for ever and he and the brethren of the hospital shall wear a religious habit of russet with a figure of a staff (baculus) in red cloth on the breast. A bell in the chapel shall summon the brethren, who shall receive the sacraments from the chaplain. Servants of the hospital who are not lay-brothers (conversi) and all the rest resorting there shall receive the sacraments at the mother church like other parishioners. The hospital shall have its own cemetery in which the lay-brothers (conversi) and the poor and sick can be buried, except for parishioners of Polebrook who die there. The mother church of Polebrook is to receive all the offerings and obventions from the hospital, except the offerings made on the two feasts of St John the Baptist [24 June, 29 August], which shall be for the use of the hospital and the poor. The superior of the hospital shall be pre-

sented to the bishop for institution, and at his admission shall make obedience to the bishop and his officials and fealty to the rector of Polebrook for the time being. As a sign of subjection Ralph and Alice have assigned in perpetuity to the mother church of Polebrook an annual rent of three shillings, which the rector shall receive from Solomon of Stanground and his heirs.

Fingest, 13 April 1232

B = LAO Wells roll ix, m. 8d.   C = LAO Episcopal Register I (register of Bp Oliver Sutton 1280–99), fo. 275r–v.
Pd from B in *RHW* ii 256–8; from C in *Reg. Sutton* ii 149–51(probably taken from original rather than Wells roll copy).

Hiis testibus: Iohanne archidiacono Norh't[a], Warino de Kirk'[b] et R.[c] de Bolesour'[d] capellanis, magistris W.[e] de Werm'[f] et R.[g] de Wendour'[h], W.[i] de Winch'[j], R.[k] de Oxon' et T.[l] de Askeby, canonicis Linc'[m], magistro A.[n] de Arund'[o], G.[p] de Moris[q] et S.[r] de Castell', clericis. Dat' per manum nostram apud Tingherst'[s] idibus Aprilis pontificatus nostri anno xxiii°.[t]

[a] Norhamt' C.   [b] Kirketon' C.   [c] Roberto C.   [d]Bolsour' C.   [e] Waltero C.
[f] Wermynton' C.   [g] Ricardo C.   [h] Wendoure C.   [i] Willelmo C.   [j] Winchecumb' C.   [k] Ricardo C.   [l] Thoma C.   [m] Lincoln' C.   [n] Alardo C.   [o] Arundel' C.
[p] Galfrido C.   [q] Mouns C.   [r] Stephano C.   [s] Tyngehirst C.   [t] vicesimo tertio C.

For details of the hospital of St John the Baptist, Armston, see *VCH Northants* ii 149. Amaury of Shelton, chaplain, was admitted as the first master at this time (*RHW* ii 172).

371.   Lincoln cathedral

Confirmation of what was ordained concerning the church of Hambleton, the advowson of the same church, a pension of twenty shillings from the church of St Peter, Stamford, and the chapel of Braunston, unless before his death the bishop ordains otherwise.   London, Old Temple, 17 May 1232

A = LAO Lincoln D. & C. Dij/89/1/24. No ancient endorsement; approx. 195 mm. x 64 mm. + 10 mm.; seal and tag missing, sealing method 1.
B = LAO Wells roll ix, m. 8d. C = Wells D. & C. Liber Albus II fo. 192v. s. xvi in.
Pd from A in *Reg. Ant.* iii no. 1010; from B in *RHW* ii 258; (calendar) from C in *HMC* Wells i 404.

Omnibus Cristi fidelibus ad quos presens scriptum pervenerit, Hugo Dei gratia Lincoln' episcopus salutem in domino. Noverit universitas vestra nos ordinasse, concessisse et hac presenti carta nostra confirmasse successoribus nostris episcopis Linc' qui pro tempore fuerint, quod de ecclesia de Hameldun' et de iure patronatus eiusdem, et de pensione viginti solidorum de ecclesia beati Petri Stanford' et de omnibus aliis pertinentiis suis, et de capella de Branteston' cum eas vacare contigerit, ordinent secundum Deum prout viderint expedire, nisi ante decessum nostrum aliter de eisdem duxerimus ordinandum: salvis in omnibus episcopalibus[a] consuetudinibus et Linc' ecclesie dignitate. In huius autem ordinationis, concessionis et confirmationis nostre testimonium, presenti scripto sigillum nostrum duximus apponendum. Act' apud Vetus Templum London' sextodecimo kalendas Iunii pontificatus nostri anno vicesimo tertio.

[a] epispalibus A.

For the earlier dealings over Hambleton (and Oakham) see above nos. 345 and 348 and for the 1231 settlent *Reg. Ant.* ii no. 374).

372. Hospitallers

Institution of master Richard of Wendover, clerk, to the church of Yardley [Hastings], on the presentation of brother Robert de Dive, the prior and the Hospitallers in England, saving to the prior and brethren their due and ancient pension.

Thurning, 20 May 1232

B = LAO Wells roll ix, m. 8.
Pd *RHW* ii 248.

Hiis testibus: Warino de Kirket' et Roberto de Bolesour', capellanis, magistro Ricardo de Wendour', W. de Winchecumb' et R. de Oxon', canonicis Linc', magistro Alardo de Arundell', G. de Moris et S. de Castell', clericis. Dat' per manum R. de Warr', canonici Linc', apud Tunrig' xiii kalendas Iunii pontificatus nostri anno xxiiiº.

A note after this charter records that it was duplicated, one copy being made for the patrons, the other for the rector (ibid. 249). The institution is recorded in the institution roll (ibid. 167).

373. Northampton, abbey of St James

Institution of Warner the chaplain to the vicarage of Duston, on the presentation of the abbot and convent of St James, Northampton. He is to serve personally. The vicarage consists of the entire altarage of the church and a manse, and the vicar shall pay to the abbey a pension of one mark a year. He also has all the chapel of St Margaret and a manse, paying two marks a year to the abbey. He shall have a suitable chaplain to serve continually in the chapel and he shall pay synodal dues.

Lyddington, 4 July 1232

B = LAO Wells roll ix, m. 8.
Pd *RHW* ii 249.

Hiis testibus: Warino de Kirketon' et Roberto de Bollesour', capellanis, magistris Waltero de Werm' et Ricardo de Wendour', W. de Winchecumb' et R. de Oxon', canonicis Linc', magistris A. de Arundell', Iohanne de Krakehal' et aliis. Dat' per manum R. de Warr', canonici Linc', apud Lidingt' iiii nonas Iulii pontificatus nostri anno xxiii.

The institution is recorded in the institution roll among entries for the bp's eighteenth pontifical year, 20 December 1226 x 19 December 1227 (ibid. 135).

374. Wootton church

Institution of Walter of Horton, clerk, to the church of Wootton, on the presentation of Amabel of Wootton.

Kilsby, 31 July 1232

B = LAO Wells roll ix, m. 8.
Pd *RHW* ii 250.

Testibus ut supra in carta proxima [no. 384]. Dat' apud Kildeby per manum

Radulfi de Warr', canonici Linc', ii kalendas Augusti pontificatus nostri anno xxiiiº.

The institution is recorded in the institution roll (ibid. 168).

375. Northampton, priory of St Andrew

Institution of Thomas of Leicester, clerk, to the church of Quinton, on the presentation of the prior and convent of St Andrew, Northampton.

Kilsby, 31 July 1232

B = LAO Wells roll ix, m. 8.
Pd *RHW* ii 250.

Testibus et dat' ut supra in carta proxima [no. 374].

The institution is recorded in the institution roll among entries for the bp's twenty-second pontifical year, 20 December 1230 x 19 December 1231 (ibid. 162). The church had previously been collated to Thomas by authority of the Council.

376. Ketton church

Indulgence of twenty days for all those of the Lincoln diocese and others, whose diocesan bishops shall approve, who shall contribute alms towards the construction and repair of St Mary's church, Ketton, as in no. 363.   9 August 1232

B = LAO Wells roll ix, m. 8d.
Pd *RHW* ii 259.

Dat' per manum R. de Warr', canonici Linc', v idus Augusti pontificatus nostri anno xxiiiº.

377. Edinburgh, Holyrood abbey

Grant, with the assent of William the dean and the chapter of Lincoln, to the abbot and convent of Holyrood, Edinburgh, of twenty marks a year, in the name of a perpetual benefice, from the church of Great Paxton, which is in the bishop's patronage, the six marks which formerly they were accustomed to receive from that church being included. The said twenty marks shall be handed over to the sacrist of Lincoln by those who shall be instituted to the church. The latter shall bear the due and customary charges of the church. The sacrist of Lincoln shall pay the pension of twenty marks, together with any sum that may be due for default, to the canons of Edinburgh or their messenger.

Lincoln, in chapter, 8 September 1232

B = LAO Lincoln D. & C. A/1/6 (Registrum) no. 303. s. xiv med.
Pd *Reg. Ant.* iii no. 826.

Hiis testibus: Willelmo decano, Roberto archidiacono, Iohanne precentore, Willelmo cancellario et Waltero thesaurario Linc', Iohanne Northampton', Gilberto Huntingdon', Amaurico Bedeford' archidiaconis, Willelmo subdecano Lincoln', magistris Roberto de Gravel', Stephano de Cicestr', Roberto de Brincl', Theobaldo et Ricardo de Cantia, Thoma de Norton', Warino de Kirketon' et Roberto de Bollesovere, capellanis, magistris Willelrno de Linc' et Waltero de Welle, Radulfo de Warravill', Willelmo de Winchecumbe diaconis, magistro Ricardo de

Wendour', Ricardo de Oxon' et Thoma de Askeby subdiaconis, canonicis Linc'. Dat' per manum nostram in capitulo Linc' sexto idus Septembris pontificatus nostri anno vicesimo tertio.

> The advowson of Great Paxton was transferred to the bp about this time by abbot W. and the convent of Holyrood (ibid., no. 825). The sacrist was the sub-treasurer of the cathedral (K. Edwards, *The English secular cathedrals in the middle ages* (2nd edn, Manchester, 1967), p. 223).

378.   Lincoln cathedral: Asfordby church

Ordination, with the assent of William the dean and the chapter of Lincoln, touching ten marks to be paid yearly from the church of Asfordby by the hands of master Alard of Arundel, the parson of the church and his successors, for distribution on each anniversary of the bishop's death, to the canons and other ministers of the church of Lincoln and to feed the poor. Until the church of Riseholme becomes vacant, two and a half marks are to be taken out of the ten marks for the chaplains who shall celebrate for the bishop and all the faithful.

Lincoln, in chapter, 9 September 1232

> B = LAO Lincoln D. & C. A/1/5 (Registrum Antiquissimum), no. 224. s. xiii in. C = ibid., no. 998. D = LAO Lincoln D. & C. doct. Dj/20/1/1 in an inspeximus of Archbp Walter de Gray of York, 12 Nov. 1251. E = LAO Lincoln D. & C. A/1/8 (Liber de ordinationibus cantariarum), no. 59. s. xiv. F = ibid., no. 374. G = CUL ms. Dd. 10. 28 (Vetus Repertorium), f. 77r. s. xiv.
> Pd from B in *Reg. Ant.* ii no. 361.

Hiis testibus: Willelmo decano, Roberto archidiacono, Willelmo cancellario et Waltero thesaurario Linc', Iohanne Norhampton', Gilberto Huntendon' et Amaurico Bedeford' archidiaconis, Willelmo subdecano, magistris Roberto de Gravell' et Stephano de Cicestr', [Theobaldo et Ricardo de Cantia, Galfrido Scoto, Warino de Kirketon', Thoma de Norton' et Roberto de Bollesover capellanis, magistris Willelmo de Lincoln', Roberto de Brincla et Waltero de Well', Petro de Hungar', Radulfo de Warravill' et Willelmo de Wynchecumb' diaconis, magistro Nicholao de Evesham et Ricardo de Wendover, Ricardo de Oxon' et Thomas de Askeby subdiaconis]ª, canonicis Linc'. Dat' per manum nostram in capitulo Linc' quinto idus Septembris pontificatus nostri anno xx° tertio.

ª *additional witnesses in square brackets provided from* F.

> Master Alard of Arundel was a household clerk of Bp Hugh. The church of Asfordby was collated to him during the bp's twenty-third pontifical year, 20 December 1231 x 19 December 1232 (*RHW* ii 321). Asfordby and Riseholme were both in the bp's gift.

379.   Lincoln cathedral

Grant, made with the assent of William the dean and the chapter of Lincoln, to the canons of Lincoln, as an augmentation of their common fund, of a yearly render of forty-five marks from the church of Hambleton when next it shall fall vacant, to be paid at Lincoln to the provost of the common, half at Martinmas and half at Whitsun, together with five marks from the church of Brattleby, otherwise granted to them by the bishop.

Lincoln, in chapter, 9 September 1232

B = LAO Wells roll ix, m.7 (slightly abridged). C = LAO Lincoln D. & C. A/1/5 (Registrum Antiquissimum) no. 223. s. xiii in. D = ibid., no. 997. E = ibid., Dj/20/1/1 (in an inspeximus of Walter de Gray, archbp of York, dated 12 November 1251).
Pd from B in *RHW* ii 251–2; from CDE in *Reg. Ant.* ii no. 359.

Hiis testibus:[a] Willelmo decano, Roberto archidiacono, Willelmo cancellario, et Waltero thesaurario Linc', Iohanne Norhampton', Gilberto Huntindon' et Amaurico Bedeford' archidiaconis, Willelmo subdecano, magistris Roberto de Gravell', Stephano de Cicestr'[b], canonicis Linc'. Dat' per manum nostram in capitulo Linc' quinto idus Septembris pontificatus nostri anno xx° iii°.

[a] *Witness list taken from C.* B *has* testibus et dat' ut in carta de xxxii marcis et dimidia assignatis ad trium capellanorum sustentationem etc. in archidiaconatu Lincolniensi.   [b] Cycestr' E.

The Brattleby grant referred to is no. 420 below. The grant for the maintenance of three chaplains mentioned in the dating clause of B probably represents the earlier version of the augmentation of 16 August 1234 (no. 431).

380. Goring priory

Grant, with the assent of William the dean and the chapter of Lincoln, to the prioress and nuns of Goring of an annual pension of four and a half marks, in the name of a perpetual benefice, from the church of Moulsoe, which is of their patronage. The thirty shillings that used to be paid is to be reckoned in with it. The pension is to be paid by the incumbent, thirty shillings at Martinmas and thirty shillings at Whitsun.   Lincoln, in chapter, 9 September 1232

A = Castle Ashby, Compton document 37. Endorsed: Molesho (s. xiii); Garing' (s. xiii); Willelmus de Roche (s. xiv); Milsho quedam concessio facta per Hugonem episcopum cum assensu capituli Linc' super sexaginta solidis monialibus de Garinges (s. xv); approx. 188 mm. x 123 mm. + 12 mm.; episcopal seal in seal-bag, green wax, and fragment of capitular seal in seal-bag, green wax, on parchment tags.

Omnibus Cristi fidelibus ad quos presens scriptum pervenerit, Hugo Dei gratia Lincoln' episcopus salutem in domino. Noverit universitas vestra nos, interveniente dilectorum filiorum Willelmi decani et capituli nostri Lincoln' assensu, concessisse et hac carta nostra confirmasse, divine pietatis intuitu, dilectis in Cristo filiabus priorisse et monialibus de Garing' ad uberiorem ipsarum sustentationem de ecclesia de Mulesho, que de earum advocatione est, quatuor marcas et dimidiam, computatis in ipsa summa triginta solidis quos de ea prius percipere consueverunt,. percipiendas, nomine beneficii perpetui, singulis annis in duobus terminis: videlicet, in festo sancti Martini triginta solidos et tantundem in festo Penthecost', per manus eorum qui ad ipsarum monialium presentationem instituti successive dictam ecclesiam tenuerint, satisfacturi pro ea de oneribus ordinariis debitis et consuetis ipsam contingentibus; salvis in omnibus episcopalibus consuetudinibus et Lincoln' ecclesie dignitate. Quod ut perpetuam optineat firmitatem, presenti scripto sigillum nostrum una cum sigillo predicti capituli nostri Lincoln' duximus apponendum. Hiis testibus: Willelmo decano, Roberto archidiacono, Willelmo cancellario et Waltero thesaurario Lincoln', Iohanne Norhamton', Gilberto Hunted' et Amaurico Bedeford' archidiaconis, Willelmo subdecano, magistris Roberto de Gravel', Stephano de Cicestr', Theobaldo et Ricardo de Cant', Galfrido Scoto, Warino de Kirketon', Thoma de Norton' et Roberto de Bollesour' capellanis, magistris Willelmo de Lincoln', Roberto de Brincl' et Waltero de Well', Petro de Hungar', Radulfo de Waravill' et Willelmo de Winchecumb' diaconis, magistris Nicholao de Evesham et Ricardo de Wendour', Ricardo de Oxon' et Thoma de Askeb' subdiaconis, canonicis Lincoln'. Dat' per manum nostram in capitulo Lincoln' quinto idus Septembris pontificatus nostri anno vicesimo tertio.

381. Lincoln cathedral

Grant, with the assent of William the dean and the chapter of Lincoln, of six marks a year from the church of Kilsby for the maintenance of two servants to guard the cathedral church of Lincoln and all its contents by day and night. The dean and chapter shall appoint these servants. This arrangement is to come into effect on the next vacancy of the church of Kilsby and the rector of the church and his successors are to pay the sum to the sacrist of Lincoln in two instalments, half at Martinmas and half at Whitsun. This grant is not to affect the duties of the treasurer of Lincoln in respect of the provision of servants and their stipends.

Lincoln, in chapter, 9 September 1232

> B = LAO Wells roll ix, m. 8 (slightly abbreviated). C = LAO Lincoln D.& C. A/1/5 (Registrum Antiquissimum) no. 226. s. xiii in.
> Pd from B in *RHW* ii 252; from C in *Reg. Ant.* ii no. 365.

Hiis testibus:[a] Willelmo decano, Roberto archidiacono, Willelmo cancellario et Waltero thesaurario Linc', Iohanne Norhampt', Gilberto Huntendon' et Amaurico Bedeford' archidiaconis, Willelmo subdecano, magistris Roberto de Gravel', Stephano de Cicestr', Theobaldo et Ricardo de Cant', Galfrido Scoto, Warino de Kirketon', Thoma de Norton' et Roberto de Bollesover' capellanis, magistris Willelmo de Linc', Roberto de Brincl' et Waltero de Well', Petro de Hungar', Radulfo de Waravill' et Willelmo de Winchecumb' diaconis, magistris Nicholao de Evesham et Ricardo de Wendour', Ricardo de Oxon' et Thoma de Askeby subdiaconis, canonicis Linc'. Dat' per manum nostram in capitulo Linc' quinto idus Septembris pontificatus nostri anno vicesimo tertio.

> [a] *The witness list and dating clause are taken from* C; B *has* testibus et dat' ut in carta de xxxii marcis et dimidia assignatis ad trium capellanorum sustentationem etc. in archidiaconatu Lincoln'.

The church of Kilsby was in the bp's collation.

382. Lichfield cathedral

Grant, with the assent of William the dean and the chapter of Lincoln, to the dean and chapter of Lichfield, in augmentation of their common fund, of the garb tithes of the church of Thornton [by Horncastle], which is of their patronage, in the name of a perpetual benefice. The rest of the church is reserved to the vicar who shall bear all due and customary charges of the church.

Lincoln, in chapter, 9 September 1232

> B = Lichfield D. & C. ms. Lich. 28 (Magnum Registrum Album) fo. 221v. s.xiv in.
> Pd (calendar), *Magnum Registrum Album* no. 515.

Omnibus Cristi fidelibus ad quos presens scriptum pervenerit, Hugo Dei gratia Linc' episcopus salutem in domino. Noverit universitas vestra nos, de assensu et voluntate dilectorum filiorum Willelmi decani et capituli nostri Linc', concessisse et dedisse dilectis nobis in Cristo decano et capitulo Lich' in augmentum commune sue decimas garbarum pertinentes ad ecclesiam de Thorneton', que de eorum advocatione est, nomine perpetui beneficii, percipiendas inperpetuum, salvo toto residuo ipsius ecclesie vicario qui ad eorum presentationem a nobis et successoribus nostris admittendus et instituendus in eadem. Omnia onera ecclesie predicte debita et consueta sustinebit, salvis etiam in omnibus episcopalibus consuetudinibus et Linc' ecclesie dignitate. Quod ut perpetuam optineat firmitatem, presenti scripto sigillum nostrum una cum sigillo predicti capituli nostri Linc' duximus apponendum. Hiis testibus: Willelmo decano, Roberto archidiacono, Willelmo cancellario, Waltero thesaurario Linc', Iohanne Norh', Gilberto Hunting' et Amaurico Bedeford' archidiaconis et aliis. Actum in capitulo Linc' quinto idus Septembris pontificatus nostri anno vicesimo tertio.

383. Great Addington: chapel of Baldwin de Ver

Confirmation of the arrangements made between Baldwin de Ver and the abbot and convent of Crowland, patrons, and Walter the rector of the church of [Great] Addington, over the erection of a chapel in the parish by Baldwin for the use of himself and his family and household and guests and safeguarding the rights of the mother church of [Great] Addington. Lincoln, 9 September 1232

> A = Northamptonshire RO, SS. 2320. Endorsed: Carta abbatis Croulond' (s. xiii); 199 mm. x 158 mm. + 10 mm.; seal missing, sealing by parchment tag (method 1).
> B = LAO Wells roll ix, m. 8d.
> Pd from B in *RHW* ii 259–61.

Omnibus Cristi fidelibus ad quos presens scriptum pervenerit, Hugo Dei gratia Linc' episcopus salutem in domino. Noverit universitas vestra quod cum Baldewinus de Ver capellam apud Adinton' in proprio fundo construxisset assensum dilectorum filiorum abbatis et conventus Croyland' patronorum ecclesie de Adinton' et Walteri rectoris eiusdem ecclesie optinuit in hac forma: videlicet, quod infra capellam vel extra nec baptisterium nec campane nec aliquid aliud habeatur per quod preiudicium fieri possit matrici ecclesie, et in ea capella ipse Baldewinus et heredes sui et hospites eorum et tantum propria familia audiant missas et divina officia et nullum aliud sacramentum ibi fiat nisi tantum panis benedictus et aqua benedicta, diebus dominicis aspergenda tantum existentibus in capella, et in eadem capella parrochiani matricis ecclesie, alii a sua familia propria, non recipientur ad divina. Et ipse Baldewinus et heredes sui iurabunt quod nec per se nec per alium dampnum vel lesionem aliquam occasione predicte capelle matrici ecclesie inferri patientur. Ad presentationem vero Baldewini et heredum eius admittantur a rectoribus matricis ecclesie capellani in eadem capella propriis sumptibus divina officia celebraturi, sacramento ab eis prius prestito quod de oblationibus et obventionibus omnibus in dicta capella percipiendis plene et integre matricis ecclesie rectoribus respondebunt, et quod nichil in parrochia facient vel fieri procurabunt per quod fiat preiudicium matrici ecclesie vel eiusdem ecclesie rectoribus; qui si infideles inventi fuerint et super hoc coram archidiacono vel decano loci confessi vel convicti fuerint, tamquam periuri ea hac causa ammoveantur, alio idoneo successive substituendo ad presentationem dicti B. et heredum suorum de assensu rectorum ecclesie, ut predictum est. Et ipse B. et heredes sui cum tota familia sua octies per annum matricem ecclesiam visitabunt, divina ibidem audituri, videlicet: die Natalis Domini, die Purificationis beate Marie, die Pasche, die dedicationis ecclesie, die Ascensionis, die Pentech', die Assumptionis beate Marie et die Omnium Sanctorum, nisi per infirmitatem vel aeris intemperiem vel hospitum magnorum reverentiam vel aliam rationabilem et manifestam causam fuerint predictis octo festis impediti; et tunc de permissione et licentia rectoris ecclesie diebus illis in capella compleantur divina sive rector maluerit per proprium capellanum sive per illum qui in capella illa constituitur; ita videlicet quod tam diebus illis quam aliis liceat rectori ecclesie si voluerit per proprium clericum percipere ea que ad capellam perveniunt, per manum ipsius ad matricem ecclesiam deferenda, vel si maluerit per capellanum in capella ministrantem. Domino vero capelle domi non existente predictis octo festis, familia que tunc ibidem erit matricem ecclesiam visitabit. Dictus vero B. tanti memor benefitii dedit et concessit et carta sua quam inspeximus confirmavit pro se et heredibus suis matrici ecclesie de Adinton' in puram, liberam et perpetuam elemosinam pro salute anime sue, antecessorum et heredum suorum, necnon et Hawise uxoris sue, sex acras terre cum omnibus pertinentiis suis in territorio de Adinton', videlicet: in Sleng tres rodas iuxta feodum Mauricii de Andely, sub Wdefordebanlon' unam rodam iuxta terram ecclesie, et apud Grenewey duodecim selliones[a] iuxta terram decani, et unam rodam que abutat super Buttes iuxta terram decani, et sub Rigwey dimidiam acram et quatuor selliones iuxta terram decani, et duodecim seilliones que abutant super Trendelade iuxta terram Ioce, et duodecim selliones super Lidewellehill' iuxta terram decani, et dimidiam acram quatuor sulcis minus que abutant (*sic*) super caputium Alexandri iuxta terram Henrici filii Seyne, et duodecim selliones apud Mychelwell' iuxta terram Ade prepositi, et in Westfeld' super Schiterhill' tres rodas, et in Brocfurlang unam rodam iuxta terram decani, et in Brocfurlang super Rennendewesthill' unam acram iuxta terram decani, et apud Nolles tres rodas iuxta terram decani, et subtus Rigwey unam rodam iuxta terram decani. Idem vero B. et heredes sui warrantizabunt dictas sex acras terre cum pertinentiis dicte ecclesie de Adint' et eiusdem ecclesie rectoribus in perpetuum versus omnes et in omnibus, ut liberam et puram elemosinam suam. Nos autem omnia predicta rata quantum in nobis est habentes et grata, ea episcopali confirmamus auctoritate; salvis in omnibus episcopalibus consuetudinibus et Linc' ecclesie dignitate. Quod ut perpetuam optineat firmitatem, presenti scripto sigillum nostrum duximus apponendum. Hiis testibus: Warino de Kirket', Roberto de Boleshovere capellanis, magistris Waltero de Wermen' et Ricardo de Wend', Willelmo de Winch', Ricardo de Oxon' et Thoma de Askeb', canonicis, magistro Alardo de Arundel, Stephano de Castell', clericis, et aliis. Dat' Linc' per manum Radulfi de Waravill', canonici Linc', quinto idus Septembris anno pontificatus nostri vicesimo tertio.

[a] seillones B. *This text includes three spelling of selions:* seillones, selliones, seilliones.

384. Bulwick church

Institution of Aymer de Thacheworth, chaplain, to the vicarage of Bulwick, on the presentation of master Walter de Cantilupe, the parson of the church, with the consent of William de Cantilupe, the patron. He is to serve personally. The vicarage consists of the entire altarage with all small tithes and firstfruits (primitie), the whole tithe of the demesne of the church together with a meadow called Bulwick church meadow towards Laxton, all the tithe of the mill and the tithe of pannage of the manor of Bulwick, and two messuages near the church. The vicar shall find a suitable chaplain to serve continually in the chapel of St Laurence.

[20 December 1231 x 19 December 1232]

B = LAO Wells roll ix, m. 8.
Pd *RHW* ii 249–50.

Testibus et dat' ut in carta magistri Roberti, persone de Gravel', in archidiaconatu Huntingd'.

The institution is recorded in the institution roll (ibid. 165–6); the Huntingdon archdeaconry charter roll has not survived; nor has the Huntingdon archdeaconry institution roll for this period. Master Robert of Graveley, the episcopal clerk, was vicar of Graveley (ibid. iii 50). See no. 385 below.

385. Lenton priory

Institution of Thomas of Northampton, chaplain, to the church of Rushden, on the presentation of the prior and convent of Lenton, saving to the priory their portion granted by the bishop and chapter, in the name of a perpetual benefice. The parsonage consists of the entire altarage and all obventions and small tithes belonging to the church, together with the manse which belonged to Hawisia Tempernoise, and half a virgate of land which William Bunche held, free from all secular exactions and quit from the payment of tithes. It also consists of the annual pension of seven shillings and eightpence from the Hospital of St James in the same parish and twenty pence from the toft of Arnold le Tippere and the garb tithes and tithes of hay of thirteen virgates of land (namely: half a virgate of Edward le Neubonde, half a virgate of Battehulle, half a virgate of Hugh the shepherd, half a virgate of Roger the chaplain, half a virgate of Warin son of Robert, half a virgate of Thurstan son of Wlmar, half a virgate of Nicholas son of Robert, half a virgate of Richard son of Warin, half a virgate of Warin the squire, half a virgate of Richard Long, half a virgate of Hugh son of Osbert, half a virgate of Peter Attelane and Seled Bagge, half a virgate of William Hoppesort, half a virgate of Henry ad portam, Half a virgate of Matilda Suetis and Roger Lydy, half a virgate of Roger Laweite, half a virgate of William Finch, half a virgate of Richard Hunein, half a virgate of Richard Gnottere, half a virgate of Walter Fader, half a virgate of Simon Peck and Edward son of Roger, half a virgate of William son of Edric, half a virgate of Acer son of William, half a virgate of Samson, and one virgate of Fulk). The parson shall bear all ordinary charges of the church and shall serve personally in the church. The monks shall be responsible for their portion for extraordinary burdens.

[20 December 1231 x 19 December 1232]

B = LAO Wells roll ix, m. 8.

Pd *RHW* ii 250–1.

Testibus et dat' ut in carta magistri Roberti persone de Gravel' in archidiaconatu Huntingd'.

> The institution is recorded in the institution roll among entries for the bp's twenty-first pontifical year, 20 December 1229 x 19 December 1230 (ibid. 152–3). The entry concludes: Iste portiones evidentius et melius inseruntur in carta monachorum anno xxi° et etiam persone anno xxiii. The first of these charters is likely to be no. 320 in this edition and the second this present document. For Robert of Graveley see previous entry.

386.   Newport Pagnell priory

Letter to William de Beauchamp, informing him that since the priory of Newport Pagnell has been vacant for over six months, the right of appointing a prior devolves upon the bishop according to the statutes of the Council and consequently he has collated the priory to John of Colne, a monk of Spalding. He recommends John to William, who is patron of the priory.
[20 December 1231 x 19 December 1232]

> B = LAO Wells roll vii, m. 13d (no witnesses or date).
> Pd *RHW* ii 88.
>
> This and the subsequent entries are placed among the acts of the bp's twenty-third pontifical year, 20 December 1231 x 19 December 1232.

387.   Newport Pagnell priory

Letter to the subprior and convent of Newport Pagnell, informing them of the appointment of John of Colne as prior and enjoining their obedience.
[20 December 1231 x 19 December 1232]

> B = LAO Wells roll vii, m. 13d (no witnesses or date).
> Pd *RHW* ii 88.

388.   Newport Pagnell priory

Mandate to the archdeacon of Buckingham to install John of Colne as prior of Newport Pagnell.   [20 December 1231 x 19 December 1232]

> B = LAO Wells roll vii, m. 13d (no witnesses or date).
> Pd *RHW* ii 88.

*389.   Newport Pagnell priory

Letter to the prior of Bradwell directing him to install John of Colne as prior of Newport Pagnell in the event of the archdeacon of Buckingham's absence.
[20 December 1231 x 19 December 1232]

> Mention of letter in LAO Wells roll vii, m. 13d.
> Pd *RHW* ii 89.

390. Grendon church

Institution of Hugh of Stukeley, clerk, to the church of Grendon, on the presenta-
tion of John, earl of Huntingdon.   [20 December 1231 x 19 December 1232]

> B = LAO Wells roll ix, m. 8.
> Pd *RHW* ii 253.

Testibus et dat' ut in carta de Cybeceya in archidiaconatu Lincoln'.

> The institution is recorded in the institution roll among entries for the bp's twenty-
> third pontifical year, 20 December 1231 x 19 December 1232 (ibid. 168–9). It is
> possible that this letter of institution was issued before 21 November 1232 when
> earl John of Huntingdon was created earl of Chester in succession to his uncle,
> Ranulf de Blundeville. John's father, earl David of Huntingdon, died in 1219 and
> John had livery of his lands in 1227 (*Complete Peerage* iii 169–70). The Lincoln
> archdeaconry charter roll has not survived; the Sibsey charter referred to may just
> possibly have been the institution of John de Hayles to the church, recorded in the
> Lincoln archdeaconry institution roll for the bp's twenty-second pontifical year, 20
> December 1230 x 19 December 1231 (*RHW* iii 187).

391. Thornby church

Institution of Robert of Dagnall, clerk, to the church of Thornby, on the presenta-
tion of Robert of Ashby, saving to Thurstan the chaplain his perpetual vicarage.
The vicar shall hold the church for life, paying to Robert the parson and his suc-
cessors an annual pension of five marks.
                          [20 December 1231 x 19 December 1232]

> B = LAO Wells roll ix, m. 8.
> Pd *RHW* ii 255.

Testibus et dat' ut in carta de Cibecey in archidiaconatu Lincoln'.

> This letter of institution is placed among entries for the bp's twenty-third pontifical
> year (20 December 1231 x 19 December 1232) but the institution is recorded in the
> institution roll among entries for the bp's nineteenth pontifical year, 20 December
> 1227 x 19 December 1228 (ibid. 142). The Lincoln archdeaconry charter roll has
> not survived; for Sibsey see note to previous entry.

*392. Dunstable priory

Statutes issued after the visitation of Dunstable priory made on behalf of Bishop
Hugh by master Robert, archdeacon of Lincoln, the bishop's Official.   [1233]

> Mention of visitation and the subsequent statutes in the annals of Dunstable: *et tunc*
> *visitata fuit ecclesia nostra per officialem Hugonis episcopi, magistrum Rob-*
> *ertum archidiaconum Lincolnie, cuius statuta, sigillo suo signata, apud nos*
> *remanserunt*, pd *Ann. Mon.* iii 132.

393. Hospitallers

Institution of master Peter of Radnor, clerk, to the church of Ravensthorpe, on the
presentation of brother Robert de Dive, prior of the Hospitallers in England.
                          Stow Park, 7 March 1233

> B = LAO Wells roll ix, m. 8.

Pd *RHW* ii 261.

Hiis testibus: Roberto de Bollesour' capellano, magistro R. de Wendour' et W. de Wynchecumb', canonicis Linc', magistro A. de Arundell', Iohanne de Crachale, Stephano de Castello, Iohanne de Torkesey, clericis. Dat' per manum Garini de Kyrketon' capellani, canonici Linc', apud Parkum Stowe nonis Martii pontificatus nostri anno xxiiii^{to}.

The institution is recorded in the institution roll (ibid. 172).

394.   Farthingstone church

Institution of Simon of Middelton, clerk, to the church of Farthingstone, on the presentation of Walter of Gaddesden.   Stow Park, 7 March 1233

B = LAO Wells roll ix, m. 8.
Pd *RHW* ii 261.

Testibus et dat' ut supra in carta proxima [no. 393].

The institution is recorded in the institution roll, among entries for the bp's twenty-third pontifical year, 20 December 1231 x 19 December 1232 (ibid. 167–8). It is noted that abbot Walter of St James', Northampton had unsuccessfully contested the right of patronage in the king's court.

395.   Wyke Hamon tithes

Collation, by authority of the Council, of the demesne tithes of William son of Hamo in Wyke [Hamon] to Robert of Wells, clerk.   Stow Park, 7 March 1233

B = LAO Wells roll ix, m. 8.
Pd *RHW* ii 261.

Testibus et dat' ut supra [no. 394].

The collation is recorded in the institution roll, among entries for the bp's twenty-third pontifical year, 20 December 1231 x 19 December 1232 (ibid. 171).

396.   Daventry priory

Institution of William Marshal, clerk, to the church of Braybrooke, on the presentation of the prior and convent of Daventry, saving to Alexander the chaplain his vicarage as long as he shall live. Alexander shall hold the church for life paying to William and his successors as parsons an annual pension of two shillings.
Stow Park, 2 April 1233

B = LAO Wells roll ix, m. 8.   C = BL ms. Cotton Claudius D xii (Daventry cartulary) fo. 164r (clxr). s. xiv ex.
Pd from B in *RHW* ii 262; from C in *Daventry Cartulary* no. 949.

[a]-Hiis testibus: Waltero thesaurario Lincoln', Roberto de Bollesour', Waltero de Wermanister, Ricardo de Wendour', canonicis Lincolnie et pluribus aliis.[-a] Dat' per manum Garini de Kyrk'[b] capellani, canonici Lincoln', quarto[c] nonas Aprilis[d] apud Parcum Stowe pontificatus nostri anno vicesimo quarto.

^{a–a} *taken from* C. B *reads* Testibus ut in carta super ecclesia de Munby in archidi-
aconatu Linc'.   ^b Kirketon' C.   ^c iiii C.   ^d *In* C *the date follows* apud Parcum
Stowe.

The institution is noted in the institution roll among entries for the bp's twenty-third
pontifical year, 20 December 1231 x 19 December 1232 (ibid. 170).

*397. Markby priory

*? Confirmation to the prior and convent of Markby, with the assent of the chapter
of Lincoln, of an annual pension of forty shillings from the church of Mumby.*

[? April 1233]

Mention of Mumby charter as in version B of the preceding charter. The next institution to Mumby (20 December 1233 x 19 December 1234) includes the following saving clause: salvis inde patronis ipsis quadraginta solidis annuis
sibi per dominum episcopum et capitulum suum Linc' concessis et confirmatis (*RHW* iii 210). It is very likely that the allusion to the Mumby charter is to
this lost confirmation.

398. Nettleham church

Collation of the personatus *of the church of Nettleham to Warin of Kirton,
chaplain. The* personatus *consists of the entire altarage and all the small tithes of
the parish and the garb tithes and tithes of hay of twenty-four bovates of land in
the same village (namely, the four bovates of Alice de Solario, four bovates of
Ralph son of Ulsi (?Ulf), four bovates which were of Lettice, two bovates of Swain
de la Grene, two bovates which were of Roger le Paumer, two bovates which were
of Hugh son of Sibyl, two bovates of Hugh the reeve, two bovates of Godfrey son
of Ralph, and two bovates of Hugh son of Swynild). Warin is assigned an area on
the eastern side of the manse of the church (containing in breadth three perches
and in length as much as goes down the whole side of the* curia *to the curtilage),
part of the chief manse of the church towards the west and the smaller barn
(grangia), so as to be enclosed by the west side of the dean's barn.*

[?March x April] 1233

B = LAO Lincoln D. & C. A/1/5 (Registrum Antiquissimum) no. 236. s. xiii in.
Pd *Reg.Ant.* ii no. 378.

Hiis testibus: Waltero thesaurario Linc', Roberto de Bolesover' capellano, magistris Waltero de Wermen' et Ricardo de Wendour', Willelmo de Winchecumb' et
Thoma de Askeby, canonicis Linc', magistro Alardo de Arundell' et Stephano de
Cast', clericis. Dat' per manum nostram apud Parcum Stowe iiii ^{to a} Aprilis pontificatus nostri anno xx° iiii^{to}.

^a clearly 'kalendas, idus, *or* nonas *is omitted here. Hence the date could be 29
March or 2 or 10 April 1233.*

The institution of Warin is recorded *RHW* i 221–2, among entries for the bp's fifteenth pontifical year, 20 December 1223 x 19 December 1224. Warin of Kirton
was a member of the episcopal *familia* and acted as the bp's datary for the last two
years of Bp Hugh's life.

399.   Maidwell church

Institution of Peter Rabaz, clerk, to the church of St Peter, Maidwell, on the presentation of Peter Rabaz, the patron.   Stow Park, 16 April 1233

B = LAO Wells roll ix, m. 8.
Pd *RHW* ii 262.

Hiis testibus: Waltero thesaurario Linc', Roberto de Bollesour' capellano, magistro R. de Wendour', W. de Wynchecumb' et Thoma de Askeby, canonicis Linc', magistro A. de Arundell', I. de Crakehal', S. de Castell' et Iohanne de Thorkes', clericis. Dat' per manum Garini de Kyrketon' capellani, canonici Linc', apud Parcum Stowe xvi° kalendas May pontificatus nostri anno xxiiii^{to}.

The institution is noted in the institution roll (ibid. 174); this entry indicates that the presentee was the son of the patron.

400.   Launde priory

Institution of John the chaplain to the perpetual vicarage of Ashby [St Ledgers], on the presentation of the prior and canons of Launde. He is to serve personally. The vicarage consists of the entire altarage of the church, the third part of the garb tithes of the demesnes of John of Cranford and Ledger de Dive, the garb tithes of one and a half virgates of land which Richard of Harrowden holds, and the manse which the priory has of the gift of Hugh le Eyr. The vicar shall pay synodal dues only. The prior and canons shall provide hospitality for the archdeacon.   Stow Park, 16 April 1233

B = LAO Wells roll ix, m. 8.
Pd *RHW* ii 262–3.

Testibus et dat' ut supra in carta proxima [no. 399].

The institution is recorded in the institution roll among entries for the bp's eighteenth pontifical year, 20 December 1226 x 19 December 1227 (ibid. 136). See also no. 204.

401.   Boscherville, abbey of St George

Institution of William of St Lo, chaplain, to the church of [Edith] Weston, on the presentation of the abbot and convent of St George, Boscherville.   Stow Park, 16 April 1233

B = LAO Wells roll ix, m. 8.
Pd *RHW* ii 263.

Testibus et dat' ut supra in carta proxima [no. 400].

The institution is noted in the institution roll among entries for the bp's twenty-third pontifical year, 20 December 1231x 19 December 1232 (ibid. 170).

402. Launde priory

Institution of William of Arthingworth, clerk, to the church of Ashby Folville, on the presentation of the prior and convent of Launde.   Stow Park, 16 April 1233

>   B = LAO Wells roll ix, m. 8.
>   Pd *RHW* ii 263.

T(estibus) et dat' ut supra in carta proxima [no. 401].

>   The institution is noted in the institution roll among entries for the bp's twenty-third pontifical year, 20 December 1231 x 19 December 1232 (ibid. 317). This entry belongs to the Leicester archdeaconry and was obviously entered in error upon the Northampton charter roll.

403. Launde priory

Institution of John of Newbottle, clerk, to the church of Arthingworth, on the presentation of the prior and convent of Launde; saving to the priory their due and ancient pension.   Stow Park, 16 April 1233

>   B = LAO Wells roll ix, m. 8.
>   Pd *RHW* ii 263.

Testibus et dat' ut supra in carta proxima [no. 402].

>   The institution is noted in the institution roll (ibid. 173–4).

404. Helpston church

Institution of Walter de Burgo, clerk, to the church of Helpston, on the presentation of Roger of Helpston.   Stow Park, 16 April 1233

>   B = LAO Wells roll ix, m. 8.
>   Pd *RHW* ii 263–4.

Testibus et dat' ut supra in carta proxima [no. 403].

>   The institution is recorded in the institution roll among entries for the bp's twenty-second pontifical year, 20 December 1230 x 19 December 1231 (ibid. 161). The patron's name is given there as Roger, son of Pain of Helpston, knight.

405. Daventry priory

Institution of Simon de Blukevill, clerk, to the church of Gumley, on the presentation of the prior and convent of Daventry.   Stow Park, 16 April 1233

>   B = LAO Wells roll ix, m. 8
>   Pd *RHW* ii 264.

Testibus et dat' ut supra in carta proxima [no. 404].

>   Gumley is in the archdeaconry of Leicester and the letter of institution was erroneously entered on the Northampton charter roll. The institution is recorded in the Leicester institution roll among entries for the bp's twentieth pontifical year, 20 December 1228 x 19 December 1229 (ibid. 308).

406. Gosberton church

Grant to Robert de Rye, son and heir of Philip de Rye, and his heirs issuing from him, and for lack of such heirs to Alice his sister and her heirs, of the advowson of the church of Gosberton, which Philip his father gave to the bishop: saving to the common fund of the canons of Lincoln forty marks a year which the bishop had previously granted to them while he held the advowson. This sum is to be paid by the parson for the time being. At his institution, each new parson shall swear an oath to the dean and chapter regarding the full payment of this pension. If Robert and Alice should die without heirs the advowson shall revert to the bishop and his successors.   Stow Park, 8 May 1233

> B = LAO Lincoln D. & C. A/1/5 (Registrum Antiquissimum) no. 228. s. xiii in. C =
> LAO Lincoln D. & C. A/1/3/10, the fourth charter in an original inspeximus
> of King Edward III, 15 February 1329. D = PRO C53/116 (charter roll, 3
> Edward III), m. 2.
> Pd from B in *Reg. Ant.* ii no. 367; (calendar) from D in *Cal. Ch. R.* iv 149.

Hiis testibus: Waltero teshaurario[a] Linc', Willelmo archidiacono Leycestr'[b], Roberto de Bollesouer'[c] capellano, Radulfo de Waravill', Willelmo de Winchecumb', magistro Ricardo de Wendour' et Thoma de Askeb'[d], canonicis Linc', Gilberto de Treylli[e], seneschallo[f] nostro, magistro Alardo de Arundell', Iohanne de Crakall', Stephano de Castell' et Iohanne de Burgo, clericis, Willelmo de Dyva iuniore, Petro de Cotington', Iohanne de Camera, Waltero venatore, Helia[g] de la Mar'[h], Stephano de Grafham, Galfrido de Stowa[i], Rogero Marescallo et aliis. Dat' per manum Warini de Kyrketon' capellani, canonici Linc', apud Parcum Stowe viii⁰ idus Maii pontificatus nostri anno xx⁰ iiii⁰[j].

> [a] thesaurario D.   [b] Leicestr' D.   [c] Bollesour' D.   [d] Askeby D.   [e] Treilly D.
> [f] senescallo D.   [g] Helya D.   [h] Mara D.   [i] Stouwa D.   [j] vicesimo quarto D.

407. Jocelin, bishop of Bath

Grant to Bishop Jocelin of Bath and his assigns of the custody of the land of the late Ralph of Cromwell in Cromwell and the custody of Ralph the heir of the aforesaid Ralph and his marriage, with the advice of friends and without disparagement; in the case of the death of the younger Ralph, Bishop Jocelin shall have the custody of his sisters, being minors, and their marriages. Likewise the bishop grants to his brother the custody of the land in Thurning late of William de Dive, senior, until the majority of the younger William; in the case of the latter's death, the bishop shall have custody of his sister, Alice. These two grants are both to be used for the advantage of the hospital at Wells.   Stow Park, 30 May 1233

> B = PRO C53/27 (charter roll, 17 Henry III) m. 2 (slightly damaged. Words in
> square bra ckets conjectural).
> Pd (calendar) in *Cal. Ch. R.* i 185 (in an inspeximus of King Henry III, 11 July
> 1233).

Omnibus Cristi fidelibus ad quos presens scriptum pervenerit, Hugo Dei gratia Lincoln' episcopus salutem in domino. Noverit universitas vestra nos venerabili in Cristo fratri nostro domino Ioscelino Bath' episcopo [et cui] assignare voluerit concessisse, dedisse et presenti carta nostra confirmasse custodiam terre de Crumbwell', que fuit Radulfi de Crumbwell' senioris et est de feodo nostro, et custodiam Radulfi de Crumbwell' iunioris filii, scilicet, et heredis predicti Radulfi et maritagium eiusdem heredis per consilium amicorum suorum et ubi non disparagetur; habend' et tenend' cum predicta terra et omnibus pertinentiis, libertatibus et liberis consuetudinibus suis, integre, quiete et pacifice, quousque idem Radulfus iunior ad legitimam pervenerit etatem. Et si de eo interim humanitus contigerit, quod Deus avertat, concessimus[a] et presenti carta nostra confirmavimus eidem domino fratri nostro et cui assignare voluerit custodiam sororum ipsius heredis filiarum, scilicet, predicti Radulfi senioris, que non fuerint legitime etatis, et maritagium earundem ubi non disparagetur; habend' et tenend' ut predictum est donec ad legitimam pervenerint etatem ad convertendum per manus ipsius domini episcopi et assignatorum suorum quicquid inde ceperint in usus et emendationem hospitalis Well'. Concessimus insuper et presenti carta nostra confirmavimus eidem domino episcopo fratri nostro, et cui assignare voluerit, custodiam terre de Tunrig' que fuit Willelmi de Dyva senioris; habendam et tenendam integre, quiete et pacifice cum omnibus pertinentiis, libertatibus et liberis consuetudinibus suis, quousque Willelmus de Dyva iunior heres [? predicti Willelmi] ad legitimam pervenerit etatem. Et si de eo infra etatem contigerit humanitus, concessimus et presenti carta nostra confirmavimus eidem domino episcopo fratri nostro, et cui assignare voluerit, custodiam Alicie sororis sue cum predicta terra et omnibus pertinentiis suis, ut predictum [est]; habendam et tenendam integre, quiete et pacifice donec legitime fuerit etatis, ad convertendum per manus ipsius episcopi et assignatorum suorum quicquid inde ceperint in usus et emendationem hospitalis Well' supradicti. In predictorum igitur robur et testimonium, presenti scripto sigillum nostrum apposuimus. Hiis testibus: Waltero thesaurario Lincoln', Warino de Kirketun' et Roberto de Bolesour' capellanis, Radulfo de Warevill' et Willelmo de Wynchecumb', magistris Waltero de Wermenistr' et Ricardo de Wendour' et Thoma de Askeby, canonicis Lincoln', Giliberto de Treylli senescallo nostro, Iohanne de Crakehal' et Stephano de Lond', clericis. Dat' per manum nostram apud Parcum Stowe tertio kalendas Iunii pontificatus nostri anno vicesimo quarto.

[a] concessissimus B.

William de Dive, one of Bp Hugh's knights, was killed at the siege of Newark castle in 1218 (*MPCM* iii 33). In 1242–3 it was recorded that Ralph of Cromwell held half a knight's fee of the bp in Cromwell of the old feoffment (*Book of Fees* ii 984, 992). The Thurning and Cromwell wardships were also mentioned in Bp Hugh's will of 1 June 1233 (see no. 408 below).

408.   The second testament of the bishop

The second testament of Bishop Hugh of Wells   Stow Park, 1 June 1233

> A = LAO Lincoln D & C. doct. Dj/20/1/7. Endts: Testamentum Hugonis secundi Lincoln' episcopi (s. xiv). T[estamentum] Hugonis Wells olim Lincoln' episcopi (s. xviii). Size: 279 mm x 381 mm. There are no signs of sealing. The foot of the charter, in particular, has been damaged and torn. Any omissions are completed in square brackets from B.
> B = LAO Lincoln D & C. A/1/8 (Liber de ordinationibus cantariarum) no. 379. s. xiv.
> Pd from A in *Reg. Ant.* ii no. 372; *Gir. Camb.*, vii 223–230.

In nomine Patris et Filii et Spiritus Sancti Amen, ego Hugo Dei gratia Lincoln'
ecclesie [qualiscunque] minister condo testamentum meum in hunc modum.
Lego et concedo domino Bathon' episcopo fratri meo et cui assignaverit [custo-
diam meam de] Tunring cum omnibus pertinentiis [suis], habendam et tenendam
libere et quiete do[nec heres ad legitimam] pervenerit etatem, convertendo per
manus ipsius domini episcopi vel assignatorum suorum quicquid inde ceperint in
usus et emendationem hos[pitalis Wellensis], una cum ducentis marcis quas
eidem domino episcopo pridem pacavi ad opus hospital[is supradicti. Do
in]super eidem domino episcopo et cui assignaverit custodiam terre et heredum
de Crombwell', que est de feodo meo, et maritag[ia eorundem heredum ibi] non
disparagentur, volens et ordinans quod predictus dominus episcopus vel assignati
sui de exiti[bus eiusdem m]anerii faciat usque ad etatem heredum ad opus hospitalis Well' et sustentationem ipsius pro salute anime mee [et pro animabus patris
et matris] mee et omnium antecessorum et heredum meorum et pro anima
Iordani de Turri, sicut ordinavi de custodia mea de Tunring faciendum. Preterea
do eidem hospitali et fratribus ibidem Deo servientibus et servituris imperpetuum [totam terram meam de] Derneford' quam dedi cum Agatha nepte mea in
maritagium, nisi de corpore suo heredem habuerit, cui terra debeat remanere.
Item concedo et assigno Radulpho de Waravill' et Ricardo de Oxon', canonicis
Lincoln', [tanquam attornatis Galfridi] filii Baldwini et Petri de Bathon' qui in
principio firme sue ita michi concesserunt totam terram de Orresby cum
omnibus pertinentiis suis, quam Ingerardus de Bovinton' et Iohanna uxor sua
dimiserunt predictis Galfrido et Pe[tro usque ad terminum in] cirographo conten-
tum facto in curia domini regis; ut ipsi Radulphus et Ricardus, vel unus eorum si
uterque vacare non poterit vel cui vel quibus assignaverint, teneant eam in manu
sua per totum terminum et omnes fructus et exitus ex ea pro[venientes] dis-
tribuant singulis annis pauperibus domibus religiosis episcopatus mei et aliis
pauperibus pro anima mea. Item leg[o prior]i de Kaldwell' i marcam; priori de
Noketon' i [marcam]; priori de Kima i marcam; abbati de Brunna ii [marcas];
priori de Ellesham' ii marcas; abbati de Humberstain i marcam; priori de
Markeby i marcam; priori de Tornholm' i[i marcas]; abbati de Tuppeholm' i
marcam; abbati de M[e]ssenden xl solidos; abbati de Barling' xx solidos; priori
de Torkesey i marcam; abbati de Osulveston' xx solidos; priori de Landa i
marcam; abbati de N[utel' x]l solidos; priori de [Bradewell'] i marcam; priori de
Dunstap'll xl solidos; priori Sancti Neoti xl solidos; et priori [Hu]ntedon' xl
solidos; Item lego Iohanni de camera x marcas; Petro de Cotinton' x marcas;
magistro Hugoni coco x marcas; Rogero mareschallo [x] marcas; Willelmo servienti de Bugeden' c solidos; Willelmo Lu[po] x marcas; Willelmo serv[ienti
Ley]cestr' c [solidos]; Willelmo de Tunring ii marcas; Willelmo de Wodeford' ii
marcas; Iohanni servienti de Esfordeb' iii marcas; Reginaldo de Treilly v marcas;
Elye Kotele v marcas; Ricardo de Ispania ii marcas et dimidiam; Rogero filio
Willelmi x marcas; Thome marescallo v marcas; Henrico Cauchais de Tingehurst' v marcas; Gilberto de camera ii marcas; Waltero ostiario i marcam;
Iohanni de capella xx solidos; Bufeto nuntio iiii marcas; Hankino de pistrino [i]
marcam; Iohanni de curru xx solidos; Pagano i marcam; Galfredo Rom' i
marcam; Thome carecario i marcam; Reginaldo carecario i marcam; Roberto
clerico, custodi domorum Linc' xl solidos; Odino de Bugeden' xl solidos;
Roberto de Well' c[oco] de[cani] Lincoln' xx solidos; filio magistri Waleis ii
marcas. Volo insuper quod per executores meos detur de bonis meis servientibus,

nuntiis et garcionibus meis et aliis quibus non lego vel quibus minus lego, prout viderint [expedire]. Item lego canonico prebende Leicestr' ad edificia sibi construenda in prebenda sua xl marcas, nisi interim fecero grantum suum. Item lego pauperibus parentibus meis apud Well' et circa Pilton' lx marcas, ubi dominus frater meus [et] alii executores mei viderint expedire. Item lego fabrice ecclesie mee Lincoln' c marcas et totum mairemium quod habuero in decessu meo per totam episcopatum meum, ita quod reservetur usque in tempus successoris mei et detur ei pro l marcis, si voluerit, pacandis eidem fabrice antequam illud recipiat. Item lego successori meo xxvi carrucatas boum et domino Cantuar' et singulis episcopis provincie sue in Anglia [unum anulum. Item lego] ad exequias meas faciendas et ad emendum ea que necessaria fuerint altari quod est iuxta sepulturam meam c marcas et [ad in]veniendas necessarias expensas executoribus meis, qui prosequentur executionem testamenti mei [lx marcas], ut quod inde residuum fuerit cedat testamento meo. Predicto vero altari meo lego totam capellam meam, excepto parvo missali, quod vendatur et distribuatur pauperibus pro anima Rogeri de Bristoll' quondam canonici Lincoln'. Ordino insuper quod centum duodecim libre quas recepi a Willelmo decano Lincoln' depositas in custodia sua et mutuo datas Nicholao abbati et conventui Einesham super cartas suas quas penes me [habeo] reddantur ipsi decano vel cui assignaverit ad faciendum inde quod viderit faciendum; de quibus iam acquietavi me versus eundem decanum de l marcis quas recepi ab eisdem abbate et conventu et de v [solidos et] viii denarios, quos scilicet v solidos et viii denarios recepi a predicto decano ultra summam antedictam. Et sciendum quod dicti abbas et conventus solverunt michi postmodum l marcas de predicto prestito eis facto, quas adhuc debeo et ipsi debent totum residuum de predictis cxii libris. Volo autem quod tam debita quam legata mea perficiantur de bonis meis: in primis, videlicet, de blad[is et inst]auris m[ei]s et postmodum de pecunia si quam in morte mea habuero. Si[militer as]signo ad hoc faciendum omnia bona mea mobilia et omnes fructus tam de bladis in terra mea ᴅominatiꝋ antꬴ mortꬴm mꬴam quam ꜰructus vꝟgultorum et vineārum ꬴodem anno, scilicet, usque ad festum sancti Michaelis proxim[e post obitum] meum provenientes et omnia alia que me quocunque modo contingunt tam de proventibus reddituum quam de vasis, equis et iocalibus meis. Totum vero quod residuum fuerit de bonis meis, detur pauperibus domibus religiosis episcopatus m[ei, leprosis] pauperibus et magistris et scolaribus Oxon' ac conversis de Iudaismo in episcopatu meo et pauperibus hominibus maneriorum meorum, et precipue illis hominibus quorum blada habui que seminaverunt in dominicis meis per dominum regem [post]quam f[ui confirmatus] nec ea michi postmodum remiserunt et que dominus rex de iure non potuit illis warantizare; et etiam aliis hominibus meis si quos gravavi et alibi ubi executores mei cognoverint me teneri et viderint ex[ped]ire. Preterea assigno [et concedo abbati] et conventui de Parco Lude maneria de Suthelkinton' et de Kaltorp' cum omnibus pertinentiis, libertatibus et consuetudinibus suis; habend' et tenend' integre, quiete et pacifice usque ad terminum inter me et Roesiam de Kime et Philippum [filium suum con]stitutum a die videlicet beati Luce evangeliste anno domini m⁰ cc⁰. xxvii usque ad x annos proximo sequentes completos, et in eadem forma qua ipsa maneria cum pertinentiis suis michi concessa sunt et carta sua confirmata: salvis michi cata[llis meis que] fuerint in terris illis et pertinentiis et bladis que seminata fuerint in eisdem terris et pertinentiis in ultimo anno tenure mee ad executionem testamenti mei et salvo eo quod ego dicta maneria cum pertinentiis interim

tenebo in manu mea quamdiu michi placuerit: reddendo inde dictis abbati et conventui x marcas annuas in duobus anni terminis, scilicet, in festo sancti Michaelis
v marcas et in festo Penthec' v marcas. Insuper assigno et concedo eisdem abbati
et conventui v marcas annuas de custodia terre et heredis Radulfi de Wyhun,
quam Gilberto de Treilli senescallo meo et Radulfo de Waravill' concessi et
tradidi; habend' et tenend' cum pertinentiis suis usque ad legittimam ipsius
heredis etatem: reddendo inde dictis abbati et conventui v marcas annuas terminis supradictis. Ordino etiam et concedo quod computatis predictis v marcis
annuis quamdiu eas receperint [et comput]atis omnibus que de predictis maneriis
ad eosdem abbatem et conventum quocunque modo pervenerint, satisfiat eis per
executores testamenti mei usque ad summam cc marcarum, [ita quidem] quod
quicquid ultra dictarum cc marcarum summam ad ipsos [occasione dictorum]
maneriorum et custodie de Wyhun uel aliunde quocunque modo pervenerit
executoribus nostris [fideliter] restituant ad executionem testamenti mei faciendum. Item lego Waltero servienti meo de Dorkecestr' x marcas. H[uius igitur tes-
tamenti] mei executores constituo predictum dominum Bathon' fratrem meum,
Robertum archidiaconum Linc', Walterum thesaurarium, [I.] Norhampt' et W.
Leicestr' archidiacanos, Warinum et Robertum capellanos meos, Gilbertum de
Treilly, Radulphum de [Wa]ravill', [Tho]mam de Askeb', Iohannem de Crakall'
et Iohannem de Burgo clericos meos. [In] hunc modum assigno et const[ituo]
dictos Gilbertum, Radulphum, Thomam, Iohannem et Iohannem ad vendenda
bona mea et colligendam inde pecuniam per consilium predicti domini fratris mei
et aliorum executorum meorum et ad deponendam eam in tutis locis donec
provis[um fuerit] per cons[ilium] eorum [qui interesse] poterunt cum episcopo,
quid cui vel quibus et quando sit distribuendum iuxta presentis testamenti mei
ordinationem. Si vero dominus frater meus interim decessit quod Deus avertat
vel alius aut alii executorum meorum, volo [et ordino quo]d super[stites eorum
nichilomi]nus testamentum meum fideliter exequantur in fide qua Deo et michi
tenentur. Supplico igitur flexis genibus venerabili patri et domino Cant' archiepiscopo et ipsum [in vir]tu[te] Spiritus Sancti lacrimabiliter contestor quatinus
ob remissionem [peccatorum suorum non sustineat testamentum] meum,
quantum in ipso est, ab aliquo infirmari. Set si qui apparuerunt raptores, distrac-
tores vel perturbatores quom[in]us executores mei testamentum [m]e[um] libere
valeant adimplere, ipse cum super hoc requisitus f[uerit univer]sos [et singulos
per ecclesiasticam] compescat districtionem. Rogo insuper decanum et capitulum
meum Lincoln' et archidiaconos [meos univers]os et singulos [cum] omni qua
possum devotione et eos obtestor per aspersionem sanguinis Ihesu Cristi
quat[inus si qui in iurisdictione sua et potestate ap]paruerint impeditores vel perturbatores testamenti mei, ut predixi, ipsos ecclesiastica s[everitate desistere
com]pellan[t. In predictorum autem omnium] robur et testimonium, presenti testamento meo sigillum meum [una cum sigillis predictorum domini fratris mei],
decani et capituli et aliorum executorum meorum feci apponi. Actum [apud
Parcum Stowe kalendis Iu]nii anno domini [m°] cc° xxxiii° pontificatus, scilicet,
mei anno vicesimo [quarto]. Preterea [lego domino meo regi] pul[criorem] palefridum [et cuppam] pulcriorem quam [habuero in decessu meo. Item lego
Ricardo Cotele] milit[i predicti domini fratris m]ei xl marcas ad filias ipsius
Ricardo [maritandas].

The charters of King Henry III, granting the bishop permission to make his testament, are to be found in the *Reg. Ant.* ii nos. 370–1. They are dated 27 May 1227 and 15 May 1229 respectively (cf. *Cal. Ch. R.* i 42, 105; cf. *Cal. Ch. R.* iv 148). For the earlier testament of the bp see above no. 2.

409. Gilbert de Treilly and Ralph de Waravill

Grant to Gilbert de Treilly, the bishop's steward, and Ralph de Waravill, canon of Lincoln, or to the survivor of them and their assigns, of the custody of the land of Ralph de Wyham and of his heir, with the marriage of the said heir without disparagement; in the case of the death of the heir, they shall have the custody and marriage of the next heir: paying to the abbot and convent of Louth Park (? five) marks a year.   Stow Park, 1 June 1233

> B = PRO C53/27 (charter roll, 17 Henry III), m.2 (the right hand edge of the roll is badly damaged. Words in square brackets are conjectural).
> Pd (calendar) in *Cal. Ch. R.* i 186 (in an inspeximus of King Henry III, 11 July 1233).

Omnibus Cristi fidelibus ad quos presens scriptum pervenerit, Hugo Dei gratia [Lincolniensis episcopus salutem in domino. Noverit] universitas vestra nos dilectis in Cristo filiis Gilberto de Trelly senescallo nostro et Radulfo de Warevill' canonico Lincoln' vel uni eorum si de altero interim humanitus contigerit .... vel unius eorum <eam> assignaverit si de altero contigerit humanitus, concessisse, dedisse et presenti carta nostra confirmasse custodiam terre Radulfi de Wyhun, que est de feodo nostro, [et custodiam .... filii] et heredis ipsius Radulfi et maritagium eius ubi non disparagetur. Et si de eo infra etatem contigerit humanitus, custodiam heredis proximioris si legittime non fuerit etatis, et [maritagium eius] ubi non disparagetur, nisi fuerit maritatus: habend' et tenend' cum predicta terra et omnibus pertinentiis suis integre, quiete et pacifice quousque heres ad legittimam pervenerit etatem; reddendo inde [? annuatim quinque] marcas abbati et conventui de Parco Lude ad duos terminos, videlicet, medietatem in festo sancti Martini et aliam medietatem in festo Pentecost'. In huius igitur rei robur et testimonium, [presenti scripto] sigillum nostrum apposuimus. Hiis testibus: domino I. Bathon' episcopo fratre nostro, W. thesaurario Linc', I. archidiacono Norhampt',Warino de Kirketon et Roberto de Bolesour capellanis, [magistris] Waltero de Werministr' et Ricardo de Wendour', Willelmo de Winchecumb' et Thoma de Askeby, canonicis Lincoln'. Dat' per manum nostram apud Parcum Stowe kalendis Iunii [pontificatus nostri] anno vicesimo quarto.

> Ralph of Wyham held land of the bp in Wyham, Worlaby and Ormsby (*Book of Fees* i 159). An annual pension of five marks payable to Louth Park abbey is mentioned in the bp's second will (see above, no. 408). For a similar grant of wardship to the bp's brother, Bp Jocelin of Bath, issued two days before this document, see above, no. 407.

410. Rowney priory

Settlement of a dispute between Richard de Cernay, rector of the church of Great Munden and the nuns of the priory of Rowney over tithes, the parties and the church's and priory's patron, Gerard de Furnivall, having submitted to the bishop's ordination. The nuns are to possess the disputed tithes (described in detail), rendering to the church of Great Munden each year, on the Sunday before the feast of St Nicholas, six pounds of wax. If new assarts are made within the parish, any tithes are to go to the rector of the parish church.

Stow Park, 14 June 1233

B = PRO E315/62 (? register of Sir John Fray) fo. 6v. s. xv med.

Omnibus Cristi fidelibus ad quos presens scriptum pervenerit, Hugo Dei gratia Lincoln' episcopus salutem in domino. Noverit universitas vestra quod cum inter Ricardum de Cernay rectorem ecclesie de Magna Munden' actorem, et moniales prioratus de Rugenheya parte rei fungentes auctoritate domini pape super portionibus inferius annotatis questio verteretur aliquamdiu. Tandem tam dicte partes quam Gerardus de Furnivall' ipsius ecclesie necnon et dicti prioratus patronus sponte, simpliciter et absolute super portionibus ipsis ordinationi nostre se subiecerunt. Sunt autem hec portiones minute decime de curia dictarum monialium provenientes: tota decima de Tren' et de Langel' et due partes decime septem acrarum, una roda minus, de terra que fuit Gilberti le Parker in eodem campo; item tota decima illius partis de assarto que iacet inter terram dicti Gilberti et terram Nobilie et decime omnium garbarum campi iacentis citra grangiam monialium; item decime provenientes de decem acris pasture de terra Osberti iuxta parcum versus orientem et due partes decime de quatuor acris et una roda, que iacent iuxta curiam monialium quas Leffyng' tenuit; item omnes decime de augmento instauri curie de Munden' occasione forinsecarum terrarum que non pertinent[a] ad antiquum dominicum. Nos quidem pensatis pensandis et Deum habentes pre oculis quia per inquisitionem in hac parte factam de possessione dictarum monialium nobis constitit, ordinavimus in hunc modum: videlicet, quod sepedicte moniales de Rugeheya recipiant et possideant[b] omnes decimas prenotatas imperpetuum: reddendo inde supradicte ecclesie de Munden' sex libras cere singulis annis die dominica proxima ante festum sancti Nicholai. Ordinavimus etiam quod si de novo fiant assarta vel alterius modi augmenta infra parrochiam predictam unde decime dari debeant, ille decime totaliter et libere dicte matricis ecclesie rectoribus persolvantur: salvis in omnibus episcopalibus consuetudinibus et Lincoln' ecclesie dignitate. Ut autem hec ordinatio nostra a supradictis partibus admissa et accepta perpetuam optineat firmitatem, presenti scripto sigillum nostrum duximus apponendum. Hiis testibus: Waltero thesaurario Lincoln', Roberto de Boselour'[d] capellano, Radulfo de Warravill', Willelmo de Winchecumb et Thoma de Askeby, canonicis Lincoln', magistro Alardo de Arundell', Iohanne de Crakehall', Eustachio de Westunlun[d] et Stephano de Castello, clericis. Dat' per manum Garini de Kirketon' capellani, canonici Lincoln', apud Parkum Stowe xviii kalendas Iulii pontificatus nostri anno vicesimo quarto.

[a] pertinet B. [b] possidiant. [c] *The letter 'l' inserted between these two words.*
[d] sic.

411. Peterborough abbey

Institution of master Ralph of Collingham, clerk, to the church of Kettering, on the presentation of the abbot and convent of Peterborough

[? Stow Park, 14 June 1233]

B = LAO Wells roll ix, m. 9.
Pd *RHW* ii 264.

Testibus et dat' ut in carta monialium de Ruhenh' in archidiaconatu Huntingdonie.

> The institution is recorded in the institution roll (ibid. 173). The Rowney charter referred to on the lost Huntingdon archdeaconry charter roll is most probably to be identified with no. 410.

412. Crowland abbey

Institution of Peter of Brampton, chaplain, to the perpetual vicarage of Wellingborough, on the presentation of the abbot and convent of Crowland. He is to serve personally. The vicarage consists of the entire altarage of the church and half a virgate of land. Stow Park [? 25 July/6 August] 1233

> B = LAO Wells roll ix, m. 9.
> Pd *RHW* ii 264–5.

Testibus: Waltero thesaurario Linc', Roberto de Boll', capellano, Willelmo de Winch' et Thoma de Ask', canonicis Linc', Stephano de Cast' et Thoma de Norfolch', clericis. Dat' per manus Warini capellani apud Parcum Stowe viii nonas Augusti pontificatus nostri anno vicesimo quarto.

> The date given in the entry is impossible. Possibly 8th calends (25 July) or 8th ides (6 August) is meant. The institution is recorded in the institution roll among entries for the bp's twenty-third pontifical year, 20 December 1231 x 19 December 1232 (ibid. 169).

413. Goring priory

Institution of Nicholas of Bledington, chaplain, to the church of Moulsoe, on the presentation of the prioress and nuns of Goring, saving to the nuns an annual pension of sixty shillings. Nicholas is to serve personally.

Stow, 11 November 1233

> A = Castle Ashby, Compton document 38. Endorsed: Mulesho (s. xiii); Mulesho. Institutio per dominum Hugonem Lincol' episcopum ad ecclesiam salva pensione lx solidorum inde monialibus de Garinges (s. xv); approx. 156 mm. x 76 mm. + 12 mm.; episcopal seal (now powdery, brownish-white wax) in a black seal-bag, on parchment tag (method 1).

Omnibus Cristi fidelibus ad quos presens scriptum pervenerit, Hugo Dei gratia Lincoln' episcopus salutem in domino. Noverit universitas vestra nos, ad presentationem dilectarum filiarum priorisse et monialium de Garing' patronarum ecclesie de Mulesho, dilectum in Cristo filium Nicholaum de Bladint' capellanum ad eandem ecclesiam admisisse ipsumque in ea canonice personam instituisse, cum onere ministrandi personaliter in eadem; salvis inde dictis monialibus sexaginta solidis annuis, secundum quod in carta quam de nobis habent continetur [no. 380]; salvis etiam in omnibus episcopalibus consuetudinibus et Linc' ecclesie dignitate. Quod ut perpetuam optineat firmitatem, presenti scripto sigillum nostrum duximus apponendum. Hiis testibus: Waltero thesaurario Linc', Roberto de Bolesour' capellano, Radulfo de Warevill', Willelmo de Winchecumb' et Thoma de Askeby, canonicis Linc', magistro Ricardo de Windesor' et Willelmo de Bladint', clericis. Dat' per manum Warini de Kyrketon' capellani, canonici Linc', apud Stowam tertio idus Novembris pontificatus nostri anno vicesimo quarto.

The institution is recorded in *RHW* ii 91.

414. Great Paxton church

Collation of the church of Great Paxton, which is in the bishop's gift, to master Reginald of Bath, clerk, saving an annual pension of forty marks, payment of which is to be made at Lincoln in two instalments, twenty marks at Martinmas, twenty at Whitsun.   Stow Park, 11 November 1233

> B = LAO Lincoln D. & C. A/1/6 (Registrum) no. 302. s. xiv med.
> Pd *Reg. Ant.* iii no. 827.

Hiis testibus: Roberto de Bollesovere, capellano, Radulfo de Warravill', domino[a] de Winchecumbe et Thoma de Askeby, canonicis Lincoln', magistro Ricardo de Windlesor' et Willelmo de Bladington', clericis. Dat' per manum Garini de Kirketon', capellani, canonici Lincoln', apud Parcum Stowe iii idus Novembris pontificatus nostri anno vicesimo quarto.

> [a] *for* Willelmo.

For the grant of the pension see no. 377.

415. John of Banbury

Inspeximus and confirmation of a charter of John of Banbury, rector of Litchborough, granting to Nicholas de Wythibroc all the profits of his church until a debt incurred in Bologna, for which Nicholas stood surety, shall have been repaid in full. Richard the clerk, proctor of Nicholas, has been inducted into corporal possession of the church.   Stow Park, 12 December 1233

> B = LAO Wells roll ix, m. 8d (no witnesses).
> Pd *RHW* ii 266–7.

Dat' apud Parcum Stowe ii idus Decembris pontificatus nostri anno xxiiii[to].

416. Roade church

Institution of William de Esse, clerk, to a portion of the church of Roade, last held by Peter Lupus, on the presentation of Robert Lupus.
                                    [20 December 1232 x 19 December 1233]

> B = LAO Wells roll ix, m. 9.
> Pd *RHW* ii 265.

Testibus et dat' ut in carta super ecclesia de Saxeby in archidiaconatu Linc'.

> The institution (entered here under the bp's twenty-fourth pontifical year) is recorded in the institution roll among entries for the bp's twenty-third pontifical year, 20 December 1231 x 19 December 1232 (ibid. 265). The Lincoln archdeaconry charter roll has not survived; no Saxby charter survives for the twenty-fourth pontifical year (20 December 1232 x 19 December 1233) in the Lincoln archdeaconry institution roll - the closest one recorded is an institution during the twenty-first pontifical year, 20 December 1229 x 19 December 1230 (ibid. iii 177–8).

417. Dunstable priory

Institution of Robert of Torksey, chaplain, to the vicarage of a mediety of the church of Pattishall, on the presentation of the prior and convent of Dunstable. He is to serve personally. The vicarage consists of half of the entire altarage and three virgates of land with a suitable manse. The vicar shall pay synodal dues only. [20 December 1232 x 19 December 1233]

B = LAO Wells roll ix, m. 9.
Pd *RHW* ii 265.

Testibus et dat' ut in carta super ecclesia de Saxeby in archidiaconatu Linc'.

The institution (entered here under the bp's twenty-fourth pontifical year) is recorded in the institution roll among entries for the bp's seventeenth pontifical year, 20 December 1225 x 19 December 1226 (ibid. 130). The Lincoln archdeaconry charter roll has not survived; for Saxby see note to previous entry.

418. Wappenham church

Institution of John the chaplain to the perpetual vicarage of Wappenham, on the presentation of Thomas de Picquigny, the rector of the church, with the consent of Lettice de Lucy, the patron. John is to serve personally. The vicarage consists of the entire altarage and the corn of five acres, together with a manse. The vicar shall pay annually to the parson twenty shillings in four instalments and two pounds of wax in two instalments. He shall also pay synodal dues. [20 December 1232 x 19 December 1233]

B = LAO Wells roll ix, mm. 8–9 (entered here under the bp's twenty-fourth pontifical year).
Pd *RHW* ii 264.

Testibus et dat' ut in carta ecclesie de Brantefed' in archidiaconatu Huntingd'

The Huntingdon archdeaconry charter roll is lost, as is the Huntingdon archdeaconry roll for this period.

419. Nuneaton priory

Institution of Geoffrey de Lodbroke, chaplain, to the vicarage of Burley[-on-the-Hill], on the presentation of the prioress and convent of Nuneaton. He is to serve personally. The vicarage consists of the entire altarage except lambs and the offerings pertaining to the altar for fifteen days on the two feasts of the Holy Cross; also the tithes of hay and mills which Th. the last vicar obtained from the lord and the parishioners, together with a certain part of the lord's wood and pasture. The vicar shall have the demesne land of the church with appurtenances and a manse, except for a barn (horreum) in which to place the garb tithes of the aforesaid nuns, from whom the vicar shall receive three shillings a year for half a bovate of land. He shall pay synodal dues. [20 December 1232 x 19 December 1233]

B = LAO Wells roll ix, m. 9.
Pd *RHW* ii 265–6.

Testibus et dat' ut in carta super ecclesia de Wassingeburk' in archidiaconatu Linc'.

The institution (entered here under the bp's twenty-fourth pontifical year) is
recorded in the institution rolls among entries for the twenty-third pontifical year,
20 December 1231 x 19 December 1232 (ibid., 166–7). The Lincoln archdeaconry
charter roll is lost; the Washingborough charter in question is likely to have been
the letter of institution of Gerard, chancellor of the duke of Brittany, to the church,
recorded in the Lincoln archdeaconry institution roll for the twenty-fourth pontifical year, 20 December 1232 x 19 December 1233 (ibid. iii 207–8).

420.   Lessay abbey

*Ordination, made with the assent of William the dean and the chapter of Lincoln,
touching the churches of Fillingham, Brattleby, Riseholme, and [Great] Carlton,
all in the patronage of the abbot and convent of Lessay. Abbot Robert and the
convent had, with the assent of bishop Hugh of Coutances their diocesan, submitted to the ordination of the bishop of Lincoln and had sent prior Anketil of Box-
grove as their proctor. The abbot and convent shall have twenty marks a year
from the church of Fillingham, from the next vacancy onwards, in the name of a
perpetual benefice, to be paid by the rector in two instalments, namely ten marks
at Martinmas and ten at Whitsun (with a penalty of twenty shillimgs for every
non-payment of an instalment). Whenever the church is vacant the abbot and
convent shall present a suitable clerk to the bishop and his successors for institution. The rector shall bear all ordinary and customary charges. Furthermore, the
bishop ordains that from the next vacancy onwards two and a half marks from the
church of Riseholme and five marks from the church of Brattleby shall go each
year to augment the common fund of the canons of Lincoln, to be received from
the rectors who shall be instituted on the presentation of the abbot and convent.
Likewise these rectors shall bear all ordinary and customary charges of their
churches. The bishop reserves the church of [Great] Carlton for his own disposi-
tion in perpetuity. Meanwhile, until the time this ordination takes effect, the abbot
and convent are to continue to receive the annual payments which they used to
receive from these churches. If, however, the churches of Brattleby or Riseholme,
or either of them, should fall vacant before the Fillingham ordination takes effect
the dean and chapter of Lincoln are to receive the benefits granted to them above,
but in the meantime are to pay to the abbot and convent one mark for Brattleby
and three shillings for Riseholme.*   [20 December 1226 x 9 September 1232]

> B = LAO Lincoln D. & C. Dij/68/2/30 (in an inspeximus of Hugh de Morville, bp
> of Coutances (1208–36), ratifying the ordination).
> Pd *Reg. Ant.* ii no. 369.

When master John de Leonibus was instituted to the church of Great Carlton in the
course of the bp's eighteenth pontifical year (20 December 1226 x 19 December
1227), the patrons were the abbey of Lessay; the next vacancy was in 20 December
1233 x 19 December 1234 when the bp was the patron (*RHW* iii 154, 210). This
ordination must have been made before 9 September 1232, however, since the Brattleby payment is referred to in an actum of that date (no. 379).

421.   Luffenham church

*Institution of Richard de la Thurne, clerk, to the church of South Luffenham, on
the presentation of William Mauduit.*   Stow Park, 28 January 1234

> B = LAO Wells roll ix, m. 9.

Pd *RHW* ii 267.

Hiis testibus: Waltero thesaurario Linc', Roberto de Bol', capellano, magistro W. de Werminist', W. de Winchic' et Thoma de Askeby, canonicis Linc', magistro A. de Arundell' et W. de Bladinton', clericis. Data per manum Gwarini de Kirketon', capellani, canonici Linc', apud Parcum Stowe v kalendas Februarii pontificatus nostri anno xxv^{to}.

> The institution is recorded in the institution roll among entries for the bp's twenty-fourth pontifical year, 20 December 1232 x 19 December 1233 (ibid. 175).

422. Bury St Edmunds abbey

Institution of master John de Histon, clerk, to the church of Warkton, on the presentation of the abbot of Bury St Edmunds.   Stow Park, 21 March 1234

> B = LAO Wells roll ix, m. 9.
> Pd *RHW* ii 267–8.

Hiis testibus: Waltero thesaurario Linc', Iohanne archidiacono Norhampt', Roberto de Bolesour', capellano, Willelmo de Winchicumb', Thoma de Askeby et Iohanne de Crakehal', canonicis Linc', Philippo de Sideham, capellano, magistris Alardo de Arundel, Ricardo de Wyndelesour', Stephano de Castell', Willelmo de Bladinton', clericis. Dat' per manum Gwarini de Kirketon' capellani, canonici Linc', apud Parcum Stowe xii kalendas Aprilis pontificatus nostri anno vicesimo quinto.

> The institution is recorded in the institution roll (ibid. 177).

423. Daventry priory

Institution of master Roger de Weseham, clerk, to the church of Walgrave, on the presentation of the prior and convent of Daventry.   Stow Park, 21 March 1234

> B = LAO Wells roll ix, m. 9.
> Pd *RHW* ii 268.

Testibus et dat' ut supra in carta de Werketon' [no. 422].

> The institution is recorded in the institution roll among entries for the bp's twenty-third pontifical year, 20 December 1231 x 19 December 1232 (ibid. 169). Roger is probably the future bp of Coventry and Lichfield 1245–56.

424. East Farndon church

Institution of Simon de Dyngale, clerk, to the church of [East] Farndon, on the presentation of Hugh de Dyngale.   Stow Park, 21 March 1234

> B = LAO Wells roll ix, m. 9.
> Pd *RHW* ii 268.

Testibus et dat' ut supra [no. 423].

> The institution is recorded in the institution roll among entries for the bp's twenty-first pontifical year, 20 December 1229 x 19 December 1230 (ibid. 156–7). There had been a dispute over the advowson in the king's court between Hugh and William of Knapwell.

425. Northampton, priory of St Andrew

Institution of William le Butiller of Sydenham, chaplain, to the perpetual vicarage of Hardingstone, on the presentation of the prior and convent of St Andrew, Northampton. The vicarage consists of all altar offerings and small tithes (except the tithe of lambs), one virgate of land in the same village, the tithes of mills and sixty thraves of corn, namely fifteen thraves of wheat, fifteen of rye, fifteen of barley, and fifteen of oats, to be received annually from the prior and convent. A suitable manse beside the church is assigned to the vicar, who shall pay synodal dues. The monks shall bear all ordinary, due and customary charges of the church.   Stow Park, 21 March 1234

> B = LAO Wells roll ix, m. 9.
> Pd *RHW* ii 268.

Testibus et dat' ut supra [no. 424].

> The institution is recorded in the institution roll among entries for the bp's twenty-fourth pontifical year, 20 December 1232 x 19 December 1233 (ibid. 174–5).

426. Kislingbury church

Institution of Thomas the chaplain to the vicarage of Kislingbury, on the presentation of David de Armenters, parson of the church, with the assent of the queen dowager, patron by reason of her dowry. The vicar is to serve personally. He shall hold the whole church as long as he lives, paying to David the parson and his successors an annual pension of one hundred shillings.
Stow Park, 11 April 1234

> B = LAO Wells roll ix, m. 9.
> Pd *RHW* ii 269.

Testibus: Waltero thesaurario Linc', Roberto de Bolesour', capellano, Willelmo de Winchecumb', Thoma de Askeby et Iohanne de Crak', canonicis Linc', magistris R. de Windl' et A. de Arund', Stephano de Castell' et Willelmo de Bladin', clericis. Dat' apud Parkum Stowe per manus Garini de Kyrket' capellani, canonici Linc', iii° idus Aprilis pontificatus nostri anno xx^{mo} v^{to}.

427. Cotterstock church

Institution of Alan of Tilbrook, chaplain, to the perpetual vicarage of Cotterstock, on the presentation of Thomas de Torpel, the rector, with the consent of Ralph [Neville], bishop of Chichester and the king's chancellor, patron by reason of his custody of the land and heir of Roger de Torpel. Alan is to serve personally. The vicarage is described.   [Stow Park, 11 April 1234]

> B = LAO Wells roll ix, m. 9.

Omnibus etc. Noverit universitas vestra nos, ad presentationem Thome de Torpel rectoris ecclesie de Godestoke factam de assensu venerabilis fratris Radulfi Cycestr' episcopi, domini regis cancellarii, custodis terre et heredis Rogeri de Torpel eiusdem ecclesie patroni, dilectum in Cristo filium Alanum de Tilebroc capellanum ad ipsius ecclesie vicariam admisisse, ipsumque in ea canonice vicarium perpetuum instituisse, cum onere ministrandi personaliter in eadem. Consistit autem ipsa vicaria in omnibus minutis decimis, oblationibus et obventionibus altaris et in terris ecclesie predicte cum decimis molendinorum; salvis in omnibus etc. Quod ut perpetuam etc. Testibus et dat' ut supra in carta proxima.

> This entry was omitted from *RHW.* It should immediately follow the Kislingbury charter, ibid., ii 269. The institution is recorded in the institution roll ibid. 173, under the twenty-fourth pontifical year (20 December 1232 x 19 December 1233).

428. Ramsey abbey

Institution of Richard of Houghton, chaplain, to the perpetual vicarage of St Ives, on the presentation of the abbot and convent of Ramsey. He is to serve personally. The vicarage consists of all the small tithes and altar offerings, both of the mother church and its chapels, and generally of everything connected with the church and the chapels by parochial right, except for the land of the church, the garb tithes, and the tithes of hay. The vicar shall bear all ordinary and customary charges of the church and chapels, except for providing hospitality for the arch-deacon which is the abbey's responsibility. The vicar and the abbey shall be jointly responsible for any extraordinary charges. The vicar shall pay one hundred shillings a year to the prior of St Ives, twenty-five shillings at Michael-mas, Christmas, Easter, and the Nativity of St John the Baptist.

Stow Park, 11 April 1234

> B = PRO E164/28 (Ramsey cartulary) fo. 192v. s. xiv med.
> Pd *Ramsey Cartulary* ii no. ccc.

Omnibus Cristi fidelibus ad quos presens scriptum pervenerit, Hugo Dei gratia Lincoln' episcopus salutem in domino. Noverit universitas vestra nos, ad presen-tationem dilectorum filiorum abbatis et conventus Rames' patronorum ecclesie de Slepa, dilectum in Cristo filium Ricardum de Houghtone capellanum ad per-petuam ipsius ecclesie vicariam admisisse, ipsumque in ea canonice vicarium perpetuum instituisse, cum onere ministrandi personaliter in eadem. Consistit autem ipsa vicaria in omnibus minutis decimis et obventionibus altarium tam matricis ecclesie quam capellarum, et generaliter in omnibus dictas matricem ecclesiam et capellas iure parochiali contingentibus, exceptis terra ecclesie et decimis garbarum et feni, et sustinebit vicarius omnia onera ordinaria, debita et consueta dictas ecclesiam et capellas contingencia, preter hospitium archidiaconi quod patroni procurabunt, de extraordinariis cum contigerint pro rata sua respon-dentes. Solvet etiam vicarius priori de sancto Ivone, qui pro tempore fuerit[a], centum solidos annuos, in quatuor anni terminos: in festo sancti Michaelis xxv solidos; in festo Natalis Domini xxv solidos; in festo Pasche xxv solidos et in Nativitate sancti Iohannis Baptiste xxv solidos: salvis in omnibus episcopalibus consuetudinibus et Linc' ecclesie dignitate. Quod ut perpetuam optineat firmita-tem, presenti scripto sigillum nostrum duximus apponendum. Hiis testibus: Waltero thesaurario Linc', Roberto de Bolesour' capellano, et aliis. Dat' per manum Guarini de Kirketon' capellani, canonici Linc', apud Park' Stowe iii⁰ idus Aprilis pontificatus nostri anno xxv⁰.

[a] fuerunt *sic* B.

429. Great Houghton church

Institution of Michael of Quorndon, clerk, to the church of Great Houghton, on the presentation of William of Houghton, knight. Stow Park, 22 May 1234

> B = LAO Wells roll ix, m. 9.
> Pd *RHW* ii 269.

Hiis testibus: Roberto de Bolesour', capellano, Radulfo de Warevill', Willelmo de Winchecumb' 'et' Thoma de Askeby, canonicis Linc', Stephano de Castello et Willelmo de Bladinton', clericis. Dat' per manum Warini de Kirketon', capellani, canonici Linc', apud Parcum Stowe xi kalendas Iunii pontificatus nostri anno xxv^{to}.

> The institution is recorded in the institution roll (ibid. 178).

430. Cirencester abbey

Institution of master William de Hoveton', chaplain, to the church of Oxendon, on the presentation of the abbot and convent of Cirencester, saving to the abbey their due and ancient pension. Stow Park, 5 June 1234

> B = LAO Wells roll ix, m. 9. C = Oxford, Bodl. ms. Dep. C392 (Cirencester cartulary) fo. 175r. s. xiii med.
> Pd from B in *RHW* ii 269–70; from C in *Cirencester Cartulary* ii no. 705.

Hiis testibus: Waltero thesaurario Linc', Roberto de Bolesour^a, capellano, Willelmo de Winchecumb', Thoma de Askeby^b et Iohanne de Crakehal'^{c}, canonicis Linc', magistris Ricardo de Windlesor' et Alardo de Arundell', clericis. Dat' per manus^d Guarini de Kirketon' capellani, canonici Linc', apud Parkum Stowe^e nonis^f Iunii pontificatus nostri anno vicesimo quinto.

> ^{a} Bolosourum C. ^{b} Askebi C. ^{c} Crakeh C. ^{d} manum C. ^{e} Barkestowe C.
> ^{f} nono C.

> The institution is recorded in the institution roll among entries for the bp's twenty-second pontifical year, 20 December 1230 x 19 December 1231 (ibid. 159). This entry notes that the customary pension was three marks.

431. Lincoln cathedral

Grant, with the assent of William the dean and the chapter of Lincoln, as an augmentation of the maintenance of three chaplains, one deacon and one subdeacon, being vicars choral of Lincoln, who shall celebrate daily for the soul of the bishop and others, of thirty-four and a half marks (two and a half marks from Riseholme church; twenty marks from Paxton church and twelve marks from Great Carlton church) and an assignment of eight pounds of wax yearly from one bovate of land at Owersby. The duties of the chaplains are laid down. Stow Park, 16 August 1234

> A1 = LAO Lincoln D. & C. doct. Dj/20/1/2. No surviving seal. Slits for two seal tags. Size: 279 mm. x 344 mm. Endts: Carta super ordinatione altaris beati Hugonis (s. xiii).
> A2 = LAO Lincoln D. & C. doct. Dj/20/1/3. Slit for one seal-tag. Size: 204 mm. x 318 mm. No endorsement.

B = LAO Lincoln D. & C. A/1/5 (Registrum Antiquissimum), no. 225. s. xiii in. C = LAO Lincoln D. & C. A/1/8 (Liber de ordinationibus cantariarum) no. 58. s. xiv. D = ibid., no. 373. E = CUL ms. Dd. 10. 28 (Vetus Repertorium), fos. 76r–77r. s. xiv.

Pd from A1 in *Reg. Ant.* ii no. 363; H. Bradshaw & C. Wordsworth, *Statutes of Lincoln Cathedral* ii pp. lxv–lxvi (in part, incorrectly dated to 1221).

Omnibus[a] Cristi fidelibus ad quos presens scriptum pervenerit, Hugo Dei gratia Lincoln'[b] episcopus salutem in domino[c]. Cum sine diei certi seu temporis prefinitione soluturi simus nature debitum, cupientes ut expedit nobis itinerantibus providere viaticum in presenti et in futuro remedium, interveniente dilectorum filiorum Willelmi decani et capituli nostri[d] Lincoln'[e] assensu, dedimus et assignavimus perpetuo ad trium capellanorum unius diaconi et unius subdiaconi vicariorum de choro Lincoln'[e] per decanum et capitulum successive sicut expedire viderint assumendorum perpetue sustentationis augmentum et ad alios pios usus subscriptos triginta quatuor[f] marcas et dimidiam, scilicet: duas marcas et dimidiam de ecclesia de Rysum cum primo vacaverit, que est de patronatu abbatis et conventus de Exaquio, non obstante ordinatione nostra de dictis[g] duabus marcis et dimidia alias facta; item viginti marcas de ecclesia de Paxton' et duodecim[h] marcas de ecclesia de Karleton'[i] , que quidem ecclesie de advocatione nostra sunt, annuatim apud Lincoln'[e] per manus rectorum ipsarum pro tempore qui per nos et successores nostros patronos earumdem instituendi, ipsarum ecclesiarum cum pertinentiis omnia onera ordinaria, debita et consueta sustinebunt: solvendas periculo et sumptibus eorundem rectorum in duobus anni terminis: videlicet, in festo sancti Martini de ecclesia de Rysum sexdecim[j] solidos et octo[k] denarios; de ecclesia de Paxton' decem[l] marcas; et de ecclesia de Karleton' sex[m] marcas; et tantumdem in festo Penthecost'[n] ille de predictis capellanis qui perpetuus erit ad id per nos et successores nostros, vel sede vacante per dictos decanum et capitulum Lincoln'[e], preficiendo. De qua quidem pecunia[o] idem capellanus quatuor denarios singulis diebus ad opus suum retinebit et solvet dictis duobus capellanis, qui quasi ebdomadarii erunt per circuitum, utrique denarios tres[p], diacono autem et subdiacono similiter quasi ebdomadariis utrique duos denarios; et singulis sabbatis fiet solutio supradicta: salvis nichilominus omnibus ipsis stipendiis suis et aliis que eos ratione vicariarum suarum contingunt. Et hii omnes vespertinum ac matutinum officium mortuorum cum commendatione tanquam pro corpore presenti pro nobis in loco[q] deputato ad hoc in profestis[r] diebus ante vesperas. In festis etiam post vel[s] ante, cum commodius poterunt et melius sine dampno vel nocumento servitii ecclesie simul inperpetuum decantabunt. Predictus vero sacerdos principalem missam pro nobis specialiter et pro cunctis fidelibus defunctis singulis diebus priusquam canonici ingrediantur chorum ad primum, cum diacono et subdiacono indutis albis et sericis celebrabit, et cum sollempnitate tanquam pro corpore presenti secundus pro animabus regum et aliorum patronorum ecclesie nostre[t] predecessorum nostrorum, patrum et matrum, parentum[u], amicorum et benefactorum nostrorum et eiusdem ecclesie nostre et omnium fidelium defunctorum, cum oratione speciali pro nobis et cum cantu si voluerit. Tertius etiam pro canonicis, fratribus et sororibus ecclesie nostre Lincoln'[e] et pro cunctis fidelibus defunctis. Et hii duo singulis diebus celebrabunt ante primum vel post, cum commodius poterunt, et uni serviet diaconus et alii subdiaconus prenotati. Et si forte aliquis eorum infirmitate vel alia de causa prepeditus officium istud ut dictum est temporibus suis exequi non valeat, alius de choro ydoneus ad ipsius instantiam illud interim exequetur. Alioquin, de solutione predicta pro tempore quo defuerit nequaquam sibi respondeatur. Ad quod quidem cum predictis assignavimus annuas octo^k libras cere de bovata terre in Ouresby, que fuit Willelmi de Copland'^{v}, per manum Stephani de Grafham^w et heredum vel assignatorum suorum in festo beati Laurentii martyris^x singulis annis Lincoln'^{e} reddendis, prout in carta ipsius Stephani quam de nobis habet continetur. $^{y-}$Prefatus etiam sacerdos principalis habebit custodiam altaris illius, ubi premissa fient librorum etiam et vasorum, vestimentorum quoque atque aliorum que ad officium illud pertinent et ad id luminaria duos videlicet cereos trium librarum ad vespertinum ac matutinum officium et dum misse celebrantur et candelas, cum necesse fuerit, incensum etiam et alia ad predictum officium pertinentia sifficienter inveniet et honorifice-^{y}. Si autem ad aliquam missam de predictis oblatio pervenerit, tota simul cum eo quod de predictis triginta quatuor^f marcis et dimidia supererint post predictorum onerum deductionem, cedet in usus sepedicti principalis sacerdotis, salvo uno denario ei qui missam celebraverit. Illi quoque qui pro tempore dictarum ecclesiarum rectores^z futuri fuerint instituentur in hac forma: scilicet, quod predictam pecuniam annuatim terminis statutis, sicut predictum est, integre solvent et fideliter et hoc etiam coram dictis decano et capitulo iurabunt corporaliter cum per eos inde fuerint requisiti. Et si forte quod absit peccuniam^{aa} sepedictam predicto modo non solverint, ad ipsam persolvendam^q cum satisfactione canonica de termino quolibet non observato et de expensis ob id factis et dampnis que propter hoc evenerint per nos et successores nostros prout iustum fuerit compellentur. Nos autem et predicti decanus et capitulum communi assensu sollempniter excommunicavimus omnes illos quicunque contra hanc nostram ordinationem aliquo tempore malitiose venire presumpserint, nisi commoniti resipuerint et de contemptu satisfecerint competenter: salvis in omnibus episcopalibus consuetudinibus et Lincoln'^{b} ecclesie dignitate. Quod ut perpetuam optineat firmitatem, presenti scripto sigillum nostrum una cum sigillo predicti capituli nostri Lincoln'^{e} duximus apponendum. Hiis testibus^{bb}: Willelmo decano, Roberto archidiacono, Willelmo cancellario et Waltero thesaurario Linc', Iohanne Norhampton', Gilberto Huntingd'^{cc} et Amaurico Bedeford' archidiaconis, [Willelmo] subdecano, magistris Roberto de Gravel', Stephano de Cycestr'^{dd}, Theobaldo et Ricardo de Cantia, Galfrido Scoto et Roberto de Bolesover'^{ee} capellanis, [magistris] Roberto de Brincl' et Waltero de Well', Radulfo de Warravill'^{ff}, Petro de Hungar' et Willelmo de Winchecumb'^{gg} diaconis, Ricardo de Oxon' et Thoma de Aske[by^{hh} subdiaconis], canonicis Lincoln'^{b}. Dat' per manum Guarini de Kirketon' capellani, canonici Lincoln', apud Parkum^{ii} Stowe xvij^o kalendas Septem[bris ponti]ficatus nostri anno vicesimo quinto.

^{a} *The initial* O *is illuminated in red and green* B. ^{b} Linc' B. ^{c} in domino *omitted* B. ^{d} nostri *omitted* E. ^{e} Linc' B E. ^{f} xxxiiij E. ^{g} de dictis *repeated* B. ^{h} xij E. ^{i} Carleton' B E. ^{j} xvj E. ^{k} viij E. ^{l} x E. ^{m} vj E. ^{n} Penth' B; Pentecost' E. ^{o} peccunia B. ^{p} iij E. ^{q} in loco *repeated* E. ^{r} festis E. ^{s} *for* vel *read* hoc B. ^{t} nostre *omitted* E. ^{u} et *inserted* B E. ^{v} Coppeland' E. ^{w} Graham B. ^{x} martiris B. $^{y-y}$ BCE *this clause is placed in front of* Ad quod quidem cum predictis assignavimus . . . ^{z} facti *cancelled here* B. ^{aa} pecuniam B. ^{bb} Hiis testibus etc *entry ends here* E. ^{cc} Huntendon' B. ^{dd} Cicestr' B. ^{ee} Bollesovere B. ^{ff} Warauill' B. ^{gg} Wyndhecumb' B. ^{hh} Ascheby A2. ^{ii} Parchum B.

All words in square brackets are supplied from A2, the first original having been slightly injured.

432. Little Wymondley hospital

Ordination by the bishop and the dean and chapter of Lincoln respecting the hospital in Little Wymondley. The patronage of the hospital had been given to the bishop and his chapter by Richard de Argentein, the founder. Provisions are made respecting the appointment of a master and the admission of new brethren.

Stow Park, 16 August 1234

B = BL ms. Add. 43972 (Little Wymondley cartulary) fo. 13r (12r). s. xiii med. C = LAO, Ep. Reg. XXV (register of Bp William Atwater, 1514–21) fo. 97r (abridged). D = ibid., Ep. Reg. XXVI (register of Bp John Longland, 1521–47) fo. 225r–v.

Omnibus Cristi fidelibus ad quos presens scriptum pervenerit, Hugo Dei gratia Lincoln' episcopus et Willelmus de Tornaco decanus et capitulum Lincoln' salutem in domino. Noverit universitas vestra quod cum dilectus in Cristo Ricardus de Argent' patronatum hospitalis quod fundavit[a] in Parva Wilemundeleya[b] nobis contulerit, volumus et concedimus et firmiter statuimus quod tam magister, qui pro tempore in eodem hospitali ex fratribus eiusdem domus, si idoneus inveniatur, auctoritate nostra preficiendus, quam alii fratres canonici sub habitu regulari secundum regulam beati Augustini communiter vivant ibidem et secundum quod loci suppetunt facultates, hospitales se exibebunt[c] infirmis et tribulatis et pauperibus maxime in hospitali suo caritative hospitandis. Idem etiam magister potestatem habeat de consensu fratris vel fratrum superstitum confratres sibi in locum decedentium eligendi et admittendi, ita quod non admittantur[d] ibidem canonici ultra numerum septenarium, nisi devotione seu pia largitione fidelium eiusdem loci in futurum excreverint facultates secundum quas prefatus numerus canonicorum augeri merito poterit et debebit; ita tamen quod per huiusmodi multiplicationem nullo modo hospitalitatis[c] opera minuantur ibidem. Et siquis predictorum fratrum ante conversionem nondum ad sacerdotii gradum fuerit promotus, post habitus susceptionem quamcitius poterit ad ordinem sacerdotii promoveatur. Mortuo vero magistro dicti hospitalis, unus de fratribus cum litteris domus sigillo eius signatis infra tres septimanas mortem eius nobis denuntiet, electione tamen magistri sicut premissum est indifferenter nobis reservata. Si autem casus talis se ingesserit ut omnes fratres ante magistri substitutionem debitum conditionis humane exolverint, nos immediate subiacet et ad quos pleno iure quibus dictum hospitale pertinet circa[f] substitutionem tam fratrum quam magistri plena gaudeamus libertate. Ita quidem quod sede Lincoln' quandocumque vacante, decanus qui pro tempore fuerit et capitulum Lincoln' circa ordinationem domus prefate plenum ius habeant in omnibus premissis. Ordinata vero ecclesia Lincoln', is qui pro tempore fuerit episcopus[g] decanus et capitulum Lincoln' in ordinatione domus memorate premisso iure gaudeant inperpetuum[h], salvo pleno iure decani et capituli Lincoln' ut predictum est, quandocumque contigerit ecclesiam Lincol' vacare. Quod ut ratum sit et firmum, presens scriptum sigillorum nostrorum appositione duximus roborandum. Hiis testibus etc. Dat' per manum Guarini de Kirket'[i] capellani, canonici Linc', apud Parkum[j] Stowe xvii kalendas Septembris pontificatus nostri anno vicesimo quinto.

^a fundat C. ^b Wildmundelera C. ^c exhibebunt CD. ^d admittatur D. ^e hospitalis D. ^f carta C. ^g C *ends here* ^h imperpetuum D. ⁱ Kirk' et D. ^j Parcum D.

For the grant of the church of St Peter, Wymondley, to Richard de Argentein's new hospital foundation in 1214 see above, no. 6.

433. Peterborough abbey

Institution of Ralph of Norwich, clerk, to the church of Stanwick, on the presentation of the abbot and convent of Peterborough.   Stow Park, 2 October 1234

> B = LAO Wells roll ix, m. 9.
> Pd *RHW* ii 270.

Hiis testibus: Roberto de Bollesour', capellano, Radulfo de Waravill', Willelmo de Winch', Ricardo de Oxon', Iohanne de Crakehal', canonicis Linc', Iohanne de Burgo, Willelmo de Ingoldemel, et Stephano de Castell', clericis. Dat' per manum Gwarini de Kirketon' capellani, canonici Linc', apud Parkum Stowe vi^o nonas Octobris pontificatus nostri anno xxv^o.

> The institution is recorded in the institution roll among entries for the bp's twenty-fourth pontifical year, 20 December 1232 x 19 December 1233 (ibid. 174).

434. Crowland abbey

Institution of Robert of Weldon, chaplain, to the vicarage of Gedney, on the presentation of Thomas, the rector of the church, made with the assent of the abbot and convent of Crowland, the patrons. The endowments of the vicarage are described.   Stow Park, 16 October 1234

> B = Spalding Gentlemen's Society, Crowland cartulary fos. 112v–113r, no. xxvi. s. xiv med.

Omnibus Cristi fidelibus ad quos presens scriptum pervenerit, Hugo Dei gratia Lincoln' episcopus salutem in domino. Noverit universitas vestra nos, ad presentationem dilecti filii Thome rectoris ecclesie de Gedeney factam de assensu abbatis et conventus Croiland' patronorum [fo. 113r] eiusdem, dilectum in Cristo filium Robertum de Weldon' capellanum ad ipsius ecclesie vicariam admisisse, ipsumque in ea canonice vicarium perpetuum instituisse. Consistit autem ipsa vicaria in toto altaragio et in decimis feni preterquam de feno dominici eiusdem ville et in quatuor acris eidem vicario pro tofto assignatis; qui quidem omnia onera illius ordinaria, debita et consueta sustentabit, preter hospitium archidiaconi quando dictus Thomas et successores sui procurabunt: salvis in omnibus episcopalibus consuetudinibus et Lincoln' ecclesie dignitate. Quod ut perpetuam optineat firmitatem, presenti scripto sigillum nostrum duximus apponendum. Hiis testibus etc. Dat' apud Park Stowe xvii kalendas Novembris pontificatus nostri anno^a vicesimo quinto.

^a *word omitted* B.

> The institution is recorded in *RHW* iii 214.

435. Lytham priory

Institution of Thornas Dandely, clerk, to the church of Appleby, on the presentation of the prior of Lytham.   Stow, 13 December 1234

> A = Durharn D. & C. 3.4. Ebor.6. Endorsed: De Appelby (s. xiii); Admissio eiusdem 'T. Andeley' ad ecclesiam de Apelby per episcopum Lincol' ad presentationem prioris et conventus Dunelm' (s. xiv); Lethom (s. xv); approx. 183 mm. x 41/27 mm.; tongue and tie, fragment of seal (upper half only), whitish-brown wax, counterseal.
> B = ibid. Loc.II.7. s. xiii ex. C = ibid. 4.3. Ebor.3d. ss. xiii ex–xiv in. D = ibid. 4.3. Ebor.3e. ss. xiii ex–xiv in. E = BL ms. Stowe 930 (Durham register) fo.19r. ss. xiii–xiv.
> Pd from E in *Durham Annals and Documents* 120.

Omnibus Cristi fidelibus ad quos presens scriptum pervenerit, Hugo Dei gratia Lincoln' episcopus salutem in domino. Noverit universitas vestra nos, ad presentationem prioris de Lythun patroni ecclesie de Appelby, dilectum in Cristo filium Thomam de Andely clericum ad eandem ecclesiam admisisse, ipsumque in ea canonice personam instituisse: salvis in omnibus episcopalibus consuetudinibus et Lincoln' ecclesie dignitate. Et in huius rei testimonium, presenti scripto sigillum nostrum duximus apponendum. Dat' per manum Guarini de Kirketon' capellani, canonici Lincoln', apud Stowam idibus Decembris pontificatus nostri anno vicesimo quinto.

> The collation of the church to Thomas 'by authority of the Council' is recorded in *RHW* ii 322–3; his institution on the presentation of Lytham priory ibid. 324.

436. Templars

Institution of master Alard of Arundel, clerk, to the church of Althorpe, on the presentation of the master and brethren of the Templars in England, patrons of one mediety of the church, with the consent of the prior and brethren of the hospital of St Leonard, York, patrons of the other mediety.

Stow Park, 13 December 1234

> A = LAO Misc. Dep. 456 (formerly Phillipps 41058). Endorsed: De institutione Alardi in ecclesia de Altorp' (s. xiii); Aletorp' (s. xiii); R. (s. xiii); approx. 153 mm. x 60 mm. + 10 mm. tongue (tie torn away); some staining on the face of the document; small fragment of seal (natural wax) on tongue (nothing legible).
> B = BL ms. Cotton Nero D iii (St Leonard's, York cartulary) fo. 16r (14r). ss. xiv–xv.

Omnibus Cristi fidelibus ad quos presens scriptum pervenerit, Hugo Dei gratia Lincoln' episcopus salutem in domino. Noverit universitas vestra nos, ad presentationem fratris Roberti de Sanford' magistri et fratrum Militie Templi in Anglia patronorum unius medietatis ecclesie de Alethorp', factam de assensu prioris et fratrum hospitalis sancti Leonardi Eborac' patronorum alterius medietatis eiusdem, dilectum in Cristo filium magistrum Alardum de Arundell' clericum ad ipsam ecclesiam admisisse, ipsumque in ea canonice personam instituisse, salvo iure cuiuslibet et salvis in omnibus episcopalibus consuetudinibus et Lincoln' ecclesie dignitate. In cuius rei testimonium, presenti scripto sigillum nostrum duximus apponendum. Dat' per manum Garini de Kirketon', capellani, canonici

Lincoln', apud Park' Stowe idibus[a] Decembris pontificatus nostri anno vicesimo quinto.

[a] idus A.

The institution is recorded in the Stow archdeaconry institution roll (*RHW* i 237).

437.   Master Peter of Northampton

Letter from the bishop to the abbot of Cirencester and his fellow judges, inform-ing them that the vicarage of Little Houghton had been sequestered at Michael-mas 1231 on account of the contumacy of master Peter of Northampton, then vicar of the church. He had been deprived of his benefice because he had not come to be ordained, although summoned several times; he did not reside in person or minister in the priestly office.

[20 December 1233 x 19 December 1234]

B = LAO Wells roll ix, m. 9d.
Pd *RHW* ii 270–1.

This letter is placed among entries for the bp's twenty-fifth pontifical year, 20 December 1233 x 19 December 1234, although the record of the bp's institution of Peter's successor as vicar of Little Houghton is to be found in the Northampton archdeaconry institution roll for the preceding pontifical year (ibid. 175). In that entry it states that Peter had been removed by definitive sentence of the archdeacon of Northampton.

438.   Thistleton church

Institution of John de Bussay to the church of Thistleton, on the presentation of Lambert de Bussay.   [20 December 1233 x 19 December 1234]

B = LAO Wells roll ix, m. 9.
Pd *RHW* ii 270.

Testibus et dat' ut in carta de Helmeswell' in archidiaconatu Stowe.

The entry is placed among those for the bishop's twenty-fifth pontifical year. The institution of Bussay is recorded ibid. 133 under the seventeenth pontifical year (20 December 1225 x 19 December 1226). The Stow archdeaconry charter is no longer extant; the only Hemswell entry noted in the Stow archdeaconry institution roll is the institution of Simon de Offeham to the church during the bp's twenty-second pontifical year, 20 December 1230 x 19 December 1231 (ibid. i 230).

439.   Northampton, priory of St Andrew

Institution of John of St Medard, clerk, to the church of St Gregory, Northampton, on the presentation of the prior and convent of St Andrew, Northampton, saving to the prior their due and ancient pension.   Stow Park, 25 January 1235

B = LAO Wells roll ix, m. 9.
Pd *RHW* ii 271.

Hiis testibus: Roberto de Bolesover', capellano, magistro Waltero de Wer-ministr', Radulfo de Waravill', Willelmo de Winchecumb', Ricardo de Oxon' et Thoma de Askeby, canonicis Lincoln'. Dat' apud Parkum Stowe per manum

Garini de Kirketon', capellani, canonici Linc', viii kalendas Februarii pontificatus nostri anno vicesimo sexto.

> The institution to St Gregory's is not recorded on the Northampton archdeaconry
> institution roll, although the institution of John of St Medard to the church of St
> Edmund, Northampton, is noted among entries for the bp's twenty-fifth pontifical
> year, 20 December 1233 x 19 December 1234 (ibid. 179).

440.   Kingsthorpe, Holy Trinity hospital outside Northampton

*Collation, by authority of the Council, of John of Brampton, chaplain, as master
and rector of the hospital of the Holy Trinity, Northampton, saving in future the
right of patronage.*   Stow Park, 25 January 1235

> B = LAO Wells roll ix, m.9.
> Pd *RHW* ii 272.

Testibus et dat' ut in carta proxima supra [no. 439].

> The collation is recorded in the institution roll (ibid. 176). The hospital had been
> vacant for seven months as a result of a dispute between the priory of St Andrew,
> Northampton, and Philip, son of Robert of Northampton. The date of John of
> Brampton's collation is given as 10 December 1234. The hospital is also known as
> Kingsthorpe.

441.   Gayton church

*Institution of William d'Aubigny, clerk, to the church of Gayton, on the presenta-
tion of King Henry III by virtue of the land of the advocate of Béthune being in
his hands.*   Stow Park, 25 January 1235

> B = LAO Wells roll ix, m. 9.
> Pd *RHW* ii 272.

Testibus et dat' ut in carta super ecclesia sancti Gregorii Norhampt' supra [no.
439].

> The institution is recorded in the institution roll among entries for the bp's twenty-
> fifth pontifical year, 20 December 1233 x 19 December 1234 (ibid. 180–1).

442.   Peterborough abbey

*Institution of master William de Burgo [Peterborough], clerk, to the church of
Paston, on the presentation of the abbot and convent of Peterborough, saving to
the abbey their due and ancient pension.*   Stow Park, 25 January 1235

> B = LAO Wells roll ix, m. 9.
> Pd *RHW* ii 272.

Testibus et dat' ut in carta supra [no. 441].

> The institution is recorded in the institution roll among entries for the bp's twenty-
> fifth pontifical year, 20 Decernber 1233 x 19 December 1234 (ibid. 179–80).

443. Sulby abbey

Institution of William [Blund], chancellor of the church of Lincoln, to the church of [Great] Harrowden, on the presentation of the abbot and convent of Sulby, saving to the patrons an annual pension of two marks, in the name of a perpetual benefice, payable at the feast of All Saints and at Easter.
[20 December 1234 x 7 February 1235]

B = LAO Wells roll ix, m. 9 (among entries for the bp's twenty-sixth pontifical year).
Pd *RHW* ii 271.

Testibus et dat' ut in carta de Magna Gathesden' in archidiaconatu Huntingdon'.

The institution is recorded in the institution roll among entries for the bp's twenty-fifth pontifical year, 20 December 1233 x 19 December 1234 (ibid. 181). The bp died on 7 February 1235. For the bp's grant of the pension, see no. 280. The Huntingdon archdeaconry charter roll has not survived, nor has the Huntingdon institution roll for this year, so there is no clue as to the contents of the Great Gaddesden charter alluded to in the dating clause.

444. Master William

A recital of a dispensation from Pope Gregory IX to master William de L[rest illegible].
[20 December 1234 x 7 February 1235]

B = LAO Wells roll ix, m. 9d (an entry of fourteen lines, badly stained and damaged and nearly illegible, not pd in *RHW*).

Omnibus Cristi fidelibus ad quos presens scriptum pervenerit, Hugo Dei gratia Lincoln' episcopus salutem in domino. Mandatum domini pape suscepimus in hec verba: Gregorius episcopus servus servorum Dei venerabili fratri Lincoln' episcopo salutem et apostolicam benedictionem. Dilectus filius magister Willelmus de L......... clericus tue diocesis in nostra presentia constitutus ... (*rest almost completely illegible, except that under ultra-violet light the date of the papal mandate is 8 calends of October [24 September]*).

The entry is recorded among those for the bp's twenty-sixth pontifical year, beginning 20 December 1234.

445. Crowland abbey

Institution of John son of Ilbert to the perpetual vicarage of Baston, on the presentation of the abbot and convent of Crowland. John shall receive all the altar offerings and the rest of the income, save for garbs, and shall pay two marks a year to the monks of Crowland.
[?20 December 1209 x 7 February 1235]

B = Spalding Gentlemen's Society, Crowland cartulary fo. 157r, no. i. s. xiv med.

Omnibus Cristi fidelibus ad quos presens scriptum pervenerit, Hugo Dei gratia Lincoln' episcopus salutem in domino. Ad universitatis vestre notitiam volumus pervenire nos, ad presentationem dilectorum in Cristo filiorum abbatis et conventus de Croiland', recepisse dilectum filium nostrum Iohannem filium Ilberti ad perpetuam vicariam ecclesie de Baston' cum omnibus pertinentiis et ipsum in ea canonice vicarium instituisse, ita quidem quod prefatus Iohannes percipiet omnes obventiones altaris cum ceteris provenientibus preter garbas: reddendo monachis de Croiland' duas marcasª annuatim: salvis episcopalibus consuetudinibus et Lincoln' ecclesie dignitate. Quod ut ratum habeatur et firmum, presenti scripto et sigillo nostro duximus confirmandum. Hiis testibus etc.

ª *followed by an erasure* B.

Since the witnesses have been omitted and there is no indication as to whether there was a dating-clause, which would have identified the Bp Hugh as Hugh of Wells, it is virtually impossible to say whether this *actum* belongs to Hugh I or Hugh II. Unfortunately, *RHW* does not contain a single reference to Baston, although from another source it is known that the vicar in 1222 was called William (Crowland cartulary fo. 157r, no. ii). Similarly the diplomatic of the document does not aid identification.

446.   Lincoln cathedral

? Indulgence of twenty days for those contributing alms to Lincoln cathedral.
[20 December 1209 x 7 February 1235]

Mention of indulgence in *Gir. Camb.* vii 218, app. F. It is not entirely certain that Hugh II is the bp concerned, although there is another record of a similar indulgence of eighty days granted by Hugh I (*EEA* 4 no. 98). See also *Gir. Camb.* vii 218, n. 4 for further comments on the identification of the bp.

447.   Nun Cotham priory

Visitation injunctions made for the nuns of the priory of Nun Cotham. The number of nuns shall not exceed thirty, [lay] sisters ten, with twelve lay brethren for outdoor work. There are to be two chaplains, besides the master, attached to the house. Provision is made for the showing of the priory's accounts and the custody and use of the conventual seal. The nuns, chaplains, and lay brethren and sisters, as well as guests, shall all have the same food: special provision is made for the sick. No secular guests are to be admitted for more than one night at a time. No nun may speak alone with a stranger and no lay sister may live at the priory's granges. Special provisions are made for visits to relatives and friends and absences of nuns from the priory. No nun or sister is to possess anything of her own or receive money or property.   [?20 December 1209 x 7 February 1235]

B = Oxford, Bodl., ms. Top. Lincs d. 1 (Nun Cotham cartulary), fo. 38r. *rubric*: Hec sunt littere constitutionum Hugonis Linc' episcopi in visitatione. s. xiii in.
Pd *Mon. Angl.*, v 677–8, no. vii; *PL* cliii, cols. 1113–16 (ascribed to St Hugh, bp of Lincoln 1186–1200).

[O]mnibus Cristi fidelibus ad quos presens scriptum pervenerit, H. Dei gratia Linc' episcopus salutem in domino. Cum ad congregationem ancillarum Cristi de Cot', causa visitationis, ex officii nostri debito faciende accederemus, ad ea que didiscimus ibidem corrigenda, remedium studuimus adhibere. Advertentes igitur multitudinem monialium ampliorem quam sustinere valeant domus illius facultatis, habita deliberatione statuimus, cum concensu (*sic*) magistri, priorisse et conventus, quod congregatio monialium de cetero xxxᵣⁱᵘᵐ numerum non excedat, sororum numerus sub denario concludatur, duodecim fratres conversi ad officia ruralia sint ibidem excercenda. Magister capellanus cum duobus capellanis tantum ad divina deputentur ad implenda.[a] Nulli vero religionis habitus in eadem domo tribuatur donec diminutus fuerit presens conventus ad numerum pretaxatum, nisi propter manifestam domus utilitatem, et hoc ex speciali licentia dyocesani. Sigillum domus sub custodia magistri, priorisse et monialium ad hoc communiter electe, cuius religio fuerit et discretio approbata, sub clave triplici, reservetur, nec aliquid scriptum inde signetur sine conscientia totius capituli vel maioris et sanioris partis eiusdem. Redditus omnes, instaura, proventus quicunque, singulis annis redigantur in scriptum, quod priorisse et subpriorisse et ceteris iiii[or] de melioribus et prudentioribus a toto capitulo vel maiori ac saniori parte communiter electis tradatur custodiendum. Magister et procuratores domus totam pecuniam domus in denariis vel huiusmodi ex quacunque causa domui <sue> provenientem[b], cum coram eisdem sex numerata fuerit, sub sigillo magistri signatam ipsis tradent, quam eedem ad negotia domus expedienda quotiens necesse fuerit et quantum opus fuerit, sub fideli testimonio tam magistri quam aliorum sine difficultate liberabunt, et residuum sigillo magistri signatum iterato reponent. Singulis autem mensibus, eedem sex compotum audient de simplicibus eiusdem domus expensis. Et quoniam abdicatio proprietatis professioni religiosorum est annexa, firmiter inhibuimus ne qua vel quis in eadem domo, post susceptum religionis habitum, aliquid proprium habere presumat sed sint eis omnia communia. Eodem etiam pane tam moniales, capellani, fratres et sorores quam hospites vescantur et potum habeant eundem, excepto quod infirmorum necessitati prout oportunum fuerit delicatius provideatur. Quia vero per frequentiam secularium quies religiosorum turbari solet, prohibuimus ne vir vel mulier recipiatur in habitu seculari moram facturus in domo memorata, nisi forsan hospitalitatis gratia quis ibi pernoctaverit. Item ne quis vel qua sive secularis persona sive religiose professionis aliunde veniens, cum sola moniali solus vel sola loquatur, sed honesto testimonio tali quod sinistra careat suspicione, et cum licentia secundum regulam suam ab hiis que presunt optenta. Preterea quia religiosis et presertim in sexu mulieri discurrere vel vagari modis omnibus est inhonestum, constituimus ne soror vel monialis apud grangiam moretur, causa nutrimentorum animalium, vel aliqua qualibet occasione. Moniales etiam, causa visitandi proximos aut parentes, nullatenus extramittantur ex earum sola voluntate vel levi qualibet occasione nec tandem ullo modo, sine magistri et priorisse licentia speciali, et maxima ac cognita necessitate. Quia simoniaca pravitas plures in errorem et interitum adduxit, animarum saluti providere volentes, districte prohibuimus ne vir vel mulier pro pecunia vel re qualibet temporali recipiatur unquam ibidem ex pacto, sub anathematis interminatione precipientes quod omnia premissa salubriter a nobis constituta firmiter ab omnibus utriusque sexus in eadem domo serventur inperpetuum.

[a] implentur *originally written and the last three letters dotted for deletion and* da *interlined* B.   [b] *domus venientes inserted* B.

For notes on the date etc. and on the likelihood that Bp Hugh is Hugh of Wells rather than St Hugh see C.R. Cheney, *Episcopal Visitation of Monasteries in the thirteenth century* (Manchester 1931), p. 98, n. 2.

448. Leicester abbey

*Grant to the abbey of Leicester in proprios usus of the church of Sharnbrook,
saving a suitable vicarage ordained by the bishop.*

[?20 December 1209 x 7 February 1235, possibly 20 December 1226 x
7 February 1235]

> Mention of charter in Bodl. ms. Laud misc. 625 (Charyte's Leicester abbey rental),
> fo. 182v. s. xvi in.: Concessio Hugonis episcopi Linc' de possidendo eccle-
> siam de Sharnbrok' in proprios usus, salva vicaria competente in eadem in
> qua concessione portio vicarie taxata est per episcopum.

> An earlier part of Charyte's Rental (fo. 121v) gives further details. The church was
> given to the abbey, after the decease of Richard the rector, by William Triket and
> Baldwin his son and heir, by grant of Hugh of Wells and the dean and chapter
> (*Leicester Abbey*, 186). During the bp's eighteenth pontifical year (20 December
> 1226 x 19 December 1227), Sharnbrook is not described as a vicarage. On this
> occasion Leicester abbey's presentee, Richard de Trippelawe (? the same as
> Richard the rector above), was instituted to the church, and an annual pension of 8
> marks was confirmed to the abbey, in the name of a perpetual benefice (*RHW* iii
> 13). It is probable that the appropriation and vicarage ordination dates from after
> this pontifical year.

449. Luffield priory

[?] General confirmation of possessions for the priory of Luffield.

[20 December 1209 x 7 February 1235]

> Mention of charter in CUL ms. Ee. 1. 1, fo. 274v: Item Alexander papa tertius et
> secundus Hugo Linc' episcopus donationes et confirmationes antedictas
> confirmaverunt.

> From the context this sounds very much like a general confirmation but no such
> document of Bp Hugh is to be found in the Luffield cartulary. It is just possible that
> this is a reference to Bp Hugh's confirmation of the church of Water Stratford in
> 1217 (see above no. 63). The general confirmation of Pope Alexander III is likely to
> be *Luffield Priory Charters* i no. 8 (dated 10 June 1174).

450. Spalding priory: chantry at Lea

*Grant, with the assent of the prior and convent of Spalding, the patrons of the
church of Lea, and of Thomas de Hardres the rector, that Ralph of Trehampton
shall have a chantry at his chapel in his* curia *at Lea: the detailed arrangement
safeguard the rights of the mother church of Lea.*

[20 December 1209 x 7 February 1235]

> B = BL Add. ms. 35296 (Spalding cartulary), fos. 394v–395v (v^{xx}xiii v–v^{xx}xiiii v,
> 396v–397v). s. xiv in.

Omnibus Cristi fidelibus ad quos presens scriptum pervenerit, Hugo Dei gratia
Linc' episcopus salutem. Noverit universitas vestra nos, de assensu et voluntate
prioris et conventus de Spald' patronorum ecclesie de Lee et Thome de Hardis
rectoris ecclesie eiusdem, concessisse et presenti carta nostra confirmasse dilecto
filio Radulfo de Trehamton' et heredibus suis inperpetuum, ut habeant cantariam
sibi et libere familie sue et hospitibus suis in capella sua [fo. 395r] in curia sua de

Lee; salvis in omnibus matricis ecclesie de Lee rectoribus oblationibus debitis et consuetis et maxime diebus Natalis Domini, Purificationis, Parasceve, Pasche et Omnium Sanctorum, quibus quidem diebus ipsi rectores[a] ad dictam capellam venient vel mittent omnimodas[b] oblationes provenientes ibidem sine difficultate recepturi. Die vero sancte Elene dictus Radulfus et heredes sui cum uxoribus suis et familia sua predicta, cum in partibus illis fuerint[c], venient ad matricem ecclesiam cum oblationibus debitis et consuetis. Dictus etiam Radulfus fideliter promisit quod occasione concessionis huius nichil unquam in preiudicium iuris predicte matricis ecclesie vel vicinarum ecclesiarum faciet vel fieri procurabit vel sustinebit quantum in ipso est procurari, nec impetrabit nec licet impetratum fuerit utetur impetratis sed et omnes ipsius heredes in initio possessionis sue sufficientem super hiis coram archidiacono loci facient securitatem, si legitime fuerint etatis cum ad eos devolvetur hereditas. Si vero etatem legitimam non habuerint, custodes eorum prestabunt securitatem predictam et nichilominus heres, cum ad etatem plenam pervenerint, ita quidem quod eadem capella cessabit donec ab ipsis heredibus vel eorum custodibus, si fuerint in custodia, facta fuerit securitas prenotata, capellanus vero sumptibus ipsius Radulfi et heredum suorum ibidem pro tempore ministraturus, de consensu rectorum matricis ecclesie predicte, ad illud officium per archidiaconum loci admittendus, rectoribus ipsis priusquam ibi ministret iuramentum prestabit corporaliter quod nullum parochianum suum ad confessiones, sponsalia, purificationes et huiusmodi recipiet nec aliquid ecclesiasticum ius aliqui de eis impedit, nec aliquem parochianum suum divina dicta capella sine licentia ipsorum rectorum admittet, seu aliquid ab eis sive legatum sive privatum vel quemcumque proventum per se vel per alium pro tricenalibus vel aliis huiusmodi recipiet immo quod matricem ecclesiam in hiis omnibus indempnem conservabit. Hoc tamen sibi licito quod oblationes in dicta capella die beati Andree ad manum suam provenientes simul cum oblationibus aliis a supradictis consuetis et matrici ecclesie debitis ad opus suum[d] possit retinere, tota autem familia predicti Radulfi et heredum suorum alia a predicta sequetur matricem ecclesiam iure parochiali in omnibus. Idem etiam et heredes sui similiter in omnibus subiecti erunt matrici ecclesie supradicte tanquam parochiani et eius rectoribus omnia iura ecclesiastica, decimas, scilicet, [fo. 395v] maiores et minores persolvent. Hoc igitur concesso quod liceat eis divina audire in dicta capella sicut prenotatum est et ut per hanc concessionem liberaliter factam dicte matricis ecclesie honor accrescat; sepedictus Radulfus et heredes sui dabunt singulis annis inperpetuum eidem ecclesie nomine subiectionis duos cereos ii librarum in vigilia Natalis Domini ad vesperas, unum scilicet inponendum[e] ad altare maius et alium ad altare beate Marie Virginis. Si autem contra hanc formam per ipsum Radulfum vel per aliquem heredum suorum vel capellanum in dicta capella ministrantem pro tempore matrix ecclesia dampnificata fuerit[f] in aliquo et hoc ad notitiam rectoris eius pervenerit ad ipsorum unicam monitionem cessabit capella donec ecclesia de dicto dampno competenter fuerit et plene satisfactum. Ut autem predicta robur perpetue firmitatis optineant utrique parti scripti huius in modo cirographi confecti sigillum nostrum una cum sigillo partium duximus apponendum; cuius quid alia pars cui sigillo sepedicti Radulfi appensum fuerit penes priorem et conventum Spald', patronos ecclesie de Lee, remaneat, et altera penes dictum Radulfum et heredes suos sigillo[g] patronorum suorum et supradicti Thome rectoris ecclesie ipsius consignata; salvis in omnibus episcopi consuetudine et Linc' ecclesie dignitate. Precipimus etiam quod huius cirographi tenor in missali ecclesie de Leea vel alio libro et in matricula archidiaconi distincte conscribatur. T(estibus) etc.

^a rectoris B.   ^b omnimdas B.   ^c fuerunt B.   ^d suam B.   ^e inponedum B.
^f ab *dotted for deletion.*   ^g sigillum B.

On fo. 395v is a letter from Thomas de Hardres, rector of Lea, consenting to the above arrangement. There is no record of the institution of Thomas to Lea, but he occurs frequently in charters of the time of Bp Hugh II (*Reg. Ant.* ii nos. 570–1; iv nos. 1109–10, 1132, 1139, 1156, 1158 (capellanus Linc' ecclesie), 1208, 1211–12, 1262–3, 1309, 1387; v nos. 1476, 1702; vi nos. 1811, 1905, 1920, 1931; vii nos. 1996–7, 2027–31, 2095, 2134; ix nos. 2437, 2498, 2503, 2506 (rector of Lea) and n.). For Trehampton see *EYC* iv pp. xxx–xxxi.

451.   Thurgarton priory

Grant, made with the assent of the dean and chapter of Lincoln, to the prior and convent of Thurgarton of twenty shillings a year from the church of Potterhanworth in the name of a perpetual benefice. This arrangement is to take effect after the death or cession of the present rector, master Richard of Windsor; until then the priory shall receive ten shillings a year from the rector.

[20 December 1224 x 7 February 1235]

B = Southwell Minster ms. 3 (Thurgarton cartulary) fo. 145v, no. 988 (witnesses and date omitted). s. xiii med.
Pd *Thurgarton Cartulary* no. 1006.

Master Richard of Windsor was instituted to Potterhanworth during the bp's sixteenth pontifical year, 20 December 1224 x 19 December 1225 (*RHW* iii 139).

APPENDIX

Settlements, chirographs and final concords in which Bishop Hugh is a party

1. Settlement of a dispute between Bp Hugh and the dean and chapter of Lincoln on the one part, and the abbess and nuns of Fontevraud on the other. The bp and dean and chapter have granted licence to the nuns to have an oratory within the bounds of their *curia* at Grovebury (*Grava*) in the parish of Leighton Buzzard, which is a prebend of Lincoln, and also a cemetery and right of burial, saving the rights of the church of Leighton, undated.
    Pd *Reg. Ant.* iii no. 645, cf. ibid., no. 646.

2. Agreement made between Bp Hugh and Henry de Nevill that, whereas the bp claimed aganst Henry the guard of five knights at his castle of Newark in respect of the five knights that Henry holds of him, the bp has agreed that Henry during his life shall henceforth perform the guard of three knights at the bishop's castle of Sleaford, in war or when the peace of the realm is disturbed, for forty days in a year; and the bp remits to Henry for his lifetime the guard of two of the five knights, saving the bp's right to the guard of the two knights after Henry's death, undated.
    Pd *Reg. Ant.* ii no. 379.

3. Award of the bishop of Salisbury and the abbots of Westminster and Waltham, settling the dispute between Bp Hugh and the abbot and convent of St Albans over the vicarage of Luton, the status of the bp regarding churches appropriated to the abbey, and similarly his status regarding the admission and recall of heads of cells of St Albans within the Lincoln diocese.   1219
    Pd *Reg. Ant.* iii no. 653; *Gesta Abbatum monasterii Sancti Albani* (Rolls ser., 1867–9), i 275–7, cf. *MPCM* iii 44.

4. Final concord between Bp Hugh, petent, and Robert Haldein, tenant, about 42 virgates and two rods of land in Banbury. Robert acknowledged the land to be the right of the bp and his church of St Mary, Lincoln, and for this the bp has granted part of the land to Robert for an annual rent of twenty shillings.   20 January 1221
    Pd *Reg. Ant.* iii no. 926.

5. Final concord between Bp Hugh, petent, and Oliver de Aencurt, tenant, concerning the manor of Woburn.   20 January 1222
    Pd, *Reg. Ant.* iii no. 670, inspected by Bp Hugh, in chapter at Lincoln, 13 March 1222 (see above, no. 180); M.W. Hughes ed., *A calendar of feet of fines for the county of Buckingham 7 Richard I to 44 Henry III* (Bucks Record Society 4, 1940), p. 47, no. 17.

6. Final concord between William of Hedsor, petent, and Bp Hugh, tenant, by Roger de Capella his attorney, regarding 30 acres of land in Hedsor. William acknowledged the right of the bp and granted the land to the bp to hold in

pure and perpetual alms. The bp was to be quit of the payment of six pence which the land formerly owed. For this the bp gave William five silver marks.   29 October 1222
Pd *A calendar of feet of fines for Bucks*, p. 487, no. 5.

7. Final concord between Bp Hugh, petent, and Ralph of Wickham, tenant, over 16 acres of meadow and pasture in Banbury. Ralph acknowledged this land to be the right of the bp and his church of Lincoln, for which the bp has granted him twenty silver marks.   19 May 1224
Pd *Reg. Ant.* iii no. 927.

8. Final concord between Bp Hugh, guardian of Robert son and heir of Philip de Rya, plaintiff, and William de Burg and Kemia his wife. William, without licence of the bp, took to wife Kemia who was of the donation of the bp by reason of the custody of the land and heir of Philip de Rya, and Kemia had allowed herself to be married to William without the bp's licence. The bp, for himself and his successors, remitted to William and Kemia their transgression of that marriage and for that William and Kemia granted to Robert 282 acres of land in Gosberton, of the land that was assigned to Kemia in dower, of the inheritance of Philip de Rya, formerly her husband, in the same vill, viz. 13 acres and a perch in Lickinges, 11 acres and a perch in Gangetoft, and 4 acres in Algaretoft. William and Kemia also quitclaimed to Robert and his heirs all their right in a certain marsh in the same vill, called Frid, of which marsh they once had a third part pertaining to the dower of Kemia.
6 Oct. 1226
Pd *Lincs Final Concords* i pp. 218–19, no. 207; *Cal.Ch.R. !327–41*, p. 150.

9. Chirograph between Bp Hugh and Roseia de Kyme and Philip de Kyme her son and heir. Roesia granted her manors of South Elkington and Cawthorpe in Lindsey to the bp and his assigns on the Monday before the feast of the Exaltation of the Holy Cross (13 Sept. 1227) for ten years at an annual farm of 20 marks. The bp had paid the whole farm for the ten years (200 marks) beforehand.   1227
Pd *Cal.Ch.R. 1226–57*, pp. 62–3.

10. Chirograph concerning a final concord made between Bp Hugh and Oliver de Aencurt over certain pieces of land in Woburn. 16 April 1228
Pd *Reg. Ant.* iii no. 671.

11. Final concord between William Godswain and Christiana his wife, and Mabel, sister of Christiana, plaintiffs, and Bp Hugh, tenant, of a stall (*selda*) in Stow. The plaintiffs quitclaimed all right to the bp and his successors and for this the bp gave them ten shillings.   13 July 1231
Pd *Lincs Final Concords* i p. 245, no. 89.

12. Final concord between Simon de Scures, plaintiff, and Bp Hugh, tenant, by John de Crachall put in his place, of a tenth part of a knight's fee in Baketon, Huwell and Asgarby. Simon quitclaimed all right to the bp and his successors for ever, and for this the bp gave Simon one hundred pounds.
1 May 1232
Pd *Lincs Final Concords* i p. 250, no. 103.

13. Agreement made between Bp Hugh and prior Simon and the convent of Spalding on the one part, and Ranulph, earl of Chester and Lincoln, and abbot Constantius and the convent of St Nicholas, Angers, on the other. In future the priors of Spalding were to be elected in England and instituted by the bp of Lincoln. The right of visitation of the priory was reserved to the abbot of Angers. Four monks from Angers were to be maintained at Spalding, owing obedience to the prior but liable to be recalled by the abbot from time to time. Novices were still to be professed at Angers unless the abbot permitted them to make their profession at Spalding. Four copies of this agreement were made, to be kept by the abbey, the priory, the bp and the earl.

At Brampton by Huntingdon, 8 June 1232

Pd *Mon. Angl.*, iii 220, no. xv. The earl's copy is now PRO, DL25/49; a copy is in BL, Add. ms. 35296, fos. 11v–12v.

14. Final concord between John Brun, plaintiff, and Bp Hugh, tenant, by John de Crakehale put in his place, of three shops in Stow. John quitclaimed all right to the bp and his successors and for this the bp gave him twenty shillings.

21 October 1234

Pd *Lincs Final Concords* i p. 259, no. 130.

INDEX OF PERSONS AND PLACES

Roman numbers relate to page numbers in the Introduction; Arabic numbers relate to the numbered entries in the text. All references to Lincolnshire and other British counties are to the pre-1974 historic counties. The following abbreviations have been used in this index: app. = appendix; archbp = archbishop; archdn = archdeacon; bp = bishop; can. = canon; mr = master; n(n). = note(s); preby = prebendary.

INDEX OF SUBJECTS

salutation, xxxv

scribe, of bp, 2; papal, 314

seal, episcopal, xxxv–viii; size of, xxxviii

sealing in episcopal absence, xxxviii

sealing methods, xxxvii

second legacy, *see* legacy

sede vacante, see vacancy

sequestration, 437

sequestrators, xxxvi, 352

servant(s) of bp, 408; of hospital, 370; of nunnery, 330; of vicar, 342; to guard cathedral, xli, 381

serviens/servientes, 88, 106, 408

sesters (of salt), 60

settlement of dispute, 60, 177, 195, 198–9, 227, 292, 410, app., pp. 219–21

sheriff, *see* Buckinghamshire; Lincolnshire; Northamptonshire

shops, app. no. 14

sick, 370, 447

signification of excommunication, 315–17

staff (*baculus*), 370

stall (*selda*), app. no. 11

statutes, 188, 344, 392

steward, bp's, *see* Baldwin, Geoffrey son of; Treilly, Gilbert de; of abbot of Westminster, *see* Ulian; of bp of Durham, *see* Pinzun, Hugh son of; of count of Aumale, *see* Oyry, Fulk d'

stipend, 342, 381

stock, 114, 146, 447

style, episcopal, xxxv

surety, 415

suspendium clericorum, 7

synod(s), 208

synodals, synodal dues, 77–8, 84, 86, 104, 147, 150, 154, 167, 176, 183, 188–9, 204, 208, 254, 268, 308, 327, 331, 365, 373, 400, 417–19, 425

tenements, 72, 120

testament of bp Hugh, xxxi, 2, 408

testimonial, letters, xliii, li, 24–5

thicket (*riffletum*), 343

thraves, 425

tithe-barn, 105

tithes, xlii, 112, 150, 331, 360, 410; of calves, 167, 312; of cheese, 167; of chickens, 312; of corn 36, 118, 187; demesne, 71–2, 78, 104, 138, 149, 204, 218, 281, 384, 395, 400; of flax, 312; of fodder, 308; of fruits, 167; garb, 29, 36, 40, 51, 72, 77–8, 84, 86, 91, 99, 103, 105, 114, 117, 146, 161, 177, 183, 187, 198–9, 204, 227, 245, 288, 292, 308, 311, 320, 327, 357, 366, 382, 384–5, 398, 400, 410, 419, 428, 445; of gardens, 167, 312; of geese, 167, 312; of hay, 147, 187, 308, 311, 320, 330, 346, 357, 385, 398, 419, 428, 434; of hedges, 245; of labourers and

merchants, 313; of lambs, 160, 167, 312, 332, 425; of merchandise, 312; of milk, 312; of mills, 72, 245, 311, 331, 384, 419, 425, 427; of pannage, 384; of piglets, 167, 312; of quarries, 245; of salt, 187; small, 64, 77, 85, 91, 103, 114, 146, 161, 177, 198–9, 308, 320, 330, 332, 357, 366, 384–5, 398, 410, 425, 427–8; of vegetables, 187; of windmill, 319; of wool, 160, 167, 312, 332

toft, 104, 106, 117, 136, 154, 198–9, 279, 306, 434

tower, building of, 344

travellers/pilgrims, 64, 125, 131, 256

treaties, 269

Trinitarian order, 30n.

turbaries, 84, 86, 105

undersheriff, *see* Bonet, John

usury, 344

vacancy jurisdiction, xxx

vacancy of benefice, 268

vespers, 431, 450

vestments, 177

vicarage rolls, xxxi, xliv

vicarages, ordination of, or description of endowment of, xxvii, xxxi, xli, 3, 29, 35, 40–1, 44, 64, 69, 84, 86, 91, 104–5, 112, 114, 142–3, 146–7, 150, 167, 189, 204, 235, 308, 311–13, 326, 331–2, 342, 361, 365–6, 373, 384, 400, 412, 417–19, 425–8, 434, 445, 448

vice-archdeacon, *see* Hardres, Robert de

vice-chancellor (of England), 4n.

villeins, 180

vineyard, 82

virgate, 77, 114, 138, 146, 150, 180, 183, 204, 207n., 227, 244n., 308, 311, 320, 327, 346, 366, 385, 400, 412, 417, 425

visitation injunctions, 344, 392, 447; of monastic houses, xxx; rights of, app. no. 13

visits of nuns to relatives and friends, 447

wardship, (grants of), xl, 155, 205, 238, 264, 289, 334, 368, 407–8, 409n., 427

water, holy, 383

wax, 410, 418, 431, 450

wax, colours of, used in sealing, xxxvii

wax-scot, 312

wheat, 425

widowhood, grant in free, 293

will, *see* testament

windmill, 319

witness-lists, xxxvi

wood, 6, 227, 279, 343, 419; bp's, 111, 174

writ *certiorari*, xliv

yardlands (*virgulte*), 82